AICPA

AF778902

Audit and Accounting Guide

Construction Contractors

July 1, 2018

23574-349

1 2 3 4 5 6 7 8 9 0 AAP 1 9 8

ISBN 978-1-94830-601-0

Preface

(Updated as of July 1, 2018)

This guide was prepared by the Construction Contractors Guide Committee.

About AICPA Guides

This AICPA Guide has been developed by the AICPA Construction Contractors Guide Committee to assist practitioners in performing and reporting on their audit engagements and to assist management in the preparation of their financial statements in conformity with U.S. generally accepted accounting principles (GAAP).

An AICPA guide containing auditing guidance related to generally accepted auditing standards (GAAS) is recognized as an interpretive publication as defined in AU-C section 200, *Overall Objectives of the Independent Auditor and the Conduct of an Audit in Accordance With Generally Accepted Auditing Standards.*[1] Interpretive publications are recommendations on the application of GAAS in specific circumstances, including engagements for entities in specialized industries.

Interpretive publications are issued under the authority of the AICPA Auditing Standards Board (ASB) after all ASB members have been provided an opportunity to consider and comment on whether the proposed interpretive publication is consistent with GAAS. The members of the ASB have found the auditing guidance in this guide to be consistent with existing GAAS.

Although interpretive publications are not auditing standards, AU-C section 200 requires the auditor to consider applicable interpretive publications in planning and performing the audit because interpretive publications are relevant to the proper application of GAAS in specific circumstances. If the auditor does not apply the auditing guidance in an applicable interpretive publication, the auditor should document how the requirements of GAAS were complied with in the circumstances addressed by such auditing guidance.

The ASB is the designated senior committee of the AICPA authorized to speak for the AICPA on all matters related to auditing. Conforming changes made to the auditing guidance contained in this guide are approved by the ASB Chair (or his or her designee) and the Director of the AICPA Audit and Attest Standards Staff. Updates made to the auditing guidance in this guide exceeding that of conforming changes are issued after all ASB members have been provided an opportunity to consider and comment on whether the guide is consistent with the Statements on Auditing Standards (SASs).

Any auditing guidance in a guide appendix or exhibit (whether a chapter or back matter appendix or exhibit), though not authoritative, is considered an "other auditing publication." In applying such guidance, the auditor should, exercising professional judgment, assess the relevance and appropriateness of such guidance to the circumstances of the audit. Although the auditor determines the relevance of other auditing guidance, auditing guidance in a guide

[1] All AU-C sections can be found in AICPA *Professional Standards*.

appendix or exhibit has been reviewed by the AICPA Audit and Attest Standards staff and the auditor may presume that it is appropriate.

The Financial Reporting Executive Committee (FinREC) is the designated senior committee of the AICPA authorized to speak for the AICPA in the areas of financial accounting and reporting. Conforming changes made to the financial accounting and reporting guidance contained in this guide are approved by the FinREC Chair (or his or her designee). Updates made to the financial accounting and reporting guidance in this guide exceeding that of conforming changes are approved by the affirmative vote of at least two-thirds of the members of FinREC.

This guide does the following:

- Identifies certain requirements set forth in the FASB *Accounting Standards Codification*® (ASC).
- Describes FinREC's understanding of prevalent or sole industry practice concerning certain issues. In addition, this guide may indicate that FinREC expresses a preference for the prevalent or sole industry practice, or it may indicate that FinREC expresses a preference for another practice that is not the prevalent or sole industry practice; alternatively, FinREC may express no view on the matter.
- Identifies certain other, but not necessarily all, industry practices concerning certain accounting issues without expressing FinREC's views on them.
- Provides guidance that has been supported by FinREC on the accounting, reporting, or disclosure treatment of transactions or events that are not set forth in FASB ASC.

Accounting guidance for nongovernmental entities included in an AICPA Guide is a source of nonauthoritative accounting guidance. As discussed later in this preface, FASB ASC is the authoritative source of U.S. accounting and reporting standards for nongovernmental entities, in addition to guidance issued by the SEC.

Purpose and Applicability

Limitations

This guide does not discuss the application of all GAAP or GAAS that are relevant to the preparation and audit of financial statements of construction contractors. This guide is directed primarily to those aspects of the preparation and audit of financial statements that are unique to construction contractors or those aspects that are considered particularly significant to them.

Recognition

2018 Guide Edition

AICPA Senior Committees

Auditing Standards Board

Alan Long, ASB Member
Mike Santay, *Chair*

Financial Reporting Executive Committee

Dan Noll, AICPA Director of Accounting Standards
Jim Dolinar, *Chair*

The AICPA gratefully acknowledges those who reviewed and otherwise contributed to the development of this guide: Adam Canosa, William A. Clark, Jr., Robert S. Mercado, James Miller, Joseph Natarelli, Bret Rutter, Robert Schroell, and James Wiedemann.

AICPA Staff

Dave Arman
Technical Manager
Accounting and Auditing Content Development

Guidance Considered in This Edition

This edition of the guide has been modified by the AICPA staff to include certain changes necessary due to the issuance of authoritative guidance since the guide was originally issued, and other revisions as deemed appropriate. Relevant guidance issued through July 1, 2018, has been considered in the development of this edition of the guide. However, this guide does not include all audit, accounting, reporting, regulatory, and other requirements applicable to an entity or a particular engagement. This guide is intended to be used in conjunction with all applicable sources of relevant guidance.

Relevant guidance that is issued and effective on or before July 1, 2018, is incorporated directly in the text of this guide. Relevant guidance issued but not yet effective as of July 1, 2018, but becoming effective on or before December 31, 2018, is also presented directly in the text of the guide, but shaded gray and accompanied by a footnote indicating the effective date of the new guidance. The distinct presentation of this content is intended to aid the reader in differentiating content that may not be effective for the reader's purposes (as part of the guide's "dual guidance" treatment of applicable new guidance).

Relevant guidance issued but not yet effective as of the date of the guide and not becoming effective until after December 31, 2018, is referenced in a "guidance update" box; that is, a box that contains summary information on the guidance issued but not yet effective.

In updating this guide, all guidance issued up to and including the following was considered, but not necessarily incorporated, as determined based on applicability:

- FASB Accounting Standards Update (ASU) No. 2018-06, *Codification Improvements to Topic 942, Financial Services—Depository and Lending*
- SAS No. 133, *Auditor Involvement With Exempt Offering Documents* (AU-C sec. 945)

Users of this guide should consider guidance issued subsequent to those items listed previously to determine their effect, if any, on entities and engagements covered by this guide. In determining the applicability of recently issued guidance, its effective date should also be considered.

The changes made to this edition of the guide are identified in the "Schedule of Changes" appendix. The changes do not include all those that might be considered necessary if the guide were subjected to a comprehensive review and revision.

FASB ASC Pending Content

Presentation of Pending Content in FASB ASC

Amendments to FASB ASC (issued in the form of ASUs) are initially incorporated into FASB ASC in "pending content" boxes following the paragraphs being amended with links to the transition information. The pending content boxes are meant to provide users with information about how the guidance in a paragraph will change as a result of the new guidance.

Pending content applies to different entities at different times due to varying fiscal year-ends, and because certain guidance may be effective on different dates for public and nonpublic entities. As such, FASB maintains amended guidance in pending content boxes within FASB ASC until the roll-off date. Generally, the roll-off date is six months following the latest fiscal year end for which the original guidance being amended could still be applied.

Presentation of FASB ASC Pending Content in AICPA Guides

Amended FASB ASC guidance that is included in pending content boxes in FASB ASC on July 1, 2018, is referenced as "Pending Content" in this guide. Readers should be aware that "Pending Content" referenced in this guide will eventually be subjected to FASB's roll-off process and no longer be labeled as "Pending Content" in FASB ASC (as discussed in the previous paragraph).

Terms Used to Define Professional Requirements in This AICPA Audit and Accounting Guide

Any requirements described in this guide are normally referenced to the applicable standards or regulations from which they are derived. Generally, the terms used in this guide describing the professional requirements of the referenced standard setter (for example, the ASB) are the same as those used in the applicable standards or regulations (for example, "must" or "should"). However, where the accounting requirements are derived from FASB ASC, this guide uses "should," whereas FASB uses "shall." In its resource document "About the Codification" that accompanies FASB ASC, FASB states that it considers the terms "should" and "shall" to be comparable terms and to represent the same concept—the requirement to apply a standard.

Readers should refer to the applicable standards and regulations for more information on the requirements imposed by the use of the various terms used to define professional requirements in the context of the standards and regulations in which they appear.

Certain exceptions apply to these general rules, particularly in those circumstances where the guide describes prevailing and/or preferred industry practices for the application of a standard or regulation. In these circumstances, the applicable senior committee responsible for reviewing the guide's content believes the guidance contained herein is appropriate for the circumstances.

Applicability of Generally Accepted Auditing Standards and PCAOB Standards

Appendix A, "Council Resolution Designating Bodies to Promulgate Technical Standards," of the AICPA Code of Professional Conduct recognizes both the ASB and the PCAOB as standard setting bodies designated to promulgate auditing, attestation, and quality control standards. Paragraph .01 of the "Compliance With Standards Rule" (ET sec. 1.310.001 and 2.310.001) requires an AICPA member who performs an audit to comply with the applicable standards.[2]

Audits of the financial statements of those entities not subject to the oversight authority of the PCAOB (that is, those audit reports within the PCAOB's jurisdiction as defined by the Sarbanes-Oxley Act of 2002, as amended) are to be conducted in accordance with standards established by the PCAOB, a private sector, nonprofit corporation created by the Sarbanes-Oxley Act of 2002. The SEC has oversight authority over the PCAOB, including the approval of its rules, standards, and budget. In citing the auditing standards of the PCAOB, references generally use section numbers within the reorganized PCAOB auditing standards and not the original standard number, as appropriate.

Audits of the financial statements of those entities subject to the oversight authority of the PCAOB (that is, those audit reports not within the PCAOB's jurisdiction as defined by the Act, as amended)—hereinafter referred to as *nonissuers*[3]—are to be conducted in accordance with GAAS as issued by the ASB. The ASB develops and issues standards in the form of SASs through a due process that includes deliberation in meetings open to the public, public exposure of proposed SASs, and a formal vote. The SASs and their related interpretations are codified in AICPA *Professional Standards*. In citing GAAS and their related interpretations, references generally use section numbers within the codification of currently effective SASs and not the original statement number, as appropriate.

The auditing content in this guide primarily discusses GAAS issued by the ASB and is applicable to audits of nonissuers. Users of this guide may find the tool developed by the PCAOB's Office of the Chief Auditor helpful in identifying comparable PCAOB standards. The tool is available at https://pcaobus.org/standards/auditing/pages/findanalogousstandards.aspx.

Applicability of Quality Control Standards

QC section 10, *A Firm's System of Quality Control* (AICPA, *Professional Standards*), addresses a CPA firm's responsibilities for its system of quality control for its accounting and auditing practice. A system of quality control consists of policies that a firm establishes and maintains to provide it with reasonable assurance that the firm and its personnel comply with professional standards, as well as applicable legal and regulatory requirements. The policies also provide the firm with reasonable assurance that reports issued by the firm are appropriate in the circumstances.

---

[2] All ET sections can be found in AICPA *Professional Standards*.

[3] See the definition of the term *nonissuer* in the AU-C Glossary.

QC section 10 applies to all CPA firms with respect to engagements in their accounting and auditing practice. In paragraph .13 of QC section 10, an *accounting and auditing practice* is defined as "a practice that performs engagements covered by this section, which are audit, attestation, compilation, review, and any other services for which standards have been promulgated by the ASB or the AICPA Accounting and Review Services Committee (ARSC) under the "General Standards Rule" (ET sec.1.300.001) or the "Compliance With Standards Rule" (ET sec. 1.310.001) of the AICPA Code of Professional Conduct. Although standards for other engagements may be promulgated by other AICPA technical committees, engagements performed in accordance with those standards are not encompassed in the definition of an *accounting and auditing practice*."

In addition to the provisions of QC section 10, readers should be aware of other sections within AICPA *Professional Standards* that address quality control considerations, including the following provisions that address engagement level quality control matters for various types of engagements that an accounting and auditing practice might perform:

- AU-C section 220, *Quality Control for an Engagement Conducted in Accordance With Generally Accepted Auditing Standards*
- AT-C section 105, *Concepts Common to All Attestation Engagements* (AICPA, *Professional Standards*)
- AR-C section 60, *General Principles for Engagements Performed in Accordance With Statements on Standards for Accounting and Review Services* (AICPA, *Professional Standards*)

Because of the importance of engagement quality, this guide includes an appendix, "Overview of Statements on Quality Control Standards." This appendix summarizes key aspects of the quality control standard. This summarization should be read in conjunction with QC section 10, AU-C section 220, AT-C section 105, AR-C section 60, and the quality control standards issued by the PCAOB, as applicable.

Alternatives Within GAAP

The Private Company Council (PCC), established by the Financial Accounting Foundation's Board of Trustees in 2012, and FASB, working jointly, will mutually agree on a set of criteria to decide whether and when alternatives within U.S. GAAP are warranted for private companies. Based on those criteria, the PCC reviews and proposes alternatives within U.S. GAAP to address the needs of users of private company financial statements. These U.S. GAAP alternatives may be applied to those entities that are not public business entities, not-for-profits, or employee benefit plans.

The FASB ASC Master Glossary defines a *public business entity* as:

> A public business entity is a business entity meeting any one of the criteria below. Neither a not-for-profit entity nor an employee benefit plan is a business entity.
>
> a. It is required by the U.S. Securities and Exchange Commission (SEC) to file or furnish financial statements, or does file or furnish financial statements (including voluntary filers), with the SEC (including other entities whose

financial statements or financial information are required to be or are included in a filing).

b. It is required by the Securities Exchange Act of 1934 (the Act), as amended, or rules or regulations promulgated under the Act, to file or furnish financial statements with a regulatory agency other than the SEC.

c. It is required to file or furnish financial statements with a foreign or domestic regulatory agency in preparation for the sale of or for purposes of issuing securities that are not subject to contractual restrictions on transfer.

d. It has issued, or is a conduit bond obligor for, securities that are traded, listed, or quoted on an exchange or an over-the-counter market.

e. It has one or more securities that are not subject to contractual restrictions on transfer, and it is required by law, contract, or regulation to prepare U.S. GAAP financial statements (including footnotes) and make them publicly available on a periodic basis (for example, interim or annual periods). An entity must meet both of these conditions to meet this criterion.

An entity may meet the definition of a public business entity solely because its financial statements or financial information is included in another entity's filing with the SEC. In that case, the entity is only a public business entity for purposes of financial statements that are filed or furnished with the SEC.

Considerations related to alternatives for private companies may be discussed within this guide's chapter text. When such discussion is provided, the related paragraphs are designated with the following title: "Considerations for Private Companies That Elect to Use Standards as Issued by the Private Company Council."

AICPA.org Website

The AICPA encourages you to visit the website at aicpa.org, and the Financial Reporting Center (FRC) at www.aicpa.org/frc. The FRC supports members in the execution of high-quality financial reporting. Whether you are a financial statement preparer or a member in public practice, this center provides exclusive member-only resources for the entire financial reporting process and provides timely and relevant news, guidance, and examples supporting the financial reporting process, including accounting, preparing financial statements and performing compilation, review, audit, attest or assurance, and advisory engagements. Certain content on the AICPA's websites referenced in this guide may be restricted to AICPA members only.

Select Recent Developments Significant to This Guide

FASB's Revenue Recognition

FASB ASU No. 2014-09, *Revenue from Contracts with Customers (Topic 606)*, was issued by FASB to improve the financial reporting of revenue from contracts with customers and related costs and to align the reporting with International Financial Reporting Standards. ASU No. 2014-09 provides a framework for revenue recognition and supersedes or amends several of the revenue recognition requirements in FASB ASC 605, *Revenue Recognition*, as well as guidance within the industry-specific topics, including FASB ASC 958, *Not-for-Profit Entities*. The standard applies to any entity that either enters into contracts with customers to transfer goods or services or enters into contracts for the transfer of nonfinancial assets unless those contracts are within the scope of other standards (for example, insurance or lease contracts).

The AICPA has formed 16 industry task forces to assist in developing a new guide on revenue recognition that will provide insights and illustrative examples on how to apply the new standards.

Chapter 2, "Accounting for Performance of Construction-Type Contracts," includes the following changes to help readers prepare for the effective date of the amendments in ASU No. 2014-09:

> Appendix A to chapter 2, "Implementation Guidance for Accounting Standards Update No. 2014-09, *Revenue from Contracts with Customers (Topic 606)*," includes excerpts from chapter 8, "Not-for-Profit Entities" of the AICPA Audit and Accounting Guide, *Revenue Recognition*. That guide, developed by the AICPA Industry Revenue Recognition Task Forces, Revenue Recognition Working Group, and Auditing Revenue Task Force, is intended to help entities and auditors prepare for changes related to revenue recognition.

Throughout the remaining guide, only the effects of ASU No. 2014-09's amendments on FASB ASC 910 are provided in gray-shaded text following the paragraph. The distinct presentation of this content is intended to aid the reader in identifying the content that will be deleted upon the effective date of the amendments in ASU No. 2014-09 as well as the text that will replace it (the guide's "dual guidance" treatment of applicable new guidance). A more comprehensive update for the effects of ASU No. 2014-09's amendments will appear in a future edition.

Appendix A, "The New Revenue Recognition Standard: FASB ASU No. 2014-09," of this guide provides additional discussion of the new standards. The appendix is prepared for informational and reference purposes only. It has not been reviewed, approved, disapproved, or otherwise acted on by any senior committee of the AICPA and does not represent official positions or pronouncements of the AICPA.

TABLE OF CONTENTS

Chapter 1

Industry Background

1.01 This chapter is intended as background for the presentation of recommendations and guidance on financial reporting and auditing in the industry. It does not contain recommendations or guidance on the technical application of generally accepted accounting or auditing standards. Recommendations and guidance on technical accounting and auditing issues are presented in the chapters that follow and include the guidance from FASB *Accounting Standards Codification* (ASC)®.

Nature and Significance of the Industry

1.02 The construction industry consists of individuals and entities that are engaged in diverse types of activities defined as construction in the North American Industry Classification System (NAICS). The 2017 U.S. NAICS Manual *North American Industry Classification System—United States* classifies construction establishments into a wide variety of subcategories. These subcategories include: Construction of Buildings (residential and nonresidential), Heavy and Civil Engineering Construction (including Utility System Construction, Land Subdivision, and Highway, Street and Bridge Contractors), and several different classes of Specialty Trade Contractors (such as Foundation, Structure, and Building Exterior Contractors, Building Equipment Contactors, Building Finishing Contractors, and Other Specialty Trade Contractors). Data from the Bureau of Economic Analysis indicates that the construction industry is a significant factor in the U.S. economy, contributing nearly 4 percent of the gross domestic product in 2015. It represents hundreds of billions of dollars of economic activity, consists of several hundred thousand business entities widely dispersed throughout the country, and employs a large labor force.

1.03 Construction contractors may be distinguished by their size, the type of construction activity they undertake, and the nature and scope of their responsibility for a construction project. Although the construction industry also encompasses large, multinational contractors that undertake construction of billion-dollar projects, most business entities in the industry are small, local businesses whose activities are limited to a small geographical area. The large number of small entities in the industry may be attributed to the ease of entry into many phases of the construction industry and to the limited amount of capital required. The diverse types of business activities conducted by construction contractors include construction of buildings, highways, dams, and bridges; installation of machinery and equipment; dredging; and demolition. Many entities are able to meet the demands of large construction projects by combining their efforts in joint ventures.

1.04 A contractor may engage in those activities as a general contractor, a subcontractor, or a construction manager. A *general contractor* is a prime contractor who enters into a contract with the owner of a project for the construction of the project and who takes full responsibility for its completion, although he or she may enter into subcontracts with others for the performance of specific parts or phases of the project. A *subcontractor* is a second-level contractor who enters into a contract with a prime contractor or an upper-tier contractor to perform a specific part or phase of a construction project. A subcontractor's performance responsibility is to the general contractor, with whom the subcontractor's relationship is essentially the same as that of the prime contractor to the owner of the project. A *construction manager* is a contractor who enters into an agency contract with an owner of a construction project to supervise and coordinate the construction activity on the project, including negotiating contracts with others for all the construction work.

1.05 The organizational structure, resources, and capabilities of contractors tend to vary with the type of activity. Each type of contractor can pose unique accounting and auditing problems.

Features of the Business Environment

1.06 Contractors operate in a business environment that differs in some respects from that of other types of businesses. The features of the business environment are discussed in this section in terms of characteristics common to contractors, types of contracts, bonding and surety underwriting, project ownership and rights of lien, contract changes, financing considerations, the use of joint ventures to accomplish objectives, and reporting for financial and income tax purposes.

Characteristics Common to Contractors

1.07 Although the construction industry is difficult to define because of its diversity, as explained in FASB ASC 910-10-15-3, certain characteristics are common to companies in the industry. The most basic characteristic is that work is performed under contractual arrangements with customers. A contractor, regardless of the type of construction activity or the type of contractor, typically enters into an agreement with a customer to build or to make improvements on a tangible property to the customer's specification. The contract with the customer specifies the work to be performed, specifies the basis of determining the amount and terms of payment of the contract price, and generally requires total performance before the contractor's obligation is discharged. Unlike the work of many manufacturers, the construction activities of a contractor are usually performed at job sites owned by customers, rather than at a central place of business, and each contract usually involves the production of a unique property rather than repetitive production of identical products.

1.08 As noted in FASB ASC 910-10-15-4, other characteristics common to contractors and significant to accountants and users of financial statements include the following:

- A contractor normally obtains the contracts that generate revenue or sales by bidding or negotiating for specific projects.
- A contractor bids for or negotiates the initial contract price based on an estimate of the cost to complete the project and the desired profit margin, although the initial price may be changed or renegotiated.
- A contractor may be exposed to significant risks in the performance of a contract, particularly a fixed-price contract.
- Customers (usually referred to as *owners*) may require a contractor to post a performance and payment bond as protection against the contractor's failure to meet performance and payment requirements. This requirement commonly depends on the type of work

being performed. If a bond is required, most governmental owners, by law, are required to have the contractor post these bonds; other owners have the option of either having the contractor post the bonds or not. Recently, a trend has developed whereby owners, or general contractors, prequalify with contractors by providing financial statements and other information, such as safety records and evidence of experience on similar projects.

- The costs and revenues of a contractor are typically accumulated and accounted for by individual contracts or contract commitments extending beyond one accounting period, which complicates the management, accounting, and auditing processes.

Types of Contracts

1.09 The nature of a contractor's risk exposure varies with the type of contract. As identified in FASB ASC 605-35-15-4, the four basic types of contracts used in the construction industry based on their pricing arrangements are fixed-price or lump-sum contracts, cost-type (including cost-plus) contracts, time-and-materials contracts, and unit-price contracts, which are defined in the FASB ASC Master Glossary and further described as follows:

- A *fixed-price contract*, also known as a *lump-sum contract*, provides for the contractor's performance of all work to be performed under the contract for a stated price. The stated price may be subsequently adjusted, as deemed necessary by the parties to the contract, via a *change order*, which is a written agreement between the contractor and owner to adjust the terms of the contract. This type of contract is usually the safest option for the owner, but the riskiest for the contractor.
- A *cost-type* (including a *cost-plus*) *contract* provides for reimbursement of allowable or otherwise defined costs incurred plus a fee for the contractor's services that represents profit. Usually, the contract only requires that the contractor's best efforts be used to accomplish the scope of the work within some specified time and stated dollar limitation. Cost-type contracts take a variety of forms, including *guaranteed max* contracts, which are "cost plus a fee" up to a certain maximum price contract, and are gaining popularity in practice. The contracts often contain terms specifying reimbursable costs, overhead recovery percentages, and fees. The fee may be fixed or based on a percentage of reimbursable costs. These types of projects can pose a higher risk for contractors, based on whether a cost is reimbursable or not.
- A *time-and-materials contract* is similar to a cost-plus contract and generally provides for payments to the contractor on the basis of direct labor hours at fixed hourly rates (the rates cover the costs of indirect labor and indirect expenses and profit) and cost of materials or other specified costs. This type of contract is usually the safest option for the contractor, but the riskiest for the owner. Some time-and-material contracts have provisions in the contract that convert the contracts from a time-and-material to a guaranteed maximum contract, in essence the contract becomes a fixed-price contract.

- A *unit-price contract* provides for the contractor's performance of a specific project at a specified price per each unit of output. Unit-price contracts are seldom used for an entire major construction project, but are frequently used for agreements with subcontractors. This type of contract is commonly associated with road building and it is not unusual to combine a unit-price contract for parts of the project with other types of contracts.

1.10 Although not specifically defined in the FASB ASC Master Glossary, the number of *design-build contracts*, over the last two decades, has dramatically increased. Design-build contracts differ from traditional contracts because one entity works under a single contract to provide both the design of the work and the performance of the construction services. This combination of the design work and actual construction work may be accomplished via a joint venture, a corporation or limited-liability company comprising two separate specialty entities, although the number of single contractors developing the expertise to handle both types of work is growing. Alternatively, the work may be done via a design subsidiary of a construction parent or a construction and design subsidiary established under a holding company.

Contract Modifications and Changes

1.11 All types of contracts may be modified by target penalties and incentives relating to factors such as completion dates, plant capacity on completion of the project, and underruns and overruns of estimated costs.

1.12 Management control of change orders, claims, extras, and back charges is of critical significance in construction activity. Modifications of the original contract frequently result from change orders that may be initiated by either the customer or the contractor. The nature of the construction industry, particularly the complexity of some types of projects, is conducive to disputes between the parties that may give rise to claims or back charges. Claims may also arise from unapproved change orders. In addition, customer representatives at a job site sometimes authorize the contractor to do work beyond contract specifications, and this gives rise to claims for extras. The ultimate profitability of a contract often depends on control, documentation, and collection of amounts arising from such items.

Bonding and the Surety Underwriting Process

1.13 Contractors bidding on or negotiating a contract may be required to make a deposit for the use of the plans and specifications for the project. Before they are allowed to submit bids, those seeking prime contracts may be required to post a bid bond or make a deposit, usually in the form of a bank-guaranteed check, equal to a percentage of the total cost estimated in the feasibility study. On virtually all public work and on some private work, bid security is usually required to provide some assurance that only qualified, responsible contractors submit bids. In the construction industry, bid bonds, as well as performance bonds and payment bonds, are provided by surety companies. A surety company makes itself jointly and severally responsible for the performance of the contractor via the execution of the bond.

1.14 A bid bond issued by a surety does not guarantee that the contractor will sign a contract or guarantee that the surety will issue a performance bond. The contractor and surety promise the owner that if the contractor who is awarded the contract does not sign the contract or cannot provide a performance bond, the surety will pay, subject to the maximum bid bond penalty, the difference between the contractor's bid and the bid of the next lowest responsible bidder. The bid bond or deposit protects the owner from bidders without the resources necessary to complete the work and gives the owner a certain amount of indemnity against the cost of rebidding or finding another contractor who can complete the work. Owners many times will use the bid bond requirement on a job to reduce the amount of bidders on a job and use the surety as a prequalification of the contractor. A surety required to pay on a defaulted bid usually has the right of recovery against the contractor's assets.

1.15 After being awarded a contract, a contractor may be required to post payment and performance bonds, also issued by a surety. The payment and performance bond provides protection against the contractor's failure to perform the contract in accordance with its terms. The surety's obligation under the bond terminates on satisfactory completion of the work required by the contract. However, if the contractor should fail to perform in accordance with the contract, the surety is obligated to the owner for losses or to assure performance but usually has recourse against the contractor's assets.

1.16 A payment, or labor-and-materials, bond is commonly provided by sureties as a companion (or as a combined item) to the performance bond. The protection provided by a payment bond is governed by state laws, which vary widely but generally cover the contractor's labor, subcontractors, and suppliers. The Miller Act of 1935 requires general contractors on federal government projects to post payment bonds to protect suppliers of labor, materials, and supplies to those projects. This type of bond generally applies to work already performed.

1.17 In providing the various types of bonds required in the construction industry, the primary function of sureties is to prequalify the contractor. The surety examines the contracting entity to determine if it has the management, experience, equipment, and financing capability to get the job done. This due diligence, amongst other procedures, involves the surety reviewing the contractor's financial statements. As such, sureties are one of the primary users of contractors' financial statements.

1.18 If, in the judgment of the surety, the contractor can perform the contract, the surety will provide the required bonds. Similarly, the contractor may wish to evaluate the quality and capability of the surety, including the financial stability of the surety.

1.19 Surety underwriting is similar to, yet different from, insurance. Insurance involves a two-party agreement in which a premium is paid to protect an insured party from the risk of certain types of losses. In contrast, a surety bond involves a three-party agreement in which the surety and the contractor join together to provide protection against losses to a third party. Surety underwriting is also similar to extending credit. For a fee, the surety provides a guarantee to third parties that the contractor will fulfill obligations of performance and payment. Just as a banker will not knowingly make a loan without satisfying himself regarding a borrower's ability to repay the loan in accordance with its terms, a surety will not knowingly issue a surety bond without similar knowledge of the contractor's ability to meet obligations in accordance with the terms of a contract. The financial strength of the contractor is critical to the surety underwriting process.

Project Ownership and Rights of Lien

1.20 A contractor may be required to make a significant commitment of resources to a project under construction. His ability to recover his investment may be impaired by certain peculiar considerations. The project is ordinarily one of a kind and is built on the owner's site. The owner has title to the real estate as well as all improvements as the contractor provides them. The contractor acquires materials for specific projects and has no direct ownership claims to the work in progress. Subassemblies fabricated on the contractor's premises usually have little value to him or her because of the uniqueness of the project.

1.21 As a special remedy for these conditions, the laws of most states protect providers of labor and materials, such as contractors, from the failure of the owner to pay by granting a right of lien. Under a right of lien, contractors have a claim against the real property, although that right is not necessarily senior to other claims, such as the rights of mortgage holders. Because lien rights are lost if they are not perfected within a limited time period, contractors ordinarily have an established procedure for filing claims before the expiration of those rights. Federal government property ordinarily is not subject to lien under state law, but suppliers, other than general contractors, of labor and material for such property are normally protected by payment bonds that the general contractor is required to post under the Miller Act of 1935.

Financing Considerations

1.22 The methods of financing operations in the construction industry have developed in response to the nature of the industry and the business environment in which it functions. The cost and availability of financing are affected by the risks to which contractors are susceptible. The greatest risk factor in the industry stems from the method of pricing. A contractor, unlike a businessperson in most other industries, normally must set his or her prices in the bidding or negotiating process before product costs are absolutely determined; and the prices, particularly for fixed-price contracts, are not necessarily subject to modifications solely because of changes in costs.

1.23 A contractor's greatest financing need is working capital. Term loans to support working capital needs are rare because expansion can usually be supported by working capital loans on a contract-by-contract basis. Banks and other credit grantors typically require more tangible types of security for term loans than most contractors can furnish. However, contractors use chattel loans, which may be tailored to match payments with cash receipts (such as by a waiver of payments during off-season periods), to finance equipment purchases.

1.24 In addition to a traditional line of credit, a working capital line of credit on specific contracts is another short term financing option often available to contractors. Working capital loans are usually advanced on a contract as needed to pay for materials, labor, and subcontract costs. Such loans are a necessary means of financing for most contracts because of the lag between expenditures and the receipt of cash. The credit grantor may take an assignment of the contract and the related receivables; however, a bonding company, if one is involved, has rights to the receivables that take precedence over those of other creditors, including a secured lender. Credit grantors often require that the proceeds of contracts be assigned to them and may also require that the proceeds of the loan be paid directly to suppliers as invoices are submitted.

1.25 Contractors may qualify for government-sponsored programs that support or guarantee financing for small or minority-owned businesses. The programs generally guarantee lines of credit on a contract-by-contract basis. Those programs, under which the contract proceeds are usually assigned to the creditor, are ordinarily available only to contractors that would not qualify for working capital loans from banks without some form of government guarantee.

1.26 Some contractors finance bid deposits with temporary bank loans that are usually repaid by the return of the bid check. Because a bank-guaranteed check used as a bid deposit can be forfeited if a contractor who is awarded a contract cannot obtain the required bonding or withdraws from the contract, a contractor usually obtains a commitment for the required bonding before bidding on a project.

1.27 Billing practices in the industry have evolved from the need to generate cash flows in order to finance the progress of construction projects. In contrast to manufacturing entities, whose billing practices are fairly standard, with the customer billed on shipment of the goods, billing practices in the construction industry vary widely and often are not correlated with the performance of the work. Billing arrangements are usually specified in the contract and vary with the different types of contracts used in the industry. The amount and timing of billings under contract may be based, for example, on such measures as

- completion of certain stages of the work.
- costs incurred on cost-plus contracts.
- architects' or engineers' estimates of completion.
- specified time schedules.
- quantity measures of unit price contracts, such as cubic yards excavated.

1.28 In any event, progress billings or customer advances on contracts provide a significant source of financing for most construction contractors. Most contracts, however, call for retention by the owner of a specified amount of each progress billing, often ranging from 5 percent to 10 percent, until the job reaches an agreed-upon state of completion, with a provision for a reduction thereafter. The purpose of retentions is to ensure performance of the work in accordance with acceptable quality standards or to protect the owner against the cost of obtaining another contractor if a contractor fails to complete the work.

1.29 A contractor ordinarily will try to assign a higher relative bid price to job components that he or she expects to complete early in the job. The practice of unbalanced bidding, referred to as *front-end loading*, accelerates the contractor's cash receipts on a contract and represents a significant financing strategy for many contractors.

1.30 Front-end loading and other types of unbalanced bidding are often viewed with concern by those not familiar with the industry, but they are common practices that contractors use to assist in the financing of jobs. Money management is a vital part of construction management, and unbalanced bidding is one of the key tools. Negotiation of advantageous cash payment terms at the bidding stage, and other procedures to accelerate cash collection, are significant financing considerations in the industry. However, the contractor needs to be aware that, as a result of unbalanced bidding, cash inflows at the end of the contract may be less than cash requirements. Therefore, appropriate controls and cash budgeting are an essential part of financial management. An increasing number of credit grantors are requiring contractors to furnish cash projections on contracts before they will extend credit.

Joint Ventures

1.31 According to the FASB ASC Master Glossary, a *joint venture* is an entity owned and operated by a small group of businesses (the joint venturers) as a separate and specific business or project for the mutual benefit of the members of the group. A joint venture usually provides an arrangement under which each joint venturer may participate, directly or indirectly, in the overall management of the joint venture. Joint venturers thus have an interest or relationship other than as passive investors. The ownership of a joint venture seldom changes, and its equity interests usually are not traded publicly.

1.32 In the construction industry, ownership of joint ventures may take several forms. The most common are corporate joint ventures, partnerships, limited liability corporations, and other types of pass-through entities. Contractors frequently participate in joint ventures with other parties on construction projects to share risks, combine the financial and other resources and talents of the participants, or obtain financing or bonding. In the construction industry, joint ventures often include arrangements for pooling equipment, bonding, and financing and for sharing skills such as engineering, design, and construction. Many times, these joint ventures are formed between local and nonlocal construction firms in order to share the advantages of each, for example, access to local labor and equipment, or specific expertise.

1.33 The rights and obligations of each joint venturer, the scope of the joint venture's operations, and the method of sharing profits or losses of the joint venture are typically set forth in the joint venture agreement. A joint venture provides for the sharing of profits and losses in a variety of ways and may not be related to the method of sharing management or other responsibilities. Accomplishing objectives through joint ventures is often a significant business strategy for construction contractors, and management control of such activity can have a significant effect on the contractors' operations.

1.34 Public-private partnerships, or P3s, are becoming increasingly common forms of collaboration for construction projects. Public-private partnerships take the form of contractual agreements between a public agency (federal, state, local) and a private sector entity. Due to governmental agencies struggling to obtain financing for large public works projects, these partnerships allow the private sector entity to share the risks and rewards of these public sector projects.

Reporting for Financial and Income Tax Purposes

1.35 Because of the large number of small enterprises in the construction industry, construction contractors' financial statements are used most frequently for credit and bonding purposes. Such a use is often accompanied by a request for supplemental information, including a job-by-job analysis of the recognized gross profit of both completed and uncompleted contracts allocated between reporting periods, a breakdown of general and administrative expenses, job costs, and a summary aging of accounts receivable. Recognition of revenues for these financial presentations is governed by accounting conventions described elsewhere in this guide and in FASB ASC.

1.36 On the other hand, business realities demonstrate that the gross profit is not certain, nor irrevocably earned, until the contract is actually completed and accepted. In addition, final collection, particularly of retentions, usually takes place sometime after the earning process has been completed and revenue has been recognized in the financial statements.

1.37 Some contractors adopt income tax reporting practices that are sensitive to the uncertainties of the estimating process and that more nearly relate to the timing of cash receipts and disbursements. This usually means the adoption of methods that defer income recognition until contracts are completed; the use of the modified accrual basis, which reports retentions only when received; or the use of the cash basis.

Typical Industry Operations

1.38 Because the industry consists of diverse types of entities engaged in various types of work that may change over time, users of the guide need to understand not only the industry but also the operation of the individual entity with which they are concerned. For that reason, a description of the process of obtaining and initiating a project is useful to identify unusual conditions that require special consideration in preparing, auditing, or using the financial statements of a particular construction contractor.

Preparing Cost Estimates and Bids

1.39 The process leading to the preparation of estimates and bids on a project usually is initiated by the entity that engages a construction contractor for a project. When a customer, usually referred to as an owner, decides to construct a new facility, an architect or engineer may be engaged to prepare preliminary plans and cost estimates for the project. If preliminary procedures indicate the project is feasible, plans and specifications are prepared in sufficient detail for the preparation of cost estimates.

1.40 The owner may negotiate for a price with several general contracting firms or may advertise for bids. Bidders may be limited to those who can meet specified prequalification standards regarding financial capacity, experience, and availability of specialized equipment and who can furnish a bid, payment, or performance bond or all three types of bonds. The owner may decide to use one contractor as a prime contractor responsible for all phases of the work or to grant separate prime contracts for certain specialized portions of the work, such as electrical work, mechanical work, special equipment, and elevators.

1.41 Before tendering a bid, the contractor's estimating department prepares a cost estimate by examining the plans and specifications to determine the quantities of materials, the hours of various labor classifications, and the type and hours of use of the equipment necessary to perform the work. Quantity surveys, or takeoffs of the quantities of materials required for the job, prepared by the design firm or an independent agency, are often available for the contractor to use as a check on his own estimating department.

1.42 The equipment demands of a contract affect a contractor's bidding, projected need for funds, and financing strategy. Some types of construction, such as road or heavy highway projects, require extensive use of costly equipment, and contractors are faced with decisions to buy or lease the equipment. Such decisions are often complicated because equipment may be acquired and tailored for use on a specific job and because the contractor may not be able to use the equipment on other jobs. In these situations, a contractor is then faced with a decision to either capitalize the equipment or cost it out to the specific job.

1.43 Phases of the job (such as excavating, erecting steel, and roofing) not done directly by the contractor are offered to various trade or specialty subcontractors who, in turn, prepare bids to the prime contractor for their portions of the work. Each phase of the work may be bid on by more than one subcontractor, who may submit bids to more than one prime contractor. In dealing with different prime contractors, a subcontractor may vary the amount of the bids according to his or her assessment of his or her past experience with each contractor in terms of payment policies, quality of supervision and job coordination, and negotiating pressures.

1.44 Once the estimated cost of the work is determined, the contractor determines the amount by which the estimated cost will be marked up. The markup may vary between elements of the work, such as labor, material, subcontractor costs, or equipment. In determining how much the bid will be marked up over cost, the contractor ordinarily evaluates several factors including, but not limited to, the following:

- The complexities of the job
- The volatility of the labor and materials markets
- The contractor's experience, or lack of it, in doing the kind of work involved
- The reputation of the design agency for reliability and completeness of plans, as well as its reputation for reasonableness in its dealings with contractors
- The ability to identify and negotiate change orders with the owner or design agency
- The season and weather
- The predicted working relationship with the owner
- Prior history with the owner
- The probability of opportunities to negotiate profitable changes to the contract
- The alternate construction methods or specifications included in the bid request
- The competition and the market
- The incentive or penalty provisions of the contract
- The anticipated cash flow characteristics of the job
- Other peculiar risk conditions, including warranty requirements

1.45 After determining the total bid price, the contractor normally should estimate the timing of disbursements for the job and the cash resources available to determine the allocation of the contract price among the progress billing points called for in the contract.

Entering Into the Contract

1.46 The owner evaluates the bids received and may choose to sign a contract with the low bidder or to negotiate further, depending on the terms of the invitation to bid, statutes governing the bidding process of either public or private bodies, and other possible considerations. Submitted bids may be a matter of public record, and the bids of other contractors can provide a valuable, independent check on the accuracy of the contractor's estimating department. At some stage, an agreement is reached between the owner and the contractor that enables the contractor to proceed with the work. The formal signing of a contract is usually not a specific point before which all effort is selling and after which all effort is construction. Negotiation is likely to continue during the entire cycle; the signed contract represents the basic understandings and undertakings of both parties, but many contract modifications, not necessarily in writing, may be made during the progress of the job. A given situation can be covered by different types of contracts, and the risks and concerns may be different for each contract type.

Planning and Initiating the Project

1.47 Before construction begins, the contractor usually moves equipment to the job site, erects a temporary field office, and installs temporary utilities. The purchasing department proceeds with the selection of material suppliers and subcontractors and converts their bids to written contracts or purchase orders. The authority and responsibility for the performance of the work on a project usually rest on one individual known as the *project manager*.

1.48 The management organization of construction contracting entities varies considerably, depending on the size of the contractor, the complexity of the projects performed, and other factors. In some entities, the person responsible for bidding a contract is also responsible for the performance of the job. This sometimes means that there is no separation of functions among selling, pricing, and production and that the entity is a conglomerate of small profit centers sharing, perhaps, a pool of equipment and an administrative staff. In other entities, a separate department is responsible for selecting jobs to estimate, preparing bids, and executing contracts. When the entity obtains a contract for a project, a member of the production staff is assigned the responsibility as project manager. Before accepting responsibility for the profit on the project, the project manager often prepares a schedule and budget that may include a complete reestimate of the cost of the job. This procedure provides an additional control and allows the contractor to fix the responsibility for profit on a contract.

1.49 The cost reporting system for the job is usually established at about the time the work begins. The coding system may be standard throughout the entity or redesigned for each individual job, but it should conform closely to the cost categories established in the original estimate or to the categories developed in the production plan, if one is prepared. A production plan or budget that is costed out in detail is helpful because it enables the contractor to compare costs by categories to the cost standards set before beginning the work.

1.50 On most construction projects, the major construction activity is carried out at the job site. The size and location of some projects make it necessary for a contractor to establish an administrative office at the job site and conduct most control and accounting functions from that office. Recently, a trend has developed where contractors prefabricate significant components of the project at a dedicated, off-site facility. The prefabrication is performed under controlled conditions, thus improving the efficiency of the construction. The components are then delivered to the site and installed.

Variations in Size and Methods of Operation

1.51 The preceding discussion of operations is typical of a medium-sized general contractor with a small number of significant contracts; it illustrates the importance of planning, bidding, and estimating. Construction activity, however, involves all types and sizes of contractors, and the management and operations of a contractor vary with the size and type of contractor. Many contractors have a mix of jobs that includes a few large jobs and many small jobs, including fixed-price and cost-plus contracts. Service-type contractors seldom are involved in bidding for contracts. Most of their small contracts originate as service calls, and many of their large contracts result from service calls and are negotiated rather than bid.

Project Management

1.52 The quality of management is a key determinant of the success or failure of a contractor. The management objective is to develop and maintain the ability to produce reasonable and competitive cost estimates on contracts and to complete the work required by the contracts within those cost estimates. Because success is determined by the results on contracts, many contractors project the effects that every transaction and event will have at the completion of the contract and use fluctuations of the final estimated profit as the stimulus for management action. Project management requires all the functions involved in planning, acquiring, controlling, and performing a project. All the following functions are involved:

- Resource planning
- Project start-up
- Estimating
- Scheduling
- Project administration
- Technical performance
- Procurement and material planning
- Labor planning and control
- Subcontractor management
- Support equipment and facilities
- Change order identification and management
- Project accounting
- Project management reporting
- Operations analysis

Although some of these functions overlap, all are performed on every project undertaken by a contractor, even though the specific functions may not be identified. A large contractor may assign each function to a separate department, whereas a small contractor may assign two or three people responsibility for all the functions or may engage parties outside the organization to perform some of the functions on a consulting basis.

Chapter 2

Accounting for Performance of Construction-Type Contracts

Gray shaded text in this chapter reflects guidance issued but not yet effective as of the date of this guide, July 1, 2018, but becoming effective on or prior to December 31, 2018, exclusive of any option to early adopt ahead of the mandatory effective date. Unless otherwise indicated, all unshaded text reflects guidance that was already effective as of the date of this guide.

© Update 2-1 *Accounting and Reporting*: Revenue Recognition

FASB *Accounting Standards Codification* (ASC) 606, *Revenue from Contracts with Customers*, is effective for annual reporting periods of a public business entity, a not-for-profit entity that has issued, or is a conduit bond obligor for, securities that are traded, listed, or quoted on an exchange or an over-the-counter market, and an employee benefit plan that files or furnishes financial statements with or to the SEC should apply the "Pending Content" that links to FASB ASC 606-10-65-1 for annual reporting periods beginning after December 15, 2017, including interim reporting periods within that reporting period. Earlier application is permitted only as of annual reporting periods beginning after December 15, 2016, including interim reporting periods within that reporting period.

For other entities, FASB ASC 606 is effective for annual reporting periods beginning after December 15, 2018, and interim periods within annual periods beginning after December 15, 2019. Other entities may elect to adopt the standard earlier, however, only as of either

- an annual reporting period beginning after December 15, 2016, including interim periods within that reporting period, or
- an annual reporting period beginning after December 15, 2016, and interim periods within annual periods beginning one year after the annual reporting period in which an entity first applies the "Pending Content" that links to FASB ASC 606-10-65-1.

FASB ASC 606 provides a framework for revenue recognition and supersedes or amends several of the revenue recognition requirements in FASB ASC 605, *Revenue Recognition*, as well as guidance within the 900 series of industry-specific topics, including FASB ASC 910, *Contractors—Construction*. The standard applies to any entity that either enters into contracts with customers to transfer goods or services or enters into contracts for the transfer of nonfinancial assets unless those contracts are within the scope of other standards (for example, insurance or lease contracts).

Readers are encouraged to consult the full text of FASB ASC 606 on FASB's website at www.fasb.org.

Appendix A, "Implementation Guidance for Accounting Standards Update No. 2014-09, *Revenue from Contracts with Customers (Topic 606)*," of this chapter presents accounting implementation issues developed to assist management of engineering and construction entities in applying FASB ASC 606 and related interpretations from the FASB/IASB Joint Transition Resource Group for Revenue Recognition (TRG).

The AICPA Engineering and Construction Contractors Revenue Recognition Task Force identified and developed the included accounting implementation issues, and the AICPA Revenue Recognition Working Group and AICPA Financial Reporting Executive Committee (FinREC) approved them. They are a source of nonauthoritative accounting guidance for nongovernmental entities.

For more information, see appendix A, "The New Revenue Recognition Standard: FASB ASC 606," of this guide.

2.01 This chapter covers accounting for performance of construction-type contracts and other general accounting considerations. Chapter 3, "Accounting for and Reporting Investments in Construction Joint Ventures;" chapter 4, "Financial Reporting by Affiliated Entities;" chapter 5, "Other Accounting Considerations;" and chapter 6, "Financial Statement Presentation," respectively cover joint ventures, reporting by affiliated entities, interperiod tax allocation, and financial statement presentation. The guidance on accounting for construction-type contracts set forth in FASB ASC 605-35 is summarized in this chapter of the guide.

2.02 Contracts covered are *construction-type contracts*, as defined in FASB ASC 605-35-15. The classification of contracts covered in that section and the definition of a contractor and the concept of a profit center contained in FASB ASC 605-35-20 also apply to the discussion in this guide.

Basic Accounting Policy for Contracts

2.03 The choice between the two generally accepted methods of accounting for contracts is the basic accounting policy decision for construction contractors. The circumstances in which the percentage-of-completion and the completed-contract methods are preferable are set forth in FASB ASC 605-35 and are summarized in this chapter. FASB ASC 605-35-25-1 clarifies that the determination of which of the two methods is preferable is based on a careful evaluation of circumstances because the two methods should not be acceptable alternatives for the same circumstances.

The preceding paragraph will be deleted upon the effective date of FASB Accounting Standards Update (ASU) No. 2014-09, *Revenue from Contracts with Customers (Topic 606)*.[1]

[1] FASB Accounting Standards Update (ASU) No. 2014-09, *Revenue from Contracts with Customers (Topic 606)*, was issued in May 2014. Public business entities, certain not-for-profit entities, and certain employee benefit plans should apply the guidance in ASU No. 2014-09 as amended by FASB ASU No. 2015-14, *Revenue from Contracts with Customers (Topic 606): Deferral of the Effective Date*, to annual reporting periods beginning after December 15, 2017, including interim reporting periods within that reporting period. Earlier application is permitted only as of annual reporting periods beginning after December 15, 2016, including interim reporting periods within that reporting period.

All other entities should apply the guidance in ASU No. 2014-09 to annual reporting periods beginning after December 15, 2018, and interim reporting periods within annual reporting periods beginning after December 15, 2019. All other entities may apply the guidance in ASU No. 2014-09 earlier as of an annual reporting period beginning after December 15, 2016, including interim reporting periods within that reporting period. All other entities also may apply the guidance in ASU No. 2014-09 earlier as of an annual reporting period beginning after December 15, 2016, and interim reporting periods within annual reporting periods beginning one year after the annual reporting period in which the entity first applies the guidance in ASU No. 2014-09.

Readers are encouraged to read the full text of the FASB ASU, available at www.fasb.org. Readers should apply the appropriate guidance based on their facts and circumstances.

Percentage-of-Completion Method

2.04 FASB ASC 605-35-25-57 states that the percentage-of-completion method is preferable as an accounting policy when estimates are reasonably dependable and all of the following conditions exist:

- Contracts executed by the parties normally include provisions that clearly specify the enforceable rights regarding goods or services to be provided and received by the parties, the consideration to be exchanged, and the manner and terms of settlement.
- The buyer can be expected to satisfy all obligations under the contract.
- The contractor can be expected to perform all contractual obligations.

The preceding paragraph will be deleted upon the effective date of FASB ASU No. 2014-09.

2.05 As provided in FASB ASC 605-35-25-58, the presumption is that, for entities engaged on a continuing basis in the production and delivery of goods or services under contractual arrangements and for whom contracting represents a significant part of their operations, they have the ability to make estimates that are sufficiently dependable to justify the use of the percentage-of-completion method of accounting. It also states that persuasive evidence to the contrary is necessary to overcome that presumption. FASB ASC 605-35-25-60 states that the percentage-of-completion method should be applied to individual contracts or profit centers, as appropriate, based on all of the following considerations:

a. Normally, a contractor will be able to estimate total contract revenue and total contract cost in single amounts. Those amounts should normally be used as the basis for accounting for contracts under the percentage-of-completion method.

b. For some contracts, on which some level of profit is assured, a contractor may only be able to estimate total contract revenue and total contract cost in ranges of amounts. If, based on the information arising in estimating the ranges of amounts and all other pertinent data, the contractor can determine the amounts in the ranges that are most likely to occur, those amounts should be used in accounting for the contract under the percentage-of-completion method. If the most likely amounts cannot be determined, the lowest probable level of profit in the range should be used in accounting for the contract until the results can be estimated more precisely.

c. However, in some circumstances, estimating the final outcome may be impractical except to assure that no loss will be incurred. In those circumstances, a contractor should use a zero estimate of profit; equal amounts of revenue and cost should be recognized until results can be estimated more precisely. A contractor should use this basis only if the bases in (*a*) or (*b*) are clearly not appropriate. In accordance with FASB ASC 605-35-25-69, a change from a zero estimate of profit to a more precise estimate should be accounted for as a change in an accounting estimate.

The preceding paragraph will be deleted upon the effective date of FASB ASU No. 2014-09.

2.06 FASB ASC 605-35-25-61 provides that an entity using the percentage-of-completion method as its basic accounting policy should use the completed-contract method for a single contract or a group of contracts for which reasonably dependable estimates cannot be made or for which inherent hazards make estimates doubtful. FASB ASC 605-35-50-3 indicates that such a departure from the basic policy should be disclosed.

The preceding paragraph will be deleted upon the effective date of FASB ASU No. 2014-09.

Completed-Contract Method

2.07 According to FASB ASC 605-35-25-92, the completed-contract method may be used as an entity's basic accounting policy in circumstances in which financial position and results of operations would not vary materially from those resulting from use of the percentage-of-completion method (for example, in circumstances in which an entity has primarily short-term contracts). Additionally, as provided by FASB ASC 605-35-25-94, the use of the completed-contract method of accounting is preferable in circumstances in which estimates cannot meet the criteria for reasonable dependability discussed in paragraph 2.04 or if inherent hazards would make otherwise reasonably dependable contract estimates doubtful, as discussed in paragraphs 65–66 of FASB ASC 605-35-25. Paragraphs 96–97 of FASB ASC 605-35-25 establish completion criteria for determining when a contract is substantially completed under the completed-contract method.

The preceding paragraph will be deleted upon the effective date of FASB ASU No. 2014-09.

2.08 It should be noted that most sureties and other external users of the financial statements require the use of the percentage-of-completion method. Therefore, in most situations, the use of the completed-contract method is likely to be inappropriate.

The preceding paragraph will be deleted upon the effective date of FASB ASU No. 2014-09.

Determining the Profit Center

2.09 In accordance with FASB ASC 605-35-25-4, the basic presumption should be that each individual contract is the profit center for revenue recognition, cost accumulation, and income measurement unless that presumption can be overcome as a result of the contract or series of contracts meeting the conditions for combining or segmenting as described in paragraphs 5–14 of FASB ASC 605-35-25. Because there are numerous practical implications of combining and segmenting contracts, evaluation of the circumstances, contract terms, and management intent are essential in determining contracts that may be accounted for on those bases.

The preceding paragraph will be deleted upon the effective date of FASB ASU No. 2014-09.

Measuring the Extent of Progress Toward Completion

2.10 As set forth in FASB ASC 605-35-25-70, the various approaches toward measuring progress on a contract can be grouped into input and output measures. Input measures are made in terms of efforts devoted to a contract. They include the methods based on costs (for example, the ratio of costs incurred to date to total estimated costs at completion) and on efforts expended (for example, the ratio of hours performed to date to estimated total hours at completion). Output measures are made in terms of results achieved. They include methods based on units produced, units delivered, contract milestones, and value added (that is, the contract value of total work performed to date). For contracts under which separate units of output are produced, progress can be measured on the basis of units of work completed. In other circumstances, progress may be measured, for example, on the basis of cubic yards of excavation for foundation contracts or on the basis of cubic yards of pavement laid for highway contracts. FASB ASC 605-35-25-79 notes that all of these practices are intended to conform to the income recognition provisions under the percentage-of-completion method discussed in paragraphs 51–53 in FASB ASC 605-35-25.

The preceding paragraph will be deleted upon the effective date of FASB ASU No. 2014-09.

2.11 Both input and output measures have drawbacks in some circumstances. Input is used to measure progress toward completion indirectly, based on an established or assumed relationship between a unit of input and productivity. A significant drawback of input measures is that the relationship of the measures to productivity may not hold, because of inefficiencies or other factors. Output is used to measure results directly and is generally the best measure of progress toward completion in circumstances in which a reliable measure of output can be established. However, output measures often cannot be established, and input measures must then be used.

The preceding paragraph will be deleted upon the effective date of FASB ASU No. 2014-09.

2.12 Both input and output measures require the exercise of judgment and careful application to circumstances. FASB ASC 605-35-25-78 states that the acceptability of the results of input or output measures deemed to be appropriate to the circumstances should be reviewed and confirmed periodically by alternative measures that involve observation and inspection. For example, the results provided by the measure used to determine the extent of progress may be compared to the results of calculations based on physical observations by engineers, architects, or similarly qualified personnel. That type of review provides assurance somewhat similar to that provided for perpetual inventory records by periodic physical inventory counts.

The preceding paragraph will be deleted upon the effective date of FASB ASU No. 2014-09.

Income Determination—Revenue

2.13 As set forth in FASB ASC 605-35-25-15, estimating the revenue on a contract is an involved process that is affected by a variety of uncertainties that depend on the outcome of a series of future events. The estimates must be periodically revised throughout the life of the contract as events occur and as uncertainties are resolved. The major factors that must be considered in determining total estimated revenue include (*a*) the basic contract price, (*b*) contract options, (*c*) change orders, (*d*) claims, and (*e*) contract provisions for penalty and incentive payments, including award fees and performance incentives.

The preceding paragraph will be deleted upon the effective date of FASB ASU No. 2014-09.

Impact of Change Orders on Revenue

2.14 Per paragraph 25 of FASB ASC 605-35-25, change orders are modifications of an original contract that effectively change the provisions of the contract without adding new provisions. They may be initiated by either the contractor or the customer, and they include changes in specifications or design, method or manner of performance, facilities, equipment, materials, sites, and period for completion of the work. For some change orders, both scope and price may be unapproved or in dispute.

The preceding paragraph will be deleted upon the effective date of FASB ASU No. 2014-09.

2.15 Accounting for change orders depends on the underlying circumstances, which may differ for each change order depending on the customer, the contract, and the nature of the change. Therefore, change orders should be evaluated according to their characteristics and the circumstances in which they occur.

The preceding paragraph will be deleted upon the effective date of FASB ASU No. 2014-09.

2.16 In some circumstances, change orders as a normal element of a contract may be numerous, and separate identification may be impractical. Such change orders may be evaluated on a composite basis using historical results as modified by current conditions. If such change orders are considered by the parties to be a normal element within the original scope of the contract, no change in the contract price is required. Otherwise, the adjustment to the contract price may be routinely negotiated.

The preceding paragraph will be deleted upon the effective date of FASB ASU No. 2014-09.

2.17 Many change orders are unpriced; that is, the work to be performed is defined, but the adjustment to the contract price is to be negotiated later. Accounting for unpriced change orders depends on their characteristics and the circumstances in which they occur. For all unpriced change orders, recovery should be deemed probable if the future event or events necessary for recovery are likely to occur. Some of the factors to consider in evaluating whether recovery is probable are the customer's written approval of the scope of the change order, separate documentation for change order costs that are identifiable and reasonable, and the entity's favorable experience in negotiating change orders, especially as it relates to the specific type of contract and change order being evaluated. If change orders are in dispute or are unapproved in regard to both scope and price, they should be evaluated as claims.

The preceding paragraph will be deleted upon the effective date of FASB ASU No. 2014-09.

2.18 If the percentage-of-completion method is used and the contractor and the owner agree on both the scope and price of a change order, contract revenues and costs should be adjusted to reflect the change order. FASB ASC 605-35-25-87 includes the following guidelines for accounting for unpriced change orders:

- If it is not probable that costs related to an unpriced change order will be recovered through a change in the contract price, those costs should be treated as costs related to contract performance in the period the costs are incurred adding to both total estimated costs and costs incurred and thereby reducing total estimated profit.
- If it is probable that the costs of the change order will be recovered by adjusting the contract price, the costs incurred should be deferred until the parties agree on the change in price. Alternatively, the costs can be treated as costs of contract performance in the period they are incurred, with a corresponding increase in contract revenues (that is, no margin is recognized on the change order).
- If it is probable that the contract price adjustment will exceed the costs attributable to the change order and that the excess can be reliably estimated, the contract price should be adjusted to reflect the increase when the costs are recognized as costs of contract performance. Revenue exceeding the costs should not be recorded, unless realization of the additional revenue is assured beyond reasonable doubt. Realization is assured beyond a reasonable doubt if the contract's historical experience provides such assurance or the contractor receives a bona fide offer from the customer and records only the amount of the offer as revenue.

If the contractor uses the completed-contract method, it should defer costs associated with unpriced change orders together with other contract costs if it is probable that the aggregate costs (including change order costs) will be recovered.

The preceding paragraph will be deleted upon the effective date of FASB ASU No. 2014-09.

Impact of Claims on Revenue

2.19 Accounting for claims, representing amounts in excess of the agreed contract price that a contractor seeks to collect from customers or others, depends on the underlying circumstances. Claims are normally as a result of customer-caused delays, errors in specifications and designs, contract terminations, change orders in dispute or unapproved concerning both scope and price, or other causes of unanticipated additional costs.

The preceding paragraph will be deleted upon the effective date of FASB ASU No. 2014-09.

2.20 Recognition of the amounts of additional contract revenue relating to claims is appropriate only if it is probable that the claim will result in additional contract revenue and if the amount can be reliably estimated, as evidenced by satisfying the following conditions:

- The contract or other evidence provides a legal basis for the claim; or a legal opinion has been obtained, stating that under the circumstances there is a reasonable basis to support the claim.
- Additional costs are caused by circumstances that were unforeseen at the contract date and are not the result of deficiencies in the contractor's performance.
- Costs associated with the claim are identifiable or otherwise determinable and are reasonable in view of the work performed.
- The evidence supporting the claim is objective and verifiable, not based on management's feel for the situation or on unsupported representations.

If the foregoing requirements are met, revenue from a claim should be recorded only to the extent that contract costs relating to the claim have been incurred. Per FASB ASC 605-35-25-31, an alternative such as recording revenues from claims only when the amounts have been received or awarded may be used.

The preceding paragraph will be deleted upon the effective date of FASB ASU No. 2014-09.

Income Determination—Cost Elements

2.21 Paragraphs 32–33 of FASB ASC 605-35-25 establish that contract costs should be identified, estimated, and accumulated with a reasonable degree of accuracy in determining income earned. Moreover, an entity should be able to determine costs incurred on a contract with a relatively high degree of precision, depending on the adequacy and effectiveness of its cost accounting system. The procedures or systems used in accounting for costs vary from relatively simple, manual procedures that produce relatively modest amounts of detailed analysis to sophisticated, computer-based systems that produce a great deal of detailed analysis. Despite the diversity of systems and procedures, however, an objective of each system or of each set of procedures should be to accumulate costs properly and consistently by contract with a sufficient degree of accuracy to ensure a basis for the satisfactory measurement of earnings.

The preceding paragraph will be deleted upon the effective date of FASB ASU No. 2014-09.

Accounting for Contract Costs

2.22 The general principles applicable to the accounting for costs of construction-type contracts covered by FASB ASC 605-35 require the exercise of judgment and consist of the following, as directed in paragraphs 34–37 of FASB ASC 605-35-25:

a. All direct costs, such as material, labor, and subcontracting costs, should be included in contract costs.

b. Indirect costs allocable to contracts include the costs of indirect labor, contract supervision, tools and equipment, supplies, quality control and inspection, insurance, repairs and maintenance, depreciation and amortization, and, in some circumstances, support costs such as central preparation and processing of payrolls. However, practice varies for certain types of indirect costs considered allocable to contracts (for example, support costs such as central preparation and processing of job payrolls, billing and collection costs, and bidding and estimating costs) as discussed in FASB ASC 605-35-25-34. For government contractors, in accordance with FASB ASC 912-20-25-1, indirect costs that are allowable or allocable under pertinent government contract regulations may be allocated to federal government contracts as indirect costs if otherwise allowable under generally accepted accounting principles of the United States (U.S. GAAP). Methods of allocating indirect costs should be systematic and rational. They include, for example, allocations based on direct labor costs, direct labor hours, or a combination of direct labor and material costs. The appropriateness of allocations of indirect costs and of the methods of allocation depends on the circumstances and involves judgment.

c. Costs should be considered period costs if they cannot be clearly related to production, either directly or by an allocation based on their discernible future benefits in accordance with FASB ASC 605-35-25-35.

d. General and administrative costs ordinarily should be charged to expense as incurred. When the completed-contract method is used, it may be appropriate to allocate general and administrative expenses to contract costs rather than to periodic income. This may result in a better matching of costs and revenues than would result from treating such expenses as period costs, particularly in years when no contracts were completed.

e. Selling costs should be excluded from contract costs and charged to expense as incurred unless they meet the criteria for precontract costs in FASB ASC 605-35-25-41, as discussed in paragraph 2.24.

f. Costs under cost-type contracts should be charged to contract costs in conformity with U.S. GAAP in the same manner as costs under other types of contracts because unrealistic profit margins may result in circumstances in which reimbursable cost accumulations omit substantial contract costs (with a resulting larger fee) or include substantial unallocable general and administrative costs (with a resulting smaller fee).

g. In computing estimated gross profit or providing for losses on contracts, estimates of cost to complete should reflect all of the types of costs included in contract costs.

h. Inventoriable costs should not be carried at amounts that, when added to the estimated cost to complete, are greater than the estimated realizable value of the related contracts.

The preceding paragraph will be deleted upon the effective date of FASB ASU No. 2014-09.

Cost Attributable to Claims

2.23 Per FASB ASC 605-35-25-31, costs attributable to claims should be treated as costs of contract performance as incurred.

The preceding paragraph will be deleted upon the effective date of FASB ASU No. 2014-09.

Precontract Costs

2.24 Precontract costs are deferred in anticipation of future contract sales in a variety of circumstances and typically consist of any of the following:

- Costs incurred in anticipation of a specific contract that will result in no future benefit unless the contract is obtained (such as the costs of mobilization, engineering, architectural, or other services incurred on the basis of commitments or other indications of interest in negotiating a contract)
- Costs incurred for assets to be used in connection with specific anticipated contracts (for example, costs for the purchase of production equipment, materials, or supplies)
- Costs incurred to acquire or produce goods in excess of the amounts required under a contract in anticipation of future orders for the same item
- Learning, start-up, or mobilization costs incurred for anticipated but unidentified contracts

The preceding paragraph will be deleted upon the effective date of FASB ASU No. 2014-09.

2.25 The following provisions of FASB ASC 605-35-25-41 apply to precontract costs:

a. Costs that are incurred for a specific anticipated contract and that will result in no future benefits unless the contract is obtained should not be included in contract costs or inventory before the receipt of the contract. However, such costs otherwise may be deferred, subject to evaluation of their probable recoverability, but only if the costs can be directly associated with a specific anticipated contract and if their recoverability from the contract is probable. Precontract costs that are start-up activities should be expensed as incurred if they are determined to be within the scope of FASB ASC 720-15.

b. Costs incurred for assets, such as costs for the purchase of materials, production equipment, or supplies, that are expected to be used in connection with anticipated contracts may be deferred outside the contract cost or inventory classification if their recovery from future contract revenue or from other dispositions of the assets is probable.

c. Costs incurred to acquire or produce goods in excess of the amounts required for an existing contract in anticipation of future orders for the same items may be treated as inventory if their recovery is probable.

d. Learning or start-up costs incurred in connection with existing contracts and in anticipation of follow-on or future contracts for the same goods or services should be charged to existing contracts.

e. Costs appropriately deferred in anticipation of a contract should be included in contract costs on the receipt of the anticipated contract.

f. Costs related to anticipated contracts that are charged to expenses as incurred because their recovery is not considered probable should not be reinstated by a credit to income on the subsequent receipt of the contract.

The preceding paragraph will be deleted upon the effective date of FASB ASU No. 2014-09.

Cost Adjustments for Back Charges

2.26 As explained in FASB ASC 605-35-25-42, back charges are billings for work performed or costs incurred by one party that, in accordance with the agreement, should have been performed or incurred by the party to whom billed. These are frequently disputed charges. For example, owners bill back charges to general contractors, and general contractors bill back charges to subcontractors. Examples of back charges include charges for cleanup work and charges for a subcontractor's use of a general contractor's equipment.

The preceding paragraph will be deleted upon the effective date of FASB ASU No. 2014-09.

2.27 FASB ASC 605-35-25-43 provides the following guidance on accounting for back charges:

- Back charges to others should be recorded as receivables and, to the extent considered collectible, should be applied to reduce contract costs. However, if the billed party disputes the propriety or amount of the charge, the back charge is, in effect, a claim, and the criteria for recording claims apply. See paragraphs 2.19–.20 for additional guidance on the accounting treatment of claims.

- Back charges from others should be recorded as payables and as additional contract costs to the extent that it is probable that the amounts will be paid.

The preceding paragraph will be deleted upon the effective date of FASB ASU No. 2014-09.

Estimated Cost to Complete

2.28 The estimated cost to complete is a significant variable in the process of determining income earned and is thus a significant factor in accounting for contracts. It is also one of the most challenging areas for the contractor to account for and for the auditor to audit. According to FASB ASC 605-35-25-44, the following approaches should be followed in determining and updating the estimated cost to complete:

a. Systematic and consistent procedures that are correlated with the cost accounting system should be used to provide a basis for periodically comparing actual and estimated costs.

b. In estimating total contract costs, the quantities and prices of all significant elements of cost should be identified.

c. The estimating procedures should provide that estimated cost to complete includes the same elements of cost that are included in actual accumulated costs; also, those elements should reflect expected price increases as discussed in item *d*.

d. The effects of future wage and price escalations should be taken into account in cost estimates, especially when the contract performance will be carried out over a significant period of time. Escalation provisions should not be blanket overall provisions but should cover labor, materials, and indirect costs based on percentages or amounts that take into consideration known or expected increases, experience, and other pertinent data.

e. Estimates of cost to complete should be reviewed periodically and revised as appropriate to reflect new information.

The preceding paragraph will be deleted upon the effective date of FASB ASU No. 2014-09.

Computation of Earned Income

2.29 Paragraphs 82–84 of FASB ASC 605-35-25 and appendix E, "Computing Income Earned Under the Percentage-of-Completion Method," in this guide set forth and illustrate procedures for determining earned income for a period under the percentage-of-completion method.

The preceding paragraph will be deleted upon the effective date of FASB ASU No. 2014-09.

Revised Estimates

2.30 FASB ASC 605-35-25-86 establishes that revisions in revenue, cost and profit estimates, or measurements of the extent of progress toward completion are changes in accounting estimates as defined in FASB ASC 250, *Accounting Changes and Error Corrections*. Refer to paragraph 6.28 of this guide for additional discussion of revised estimates and appendix G, "Example of Change in Accounting Estimate."

The preceding paragraph will be deleted upon the effective date of FASB ASU No. 2014-09.

Provisions for Anticipated Losses on Contracts

> **Update 2-2 *Accounting and Reporting*: Revenue Recognition**
>
> FASB ASU No. 2016-20, *Technical Corrections and Improvements to Topic 606, Revenue from Contracts with Customers*, was issued in December 2016. The amendments in this FASB ASU affect the guidance in FASB ASU No. 2014-09, which is not yet effective. The effective date and transition requirements for the amendments are the same as the effective date and transition requirements for FASB ASC 606 (and any other FASB ASC topic amended by ASU No. 2014-09). ASU No. 2015-14, *Revenue from Contracts with Customers (Topic 606): Deferral of the Effective Date*, defers the effective date of FASB ASU No. 2014-09 by one year.
>
> Readers are encouraged to read the full text of the ASU, available at www.fasb.org. Readers should apply the appropriate guidance based on their facts and circumstances.

2.31 The provision for loss arises because estimated cost for the contract exceeds estimated revenue. The following summarizes the accounting treatment of anticipated losses on contracts contained in paragraphs 45–50 of FASB ASC 605-35-25 and paragraphs 1–2 of FASB ASC 605-35-45:

- For contracts on which a loss is anticipated, the entire anticipated loss should be recognized in the period in which the loss becomes evident under either the percentage-of-completion method or the completed-contract method.
- The costs used in arriving at the estimated loss on a contract should include all costs of the type allocable to contracts under FASB ASC 605-35-25-37. Other factors that should be considered in arriving at the projected loss on a contract include (*a*) target penalties and interest, (*b*) nonreimbursable costs on cost-plus contracts, (*c*) change orders, and (*d*) potential price redeterminations.
- Provisions for losses should be shown separately as liabilities on the balance sheet, if significant, except in circumstances in which related costs are accumulated on the balance sheet, in which case the provisions may be deducted from the related accumulated costs. In a classified balance sheet, a provision for loss should be shown as a current liability.
- The provision for loss should be accounted for in the income statement as an additional contract cost rather than as a reduction of contract revenue. Unless the provision is material in amount or unusual or infrequent in nature, the provision should be included in contract cost and should not be shown separately in the income statement. If it is shown separately, it should be shown as a component of the cost included in the computation of gross profit.

The preceding paragraph will be deleted upon the effective date of FASB ASU No. 2014-09 and subsequent ASUs which amend FASB ASU No. 2014-09, replaced with the following and relocated under the heading "Provisions for Anticipated Losses on Contracts" in chapter 5, "Other Accounting Considerations."

The provision for loss arises because estimated cost for the contract exceeds estimated revenue. The following summarizes the accounting treatment of anticipated losses on contracts contained in the "Pending Content" of paragraphs 45–50 of FASB ASC 605-35-25 and paragraphs 1–2 of FASB ASC 605-35-45:

- For a contract on which a loss is anticipated,[2] the entire anticipated loss should be recognized as soon as the loss becomes evident. When the current estimates of the amount of consideration that an entity expects to receive in exchange for transferring promised goods or services to the customer, determined in accordance with FASB ASC 606, and contract cost indicate a loss, a provision for the entire loss on the contract shall be made. Provisions for losses shall be made in the period in which they become evident.
- For the purpose of determining the amount that an entity expects to receive in accordance with the above item, the entity should use the principles for determining the transaction price, set forth in the "Pending Content" in paragraphs 2–27 of FASB ASC 606-10-32 and allocating the transaction price in the "Pending Content" in paragraphs 28-41 of FASB ASC 606-10-32.
- If a group of contracts are combined based on the guidance in "Pending Content" in paragraph 9 of FASB ASC 606-10-25, they should be treated as a unit in determining the necessity for a provision for a loss. If contracts are not combined, the loss is determined at the contract level.[3]
- Losses on cost-type contracts may arise if, for example, a contract provides for guaranteed maximum reimbursable costs or target penalties. In recognizing losses for accounting purposes, the contractor's normal cost accounting methods should be used in determining the total cost overrun on the contract, and losses should include provisions for performance penalties.
- The costs used in arriving at the estimated loss on a contract should include all costs of the type allocable to contracts under paragraphs 5–8 of FASB ASC 340-40-25. Other factors that should be considered in arriving at the projected loss on a contract include (*a*) variable consideration, (for example, target penalties and rewards and potential price redeterminations), (*b*) nonreimbursable costs on cost-plus contracts and (*c*) change orders that meet the guidance to be accounted for as contract modifications in accordance with paragraphs 10–13 of FASB ASC 606-10-25.

---

[2] "Pending Content" in paragraph 7 of FASB *Accounting Standards Codification* (ASC) 605-35-25 notes that contracts should be combined to determine the need for a provision for losses in accordance with "Pending Content" in paragraphs 45–49 of FASB ASC 605-35-25 only if they meet the criteria in FASB ASC 606, specifically "Pending Content" in paragraph 9 of FASB ASC 606-10-25.

[3] Per "Pending Content" in paragraph 47 of FASB ASC 605-35-25, as an accounting policy election, performance obligations identified in accordance with "Pending Content" in paragraphs 14–22 of FASB ASC 606-10-25 may be considered separately in determining the need for a provision for a loss. That is, an entity can elect to determine provisions for losses at either the contract level (including contracts that are combined in accordance with the guidance in "Pending Content" in paragraph 9 of FASB 606-10-25) or the performance obligation level. An entity should apply this accounting policy election in the same manner for similar types of contracts.

- Provisions for losses should be shown separately as liabilities on the balance sheet, if significant, except in circumstances in which related costs are accumulated on the balance sheet, in which case the provisions may be deducted from the related accumulated costs. In a classified balance sheet, a provision for loss should be shown as a current liability.
- The provision for loss should be accounted for in the income statement as an additional contract cost rather than as a reduction of contract revenue. Unless the provision is material in amount or unusual or infrequent in nature, the provision should be included in contract cost and should not be shown separately in the income statement. If it is shown separately, it should be shown as a component of the cost included in the computation of gross profit.

Selecting a Measure of Extent of Progress

2.32 A good measure of extent of progress toward completion should give weight to all elements of a contractor's work and should consider the broad phases of a contractor's operation, such as

- designing the project (preparing blueprints to meet the owner's specifications).
- obtaining the necessary labor, materials, supplies, and equipment and mobilizing them at the construction site. Refer to FASB ASC 605-35-25-76 for a discussion of uninstalled materials as they relate to measuring the extent of progress using an input measure based on costs (for example, the ratio of costs incurred to date to total estimated costs at completion).
- managing the resources to complete the project.
- demobilizing the resources from the construction site.

The preceding paragraph will be deleted upon the effective date of FASB ASU No. 2014-09.

Costs of Equipment and Small Tools

2.33 The cost of a contractor's equipment should be allocated to the particular contract on which it is used on a reasonable basis, such as time, hours of use, or mileage. Based on the reported use of the equipment, a rate may be arrived at that will serve as a basis for charging the contracts on which the equipment is used. In determining the operating unit costs for construction equipment to be included in contract cost, paragraphs 1–2 of FASB ASC 910-20-25 and FASB ASC 910-20-30-1 establish that contractors may utilize the use rate theory. In applying this theory, the following factors should be considered: (*a*) the cost of the equipment, less estimates of its salvage value or rental if it is leased, (*b*) the probable life of the equipment, (*c*) the average idle time during the life or period of hire of the equipment, and (*d*) the costs of operating the equipment, such as repairs, storage, insurance, and taxes.

2.34 In determining a suitable indirect cost allocation method for equipment, questions arise relating to accounting for equipment charges when a contractor's equipment is idle during a winter season or related to the propriety of allocating idle equipment costs to jobs. FASB ASC 910-20-25-3 states that idle equipment time, such as when a contractor's equipment is idle during a winter season, may be, but is not required to be, considered in determining indirect cost allocations. Allocation of idle equipment costs to contracts by use of rates geared to cover all costs is appropriate. That procedure results in rates that lessors of the same type of equipment charge users in the same location, except for the profit element.

2.35 FASB ASC 910-20-25-4 states that small tools should be charged to a contract as they are consumed in performance of the contract. Operating and maintenance costs of miscellaneous small tools and equipment are usually charged to overhead accounts rather than specific contracts. However, a contractor may charge the costs directly to specific contracts if they relate to specific contracts. Small tools can frequently be charged to contracts if purchased for the contracts or if issued from a central pool. Contract costs should be credited with estimated salvage value of small tools remaining at completion of the contracts.

2.36 If small tools are significant, they may be accounted for as inventory or fixed assets. FASB ASC 910-330-40-1 states that removals of small tools from inventory may be charged to specific contracts or charged to overhead and spread over jobs on an equitable basis. FASB ASC 910-360-35-1 states that depreciation of small tools carried in fixed assets may be charged to overhead or to specific contracts.

The preceding paragraphs in the section titled "Costs of Equipment and Small Tools" will be relocated to chapter 5 upon the effective date of FASB ASU No. 2014-09.

2.37

Appendix A—Implementation Guidance for Accounting Standards Update No. 2014-09, *Revenue from Contracts with Customers (Topic 606)*

Application of the Five-Step Model of FASB ASC 606

Step 1: Identify the Contract With a Customer

Identifying the Unit of Account

This Accounting Implementation Issue Is Relevant to Step 1: "Identify the Contract With a Customer," of FASB ASC 606.

Identifying the Contracts With the Customer

A-1 FASB ASC 606-10-25-9 indicates that when two or more contracts are entered into at or near the same time with the same customer, they must be accounted for as a single contract if any of the following criteria are met: (*a*) the contracts are negotiated as a package with a single commercial objective, (*b*) the amount of consideration payable under one contract depends on the price or performance under the other contract, or (*c*) the goods or services promised in the contracts represent a single performance obligation.

A-2 FinREC believes one example of when contracts should possibly be combined is when there are separate contracts with the same customer, one for engineering services and the other for construction services, that are issued only a month apart (at or near the same time). If these two contracts are for the design and building of a single capital asset and they would be a single performance obligation had they been in a single contract, these contracts likely should be combined. Judgment is required because additional facts or different circumstances could result in a different conclusion.

Impact of Customer Termination Rights and Penalties on Contract Term

This Accounting Implementation Issue Is Relevant to Step 1: "Identify the Contract With a Customer," of FASB ASC 606.

A-3 It is common in the engineering and construction industry to have contracts that give the customer a right to cancel for convenience or other than for cause but that do not give the contractor similar rights (or that the contractor could not exercise without incurring significant consequences). Engineering and construction customers include such termination clauses to provide them an opportunity to suspend or terminate a project should unforeseen economic or political circumstances occur that significantly affect the return that would be generated by the capital project. However, unlike in industries where contracts are for much smaller value and for a series of services (for example, cellular phone services), engineering and construction contracts are rarely terminated, because partial completion of a capital project or a facility is of little value to the customer, and the customer would incur additional costs that are considered akin to termination penalties (for example, costs of shutting down the work, demobilization, storage and handling of uninstalled materials, as well as restart costs if the customer later desires to complete the project).

A-4 FASB ASC 606-10-32-4 states, "For the purpose of determining the transaction price, an entity shall assume that the goods or services will be transferred to the customer as promised in accordance with the existing contract and that the contract will not be cancelled, renewed, or modified."

A-5 In an engineering and construction contract, the promise to the customer is often a facility or capital asset, as discussed in the section, "Identifying the Unit of Account," in paragraphs 11.2.01–11.2.17.

A-6 At the November 2015 meeting of the FASB/IASB TRG, an implementation issue was discussed regarding how to determine the term of the contract when the customer has the unilateral right to terminate a contract and whether termination penalties affect that analysis.

A-7 As discussed in paragraphs 50 and 51 of TRG Agenda Ref 48, *Customer Options for Additional Goods and Services, Issue 2: Customer Termination Rights and Penalties*, the FASB and IASB staff recommended that contracts with customer termination provisions should be accounted for the same as contracts with unexercised options when the contract does not include a substantive termination penalty. That is, if the termination penalty is not substantive, this may indicate that the contract term, in accordance with FASB ASC 606, is less than the stated contractual period. FASB/IASB TRG Agenda Ref 49, *November 2015 Meeting – Summary of Issues Discussed and Next Steps*, paragraph 10 states, in part:

> At the October 31, 2014 TRG meeting, the TRG discussed the accounting for termination clauses in the contract when each party has the unilateral right to terminate the contract by compensating the other party. At that meeting, TRG members supported the view that the legally enforceable contract period should be considered the contract period. Since that meeting, stakeholders have raised further questions (Issue 2) about evaluating a contract when only one party has the right to terminate the contract. TRG members agreed with the staff analysis that the views expressed at the October 2014 TRG meeting would be consistent regardless of whether both parties can terminate, or whether only one party can terminate. TRG members highlighted that when performing an evaluation of the contract term and the effect of termination penalties, an entity should consider whether those penalties are substantive. Determining whether a penalty is substantive will require judgement and the examples in the TRG paper do not create a bright line for what is substantive.

A-8 FinREC believes that the contractor's history with terminations for different types of contracts, specific knowledge about the customer, and other facts and circumstances should be considered in assessing the impact of a termination provision on the duration of a contract. The TRG discussion regarding the concept of cancelation rights and renewal options and substantive termination penalties noted in paragraph 4 is applicable in contracts for the provision of a series of recurring goods and services (for example, operations and maintenance contracts). Most engineering and construction contracts are for the design and construction of a facility or capital asset. The contractor has enforceable rights to be compensated for work performed during the execution of the contract and upon termination. The contractor has an enforceable obligation to complete the entire facility. FinREC believes that because a contractor has an ongoing enforceable obligation, often backed by a surety bond or letter of credit, to deliver the full scope of work specified in a contract with a customer, until the scope of work is completed or the customer explicitly terminates the contract, the contractor should reflect this obligation in the accounting and disclosure of remaining unsatisfied performance obligations until such time that the contract is terminated.

A-9 The following examples are intended to be illustrative, and different facts and circumstances may change the conclusion. In each example, it is assumed that the contract meets all criteria for existence in accordance with FASB ASC 606-10-25-1.

Example 11-1-1

A customer enters into a contract with an engineering and construction company for the design and construction of a high-tech manufacturing facility. In this example, the customer would incur a substantial economic penalty to cancel for convenience (for example, significant wind-down costs would be incurred and a partially completed facility would be of no use to that customer). As a result, FinREC believes the contract price, in accordance with FASB ASC 606-10-32-4, and duration of the contract are determined based on the defined scope in the contract (design and build a high-tech manufacturing facility), as opposed to a service contract, which would have a term based on the passage of time.

Example 11-1-2

A customer enters into a contract for recurring maintenance services with a contractor. The contract is for an indefinite term and includes a termination provision that allows either party to cancel for convenience upon 30 days' notice. The contract states that the customer will compensate the contractor in accordance with the terms of the contract for services provided through the termination date. In accordance with the guidance in paragraph 10 of TRG Agenda Ref No. 49, this contract would be accounted for on a month-to-month basis because there is not a substantial (contractual or economic) termination penalty.

Example 11-1-3

A customer enters into a contract to perform small capital projects at the customer's facilities for a period of three years, with an option to renew for another three years. The renewal option is assumed not to represent a material right. There is no termination for convenience clause in the contract. FinREC believes that, at inception, the term of this contract is three years because there is no termination for convenience clause (neither party has a right to terminate early except in the case of default).

Step 2: Identify the Performance Obligations in the Contract

Identifying the Unit of Account

This Accounting Implementation Issue Is Relevant to Step 2: "Identify the Performance Obligations in the Contract," of FASB ASC 606.

Identifying the Performance Obligations in the Contract

A-10 Paragraphs 14–22 of FASB ASC 606-10-25 discuss how to determine whether promised goods and services in the contract represent performance obligations.

A-11 FASB ASC 606-10-25-14 establishes that a contractor should assess goods or services promised in a contract and identify as performance obligations each promise to transfer to the customer either

a. a good or service (or bundle of goods or services) that is distinct or

b. a series of distinct goods or services that are substantially the same and that have the same pattern of transfer to the customer.

A-12 FASB ASC 606-10-25-15 explains that a series of distinct goods or services has the same pattern of transfer to the customer if both the following criteria are met:

a. Each distinct good or service in the series that the entity promises to transfer to the customer would meet the criteria in FASB ASC 606-10-25-27 to be a performance obligation satisfied over time.

b. In accordance with paragraphs 31–32 of FASB ASC 606-10-25, the same method would be used to measure the entity's progress toward complete satisfaction of the performance obligation to transfer each distinct good or service in the series to the customer.

A-13 Determining whether goods and services are distinct is a matter of judgment. Whereas FASB ASC 606-10-25-19(a) effectively looks to the economic substance of each good or service to determine whether a customer can benefit from that good or service either on its own or with readily available resources or those available to the customer in the marketplace, FASB ASC 606-10-25-19(b) requires the contractor to evaluate whether the promised good or service in the contract is separately identifiable from other promises in the contract (that is, the promise to transfer the good or service is distinct within the context of the contract), and FASB ASC 606-10-25-21 provides a nonexclusive list of indicators for the contractor to consider. A contractor's evaluation of the indicators may vary depending on the specific circumstances of the contract.

A-14 In many engineering and construction contracts, the finished deliverable is constructed in a number of phases (for example, front-end engineering and design, detailed engineering, procurement, fabrication, construction or construction management, and validation or start-up) that each include goods or services that normally provide benefit to the customer on their own or together with other readily available resources. Therefore, the contractor's evaluation regarding whether a promised good or service is or is not distinct will likely depend more on an evaluation of the criteria in FASB ASC 606-10-25-19(b)—that is, whether those goods or services are distinct within the context of the contract.

A-15 FASB ASC 606-10-25-21 includes factors for consideration in determining whether a contractor's promise to transfer a good or service to a customer is or is not separately identifiable; however, it does not limit a contractor's consideration only to those factors identified. As a result, an entity's evaluation of the indicators in FASB ASC 606-10-25-21 will largely be driven by the nature of the transaction and the specific facts and circumstances of the contract. Paragraph BC29 of FASB Accounting Standards Update (ASU) No. 2016-10, *Revenue from Contracts with Customers (Topic 606): Identifying Performance Obligations and Licensing*, indicates that when evaluating whether the individual goods and services are separately identifiable, "entities should evaluate whether the contract is to deliver (a) multiple goods or services or (b) a combined item or items that is comprised of the individual goods and services promised in the contract." In other words, entities should evaluate whether the individual goods and services are outputs or, instead, inputs to a combined output.

A-16 Paragraph BC105 of FASB ASU No. 2014-09, *Revenue from Contracts with Customers (Topic 606)*, explains that the principle of "separately identifiable" is based on the notion of separable risks, that is, whether the risk that an entity assumes to fulfill its obligation to transfer one of those promised goods or services to the customer is a risk that is inseparable from the risk relating to the transfer of the other promised goods or services. BC106 of FASB ASU No. 2014-09 further notes that the factors in FASB ASC 606-10-25-21 are based on the same underlying principle of inseparable risks, and that in many cases more than one of the factors might apply to a contract with a customer.

A-17 The factor in FASB ASC 606-10-25-21(a) suggests that a promised good or service in a contract is not distinct from the other promised goods or services where the contract is for the construction of a single, combined output resulting from the contractor's significant service of integrating the component goods and services in the contract. FinREC believes that an important factor for determining that goods or services should be combined with an integration service into a single performance obligation is that the risk the entity assumes in performing the integration service is inseparable from the risk relating to the transfer of the other promised goods or services. The judgment about the risk an entity assumes with respect to a promised good or service can often be inferred by certain terms of the contract, such as the contract's acceptance or warranty provisions.

A-18 Another important judgment in interpreting FASB ASC 606-10-25-21(a) is whether the integration service is significant. Paragraph BC107 of FASB ASU No. 2014-09 states that the risk of transferring individual goods or services is inseparable from an integration service because a substantial part of the entity's promise to a customer is to ensure the individual goods or services are incorporated into the combined output. Paragraph BC107 continues to explain that this factor may be relevant in many construction contracts in which the contractor provides an integration (or contract management) service to manage and coordinate the various construction tasks and to assume the risks associated with the integration of those tasks.

A-19 An integration service may be clearly evident when combining a number of subcomponents into a single deliverable (for instance, construction of a single structure). However, many engineering and construction contracts are for the provision of multiple services or structures (such as engineering and construction of a power generation facility). In these arrangements, additional judgment will be required when evaluating whether there is a substantial integration service involved. Although there is generally assumed to be a significant service of integrating engineering with construction to produce a combined output (such as a power plant), FinREC believes that, in some circumstances, the engineering may not be significantly integrated with the construction (such as when engineering and construction are performed in separate and distinct phases for which the customer has the option of awarding construction to a different contractor upon completion of the engineering). Significant judgment is required in making this assessment, and the conclusion should be based on specific facts and circumstances. Careful consideration should be given to the degree of the integration service provided in the context of the contract.

A-20 For example, if an engineering and construction company has a unit that provides fabrication services, whether the fabrication services would be a separate performance obligation from construction in a contract would depend on the significance of the integration service. If the fabrication unit is fabricating major sections of a bridge in its own fabrication yard and a substantial part of the construction services involves constructing the bridge by installing the fabricated components to produce the combined output of a single bridge, the fabrication and construction should be considered a single performance obligation if the entity concludes that the risk of fabrication of the individual components of the bridge is inseparable from the risk associated with construction of the bridge.

A-21 The factor in FASB ASC 606-10-25-21(b) suggests that a promised good or service in a contract is not distinct where it significantly modifies or customizes another good or service in the contract. Within the construction industry, although facts and circumstances vary and judgment is required, engineering frequently modifies or customizes each construction project significantly. For example, the construction would be customized because of site condition differences at each location, based on the engineering, for what might otherwise be identical power generation facilities.

A-22 The factor in FASB ASC 606-10-25-21(c) explains that a promised good or service in a contract is not separately identifiable if it is highly dependent upon, or highly interrelated with, other promised goods or services in the contract. Paragraph BC111 of FASB ASU No. 2014-09 states that this indicator was included because, in some cases, it might be unclear whether the entity is providing an integration service or whether the goods or services are significantly modified or customized. It is usually clear whether the factors in items (a) and (b) of FASB ASC 606-10-25-21 are met for engineering and construction contracts; therefore, the factor in item (c) will typically be less important in making the assessment of whether promised goods or services in the contract are not separately identifiable.

A-23 If, after having considered the factors in FASB ASC 606-10-25-21, a contractor has determined that promised goods or services are distinct, the contractor would then consider whether those distinct goods or services are substantially the same and have the same pattern of transfer to the customer, as discussed in FASB ASC 606-10-25-14(b). In making this determination, the contractor would evaluate whether both of the following criteria from FASB ASC 606-10-25-15 are met:

a. The distinct good or service in the series that the entity promises to transfer to the customer would meet the criteria in FASB 606-10-25-27 to be a performance obligation satisfied over time.

b. The same method would be used to measure the entity's progress toward complete satisfaction of the performance obligation to transfer each distinct good or service in the series to the customer.

A-24 BC113 of FASB ASU No. 2014-09 explains that the criteria in FASB ASC 606-10-25-15 were included as part of the definition of *performance obligation* to simplify the application of the model and to promote consistency in the identification of performance obligations in circumstances in which the entity provides the same good or service consecutively over a period of time. BC114 of FASB ASU No. 2014-09 identifies several examples of repetitive service contracts, including a cleaning contract, transaction processing, or a contract to deliver electricity. Within the engineering and construction industry, an example of a series of services would be an operations and maintenance contract with a manufacturing customer for maintenance services that are substantially the same from day to day.

A-25 Arrangements in the engineering and construction industry may include maintenance services. The first critical step in evaluating maintenance-type services is to identify the nature of the arrangement. As discussed in FASB/IASB TRG Agenda Ref. 16—Stand-Ready Performance Obligations, a promise to provide periodic maintenance, when and if needed, on a customer's equipment after a pre-established amount of usage, may be considered a "stand-ready" obligation. BC160 of FASB ASU No. 2014-09 supports the view that promises to "stand ready" are evaluated based on increments of time (that is, the act of standing ready) as opposed to the underlying activities of providing goods and services. As discussed in FASB/IASB TRG Agenda Ref 39—Application of the Series Provision and Allocation of Variable Consideration, if the contractor determines that the nature of the arrangement is a stand-ready obligation, the maintenance arrangement will generally be accounted for as a series in accordance with FASB ASC 606-10-25-14(b) (that is, the promise to stand ready is substantially the same from day to day). Consistent with paragraph 32 of FASB/IASB TRG Agenda Ref. 25, January 2015 Meeting—Summary Memo, arrangements to provide specific maintenance services over a period of time (as opposed to when and if needed) would not be accounted for as stand-ready obligations, and, as a result, are evaluated based on the specified goods and services promised in the contract using the distinct criteria discussed in paragraphs 11.2.01–11.2.15. These arrangements, which may be more common in the engineering and construction industry, may also be accounted for as a series if the types of services performed are substantially the same from day to day and meet the criteria in FASB ASC 606-10-25-15. Regardless of whether the arrangement is considered a series of stand-ready or specified services, the objective for measuring progress over time is to depict the contractor's performance of satisfying the performance obligation (consistent with question 2 of FASB/IASB TRG Agenda Ref 16, it is not appropriate to default to a straight-line revenue attribution method for stand-ready obligations if such attribution would not depict the contractor's performance.) (See the "Acceptable Measures of Progress" section in paragraphs 11.5.01–11.5.27 for appropriate methods of measuring progress for common types of arrangements in the engineering and construction industry.)

A-26 The following example is meant to be illustrative; the actual determination of the performance obligation(s) in a contract should be based on the facts and circumstances of an entity's specific situation.

Example 11-2-1

E&C Corporation (the contractor) has entered into a contract with State Transit Authority (the customer) to design and construct a commuter rail line and maintain this line along with other lines that are already operational. The maintenance services consist of regularly scheduled maintenance of the rail lines; major overhaul services are not within the scope of this contract. The design and construction work is expected to take five years to complete. The maintenance of the other lines that are already operational will be transitioned from being performed in-house by State Transit Authority to E&C Corp. within one year, and the maintenance portion of the contract will continue for 20 years.

E&C Corp. reviews FASB ASC 606-10-25-19 to 25-21 to identify the performance obligations in this contract. E&C Corp. determines that there are two performance obligations in this contract: (1) the design and construction activity and (2) the maintenance activity, which is a series of distinct services in accordance with FASB ASC 606-10-25-14(b).

E&C Corp. concludes that each of the promises in the contract (design, construction, and maintenance services) is capable of being distinct in accordance with FASB ASC 606-10-25-19(a). That is, the customer can benefit from the goods and services either on their own or together with other readily available resources. This is evidenced by the fact that other entities regularly sell these services separately to other customers (that is, the customer could receive the design services from one entity and separately contract for the construction or maintenance services from another entity).

However, E&C Corp. concludes that the design and construction services are not separately identifiable (that is, distinct within the context of the contract) in accordance with FASB ASC 606-10-25-19(b). This conclusion was reached by considering the indicators in FASB ASC 606-10-25-21. That is, E&C Corp. provides a significant service of integrating the design and construction services into a single output for which the customer has contracted (a commuter rail line). Additionally, the design significantly modifies or customizes construction, and construction is highly interdependent on the design. Therefore, because both criteria in FASB ASC 606-10-25-19 are not met for the design and construction services, E&C Corp. concludes that they should be combined into one performance obligation.

In determining whether the maintenance service is distinct from the design and construction, E&C Corp. concludes that the maintenance services are separately identifiable from the design and construction services in the contract itself (FASB ASC 606-10-25-19(b)). That is, the maintenance services are not highly integrated with or highly dependent on the design and construction and do not significantly modify or customize the design and construction (FASB ASC 606-10-25-21). Additionally, the maintenance services are determined to be a series of distinct goods and services that are substantially the same and have the same pattern of transfer to the customer, in accordance with paragraphs 14(b) and 15 of FASB ASC 606-10-25. E&C Corp., therefore, determines that the maintenance services are a series of distinct goods and services accounted for as a single performance obligation and distinct from the design and construction services performance obligation.

Step 3: Determine the Transaction Price

Variable Consideration and Constraining Estimates of Variable Consideration

This Accounting Implementation Issue Is Relevant to Step 3: "Determine the Transaction Price," of FASB ASC 606.

Background

A-27 Estimating the transaction price of a contract is an involved process that is affected by a variety of uncertainties that depend on the outcome of a series of future events. The estimates must be revised each period throughout the life of the contract when events occur and as uncertainties are resolved. The major factors that must be considered in determining total estimated revenue include (*a*) the basic contract price, (*b*) contract options, (*c*) change orders, (*d*) claims, and (*e*) contract provisions for penalty and incentive payments, including award fees and performance incentives.

A-28 Engineering and construction contracts often contain provisions for variable consideration from the customer in the form of change orders (including unpriced change orders), claims, back charges, extras, and contract provisions for penalty and incentive payments, including award fees and performance incentives. (See paragraphs 11.3.07–11.3.09 for discussion on the evaluation of the guidance in paragraphs 10–13 of FASB ASC 606-10-25 for contract modification accounting to determine if certain types of variable consideration should be accounted for under the variable consideration guidance.)

A-29 Change orders, claims, extras, or back charges are common in construction activity. Modifications of the original contract frequently result from change orders that may be initiated by either the customer or the contractor. The nature of the construction industry, particularly the complexity of some types of projects, is conducive to disputes between the parties that may give rise to claims or back charges. Claims may also arise from unapproved change orders. In addition, customer representatives at a job site sometimes authorize the contractor to do work beyond contract specifications, and this gives rise to claims for extras. The ultimate profitability of a contract often depends on whether appropriate authorization has been obtained and whether modifications to the original contract have been identified, documented, and related amounts collected.

A-30 In accordance with FASB ASC 606, entities are required to make estimates of variable consideration in determining the transaction price, subject to the guidance on constraining estimates of variable consideration. In addition, as required by FASB ASC 606-10-32-9, an entity should consider all the information (historical, current, and forecast) that is reasonably available to the entity and shall identify a reasonable number of possible consideration amounts. The information that an entity uses to estimate the amount of variable consideration typically would be similar to the information that the entity's management uses during the bid-and-proposal process and in establishing prices for promised goods and services. Entities are also required to update their estimates of variable consideration on an ongoing basis.

Incentives and Penalties

A-31 All types of contracts may be modified by target penalties and incentives relating to factors such as completion dates, plant capacity on completion of the project, and underruns and overruns of estimated costs. These provisions for incentives and award fees are generally based on (*a*) the relationship of actual contract costs to an agreed-upon target cost or shared savings or (*b*) some measure of contract performance in relation to agreed-upon performance targets. Consequently, the contractor's profit is increased when actual costs are less than agreed-upon cost targets or shared savings. Similarly, the profit is increased when actual performance meets or exceeds agreed-upon performance targets. Conversely, the contractor's profit is decreased when actual results (in terms of either cost or performance targets) do not meet the established cost or performance targets.

A-32 FinREC believes that the mere existence of contractual provisions for incentives or award fees should not be considered presumptive evidence that such incentives or award fees are to be automatically included in the transaction price. In the case of performance incentives, assessing whether actual performance will produce results that meet targeted performance objectives may require substantial judgment and experience with the types of activities covered by the contract. However, in many circumstances, these estimates of performance relative to targeted performance are similar to the processes used to estimate completion on long-term contracts.

Change Orders

A-33 Change orders are modifications of an original contract that effectively change the provisions of the contract without adding new provisions. They may be initiated by either the contractor or the customer, and they include changes in specifications or design, method or manner of performance, facilities, equipment, materials, sites, and period for completion of the work. For some change orders, both scope and price may be unapproved or in dispute. Many change orders are unpriced; that is, the work to be performed is defined, but the adjustment to the contract price is to be negotiated later.

A-34 Accounting for change orders depends on the underlying circumstances, which may differ for each change order, depending on the customer, the contract, and the nature of the change. FASB ASC 606-10-25-11 states,

> A contract modification may exist even though the parties to the contract have a dispute about the scope or price (or both) of the modification or the parties have approved a change in the scope of the contract but have not yet determined the corresponding change in price. In determining whether the rights and obligations that are created or changed by a modification are enforceable, an entity shall consider all relevant facts and circumstances including the terms of the contract and other evidence. If the parties to a contract have approved a change in the scope of the contract but have not yet determined the corresponding change in price, an entity shall estimate the change to the transaction price arising from the modification in accordance with paragraphs 606-10-32-5 through 32-9 on estimating variable consideration and paragraphs 606-10-32-11 through 32-13 on constraining estimates of variable consideration.

A-35 In accordance with FASB ASC 606-10-25-11, judgment will be needed to evaluate a change order to determine whether it represents an enforceable obligation that should be accounted for in accordance with the guidance in paragraphs 5–9 of FASB ASC 606-10-32 on estimating variable consideration and paragraphs 11–13 of FASB ASC 606-10-32 on constraining estimates of variable consideration. FinREC believes some factors to consider include the following:

a. The customer's written approval of the scope of the change order;

b. Current contract language that indicates clear and enforceable entitlement relating to the change order;

c. Separate documentation for the change order costs that are identifiable and reasonable; or

d. The entity's favorable experience in negotiating change orders, especially as it relates to the specific type of contract and change order being evaluated

Claims

A-36 Claims represent amounts in excess of the agreed contract price that a contractor seeks to collect from customers or others and that are normally a result of customer-caused delays, errors in specifications and designs, contract terminations, disputed or unapproved change orders concerning both scope and price, or other causes of unanticipated additional costs. The contract modification guidance in FASB ASC 606-10-25-11 should be considered to determine whether a claim represents an enforceable obligation that should be accounted for in accordance with paragraphs 5–9 of FASB ASC 606-10-32 on estimating variable consideration and paragraphs 11–13 of FASB ASC 606-10-32 on constraining estimates of variable consideration.

Estimating Variable Consideration

A-37 FASB ASC 606-10-32-8 discusses two methods for estimating variable consideration. The choice of method is not intended to be a free choice and is dependent on which method the entity expects to better predict the amount of consideration to which it will be entitled. The two methods are the following:

- *a.* *The expected value method.* This method estimates variable consideration based on the sum of probability-weighted amounts in a range of possible consideration amounts. This method may be appropriate when an entity has a large number of contracts with similar characteristics or the range of possible outcomes in any one contract is wide (generally, when there are more than two possible outcomes).
- *b.* *The most likely amount.* This method estimates the variable consideration based on the single most likely amount in a range of possible consideration amounts. This method may be appropriate if the estimate of variable consideration has only two possible outcomes (for example, an entity is entitled to all variable consideration upon achieving a performance milestone or none if the performance milestone is not achieved).

The number of possible outcomes should not cause an entity to automatically use any one method, but rather the method selected should be dependent on which method the entity expects to better predict the amount of consideration to which it will be entitled.

A-38 FASB ASC 606-10-32-9 requires an entity to apply one method consistently throughout the contract when estimating the amount of variable consideration to which it is entitled. Per FASB ASC 606-10-10-3, the method selected should be applied consistently to contracts with similar characteristics and in similar circumstances. The method should also be applied to types of variable consideration with similar characteristics and in similar circumstances. That is, a single contract may have more than one uncertainty related to variable consideration (for example, a contract with both cost and performance incentives), and depending on the method the entity expects to better predict the amount of consideration to which it is entitled, the entity may therefore use different methods for different uncertainties. In estimating the amount of variable consideration under either of the methods, and as discussed in FASB ASC 606-10-32-9, the entity should consider all the information (historical, current, and forecast) that is reasonably available to the entity and shall identify a reasonable number of possible consideration amounts.

A-39 The following examples are meant to be illustrative; the actual determination of the method for estimating variable consideration as stated in FASB ASC 606-10-32-8 should be based on the facts and circumstances of an entity's specific situation. The following examples also assume for illustrative purposes that the constraint principle for variable consideration has been considered.

Example 11-3-1

A contract is negotiated with a fixed price plus an award fee that is tied directly to delivery by a specified date. The entity has subcontracted a portion of the work. The entity estimates that it will achieve the award fee because the contract is not considered complex, the subcontractor has delivered on similar timelines in the past, and both the entity and subcontractor currently estimate completion up to six months prior to the specified date. In this instance, the entity determines that the expected value method may not provide a predictive estimate of the variable consideration because the contract has only two possible outcomes. The entity's estimate of the total transaction price is therefore the sum total of the fixed price plus the award fee as the most likely consideration amount.

Example 11-3-2

An entity contracts to build a solar energy plant for a customer and receives an incentive fee from the customer that varies depending on objectively determinable key performance indicators (KPIs) associated with energy savings over a one-year period. The entity has extensive experience determining energy savings under various conditions that impact solar energy. To estimate the incentive fee, management calculates the expected value by using the data available to them to estimate the savings under the various environmental conditions. The entity believes that the estimate determined using this expected value method is predictive of the amount to which it will be entitled because of the wide range of possible outcomes.

Example 11-3-3

An entity contracts to build a road on January 1 with an agreed-upon completion date of June 30. The contract calls for liquidated damages in the event that contractor-caused delays result in the road not being completed by June 30. In this example, significant judgment is needed in terms of which method the entity expects to better predict the amount of consideration to which it will be entitled because, oftentimes, whether the completion date will be met is binary; however, the number of days of liquidated damages (that is, the number of days past the agreed-upon completion date) that will be incurred is often highly variable.

Constraining Estimates of Variable Consideration

A-40 After estimating the transaction price using one of the two methods, an entity is required to evaluate the likelihood and magnitude of a reversal of revenue due to a subsequent change in the estimate. FASB ASC 606-10-32-11 discusses when to include variable consideration in the transaction price and notes that an entity shall include in the transaction price some or all of the variable consideration amount estimated in accordance with FASB ASC 606-10-32-8 only to the extent that it is probable that a significant reversal in the amount of cumulative revenue recognized will not occur when the uncertainty associated with the variable consideration is subsequently resolved.

A-41 As discussed in BC215 of FASB ASU No. 2014-09, if the process for estimating variable consideration already incorporates the principles on which the guidance for constraining estimates of variable consideration is based, then it is not necessary for an entity to evaluate the constraint separately from the estimate of variable consideration.

A-42 As discussed in FASB ASC 606-10-32-12, when determining the amount of variable consideration to include in the transaction price, the entity should consider both the likelihood and magnitude of a revenue reversal. An estimate of variable consideration is not constrained if the potential reversal of cumulative revenue recognized is not significant. As explained in paragraph 49 of FASB/IASB TRG Agenda Ref 25, January 2015 Meeting—Summary of Issues Discussed and Next Steps,

> TRG members generally agreed that the constraint on variable consideration should be applied at the contract level. Therefore, the assessment of whether a significant reversal of revenue will occur in the future (the constraint) should consider the estimated transaction price of the contract rather than the amount allocated to a performance obligation.

The levels of revenue reversals that are deemed significant will vary across entities depending on the facts and circumstances. If the entity determines that it is probable that the inclusion of its estimate will not result in a significant revenue reversal, the estimate is included in the transaction price.

A-43 As discussed in BC218 of FASB ASU No. 2014-09, when an entity applies the guidance for constraining estimates of variable consideration, the entity might determine that it should not include the entire estimate of the variable consideration in the transaction price because it is not probable that doing so would not result in a significant revenue reversal. FinREC believes that certain types of variable consideration (such as consideration associated with claims or unapproved change orders) may be recorded when settled or received only after consideration of the both the likelihood and magnitude of a revenue reversal. However, the entity might determine that it is probable that including some of the estimate of the variable consideration in the transaction price would not result in a significant revenue reversal. In these instances, the entity should include some, but not all of the variable consideration in the transaction price. That is, subject to first assessing the contract modification guidance for enforceability, the entity is required to estimate the amount of variable consideration applying the constraint guidance and should not default to a conclusion to include no amount of variable consideration in the transaction price without a fulsome analysis.

A-44 Factors to consider in assessing the likelihood and magnitude of the revenue reversal (commonly referred to as an entity's confidence level in assessing the revenue reversal in the analysis that follows) include, but are not limited to, any of the following, as indicated in FASB ASC 606-10-32-12:

Factors in FASB ASC 606-10-32-12	*Considerations*
The amount of consideration is highly susceptible to factors outside the entity's influence. Those factors include volatility in a market, the judgment or actions of third parties, weather conditions, and a high risk of obsolescence of the promised good or service.	• Reliance on suppliers or subcontractors with a history of missing deadlines • History of union strikes that impact the timing of satisfaction of performance obligations • Requiring substantive third-party (for instance, customer or regulator) approval to meet certain milestones under the contract when the entity does not have predictive experience with that party or type of milestone • Contract fulfillment involving travel, performance, or communication over well-documented areas of risk (such as, tornado, hurricanes, or earthquakes)
The uncertainty about the amount of consideration is not expected to be resolved for a long period of time.	• Contracts with disputes, claims, or unapproved change orders that are expected to take a long period of time to resolve • Variable fees that are expected to be earned for long periods of time
The entity's experience (or other evidence) with similar types of contracts is limited, or that experience (or other evidence) has limited predictive value.	• History of similar projects that have been unsuccessful • Lack of experience with similar types of contracts and variable consideration amounts • Competing in a new market capability or technology
The entity has a practice of either offering a broad range of price concessions or changing the payment terms and conditions of similar contracts in similar circumstances.	• Pattern of contract renegotiation with resulting pricing reductions subsequent to the commencement of the project • Note: Change orders (modifications of scope or price of the contract) are common in the engineering and construction industry. FinREC believes that change orders should generally be evaluated as a contract modification and are not necessarily a "price concession" contemplated by this factor in the standard.
The contract has a large number and broad range of possible consideration amounts.	• Significant volatility in the amount of possible consideration amounts (for instance, an award fee based on key performance indicator [KPI] scores between zero and 100, where the entity has no experience of obtaining average KPI scores within a narrow range)

A-45 The following examples are meant to be illustrative; the actual conclusion should be based on the facts and circumstances of an entity's specific situation. An entity should also consider positive and mitigating factors that support the assertion that a significant reversal of cumulative revenue recognized will not occur.

Example 11-3-4

An entity has a three-year, fixed-fee contract for $10 million to perform certain environmental clean-up efforts. In addition, the contract price may be increased by up to $2 million if the entity is able to meet two performance targets. Specifically, the entity is entitled to an additional $1.4 million if it completes the work on or before three years from the contract start date. The entity expects, based on history with similar contracts, that it will earn the $1.4 million. The remaining $0.6 million can be earned by the entity if it is able to limit workforce turnover to certain agreed-upon targets as shown in the following table:

Workforce Turnover Percentage (Contract-Specific)	*Incentive Fee Available*
0%–1%	$600,000
2%–3%	$300,000
Greater than 3%	$0

This is the first time this entity has worked in this geographical area, and therefore the contractor and client will meet periodically to determine progress toward the workforce turnover criterion.

The entity determined that there is one performance obligation and that satisfaction of that performance obligation occurs over three years as control transfers. The entity uses the cost-to-cost input method to measure progress on the contract.

Although the contractor has not worked in this particular geographical region before, it considers its extensive experience with similar contracts and types of variable consideration when determining what amount, if any, of the $0.6 million incentive fee to include in the transaction price. Based on its history with workforce turnover on similar contracts and its understanding of jobs data in this geographic region, the contractor determines that it is probable that it will limit workforce turnover to less than 3 percent but not less than 1 percent (based on the fact that it does not have experience with the workforce in this particular region).

Therefore, the entity concludes that $0.3 million of the turnover-related variable consideration is the "most likely amount" to which it expects to be entitled and includes that amount in the transaction price when calculating revenue because the entity has also concluded it is not probable that a significant reversal in the amount of cumulative revenue recognized will occur when the uncertainty associated with the variable consideration is subsequently resolved.

The entity reassesses this criterion each reporting period to determine if workforce turnover experience is better or worse. At the end of year two, the contractor is near completion of the contract and it becomes probable, given that the job is so near its conclusion, that turnover on the contract will be less than 1 percent. Therefore, the entity revises its estimate of variable consideration to include the entire $600,000 incentive fee in the transaction price because, at this point, it is probable that a significant reversal in the amount of cumulative revenue recognized will not occur when including the entire variable consideration in the transaction price.

The following illustrates the impact of changes in variable consideration in example 11-3-4.

Fixed consideration	A	$10,000,000		
Estimated costs to complete	B	$9,000,000		
		Cumulative		
		Year 1	*Year 2*	*Year 3*
Total estimated variable consideration—completion date	C	$1,400,000	$1,400,000	$1,400,000
Total estimated variable consideration—workforce turnover	D	$300,000	$600,000	$600,000
Total estimated variable consideration	E	$1,700,000	$2,000,000	$2,000,000
Costs incurred	F	$2,000,000	$6,000,000	$1,000,000
Fixed revenue	G = A × F/B	$2,222,222	$6,666,667	$1,111,111
Variable revenue	H = E × F/B	$377,778	$1,400,000	$222,222
Cumulative catch-up adjustment	I		$266,667	
Contract margin	J = G + H − F	$600,000	$2,066,667	$333,333
		23%	26%	25%

Example 11-3-5

An entity enters into a contract to design and build a pharmaceutical production facility for $100 million. Estimated costs are $90 million. As the contract progresses, due to customer-caused delays (that is, delays outside the control of the contractor), the expected cost of the contract far exceeds original estimates, although the contract will have a positive margin overall. The contractor submits a claim as permitted in the contract to recover "not at fault" costs incurred by the contractor. The customer, in turn, submits a counterclaim. Claims of this nature are typical in these types of contracts and history suggests that resolution in favor of the contractor is probable (although the amounts are often net settled inclusive of the counterclaim and can vary).

Claims (*a*) are inherently susceptible to factors outside the entity's influence (most often the judgment of an unrelated third party); (*b*) can take a long period of time to resolve; and (*c*) include possible outcomes that often involve a broad range of possible consideration amounts. In addition, claims are often net settled inclusive of customer counterclaims. Although there is evidence in this fact pattern supporting successful resolution of claims, this experience on a stand-alone basis may not be sufficient to support a conclusion that it is probable that the claimed amount of revenue would not be subject to significant reversal when the uncertainty is resolved, and additional factors would need to be considered to make a final determination.

Although oftentimes claim revenue will be recorded in full when amounts are either received or awarded, it could be probable that some portion of the claim will not result in a significant revenue reversal, such as when contractual terms clearly demonstrate an enforceable right to receive payment from a customer for certain situations (such as objectively determinable customer-caused delays).

Updating Estimates of Variable Consideration

A-46 Given the long-term nature of many engineering and construction contracts, it is common for circumstances to change throughout the contract. Circumstances change as contract modifications occur, as more experience is acquired, as additional information is obtained, as risks are retired or additional risks are identified, and as performance progresses on the contract. The nature of accounting for long-term contracts is a process of continuous refinements of estimates for changing conditions and new developments. FASB ASC 606-10-32-14 requires that the estimated transaction price be updated for changes in circumstances at each reporting period. As part of updating the transaction price, an entity would evaluate the factors listed in FASB ASC 606-10-32-12. In addition, when updating the estimated transaction price, an entity should consider whether there is a revision to the measure of progress (for example, estimated costs to complete the contract) as stated in FASB ASC 606-10-25-35.

A-47 The following example is meant to be illustrative; the determination of the method for updating estimates of variable consideration should be based on the facts and circumstances of an entity's specific situation.

Example 11-3-6

An entity enters into an engineering, procurement, and construction (EPC) contract for the design and construction of an industrial manufacturing facility for a fixed price of $100 million plus an award or penalty fee of $5 million tied directly to certain objective metrics around quality, schedule, and productivity (that is, the variable fee or penalty could increase or decrease the overall consideration received by the contractor). The contractor was inexperienced in this type of project and potential turnover in key positions was a concern. Accordingly, when bidding the contract, the entity did not expect to successfully attain positive metrics tied to the award fee or penalty and estimated a penalty of $5 million. The most likely transaction price at the start of the contract was therefore $95 million. As the contract neared completion, the contractor became confident that all key metrics were going to be met or exceeded. Based on this updated information, the entity concludes that they will not be in a position of incurring a penalty but rather will benefit from the full potential award, and it is probable that a significant reversal in the cumulative amount of revenue will not occur when the uncertainty is resolved; therefore, the entity includes the $5 million award fee in the transaction price. Accordingly, the most likely transaction price is updated to $105 million, and a cumulative catch-up adjustment in revenue is recorded.

Step 5: Recognize Revenue When (or as) the Entity Satisfies a Performance Obligation

Acceptable Measures of Progress

This Accounting Implementation Issue Is Relevant to Step 5: "Recognize Revenue When (or as) the Entity Satisfies a Performance Obligation," of FASB ASC 606.

Measuring Progress Toward Complete Satisfaction of a Performance Obligation

A-48 In measuring progress toward complete satisfaction of a performance obligation, FASB ASC 606-10-25-31 states that the objective when measuring progress is to depict an entity's performance in transferring control of goods or services promised to a customer (that is, the satisfaction of an entity's performance obligation). For each contract, it is important to assess the nature of the arrangement and determine the distinct goods or services, or series of goods or services, under the guidance in "Identifying the Unit of Account" included in paragraphs 11.1.01–11.1.02 and paragraph 11.2.17 of this guide.

A-49 As discussed in FASB ASC 606-10-25-33, there are various appropriate methods of measuring progress that are generally categorized as *output methods* and *input methods*. FASB ASC 606-10-55-17 explains that output methods include surveys of performance completed to date, appraisals of results achieved, milestones reached, and units produced or units delivered. FASB ASC 606-10-55-20 explains that input methods include resources consumed, labor hours expended, costs incurred, time lapsed, or machine hours used relative to the total expected inputs to the satisfaction of that performance obligation. Considerations for selecting those methods are discussed in paragraphs 16–21 of FASB ASC 606-10-55. As required in FASB ASC 606-10-25-32, for each performance obligation, the entity shall apply a single method of measuring progress that is consistent with the objective in FASB ASC 606-10-25-31 and shall apply that method consistent with similar performance obligations and in similar circumstances.

A-50 For engineering and construction entities, a careful evaluation of the facts and circumstances is required to determine which method best depicts the entity's performance in transferring control of goods or services to the customer. The entity should carefully consider the nature of the product or services provided and the terms of the customer contract, such as contract termination rights, the right to demand or retain payments, and the legal title to work in process, in determining the best input or output method for measuring progress toward complete satisfaction of a performance obligation. As noted in FASB ASC 606-10-25-36, a contractor should use one of the recognition-over-time methods only if the contractor can reasonably measure progress.

United States Federal Government Contracts

A-51 Engineering and construction contracts with the United States federal government typically provide the government the ability to terminate a contract for convenience, which is the unilateral right to cancel the contract whenever the federal buying agency deems the cancelation is in the public interest. Under a termination for convenience clause, the contractor generally is entitled to recover all costs incurred to the termination date, plus other costs not recovered at termination (such as ongoing costs not able to be discontinued, for example, rental costs), as well as an allowance for profit or fee. The U.S. federal government also typically has the right to the goods produced and in process under the contract at the time of a termination for convenience.

A-52 FASB ASC 606-10-55-17 states,

> An output method would not provide a faithful depiction of the entity's performance if the output selected would fail to measure some of the goods or services for which control has transferred to the customer. For example, output methods based on units produced or units delivered would not faithfully depict an entity's performance in satisfying a performance obligation if, at the end of the reporting period, the entity's performance has produced work in process or finished goods controlled by the customer that are not included in the measurement of the output.

A-53 BC165 of FASB ASU No. 2014-09 further notes that

> In the redeliberations, some respondents, particularly those in the contract manufacturing industry, requested the Boards to provide more guidance on when units-of-delivery or units-of-production methods would be appropriate. Those respondents observed that such methods appear to be output methods and, therefore, questioned whether they would always provide the most appropriate depiction of an entity's performance. The Boards observed that such methods may be appropriate in some cases; however, they may not always result in the best depiction of an entity's performance if the performance obligation is satisfied over time. This is because a units-of-delivery or a units-of-production method ignores the work in process that belongs to the customer. When that work in process is material to either the contract or the financial statements as a whole, the Boards observed that using a units-of-delivery or a units-of-production method would distort the entity's performance because it would not recognize revenue for the assets that are created before delivery or before production is complete but are controlled by the customer.

A-54 A distinction between the cost-to-cost method and an output method such as units-of-delivery is that the cost-to-cost method includes work in process in the measurement toward complete satisfaction of the performance obligation.

A-55 A termination for convenience clause that gives the customer the right to the goods produced and in process under the contract at the time of termination may indicate that the customer has effective control over the goods produced and work in progress, even if those goods and work in progress are not in the customer's physical possession. FinREC believes that in these circumstances an output method, such as units-of-delivery or units-of-production, would not be an appropriate measure of the progress toward complete satisfaction of the performance obligation because an output method would ignore the work in process that belongs to the customer, as discussed in BC165 of FASB ASU No. 2014-09. Therefore, an input method would typically be more appropriate in these circumstances.

A-56 Accordingly, the engineering and construction entity would evaluate their specific circumstances to determine whether an input method, such as cost-to-cost, is an appropriate measure of the progress toward complete satisfaction of the performance obligation and faithfully depicts the activity for which control is transferred to the customer.

Engineering and Construction Service Contracts

A-57 Because the nature of engineering and construction service contracts varies widely, the selection of the best method of measuring progress toward complete satisfaction of a performance obligation requires knowledge of the services provided to the customer as well as the contractual terms of the performance obligation, particularly those terms involving the timing of service delivery.

A-58 FASB ASC 606-10-55-18 states that, as a practical expedient, if an entity has a right to consideration from a customer in an amount that corresponds directly with the value to the customer of the entity's performance completed to date (for example, a service contract in which an entity bills a fixed amount for each hour of service provided), the entity may recognize revenue in the amount to which the entity has a right to invoice.

A-59 An engineering and construction company should consider whether the practical expedient in FASB ASC 606-10-55-18 would be applicable for its service contracts that specify the right to invoice an amount that corresponds directly with the value to the customer of the entity's performance completed to date. The practical expedient may be appropriate, for example, for an operations and maintenance contract when the amounts invoiced to the customer are based on labor hours incurred.

A-60 There are times when this practical expedient may not be appropriate. If a maintenance service contract has variable consideration, such as a significant incentive provision that is assessed and paid by the customer only once or infrequently (upon achievement of contractual milestones, upon contract completion, or only once each year) or with a fixed-price lump-sum construction contract, FinREC believes recognition of revenue based on the right to invoice may not be appropriate. In addition, because many engineering, procurement, and construction contracts result in the "delivery" of an integrated set of outputs (such as a functioning power plant) and the value transferred to date during the project may not correspond directly to the right to consideration from the customer, the use of the practical expedient in FASB ASC 606-10-55-18 may not be appropriate.

A-61 For certain service contracts, it may be appropriate to use input methods, such as cost-to-cost or labor hours expended, for measuring progress toward complete satisfaction of a performance obligation, depending on the facts and circumstances. FASB ASC 606-10-55-20 states that, if the entity's efforts or inputs are expended evenly throughout the performance period, it may be appropriate for the entity to recognize revenue on a straight-line basis. FinREC believes the straight-line basis would be expected to be used in limited circumstances in the construction industry. Because most performance obligations in engineering and construction contracts are not satisfied evenly throughout the performance period, the cost-to-cost input method may be more appropriate.

A-62 For other service contracts, it may be appropriate to use an output method related to the number of times short-duration homogeneous services are provided to the customer relative to the number of times the services are expected to be performed over the life of the service contract, for measuring progress toward complete satisfaction of a performance obligation.

A-63 The following examples are meant to be illustrative of engineering and construction service contracts that management has determined to be a single performance obligation; the actual determination of the method for measuring complete satisfaction of a performance obligation, as stated in FASB ASC 606-10-25-31, should be based on the facts and circumstances of an entity's specific situation.

Example 11-5-1

An engineering and construction company provides daily maintenance services for a manufacturing facility. These services qualify as a series of distinct services that are substantially the same and that have the same pattern of transfer in accordance with FASB ASC 606-10-25-14(b). The company bills monthly for the labor and material costs. The contract has a provision to award and pay an incentive bonus on an annual basis based on certain safety and cost-savings provisions. The criteria in paragraphs 5 and 11 of FASB ASC 606-10-32 related to variable consideration for recognition of an estimated amount of the incentive are met. Because of the annual incentive, the use of the practical expedient in FASB ASC 606-10-55-18 may not be appropriate.

Example 11-5-2

A heavy construction equipment company enters into a contract to provide routine maintenance for a fleet of heavy construction equipment for equal monthly payments over 24 months of service. The company's performance on this contract (as evidenced by costs incurred) occurs evenly over the period. The company may consider a time-based method, such as straight-line revenue recognition, to be a reasonable depiction of the amount of the entity's performance and transfer of control of the services to the customer because the efforts are expended evenly throughout the performance period (and not because the same amount is paid to the company each month).

Example 11-5-3

The same heavy construction equipment company, under a different contract with a different customer, provides a major equipment maintenance overhaul on a time and materials basis. In this case, the level of effort necessary for an overhaul and the pattern of performance over time vary depending on the condition of the equipment. In these circumstances, an input method may be a reasonable depiction of the amount of the entity's performance and transfer of control of the service to the customer.

Use of Units-of-Delivery Method to Measure Progress

A-64 If the entity determines that revenue should be recognized over time and the customer has control of the goods as the performance occurs, based on the guidance described in paragraph 11.5.08, a units-of-delivery or units-of-production method that has not been modified to take into account the assets that are created before delivery occurs or production is complete would not result in the best depiction of an entity's performance because such unmodified methods ignore the work in process for which control has been transferred to the customer. When that work in process is material to the contract, using a units-of-delivery or a units-of-production method would distort the entity's performance because it would not recognize revenue for the assets that are created before delivery or before production is complete but that are controlled by the customer.

A-65 Furthermore, units-of-delivery or units-of-production may not be appropriate for contracts providing design and production services because an equivalent amount of value is not delivered to the customer with each unit. BC166 of FASB ASU No. 2014-09 states that "the Boards also observed that a units-of-delivery or a units-of-production method may not be appropriate if the contract provides both design and production services because, in this case, each item produced or delivered may not transfer an equal amount of value to the customer."

A-66 BC166 of FASB ASU No. 2014-09 goes on to state that a units-of-delivery method may be an appropriate method for measuring progress for a long-term manufacturing contract of standard items that individually transfer an equal amount of value to the customer on delivery.

A-67 FinREC believes a units-of-delivery method may be appropriate in situations where the entity has a production-only contract, producing homogenous products, and the method would accurately depict the entity's performance. When selecting a method for measuring progress and considering whether a units-of-delivery method is appropriate, an entity should consider its facts and circumstances and select the method that depicts the entity's performance and the transfer of control of the goods or services to the customer. For example, for a highway paving contract for which output is cubic yards of pavement laid, a units-of-delivery method may be a reasonable depiction of the amount of the entity's performance and transfer of control of the goods and services to the customer.

Inputs That Do Not Depict an Entity's Performance

A-68 Paragraphs 20–21 of FASB ASC 606-10-55 provide guidance about measuring progress toward complete satisfaction of a performance obligation using input methods. The paragraphs state that the entity should exclude from an input method the effects of inputs that do not depict the entity's performance in transferring goods or services to the customer.

Consideration of Significant Inefficiencies in Performance

A-69 For entities using a cost-based input method for measuring progress toward complete satisfaction of performance obligations, an adjustment to the measure of progress may be required in certain circumstances. FASB ASC 606-10-55-21(a) states that, an entity would not recognize revenue on the basis of costs incurred that are attributable to significant inefficiencies in the entity's performance that were not reflected in the price of the contract (for example, the costs of unexpected amounts of wasted materials, labor, or other resources which were incurred to fulfill the performance obligation).

A-70 Determining which costs represent unexpected "wasted" materials, labor, or other resources requires significant judgment and varies depending upon the facts and circumstances. Engineering and construction projects normally have some areas of expected inefficiencies, and contingencies are included in the original project forecast for these types of risks.

A-71 There are circumstances, however, where unexpected significant inefficiencies may occur that were not considered a risk at the time of entering into the contract, such as extended labor strikes or design or construction execution errors that result in significant wasted resources that may require adjustment to a cost-based input method for measuring progress. These wasted materials should be excluded from the measure of progress toward completion and the costs should be expensed as incurred.

Costs Incurred That Are Not Indicative of Performance

A-72 There may also be circumstances in which the cost incurred on an engineering and construction contract is not proportionate to the entity's progress in satisfying the performance obligation. For example, engineering and construction entities may enter into contracts where they procure equipment and material. The procurement alone of those products likely would not be indicative of the entity's performance, unless the company has the right to payment for the cost for the procurement plus a reasonable profit, such that the procurement itself represents progress toward completion.

A-73 FASB ASC 606-10-55-21 explains that an entity should exclude from an input method the effects of any input that does not depict the entity's performance in transferring control of goods or services to the customer. FASB ASC 606-10-55-21(b) states that when a cost incurred is not proportionate to the entity's progress in satisfying the performance obligation, the best depiction of the entity's performance may be to adjust the input method to recognize revenue only to the extent of the cost incurred. For example, a faithful depiction of an entity's performance might be to recognize revenue at an amount equal to the cost of a good used to satisfy a performance obligation if the entity expects at contract inception that all of the following conditions would be met:

a. The good is not distinct.

b. The customer is expected to obtain control of the good significantly before receiving services related to the good.

c. The cost of the transferred good is significant relative to the total expected costs to completely satisfy the performance obligation.

d. The entity procures the good from a third party and is not significantly involved in designing and manufacturing the good (but the entity is acting as a principal in accordance with paragraphs 36–40 of FASB ASC 606-10-55).

A-74 For these types of contracts, if a contractor is using a cost-based input method for measuring progress toward complete satisfaction of performance obligations and the purchase of the material meets the conditions in FASB ASC 606-10-55-21(b), an entity should exclude the costs incurred for the product from the measurement of progress for the performance obligation in accordance with the objective of measuring progress in FASB ASC 606-10-25-31. Refer to the "Uninstalled Materials" section, in paragraphs 11.5.28–11.5.38, for further discussion of application of the criteria in FASB ASC 606-10-55-21.

Uninstalled Materials

This Accounting Implementation Issue Is Relevant to Step 5: "Recognize Revenue When (or as) the Entity Satisfies a Performance Obligation," of FASB ASC 606.

A-75 A typical construction project will require a wide range of different goods to be assembled by a contractor to produce a combined unit of output (that is, a single performance obligation). These goods may include standard materials such as steel, concrete, and copper wire, as well as components that require a high level of customization to fit the requirements of the asset, such as a turbine generator for a power plant or specifically designed and fabricated pipe modules for a refinery. Such goods are often procured from third parties on an as-needed basis throughout the duration of the contract. In most cases, construction contractors attempt to schedule the receipt of those goods shortly before integrating them into the project. However, in some cases, due to extended lead times or delay of installation timing, materials may arrive on the job site in advance of the contractor's ability to install them and such materials may be significant. In these cases, the contractor should consider whether the inclusion of these uninstalled materials would result in the recording of revenue prematurely.

A-76 In the engineering and construction industry, many entities apply a costs-incurred (for example, cost-to-cost) method to measure progress in satisfying a performance obligation. However, in certain instances the cost incurred may not be proportionate to the entity's progress in satisfying the performance obligation. For example, in a performance obligation composed of goods and services, the customer may obtain control of the goods before the entity provides the services related to those goods (that is, goods are delivered to a construction site, but the entity has not yet integrated the goods into the overall project; hence, "uninstalled materials").

A-77 FASB ASC 606-10-55-21(b) provides four criteria that, if all are met, may indicate a cost incurred is not proportionate to the entity's progress in satisfying the performance obligation and, therefore, the best depiction of the entity's performance may be to adjust the input method to recognize revenue only to the extent of that cost incurred. These criteria are as follows:

a. The good is not distinct.

b. The customer is expected to obtain control of the good significantly before receiving services related to the good.

c. The cost of the transferred good is significant relative to the total expected costs to completely satisfy the performance obligation.

d. The entity procures the good from a third party and is not significantly involved in designing and manufacturing the good (but the entity is acting as a principal in accordance with paragraphs 36–40 of FASB ASC 606-10-55).

A-78 A careful evaluation of the facts and circumstances is required to determine whether the exclusion from the input method of goods that meet these criteria would be a better depiction of the measure of progress towards completion of a performance obligation. FinREC believes that such an evaluation should be performed at inception and throughout the duration of the contract.

A-79 The first criterion in FASB ASC 606-10-55-21(b)(1) relates to whether the materials procured are distinct. FinREC believes that in most cases, the procurement of materials necessary to complete a performance obligation would not typically be considered a performance obligation on its own, but such an evaluation should be made. In the situation in which materials can be readily used by the contractor in other construction projects without incurring significant costs to modify the items, FinREC believes such inventoriable materials should be considered for inclusion as an uninstalled material if control has transferred to the customer and the other criteria in FASB ASC 606-10-55-21(b) are met.

A-80 Items procured to complete a performance obligation may not immediately transfer into the control of the customer. Certain of these types of costs may qualify as an inventoriable cost under FASB ASC 330, *Inventory*. For example, as part of a contract with a customer, a contractor orders inventoriable materials such as steel, concrete, and copper wire. These materials are not unique to this contract and can be used on other construction contracts.

Materials for this contract normally arrive at the job site shortly before the contractor is expected to install these materials (that is, at inception, materials were not expected to arrive significantly in advance of installation); however, unexpected delays occur (such as weather, force majeure, technical challenges, and so on) and, as a result, these materials are now at the job site significantly in advance of the revised installation timing. In these circumstances, the contractor may determine that the customer has not obtained control of these goods, even though the goods are physically at the job site. Such standard inventoriable materials, however, can be readily used by the contractor in other construction projects without incurring significant costs. An evaluation should be performed to determine when the control of these materials might transfer to the customer. In some cases, the transfer of control may occur when the item is installed. In other cases, a transfer of control might occur prior to installation if, for example, a security interest in the materials passes to the owner through billing of the specific materials procured. FinREC believes that when control has not transferred to the customer, it would be appropriate for the contractor to recognize the goods as inventory as they meet the definition of such in FASB ASC 330.

A-81 In BC171 of FASB ASU No. 2014-09, "the Boards observed that if a customer obtains control of the goods before they are installed by an entity, then it would be inappropriate for the entity to continue to recognize the goods as inventory." If a customer obtains control of the goods before they are installed by an entity, FinREC believes it would be appropriate to evaluate whether the other criteria listed in items 2–4 in paragraph 21(b) of FASB ASC 606-10-55 are met.

A-82 The criteria in items 2 and 3 of paragraph 21(b) of FASB ASC 606-10-55 indicate that if a customer is expected to obtain control of a good significantly before receiving the services related to that good (installing the item in the project) and the cost of the transferred good is significant relative to the total expected costs, those costs do not depict the entity's performance in satisfying the single performance obligation, and therefore should be excluded from the measure of progress.

A-83 Based on the criteria in item 4 of paragraph 21(b) of FASB ASC 606-10-55, if the contractor is significantly involved in the design and manufacturing of an item, even if the item is procured from a third-party manufacturer, then the procurement of such specifically designed materials would represent progress toward satisfying a performance obligation. This is often the case when an integrated engineering and construction company designs materials that are fabricated for a specific project by a third party, such as prefabricated concrete walls of a nuclear power plant.

A-84 The boards concluded in BC171 of FASB ASU No. 2014-09 that, if it is determined that uninstalled materials meet all of the criteria in paragraph 21(b) of FASB ASC 606-10-55, the contractor should recognize revenue for the transfer of the goods but only in an amount equal to the cost of those goods. In those circumstances, the contractor also should exclude the costs of the goods from the cost-to-cost calculation to be consistent with the cost-to-cost methodology.

A-85 If a good was originally determined to have met the criteria in FASB ASC 606-10-55-21(b) and revenue was recorded equal to cost upon receipt of the item, the contractor should determine the appropriate accounting once that item is installed in the project. Such an evaluation would require significant judgment about which conclusion best depicts the entity's performance in the contract. FinREC believes that in some cases it may be appropriate to include the cost of the materials in the cost-to-cost calculation as the materials are installed (resulting in a cumulative catch-up adjustment representing margin on the performance of the installation), when to do so would result in a faithful depiction of the progress made toward satisfaction of the performance obligation. This may be the case, for example, when a large amount of pipe, or conduit, or copper wire is installed over an extended period of time. In other cases, FinREC believes it may be appropriate to exclude the costs from the cost-to-cost calculation for the entire duration of the contract, because to include the costs in the cost-to-cost calculation might result in a distortion of the progress made toward satisfaction of the performance obligation in a single accounting period. This might be the case if there was a single asset that is significant to the overall contract that is installed at a single point in time. See further discussion in the "Acceptable Measures of Progress" section in paragraphs 11.5.01–11.5.27.

Other Related Topics

Disclosures and Presentation

This Accounting Implementation Issue Is Relevant to Disclosures and Presentation Required Under FASB ASC 606.

A-86 The recognition of revenue requires the use of judgment, interpretation, and estimates. As explained in FASB ASC 606-10-50-1, the objective of the disclosures for remaining performance obligations and the changes in entity's contract balances is to allow financial statement users to understand the nature, amount, timing, and uncertainty of revenue and cash flows that result from revenues from contracts with customers. To meet this objective, an entity will be required under FASB ASC 606-10-50 to disclose qualitative and quantitative information about revenues, remaining performance obligations (backlog-like disclosure), and activities affecting contract balances so that the financial statement users understand the judgments made in applying FASB ASC 606 to the different sources of revenue from contracts with customers.

Disclosures Related to Remaining Performance Obligations

A-87 The determination of remaining performance obligations is driven by the same measurement guidance as revenue recognition. Therefore, the reporting entity should apply its accounting policy for determining contract term, transaction price, and constraint on transaction price for variable consideration in determining remaining performance obligations, as well as revenue recognition under FASB ASC 606.

A-88 For generally accepted accounting principles (GAAP) disclosures regarding remaining performance obligations, the measurement should be performed as of the end of the reporting period as required by FASB ASC 606-10-50-13(a).

A-89 Prior to creating disclosures, an engineering or construction entity should determine whether it is a public business entity, as there are certain required disclosures that will be optional for those entities that do not meet the definition of a public business entity.

A-90 An entity must first understand its sources of revenue. The presentation of the income statement should indicate those revenues that are from contracts within the scope of FASB ASC 606 (that is, revenue from contracts with customers) and those revenues from other sources. If the amounts of revenue that are from other sources are material to the financial statements and not presented separately on the income statement as other revenue, they should be disclosed separately in the notes to the financial statements. The disclosure should include appropriate information as applicable under FASB ASC 606, for revenues from contracts with customers; and other relevant guidance, for revenue from other sources.

Disaggregating Revenue

A-91 Prior to creating revenue recognition disclosures, the level of disaggregation of revenue should be determined. FASB ASC 606-10-50-2 provides guidance on satisfying the overall disclosure objective, stating that "an entity shall aggregate or disaggregate disclosures so that useful information is not obscured by either the inclusion of a large amount of insignificant detail or the aggregation of items that have substantially different characteristics." FASB ASC 606-10-50-5 provides the requirements for disclosure of disaggregated revenue, and paragraphs 89–91 of FASB ASC 606-10-55 provide examples of appropriate categories for disaggregation, as noted in paragraph 11.7.09. Although entities that do not meet the definition of a public business entity may elect not to apply certain quantitative disclosures in such guidance, at a minimum entities should disaggregate revenue according to the timing of transfer of goods or services (that is, over time and point in time) and disclose qualitative information about how economic factors affect the nature, amount, timing, and uncertainty of revenues and cash flows. Many engineering and construction entities may find it easier to prepare presentation and disclosures after revenue is disaggregated and therefore even entities that are neither a public business entity nor a not-for-profit entity that has issued, or is a conduit bond obligor for, securities that are traded, listed, or quoted on an exchange or an over-the-counter market that report under U.S. GAAP may choose to disaggregate revenue when there are significant differences in revenue sources.

A-92 FASB ASC 606 does not modify the criteria for reporting operating segments under FASB ASC 280, *Segment Reporting*.

A-93 Disaggregation of revenue does not mean disclosing individual contract information that is often requested by sureties. Engineering and construction entities that are not public business entities and that primarily focus on a single market may not find it necessary to further disaggregate revenue to achieve the objectives described in FASB ASC 606-10-50-1.

A-94 Public business entities and other entities that disclose disaggregated revenue beyond the categories of revenue recognized at a point in time and over time should consider financial information that they disclose outside the financial statements, such as presentations to investors and the information that management uses to make financial decisions for the entity in determining the appropriate categories of revenue as discussed in FASB ASC 606-10-55-90. FASB ASC 606-10-55-91 provides the following categories that might be an appropriate basis for determining the categories for disaggregation of revenue:

a. Type of good or service (for example, major product lines)

b. Geographical region (for example, country or region)

c. Market or type of customer (for example, government and non-government customers)

d. Type of contract (for example, fixed-price and time-and-materials contracts)

e. Contract duration (for example, short-term and long-term contracts)

f. Timing of transfer of goods or services (for example, revenue from goods or services transferred to customers at a point in time and revenue from goods or services transferred over time)

g. Sales channels (for example, goods sold directly to consumers and goods sold through intermediaries)

A-95 For engineering and construction entities, common categories of disaggregated revenue include residential and commercial contracts, revenue from public sources (governments, and so on) and private sources, geographic region, and contract duration. If the construction contractor reports segment information in its financial statements, FASB ASC 606-10-50-6 requires the entity to disclose sufficient information to enable users of financial statements to understand the relationship between the disclosure of disaggregated revenue (in accordance with FASB ASC 606-10-50-5) and revenue information that is disclosed for each reportable segment.

A-96 When creating disclosures, it is important to consider the needs of the users of the financial statements. The objective of the disclosures is to provide the most useful information and therefore to aggregate or disaggregate disclosures in a way that does not obscure information by providing too little or too much information. Finding the ideal balance for disclosures will require careful evaluation of all sources of revenue, including how judgments that are used to recognize revenue may differ amongst different types of revenue.

Backlog—Remaining Performance Obligations

A-97 Code of Federal Regulations (CFR) Title 17, Part 229.101, Item 101(c)(viii), *Narrative Description of Business—Backlog*, states:

> The dollar amount of backlog orders believed to be firm, as of a recent date and as of a comparable date in the preceding fiscal year, together with an indication of the portion thereof not reasonably expected to be filled within the current fiscal year, and seasonal or other material aspects of the backlog. (There may be included as firm orders government orders that are firm but not yet funded and contracts awarded but not yet signed, provided an appropriate statement is added to explain the nature of such orders and the amount thereof. The portion of orders already included in sales or operating revenues on the basis of percentage of completion or program accounting shall be excluded.)

A-98 As required by SEC regulations [17 CFR 229.101(c), *Narrative Description of Business*], to the extent material to an understanding of the registrant's business taken as a whole, such backlog information should be disclosed for the registrant's dominant segment or each reportable segment about which financial information is presented in the financial statements.

A-99 In the narrative description of business, as stated in paragraph 11.7.13, SEC regulations require public entities to disclose backlog orders (contracts with customers) by significant business segment as of a recent date and as of a comparable date in the preceding fiscal year. In addition, SEC regulations require disclosure of the portion of the backlog that is not reasonably expected to be filled within the current fiscal year, and seasonal or other material aspects of the backlog.

A-100 SEC regulations, via 17 CFR 229.101(c)(viii), permits the reporting entity to define the date that it determines the disclosure of backlog on a comparative basis over the reporting periods. This date may or may not be the fiscal year end or quarter ended date. On a prospective basis, SEC reporting of backlog will typically be limited to two time bands—backlog expected to be fulfilled in the current period and aggregate remaining backlog.

A-101 There are no changes to the required SEC disclosures described in paragraphs 11.7.12–11.7.15; however, there may be additional disclosures required under FASB ASC 606. FASB ASC 606-10-50-13 defines remaining performance obligations as "performance obligations that are unsatisfied (or partially unsatisfied) as of the end of the reporting period." Backlog, as defined by the SEC, may be similar to remaining performance obligations, as defined by FASB 606-10-50-13; however, where applicable, FinREC believes management's discussion and analysis should include a description of the differences between the remaining performance obligations total (GAAP number) and the backlog total (non-GAAP number).

A-102 Dependent upon the uncertainty of remaining performance obligations relating to engineering and construction entity contracts, entities should consider disclosing qualitative information, including accounting policies and assumptions applied, in defining the events that cause the contingent scope of work to become a component of quantified remaining performance obligations and revenue recognition. These disclosures may need to include a description of the impact that certain contractual terms (such as termination provisions, options for additional goods and services, and variable consideration) have on various types of contracts (for example, U.S. government services, and operations and maintenance type). Where applicable, separate disclosure of the dollar amount of contingent remaining performance obligations may be appropriate to meet the objectives under FASB ASC 606. In preparing such disclosures, consideration should also be given to the qualitative and quantitative disclosure requirements under the existing SEC regulation [17 CFR 229.101(c)(viii)], which states "there may be included as firm orders government orders that are firm but not yet funded and contracts awarded but not yet signed, provided an appropriate statement is added to explain the nature of such orders and the amount thereof."

A-103 For public entities, FASB 606-10-50-13(a) requires disclosure of the aggregate amount of transaction price allocated to all of its remaining performance obligations that are not satisfied (or partially satisfied) as of the end of the reporting period. FASB ASC 606-10-50-14 allows an entity to not make this disclosure if either the performance obligation is part of a contract with an expected duration of one year or less (overall contract duration—not the period from the balance sheet date to completion of the contract) or the entity's right to consideration from the customer is an amount that corresponds directly with the value to the customer of the entity's performance completed to date as explained in FASB ASC 606-10-55-18. FASB ASC 606-10-50-15 requires that the entity disclose the application of the optional exemptions in paragraphs 14 and 14A of FASB ASC 606-10-50, and whether any consideration from contracts with customers is not included in the transaction price and not included in the remaining performance obligations disclosure, such as constrained variable consideration. In assessing the optional exemptions in paragraphs 14 and 14A of FASB ASC 606-10-50, the entity should carefully consider the nature of its remaining performance obligations and the level of effort necessary to identify the contracts and performance obligations that could be excluded under the optional exemption.

A-104 FASB ASC 606-10-50-13(b) also requires public entities to disclose when the entity expects to recognize as revenue the aggregate amount of its remaining performance obligations, by either presenting the disclosure on a quantitative basis using time bands that are most appropriate for the duration of the remaining performance obligation or by using qualitative information. As there are no changes to the required SEC disclosures described in paragraphs 11.7.12–11.7.15, FASB ASC 606-10-50-13(b) may expand the disclosure regarding backlog required under 17 CFR 229.101(c)(viii) when time bands are used because the disclosure under FASB ASC 606 will likely include time bands representing multiple future periods.

A-105 Entities reporting segment information should consider the disclosure of remaining performance obligations allocable to the segments.

A-106 Certain exemptions are provided in FASB ASC 606 to simplify the disclosure requirements for entities that are neither a public business entity nor a not-for-profit entity that has issued, or is a conduit bond obligor for, securities that are traded, listed, or quoted on an exchange or an over-the-counter market that report under U.S. GAAP. However, such engineering and construction entities may consider the needs of surety and sometimes other users of their financial statements regarding remaining performance obligations in the decision to make the election to not provide the disclosure and electing to apply the practical expedients permitted for remaining performance obligations disclosure.

Revenue Recognition Policies

A-107 Once an appropriate level of disaggregation has been arrived at for revenues, a construction contractor can begin to disclose the general revenue recognition policies applied to each category of revenue.

A-108 To understand the revenue recognition policy, users of the financial statement will need to understand the significant contract terms, judgments, and elections, and changes in such judgments, made for each category of revenue. These disclosures will include the following:

a. As required by FASB ASC 606-10-50-12(c), the nature of the good or service promised in the contract (that is, the nature of the performance obligations), highlighting any performance obligations to arrange for another party to transfer goods or services (that is, if the entity is acting as an agent).

b. As required by FASB ASC 606-10-50-20(b), the methods, inputs and assumptions used to determine whether an estimate of variable consideration, such as expectations about the ability to receive bonuses for on time delivery, is constrained.

c. As required by FASB ASC 606-10-50-18(a), the method of recognizing revenue, over time or at a point in time, including the event or activity that triggers recognition, such as when services are rendered or when construction is completed. For revenue recognized over time, the entity also must disclose the method for determining the portion of revenue recognized based on an input or output method. Examples include recognition based on costs, labor hours incurred, or units installed.

d. As required by paragraphs 12(b), 12(d), and 12(e) of FASB ASC 606-10-50, implied and explicit contract terms, including the terms of payments and variable consideration as well as obligations for returns, refunds, and warranties.

A-109 Public business entities have additional disclosures that are required. These same disclosures may be elected by entities that are not public business entities. These disclosures include the following:

a. Information about remaining performance obligations as required by paragraphs 13–15 of FASB ASC 606-10-50 and further described in paragraph 11.7.18.

b. As required by paragraphs 18(b) and 19 of FASB ASC 606-10-50, explanations of why the method of recognizing revenue over time faithfully reflects the transfer of the goods or services; or for revenue recognized at a point in time, the judgments used to determine when the customer obtains control of the goods or services.

c. As required by paragraph 20 of FASB ASC 606-10-50, information about the methods, inputs, and assumptions used for all of the following:

i. Determine the transaction price, which includes, but is not limited to, estimating variable consideration, adjusting the consideration for the effects of the time value of money, and measuring noncash consideration.

ii. Assess whether an estimate of variable consideration is constrained.

iii. Allocate the transaction price, including estimating stand-alone selling prices of promised goods or services and allocating discounts and variable consideration to a specific part of the contract (if applicable).

iv. Measure obligations for returns, refunds, and other similar obligations.

d. As required by FASB ASC 606-10-50-22, the election to use the practical expedient for not recognizing a financing component within a contract.

Disclosures and Presentation—Contract Balances

A-110 The objective of the disclosures for changes in the entity's contract balances is to assist financial statement users in understanding the nature, amount, timing, and uncertainty of revenue and cash flows that result from revenues from contracts with customers. Given the complexity of the billing-to-performance relationship embedded in long-term construction contracts, specifically with regard to work-in-progress subject to retentions, contracts with termination clauses, milestone payments which may not align with performance, and revisions in estimates, understanding the relationship between revenue and changes in contract balances is critical to users of the financial statements as it provides greater transparency about revenues and cash flows in relation to current period performance.

A-111 As stated in FASB ASC 606-10-45-3, "a contract asset is an entity's right to consideration in exchange for goods or services that the entity has transferred to a customer."

A-112 FASB ASC 606-10-45-4 states that "[a] receivable is an entity's right to consideration that is unconditional. A right to consideration is unconditional if only the passage of time is required before payment of that consideration is due."

A-113 As such, in accordance with FASB ASC 606-10-45-1, the entity should separately present any unconditional rights to consideration as a receivable. Any such material reclasses from contract assets to receivables should be considered in addressing the requirements of FASB ASC 606-10-50-10 related to the explanation of significant changes in contract assets and liabilities during the reporting period.

A-114 FASB ASC 606-10-45-2 states that

> [i]f a customer pays consideration, or an entity has a right to an amount of consideration that is unconditional (that is, a receivable), before the entity transfers a good or service to the customer, the entity shall present the contract as a contract liability when the payment is made or the payment is due (whichever is earlier). A contract liability is an entity's obligation to transfer goods or services to a customer for which the entity has received consideration (or an amount of consideration that is due) from the customer.

A-115 Presentation of a contract as a contract asset or a contract liability was discussed at the October 2014 TRG meeting. Paragraph 12 of TRG Agenda Ref No. 11, *October 2014 Meeting—Summary of Issues Discussed and Next Steps*, discussed how an entity should determine the presentation of a contract that contains multiple performance obligations, as follows:

> TRG members generally agreed that a contract is presented as either a contract asset or a contract liability (but not both), depending on the relationship between the entity's performance and the customer's payment. That is, the contract asset or liability is determined at the contract level and not at the performance obligation level.

A-116 Thus, in accordance with the discussion at the October 2014 TRG meeting on presentation of a contract as a contract asset or a contract liability, engineering and construction companies should aggregate performance obligations at the contract level when determining the total contract asset balance and total contract liability balance for both presentation and disclosure purposes. Entities should also consider the appropriate classification (current versus noncurrent) of each contract asset and each contract liability.

A-117 Retention receivables should be carefully assessed to determine whether retentions are subject to restrictive conditions, such as fulfillment guarantees. Where retentions are subject to conditions other than passage of time, such as fulfillment guarantees, future performance, or achievement of stated milestones, amounts related to retention receivables would continue to be classified as a contract asset until such time that the right to payment becomes unconditional.

A-118 Where construction contracts include termination clauses such that the contractor has the right to payment, including profit, for work performed to date upon customer termination, the inherent condition to payment may relate solely to passage of time (such as, time and materials, or cost-reimbursable type contracts where no milestone or performance-based billing requirements exist), and as a result, FinREC believes unbilled work-in-progress should be reclassified to unbilled receivables.

A-119 Revisions in estimates of the percentage of completion are changes in accounting estimates, as defined in FASB ASC 250, *Accounting Changes and Error Corrections*. Although estimating is a continuous and normal process for contractors, FASB ASC 250-10-50-4, ASC 606-10-50-10, and ASC 606-10-50-8 require disclosure of the effect of revisions if the effect is material. The impacts of revisions in accounting estimates on contract balances should be considered in the entity's revenue disclosures to provide relevant information about the timing of revenue recognition that was not a result of performance in the current period.

A-120 Considering the objective of the required disclosures related to the impact of revenue transactions on contract balances, the entity should provide qualitative and quantitative disclosures to provide clarity to users of the financial statements with regard to the complexity of the billing to performance relationships embedded in long-term construction contracts and how the entity's performance in the period affects revenue and cash flows.

Transition

A-121 FASB ASC 606-10-65-1 allows two alternatives for transitioning in the first year the entity reports revenue under FASB ASC 606. FASB ASC 606-10-65-1(i) requires additional disclosures if the guidance in FASB ASC 606 is applied retrospectively with the cumulative effect of initially applying as an adjustment to the opening balance of retained earnings of the annual reporting period that includes the date of initial application.

Contract Costs

This Accounting Implementation Issue Is Applicable to Accounting for Contract Costs Under FASB ASC 340-40.

A-122 FASB ASC 340-40 provides guidance on contract costs that are not within the scope of other authoritative literature.

Incremental Costs of Obtaining a Contract

A-123 FASB ASC 340-40-25-1 explains that the costs of obtaining a contract should be recognized as an asset if the costs are incremental and expected to be recovered. FASB ASC 340-40-25-2 states, "the incremental costs of obtaining a specific contract are those costs that the entity would not have incurred if the contract had not been obtained." For example, commissions paid to sales personnel, if incurred solely as a result of obtaining the contract, would be eligible for capitalization as long as they are expected to be recovered. However, costs such as salaries related to personnel working on a proposal would most likely not be capitalized, as such costs would not be incremental because the costs would be incurred even if the contract was not obtained, unless the costs are explicitly chargeable to the customer under the contract (as described in FASB ASC 340-40-25-3). An entity is precluded from deferring costs merely to normalize profit margins throughout a contract by allocating revenue and costs evenly over the life of the contract.

A-124 As a practical expedient, FASB ASC 340-40-25-4 notes that an entity may recognize the incremental costs of obtaining a contract as an expense when incurred if the amortization period of the asset that the entity otherwise would have recognized is one year or less.

Costs to Fulfill a Contract

A-125 FASB ASC 340-40-25-5 states that costs to fulfill a contract that are not addressed under other authoritative literature would be recognized as an asset only if they meet all of the following criteria:

a. The costs relate directly to a contract or to an anticipated contract that the entity can specifically identify (for example, costs relating to services provided under renewal of an existing contract or costs of designing an asset to be transferred under a specific contract that has not yet been approved).

b. The costs will generate or enhance resources that will be used in satisfying (or in continuing to satisfy) performance obligations in the future.

c. The costs are expected to be recovered.

A-126 FASB ASC 340-40-25-6 states,

> For costs incurred in fulfilling a contract with a customer that are within the scope of another Topic (for example, Topic 330 on inventory; paragraphs 340-10-25-1 through 25-4 on preproduction costs related to long-term supply arrangements; Subtopic 350-40 on internal-use software; Topic 360 on property, plant, and equipment; or Subtopic 985-20 on costs of software to be sold, leased, or otherwise marketed), an entity shall account for those costs in accordance with those other Topics or Subtopics.

A-127 As discussed in FASB ASC 340-40-25-5, only costs incurred for resources that directly relate to a contract (or anticipated contract) that generate or enhance resources of the entity that will be used to satisfy future performance obligations and are expected to be recovered are eligible for capitalization.

A-128 Pre-contract costs, or costs incurred in anticipation of a contract, may arise in a variety of situations. Costs may be incurred in anticipation of a specific contract (or anticipated follow-on order) that will result in no future benefit unless the contract is obtained.

A-129 Precontract costs may consist of the following:

a. Engineering, design, mobilization, or other services performed on the basis of commitments or other such indications of interest

b. Costs for production equipment and materials relating to specific anticipated contracts (for example, costs for the purchase of equipment, materials, or supplies)

c. Costs incurred to acquire or produce goods in excess of contractual requirements in anticipation of follow-on orders for the same item

d. Start-up or mobilization costs incurred for anticipated but unidentified contracts

A-130 Precontract costs that are incurred for a specific anticipated contract, such as engineering, design, mobilization, or other services or production equipment, materials, or supplies should first be evaluated for capitalization under other authoritative literature, such as FASB ASC 330 on inventory,

FASB ASC 360 on property, plant, and equipment, or FASB ASC 985 on software. Pre-contract costs incurred for a specific anticipated contract that are not addressed under other authoritative literature would be recognized as an asset only if they meet all the criteria in paragraph 5 of FASB ASC 340-40-25 (for example, direct labor, direct materials, costs explicitly chargeable to the customer under the contract).

A-131 Similarly, costs to fulfill a contract that are incurred prior to when the customer obtains control (as contemplated in paragraphs 23–25 of FASB ASC 606-10-25) of the good or service are first assessed to determine if they are within the scope of other standards (such as FASB ASC 330 on inventory, FASB ASC 360 property, plant, and equipment, or FASB ASC 985 on software), in which case, the entity should account for such costs in accordance with those standards (either capitalize or expense) as explained in FASB ASC 340-40-15-3. For example, costs incurred to acquire or produce goods in excess of contractual requirements for an existing contract in anticipation of future orders for the same items would likely be evaluated under FASB ASC 330 on inventory.

A-132 For engineering and construction contracts, costs that relate directly to a contract could include direct labor, direct materials, and allocations of costs that are explicitly chargeable to the customer under the contract and other costs that were incurred only because the entity entered into the contract (for example, subcontractor arrangements). As discussed in FASB ASC 340-40-25-8(a), general and administrative costs are expensed as incurred if they are not explicitly chargeable to the customer under the contract.

A-133 Contracts with the U.S. federal government may provide the contractor with the explicit ability, usually through the provisions of the Federal Acquisition Regulations, to charge general and administrative costs directly to the U.S. federal government. In such circumstances, the entity would then apply the criteria in FASB ASC 340-40-25-5 to determine if recording an asset for these costs is appropriate. Contracts with commercial entities or direct foreign government sales (that is, not a contract structured as a foreign military sale through the U.S. federal government), should be carefully evaluated to determine if general and administrative costs are explicitly chargeable or recoverable under the terms of the contract.

A-134 FASB ASC 340-40-25-8(b) explains that costs of "wasted" materials, labor, or other resources to fulfill a contract that were not reflected in the price of the contract should be expensed when incurred. Higher quantities or costs compared to the original budget does not necessarily equate to wasted materials, labor, or other resources. Determining which costs are "wasted" will require significant judgment and vary depending on the facts and circumstances. A simplistic example to illustrate the concept: If incorrect materials are used by mistake and need to be replaced due to a construction error, the "wasted" materials would result in immediate expense, presuming the materials could not be used elsewhere. However, in another situation, an engineer may be more efficient as more drawings are produced. This does not necessarily result in the earlier engineering drawings incurring "wasted" labor. Rather, efficiency gains simply reduce costs going forward.

A-135 For performance obligations that are satisfied over time as control is transferred, the accounting for costs to fulfill a contract will generally be recognized as costs of goods sold when incurred, regardless of the method used to measure progress toward completion.

A-136 For example, entities measuring progress towards complete satisfaction of a performance obligation satisfied over time using a cost-to-cost measure will generally not have inventoried costs. In accordance with FASB ASC 606- 10-55-17, when selecting a method for measuring progress, the entity should consider whether the method would faithfully depict the entity's performance toward complete satisfaction of the performance obligation. For example, an output method would not faithfully depict an entity's performance in satisfying a performance obligation if at the end of the reporting period the entity has work in process controlled by the customer that is not included in the measurement of the output. This represents a change from the accounting prior to adoption of FASB ASC 606. See also the "Acceptable Measures of Progress" section in paragraphs 11.5.01–11.5.27.

A-137 When using an input method to measure progress toward satisfaction of a performance obligation, a contractor should exclude from the input method the effects of any inputs that do not depict the entity's performance in accordance with the guidance in FASB ASC 606-10-55-21.

Learning or Start-Up Costs

A-138 Certain types of contracts often have learning or start-up costs that are sometimes incurred in connection with the performance of a contract or a group of contracts. As discussed in BC312 of FASB ASU No. 2014-09, a learning curve is the effect of efficiencies realized over time when an entity's costs of performing a task (or producing a unit) declines in relation to how many times the entity performs that task (or produces that unit).

A-139 Such costs usually consist of materials, labor, overhead, rework, or other special costs that must be incurred to complete the existing contract or contracts in progress and are distinguished from research and development costs. As a cost activity matures over its life cycle, the expectation is that these costs would decline over time. These costs are often anticipated and contemplated between the contractor and customer, and considered in negotiating and establishing the aggregate contract price. Consistent with BC313–BC314 of FASB ASU No. 2014-09, if an entity has a single performance obligation to deliver a specified number of units and the performance obligation is satisfied over time, it may be appropriate for an entity to select a method under FASB ASC 606 (such as cost-to-cost) that results in the entity recognizing more revenue and expense for the early units produced relative to the later units.

A-140 For example, assume a contractor is engaged to construct a 10-story building. The contractor determined there is a single performance obligation that is satisfied over time and revenue will be recognized using an input measure (for example, a cost-to-cost input method). The bottom floors of the building are expected to cost more than the top floors due to the learning curve costs involved. Therefore, the contractor will recognize more revenue and contract costs for the first components produced as compared to the later components.

A-141 In accordance with the requirements of FASB ASC 340-40-25-5(a), start-up or learning costs incurred for anticipated but unidentified contracts would most likely not be capitalized before a specific contract was identified.

A-142 Contractors may incur mobilization costs to move personnel, equipment, and supplies to the project site. Contractors may also incur on-site pre-construction costs in the form of temporary facilities for a construction project (such as offices, construction parking areas, access roads, and utilities). These pre-construction costs often establish facilities on the customer's property, and the related requirements for these facilities are specified in the contractual arrangements with the customer.

A-143 Once the contractor commences performance for a performance obligation satisfied over time, contract costs incurred to satisfy the performance obligation will generally not be eligible for capitalization and should be expensed when incurred in accordance with paragraph 8c or 8d of FASB ASC 340-40-25. Contractors should analyze mobilization and pre-construction activities to determine whether they are incurred while satisfying a performance obligation(s) to a customer. For example, when mobilization or pre-construction fulfillment activities are a necessary part of satisfying a performance obligation(s) and control is continuously transferred to the customer, FinREC believes that the related costs should be recognized as costs of goods sold as incurred. Otherwise, these costs should be capitalized as fulfillment costs if all the criteria in FASB ASC 340-40-25-5 are met.

Subsequent Measurement

A-144 In accordance with FASB ASC 340-40-35-1, assets recognized for incremental costs of obtaining a contract or fulfillment costs should be amortized on a systematic basis that is consistent with the transfer to the customer of the goods or services to which the asset relates. For example, if the contractor measures progress toward satisfaction of the performance obligation(s) using the cost-to-cost input method, the amount of costs of obtaining or fulfilling a contract that qualify for capitalization should be amortized in proportion to the construction costs incurred.

A-145 In addition, FASB ASC 340-40-35-2 requires that "an entity shall update the amortization to reflect a significant change in the entity's expected timing of transfer to the customer of the goods or services to which the asset relates." FASB ASC 250-10 requires such a change to be accounted for as a change in accounting estimate. Such change could be indicative of impairment of the related assets, and entities should evaluate the facts and circumstances to determine the appropriate conclusions.

A-146 For assets accounted for in paragraphs 1–7 of FASB ASC 340-40-25, contractors should recognize an impairment loss when the condition in FASB ASC 340-40-35-3 is met. For example, if a contract is terminated prior to amortization of related costs, an impairment loss should be recognized unless the contractor expects to recover the costs as part of the termination settlement.

Chapter 3

Accounting for and Reporting Investments in Construction Joint Ventures

Gray shaded text in this chapter reflects guidance issued but not yet effective as of the date of this guide, July 1, 2018, but becoming effective on or prior to December 31, 2018, exclusive of any option to early adopt ahead of the mandatory effective date. Unless otherwise indicated, all unshaded text reflects guidance that was already effective as of the date of this guide.

3.01 As noted in chapter 1, "Industry Background," contractors frequently participate in construction joint ventures with other parties to share risks, combine financial and other resources, or obtain financing or bonding. The FASB *Accounting Standards Codification* (ASC) glossary defines a *joint venture* as an entity owned and operated by a small group of businesses (the joint venturers) as a separate and specific business or project for the mutual benefit of the members of the group. A government may also be a member of the group. The purpose of a joint venture frequently is to share risks and rewards in developing a new market, product, or technology; to combine complimentary technological knowledge; or to pool resources in developing production or other facilities. Examples of such arrangements may involve the combination of a nonlocal entity having a customer relationship or expertise with a local contractor who is qualified to construct the project and has labor in the local market, two or more contractors with unique skills, or contractors creating an arrangement to be able to have sufficient bonding capacity for very large projects. A joint venture also usually provides an arrangement under which each joint venturer may participate, directly or indirectly, in the overall management of the joint venture. Joint venturers, thus, have an interest or relationship other than as passive investors. An entity that is a subsidiary of one of the joint venturers is not a joint venture. The ownership of a joint venture seldom changes, and its equity interests usually are not traded publicly. A minority public ownership, however, does not preclude an entity from being a joint venture. As distinguished from a corporate joint venture, a joint venture is not limited to corporate entities.

3.02 Entities described as construction joint ventures vary in their legal forms. They include corporations, general and limited partnerships, limited liability companies, and undivided interests. The entities, which are usually project oriented, are often viewed as joint ventures even though one of the investors may have a majority voting interest or may otherwise have effective control of the entity. Because this chapter presents guidance on accounting for investments in entities described as construction joint ventures, questions relating to the existence of control are also addressed.

Joint Venture Accounting

Accounting Methods

3.03 According to FASB ASC 323-10-05-4, investments in the stock of entities other than subsidiaries, namely corporate joint ventures and other noncontrolled entities, usually are accounted for using either the cost method, the fair value method, or the equity method. As explained in FASB ASC 323-10-15-3, the guidance in FASB ASC 323, *Investments—Equity Method and Joint Ventures*, applies to investments in 50 percent or less of (*a*) common stock, (*b*) in-substance common stock, or (*c*) a combination of common stock and in-substance common stock. The FASB ASC glossary defines *in-substance common stock* as an investment in an entity that has risk and reward characteristics that are substantially similar to that entity's common stock.

According to FASB ASC 323-10-05-4, investments held in stock of entities other than subsidiaries, namely corporate joint ventures and other noncontrolled entities usually are accounted for in accordance with either the recognition and measurement guidance in FASB ASC 321, *Investments—Equity Securities*, or the equity method. As explained in FASB ASC 323-10-15-3, the guidance in FASB ASC 323, *Investments—Equity Method and Joint Ventures*, applies to investments in 50 percent or less of (*a*) common stock, (*b*) in-substance common stock, or (*c*) a combination of common stock and in-substance common stock. The FASB ASC glossary defines *in-substance common stock* as an investment in an entity that has risk and reward characteristics that are substantially similar to that entity's common stock.[1]

3.04 FASB ASC 323-10-05-5 establishes that the equity method tends to be the most appropriate if an investment enables the investor to exercise significant influence over the operating or financial decisions of the investee. As further explained in FASB ASC 323-10-15-8, an investment (direct or indirect) of 20 percent or more of the voting stock of an investee creates the presumption that, in the absence of predominant evidence to the contrary, an investor has the ability to exercise significant influence over an investee. Conversely, an investment of less than 20 percent of the voting stock of an investee creates the presumption that an investor does not have the ability to exercise significant influence unless such ability can be demonstrated. Determining the ability of

---

[1] FASB Accounting Standards Update (ASU) No. 2016-01, *Financial Instruments—Overall (Subtopic 825-10): Recognition and Measurement of Financial Assets and Financial Liabilities*, was issued in January 2016. For public business entities, the amendments in this ASU are effective for fiscal years beginning after December 15, 2017, including interim periods within those fiscal years. For all other entities including not-for-profit entities and employee benefit plans within the scope of FASB *Accounting Standards Codification* (ASC) 960 through 965 on plan accounting, the amendments in this ASU are effective for fiscal years beginning after December 15, 2018, and interim periods within fiscal years beginning after December 15, 2019. All entities that are not public business entities may adopt the amendments in this ASU earlier as of the fiscal years beginning after December 15, 2017, including interim periods within those fiscal years. Early application by public business entities to financial statements of fiscal years or interim periods that have not yet been issued or, by all other entities, that have not yet been made available for issuance of the following amendments in this ASU are permitted as of the beginning of the fiscal year of adoption:

1. An entity should present separately in other comprehensive income the portion of the total change in the fair value of a liability resulting from a change in the instrument-specific credit risk if the entity has elected to measure the liability at fair value in accordance with the fair value option for financial instruments.
2. Entities that are not public business entities are not required to apply the fair value of financial instruments disclosure guidance in the General Subsection of FASB ASC 825-10-50.

Except for the early application guidance previously discussed, early adoption of the amendments in this ASU is not permitted.

Readers are encouraged to read the full text of the ASU, available at www.fasb.org. Readers should apply the appropriate guidance based on their facts and circumstances.

an investor to exercise significant influence is not always clear, and applying judgment is necessary to assess the status of each investment.

3.05 FASB ASC 323-10-15-6 notes that several factors may determine the ability of an investor or entity to exercise significant influence over the entity including the following:

- Representation on the board of directors
- Participation in policy-making processes
- Material intra-entity transactions
- Interchange of managerial personnel
- Technological dependency
- Extent of ownership by an investor in relation to the concentration of other shareholdings in the investee

Paragraphs 8–11 of FASB ASC 323-10-15 contain information further defining *significant influence* and explaining how to determine if significant influence exists.

3.06 FASB ASC 323-10-25-2 cautions that the equity method is not a valid substitute for consolidation. *Consolidation* is defined by the FASB ASC glossary as the presentation of a single set of amounts for an entire reporting entity. Consolidation requires elimination of intraentity transactions and balances. FASB ASC 323-10-25-2 also cautions that there are certain other limitations to the use of the equity method identified in paragraphs 8–10 of FASB ASC 810-10-15 including, but not limited to, circumstances in which the relevant provisions applicable to variable interest entities (VIEs) in FASB ASC 810, *Consolidation*, apply.

3.07 FASB ASC 323-10-15-8 explains that investments in joint ventures of less than 20 percent of the voting stock are presumed to indicate an investor's inability to exercise significant influence in the absence of predominant evidence to the contrary, in which case the use of the cost method is generally followed. FASB ASC 323-10-15-9 clarifies that an investor's voting stock interest in an investee should be based on those currently outstanding securities whose holders have present voting privileges. Potential voting privileges that may become available to holders of securities of an investee should be disregarded.

3.08 The guidance in FASB ASC 320, *Investments—Debt and Equity Securities*, is normally not applicable to investments in joint ventures because it requires the availability of readily determinable fair values for the equity securities as noted in FASB ASC 320-10-15-5. Further, it does not apply to equity securities that, absent the election of the fair value option under FASB ASC 825-10-25, would be required to be accounted for under the equity method as discussed in FASB ASC 320-10-15-7.

The preceding paragraph will be deleted upon the effective date of FASB Accounting Standards Update (ASU) No. 2016-01, *Financial Instruments—Overall (Subtopic 825-10): Recognition and Measurement of Financial Assets and Financial Liabilities*.

Capital Contributions to Joint Ventures and Initial Measurement of Investments in Joint Ventures

3.09 Unless certain exceptions in FASB ASC 323-10-30-2 apply, under the equity method, an investor should recognize an investment in a joint venture initially at cost, in accordance with FASB ASC 805-50-30.[2]

3.10 Cash capital contributions to a venture by a venturer should be recorded by the venturer as an investment in the amount of the cash contributed. As a general rule, the contribution of other assets should be recorded as an investment equal to the contributed asset's net book value on the venturer's books. That basis should be used regardless of the nature of the interest in the venture obtained from the transaction.

3.11 FASB ASC 845-10-15-4 clarifies that the guidance in FASB ASC 845, *Nonmonetary Transactions*, does not apply to a transfer of nonmonetary assets solely between a corporate joint venture and its owners, nor does it apply to a transfer of assets to an entity in exchange for an equity interest in that entity, including the exchange of a nonfinancial asset for a noncontrolling ownership interest in a joint venture. Moreover, FASB ASC 845-10-15-14 clarifies that the guidance in FASB ASC 845 pertaining to nonmonetary exchanges involving monetary consideration (referred to as *boot*) does not apply to transfers between a joint venture and its owners. Note that the FASB ASC glossary defines *nonmonetary assets and liabilities* as assets and liabilities other than monetary ones and *monetary assets and liabilities* as assets and liabilities whose amounts are fixed in terms of units of currency by contract or otherwise. Additionally, the FASB ASC glossary defines an *exchange* (or *exchange transaction*) as a reciprocal transfer between two entities that results in one of the entity's acquiring assets or services or satisfying liabilities by surrendering other assets or services or incurring other obligations.

FASB ASC 845-10-15-4 clarifies that the guidance in FASB ASC 845, *Nonmonetary Transactions*, does not apply to a transfer of nonmonetary assets solely between a corporate joint venture and its owners. Moreover, FASB ASC 845-10-15-14 clarifies that the guidance in FASB ASC 845 pertaining to nonmonetary exchanges involving monetary consideration (referred to as *boot*) does not apply to transfers between a joint venture and its owners. Note that the FASB ASC glossary defines *nonmonetary assets and liabilities* as assets and liabilities other than monetary ones and *monetary assets and liabilities* as assets and liabilities whose amounts are fixed in terms of units of currency by contract or otherwise. Additionally, the FASB ASC glossary defines an *exchange* (or *exchange transaction*) as a reciprocal transfer between two entities that results in one of the entity's acquiring assets or services or satisfying liabilities by surrendering other assets or services or incurring other obligations.[3]

---

[2] FASB ASC 325-20-30-1 explains that under the cost method, an investee will recognize a similar investment in the stock of an investee as an asset measured initially at cost.

[3] FASB ASU No. 2017-05, *Other Income—Gains and Losses from the Derecognition of Nonfinancial Assets (Subtopic 610-20): Clarifying the Scope of Asset Derecognition Guidance and Accounting for Partial Sales of Nonfinancial Assets*, was issued in February 2017. The amendments in this ASU are effective at the same time as the amendments in ASU No. 2014-09, *Revenue from Contracts with Customers (Topic 606)*. Therefore, for public entities, the amendments are effective for annual

(continued)

3.12 A noncash contribution may be accompanied by a cash withdrawal by the contributing venturer. The receipt of cash may represent monetary consideration on which the venturer should recognize profit to the extent of the other venturers' proportionate interests.

3.13 The following illustrates a transaction in which the contributing venturer should recognize profit:

> A and B are to share equally in a new joint venture. A contributes $100,000 in cash, and B contributes equipment with carrying value to him of $140,000. To equalize the contributions, A and B agree that B will withdraw $100,000 from the venture. The conditions required for proportionate profit recognition by B are present.
>
> *Results*
>
> 1. The transaction indicates that the equipment has a fair value of $200,000.
> 2. B now effectively owns a 50 percent interest in the equipment.
> 3. B, therefore, has effectively sold a 50 percent interest in the equipment to A for $100,000 and should recognize a gain before income taxes of $30,000, that is, $100,000 – (1/2 × $140,000).
> 4. B should recognize an additional $30,000 as a gain as the venture depreciates the equipment. The venture would initially record the equipment on its books at its indicated fair value of $200,000.

3.14 A venturer may contribute assets to a venture and obtain an interest in the venture smaller than the carrying amount of contributed assets, based on the relationship of the carrying amount of the asset to the cash contributed by the other venturers. In those circumstances, the transaction might provide evidence that the cost or carrying amount of the contributed assets is greater than their fair value, and that a loss should be recognized. Under the general principle that all losses should be recognized when they become evident, an indicated loss should be recognized by the venturer, with a corresponding reduction in the carrying amount of its investment in the venture.

(footnote continued)

reporting periods beginning after December 15, 2017, including interim reporting periods within that reporting period. Public entities may apply the guidance earlier but only as of annual reporting periods beginning after December 15, 2016, including interim reporting periods within that reporting period.

For all other entities, the amendments in this ASU are effective for annual reporting periods beginning after December 15, 2018, and interim reporting periods within annual reporting periods beginning after December 15, 2019. All other entities may apply the guidance earlier as of annual reporting periods beginning after December 15, 2016, including interim reporting periods within that reporting period. All other entities also may apply the guidance earlier as of annual reporting periods beginning after December 15, 2016, and interim reporting periods within annual reporting periods beginning one year after the annual reporting period in which the entity first applies the guidance. An entity is required to apply the amendments in this ASU at the same time that it applies the amendments in FASB ASU No. 2014-09.

Refer to ASU No. 2017-05 for additional guidance regarding the effective date. Readers are encouraged to read the full text of the ASU, available at www.fasb.org. Readers should apply the appropriate guidance based on their facts and circumstances.

3.15 The following is an illustration of a transaction in which a venturer should recognize a loss:

> A and B are to share equally in a new joint venture. A contributes $100,000 in cash, and B contributes equipment with a carrying value to him of $140,000.
>
> *Results*
>
> 1. The transaction indicates that the equipment has a fair value of $100,000 (the amount of A's contribution).
> 2. B should recognize a loss of $40,000 and record its investment in the venture at $100,000.

3.16 A venturer may obtain an interest in a venture by contributing service or "know-how." If the services are to be provided in the future, the cost should not be assigned to the investment account until the services are performed. Recognition of the venturer's share of the profits on withdrawals received before the performance of the services should be deferred until the services are performed and the earning process is complete.

Sales to a Venture

3.17 Sales of materials, supplies, or services to a venture by a venturer that controls the venture, through majority voting interest or otherwise, generally should not be viewed as arm's length transactions. The venturer should not recognize as income any of the intercompany profit or loss from such transactions until it has been realized through transactions with outside third parties.

3.18 FASB ASC 323-10-35-10 states that when an investor controls an investee through majority voting interest and enters into a transaction with an investee that is not on at arm's length, none of the intraentity profit or loss from the transaction should be recognized in income by the investor until it has been realized through transactions with third parties. The same treatment also applies for an investee established with the cooperation of an investor (including an investee established for the financing and operation or leasing of property sold to the investee by the investor) if control is exercised through guarantees of indebtedness,[4] extension of credit and other special arrangements by the investor for the benefit of the investee, or because of ownership by the investor of warrants, convertible securities, and so forth issued by the investee.

3.19 However, a transaction may be deemed to be on an arm's-length basis, which means that is the price that would be received to sell the property in an orderly transaction between market participants who are independent of the reporting entity. A controlling venturer may be required to recognize profit

[4] FASB ASC 460-10-50-6 states that some guarantees are issued to benefit entities that are related parties such as joint ventures, equity method investees, and certain entities for which the controlling financial interest cannot be assessed by analyzing voting interests. In those cases, the disclosures required by FASB ASC 460, *Guarantees*, are incremental to the disclosures required by FASB ASC 850, *Related Party Disclosures*. FASB ASC 460-10-25-4 clarifies that a guarantor should recognize in its statement of financial position, at the inception of a guarantee, a liability for that guarantee. The offsetting entry depends on the circumstances in which the guarantee was issued. Among other circumstances described in FASB ASC 460-10-55-23, a guarantee issued in conjunction with the formation of a partially owned business or a venture accounted for under the equity method results in an increase to the carrying amount of the investment. FASB ASC 460-10-25-1 clarifies a guarantee issued either between parents and their subsidiaries or between corporations under common control are not subject to the recognition provisions of FASB ASC 460.

to the extent of other interests in the venture if certain conditions are met. Generally, these conditions would be satisfied if all of the following are present:

- The transaction was entered into at a price determinable on an arm's-length basis; that is, fair value can be measured by comparable sales at normal selling prices to independent third parties or by competitive bids.
- No substantial uncertainties exist regarding the venturer's ability to perform, such as those that may be present if the venturer lacks experience in the business of the venture or regarding the total cost of the services to be rendered.
- The venture is creditworthy and has independent financial substance.

3.20 A venturer that does not control the venture should recognize intercompany profit to the extent of other interests in the venture.

Subsequent Measurement and Presentation of Investments in Joint Ventures

3.21 At least five different methods of presenting a venturer's interest in a venture are followed in present practice:

- *Consolidation.* The venture is fully consolidated, with the other venturers' interests shown as noncontrolling interests.
- *Partial or proportionate consolidation.* The venturer records its proportionate interest in the venture's assets, liabilities, revenues, and expenses on a line-by-line basis and combines the amounts directly with its own assets, liabilities, revenues, and expenses without distinguishing between the amounts related to the venture and those held directly by the venturer. Paragraph 14 of FASB ASC 810-10-45 provides that an investee in the construction industry may present its investment in an unincorporated legal entity accounted for by the equity method using the proportionate gross financial statement presentation.
- *Expanded equity method.* The venturer presents its proportionate share of the venture's assets and liabilities in capsule form, segregated between current and noncurrent. The elements of the investment are presented separately by including the venturer's equity in the venture's corresponding items under current assets, current liabilities, noncurrent assets, noncurrent liabilities, revenues, and expenses, using a caption such as "investor's share of net current assets of joint ventures."
- *Equity method.* Paragraphs 1–2 of FASB ASC 323-10-45 establish that an investment accounted for under the equity method of accounting should be shown in the balance sheet of an investor as a single amount. Likewise, an investor's share of earnings or losses from its investment should be shown in its income statement as a single amount, except for an investor's share of accounting changes reported in the financial statements of the investee, which should be classified separately. An investor should recognize its share of the earnings or losses of an investee based on the shares of common stock and in-substance common stock held by

that investor, as set forth in FASB ASC 323-10-35-4, in the periods for which they are reported by the investee in its financial statements. An investor should adjust the carrying amount of an investment for its share of the earnings or losses of the investee after the date of investment and should report the recognized earnings or losses in income.[5] Paragraphs 31–32 of FASB ASC 323-10-35 explain that a loss in value of an equity method investment that is other than a temporary decline should be recognized even though the decrease in value is in excess of what would otherwise be recognized by application of the equity method. A series of operating losses of an investee or other factors may indicate that an other than temporary decrease in value of the investment has occurred. FASB ASC 323-10-35-32A states that an equity method investor should not separately test an investee's underlying asset(s) for impairment. However, an equity investor should recognize its share of any impairment charge recorded by an investee in accordance with the guidance in FASB ASC 323-10-35-13 and FASB ASC 323-10-45-1 and consider the effect, if any, of the impairment on the investor's basis difference in the assets giving rise to the investee's impairment charge.

- *Cost method.* As provided in FASB ASC 325-20-35-1, under the cost method of accounting for investments in common stock, dividends are the basis for recognition by an investor of earnings from an investment. An investor recognizes as income dividends received that are distributed from net accumulated earnings of the investee since the date of acquisition by the investor. The net accumulated earnings of an investee subsequent to the date of investment are recognized by the investor only to the extent distributed by the investee as dividends. Dividends received in excess of earnings subsequent to the date of investment are considered a return of investment and are recorded as reductions of cost of the investment. As with equity method investments, FASB ASC 325-20-35-2 explains that a loss in value of a cost method investment that is other than a temporary decline should be recognized. A series of operating losses of an investee or other factors may indicate that a decrease in value of the investment has occurred that is other than temporary.

  The preceding item, "cost method," will be deleted upon the effective date of FASB ASU No. 2016-01.

3.22 The extent of the use of those methods varies; however, they have all been used in, or have been considered acceptable for use in, accounting for investments in joint ventures in the construction industry. Combinations of those

[5] Paragraphs 37–39 of FASB ASC 323-10-35 address how an investor should account for its proportionate share of an investee's equity adjustments for other comprehensive income upon a loss of significant influence, a loss of control that results in the retention of a cost method investment, and discontinuation of the equity method for an investment in a limited partnership because the conditions in FASB ASC 970-323-25-6 are met for applying the cost method.

Paragraphs 37–39 of FASB ASC 323-10-35 address how an investor should account for its proportionate share of an investee's equity adjustments for other comprehensive income upon a loss of significant influence, a loss of control that results in accounting for the investment in accordance with FASB ASC 321, *Investments—Equity Securities*, and discontinuation of the equity method for an investment in a limited partnership because the conditions in FASB ASC 970-323-25-6 are met for accounting for the investment in accordance with FASB ASC 321.

methods have also been used in the construction industry. As noted previously, a common combination is to use the one-line equity method in the balance sheet and the proportionate consolidation method in the income statement.

Corporate Joint Ventures

3.23 Paragraph 3 of FASB ASC 323-10-15 establishes that the equity method of accounting applies to investments in the common stock of corporate joint ventures. FASB ASC 323-10 provides guidance and establishes requirements on the application of the equity method. According to FASB ASC 323-10-05-4, the equity method of accounting more closely meets the objectives of accrual accounting than does the cost method because the investor recognizes its share of the earnings and losses of the investee in the periods in which they are reflected in the accounts of the investee. The equity method also best enables investors in corporate joint ventures to reflect the underlying nature of their investment in those ventures.[6]

Paragraph 3 of FASB ASC 323-10-15 establishes that the equity method of accounting applies to investments in the common stock of corporate joint ventures. FASB ASC 323-10 provides guidance and establishes requirements on the application of the equity method. According to FASB ASC 323-10-05-4, the equity method of accounting more closely meets the objectives of accrual accounting because the investor recognizes its share of the earnings and losses of the investee in the periods in which they are reflected in the accounts of the investee. The equity method also best enables investors in corporate joint ventures to reflect the underlying nature of their investment in those ventures.[7, 8]

3.24 In its definition of a *corporate joint venture*, the FASB ASC glossary explains an entity that is a subsidiary of one of the joint venturers is not a corporate joint venture. A *subsidiary*, according to the FASB ASC glossary, is an entity, including an unincorporated entity, such as a partnership or trust, in which another entity, known as its *parent*, holds a controlling financial interest, including a VIE that is consolidated by a primary beneficiary.

3.25 With limited exceptions, all majority-owned subsidiaries—that is, all entities in which a parent has a controlling financial interest—should be consolidated in accordance with "Pending Content" in FASB ASC 810-10-15-10(a). "Pending Content" in FASB ASC 810-10-15-10(a)[1] states that a majority-owned subsidiary should not be consolidated if control does not rest with the majority owner, and provides indicators of when this situation may be present.

---

[6] FASB ASC 810-10-45-13 establishes that a parent or an investor should report a change to (or the elimination of) a previously existing difference between the parent's reporting period and the reporting period of a consolidated entity or between the reporting period of an investor and the reporting period of an equity method investee in the parent's or investor's consolidated financial statements as a change in accounting principle in accordance with the provisions of FASB ASC 250, *Accounting Changes and Error Corrections*. This issue does not apply in situations in which a parent entity or an investor changes its fiscal year-end.

[7] FASB ASC 810-10-45-13 establishes that a parent or an investor should report a change to (or the elimination of) a previously existing difference between the parent's reporting period and the reporting period of a consolidated entity or between the reporting period of an investor and the reporting period of an equity method investee in the parent's or investor's consolidated financial statements as a change in accounting principle in accordance with the provisions of FASB ASC 250, *Accounting Changes and Error Corrections*. This issue does not apply in situations in which a parent entity or an investor changes its fiscal year-end.

[8] See footnote 1.

Variable Interest Entities

Accounting Alternative

3.26 Per FASB ASC 810-10-15-17AB, a legal entity need not be evaluated by a private company under the guidance in the Variable Interest Entities subsection of FASB ASC 810-10-15 if the following (criteria *a–c* and, in applicable circumstances, criterion *d*) are met:

a. The private company lessee (the reporting entity) and the lessor legal entity are under common control.

b. The private company lessee has a lease arrangement with the lessor legal entity.

c. Substantially all activities between the private company lessee and the lessor legal entity are related to leasing activities (including supporting leasing activities) between those two entities.

In applicable circumstances, the following criterion must also be met:

d. If the private company lessee explicitly guarantees or provides collateral for any obligation of the lessor legal entity related to the asset leased by the private company, then the principal amount of the obligation at inception of such guarantee or collateral arrangement does not exceed the value of the asset leased by the private company from the lessor legal entity.

3.27 If the applicable criteria are met, application of this accounting alternative is an accounting policy election that should be applied by a private company to all legal entities. If any of the conditions in FASB ASC 810-10-15-17AB for applying the accounting alternative cease to be met, the entity should begin to apply the guidance in the Variable Interest Entities subsection of FASB ASC 810-10-15 at the date of change on a prospective basis.

3.28 FASB ASC 810-10 provides guidance and establishes requirements pertaining to the consolidation of VIEs, defined by the FASB ASC glossary as a legal entity subject to consolidation according to the applicable subsections in FASB ASC 810-10 related to VIEs. This FASB ASC subtopic explains how to apply the consolidation guidance of FASB ASC 810 to certain entities in which equity investors do not have the characteristics of a controlling financial interest or do not have sufficient equity at risk for the entity to finance its activities without additional subordinated financial support. The FASB ASC glossary term *subordinated financial support* is defined as variable interests that will absorb some or all of a VIE's expected losses. "Pending Content" in FASB ASC 810-10-15-14 states that an entity should follow the consolidation guidance for VIEs in FASB ASC 810-10 if, by design, any of the following conditions exist:

a. The total equity investment at risk is not sufficient to permit the entity to finance its activities without additional subordinated financial support provided by any parties, including equity holders.

b. As a group, the holders of the equity investment at risk lack any one of the following three characteristics:

i. The power, through voting rights or similar rights, to direct the activities of a legal entity that most significantly impact the entity's economic performance[9]

ii. The obligation to absorb the expected losses of the legal entity

iii. The right to receive the expected residual returns of the legal entity

c. The equity investors as a group otherwise lack the characteristic noted in the preceding item (*b*)(i) as a result of both of the following conditions being present:

i. The voting rights of some investors are not proportional to their obligations to absorb the expected losses of the legal entity, their rights to receive the expected residual returns of the legal entity, or both.

ii. Substantially all of the legal entity's activities (for example, providing financing or buying assets) either involve or are conducted on behalf of an investor that has disproportionately few voting rights.

3.29 FASB ASC 810-10 may affect the way construction contractors account for and report their investments in construction joint ventures. As provided in "Pending Content" in FASB ASC 810-10-25-38, an entity should consolidate a VIE when that reporting entity has a variable interest (or combination of variable interests) that provide the entity with a controlling financial interest on the basis of the provisions of "Pending Content" in paragraphs 38A–38J of FASB ASC 810-10-25.[10] The entity that consolidates a VIE is called the *primary beneficiary* of that VIE.

3.30 "Pending Content" in FASB ASC 810-10-25-38A states that an entity with a variable interest in a VIE should assess whether it has a controlling financial interest in the VIE and, thus, is the VIE's primary beneficiary. The entity is deemed to have a controlling interest if it has both of the following characteristics:

- The power to direct the activities of the VIE that most significantly impact the VIE's economic performance
- The obligation to absorb the losses of the VIE that could potentially be significant to the VIE or the right to receive benefits from the VIE that could potentially be significant to the VIE[11]

---

[9] Among other significant provisions, "Pending Content" in FASB ASC 810-10-15-14 notes that kick-out rights or participating rights held by the holders of the equity investment at risk should not prevent interests other than the equity investment from having this characteristic unless a single equity holder (including its related parties and de facto agents) has the unilateral ability to exercise such rights. Alternatively, interests other than the equity investment at risk that provide the holders of those interests with kick-out rights or participating rights should not prevent the equity holders from having this characteristic unless a single reporting entity (including its related parties and de facto agents) has the unilateral ability to exercise those rights.

[10] Paragraph 14 of FASB ASC 810-10-45 provides that an investee in the construction industry may present its investment in an unincorporated legal entity accounted for by the equity method using the proportionate gross financial statement presentation.

[11] The use of a quantitative approach, as discussed in the FASB ASC glossary definitions of *expected losses*, *expected residual returns*, and *expected variability* is not required and should not be the sole determinant about whether the entity has those obligations or rights.

Only one reporting entity is expected to be identified as the primary beneficiary of a VIE, although several may have the characteristics of the second item in the preceding list.[12] Only one entity will have the power to direct the activities of the VIE that most significantly impact the VIE's economic performance.

3.31 "Pending Content" in FASB ASC 810-10-25-38B states that an entity is not required to exercise the power it holds over a VIE in order to have power to direct the activities of a VIE.

Initial Consolidation of a Variable Interest Entity

3.32 If the primary beneficiary of a VIE and the VIE itself are under common control, the primary beneficiary should initially measure the assets, liabilities, and noncontrolling interests of the VIE at amounts at which they are carried in the accounts of the reporting entity that controls the VIE. For situations in which the initial consolidation of a VIE is a business, the transaction is a business combination and should be accounted for under the provisions of FASB ASC 805, *Business Combinations*.

3.33 "Pending Content" in paragraphs 7–9 of FASB ASC 810-10-30 provide guidance to a reporting entity that has not applied the guidance in the "Variable Interest Entities" subsections of FASB ASC to a legal entity because earlier consolidation was prevented due to a lack of information as discussed in FASB ASC 810-10-15-17(c).

3.34 According to FASB ASC 810-10-30-3, when a reporting entity becomes the primary beneficiary of a VIE that is not a business, no goodwill should be recognized. The primary beneficiary initially should measure and recognize the assets (except for goodwill) and liabilities of the VIE in accordance with FASB ASC 805-20-25 and 805-20-30. However, the primary beneficiary initially should measure assets and liabilities that it has transferred to that VIE at, after, or shortly before the date that the reporting entity became the primary beneficiary at the same amounts at which the assets and liabilities would have been measured if they had not been transferred. No gain or loss should be recognized because of such transfers.

3.35 The primary beneficiary of a VIE that is not a business should recognize a gain or loss for the difference between the following:

- The sum of
  - — the fair value of any consideration paid,
  - — the fair value of any noncontrolling interests,

---

[12] If the entity determines that power is, in fact, shared among multiple unrelated parties such that no one party has the power to direct the activities of the variable interest entity (VIE) that most significantly affect the VIE's economic performance, then no party is the primary beneficiary. Power is shared if two or more unrelated parties together have the power to direct the activities of a VIE that most significantly affect the VIE's economic performance and if decisions about those activities require the consent of each of the parties sharing power. If the entity concludes that power is not shared, but the activities that most significantly affect the VIE's economic performance are directed by multiple unrelated parties, and the nature of activities that each party is directing is the same, then the party, if any, with the power over the majority of those activities will be considered to have the characteristics in the first item in the bulleted list in paragraph 3.30.

However, if the activities that affect the VIE's economic performance are directed by multiple unrelated parties, and the nature of the activities that each party is directing is not the same, then the entity should identify which party has the power to direct the activities that most significantly affect the VIE's economic performance. Only one party will have this power.

— the reported amount of any previously held interests, and

- The net amount of the VIEs identifiable assets and liabilities recognized and measured in accordance with FASB ASC 805.

3.36 In accordance with FASB ASC 810-10-35-3, after the initial measurement, the assets, liabilities, and noncontrolling interests of a consolidated VIE should be accounted for in consolidated financial statements as if the VIE were consolidated based upon voting interests. Any specialized accounting requirements applicable to the type of business in which the VIE operates should be applied as they would be applied to a consolidated subsidiary. The consolidated entity should follow the requirements for elimination of intra-entity balances and transactions and other matters described in FASB ASC 810-10-45, FASB ASC 810-10-50-1, and FASB ASC 810-10-50-1B, as well as existing practices for consolidated subsidiaries. Fees or other sources of income or expense between a primary beneficiary and a consolidated VIE should be eliminated against the related expense or income of the VIE. The resulting effect of that elimination on the net income or expense of the VIE should be attributed to the primary beneficiary (and not to noncontrolling interests) in the consolidated financial statements.

3.37 In accordance with FASB ASC 810-10-45-16, the noncontrolling interest should be reported in the consolidated statement of financial position within equity (net assets), separately from the parent's equity (or net assets). The amount should be clearly identified and labeled, for example, as noncontrolling interest in subsidiaries. An entity with noncontrolling interests in more than one subsidiary may present those interests in aggregate in the consolidated financial statements.

General Partnerships

3.38 FASB ASC 323-30-25-1 states that investors in unincorporated entities, such as partnerships, generally should account for their investments using the equity method of accounting by analogy to FASB ASC 323-10 if the investor has the ability to exercise significant influence over the investee.

3.39 The principal difference, aside from income tax considerations, between corporate joint ventures and general partnerships is that a condition that would usually indicate control of a general partnership is ownership of a majority (over 50 percent) of the financial interests in profits or losses. The power to control a general partnership may also exist with a lesser percentage of ownership, for example, by contract, by agreement with other partners, or by court decree. On the other hand, majority ownership may not constitute control if major decisions such as the acquisition, sale, or refinancing of principal partnership assets must be approved by one or more of the other partners.

Undivided Interests in Ventures

3.40 FASB ASC 323-30-15-3 clarifies that investments in partnerships and unincorporated joint ventures may also be called *undivided interests in ventures*. According to FASB ASC 810-10-45-14, if the investor-venturer owns an undivided interest in each asset and is proportionately liable for its share of each liability, the provisions of FASB ASC 323-10-45-1 relating to the application of the equity method of accounting may not apply to investees in the construction industry. For example, proportionate consolidation using a proportionate gross financial statement presentation wherein the investor-venturer accounts in its financial statements for its pro rata share of the assets, liabilities, revenues, and expenses of the venture may be appropriate.

Determining Venturers' Percentage Ownership

3.41 Many joint venture agreements designate different allocations among the venturers of (*a*) the profits and losses, (*b*) the specified costs and expenses or revenues, (*c*) the distributions of cash from operations, and (*d*) the distributions of cash proceeds from liquidation. Such agreements may also provide for changes in the allocations at specified future dates or on the occurrence of specified future events. For the purpose of determining the amount of income or loss to be recognized by the venturer, the percentage of ownership interest should be based on the percentage by which costs and profits will ultimately be shared by the venturers. An exception to this general rule may be appropriate if changes in the percentages are scheduled or expected to occur so far in the future that they become meaningless for current reporting purposes. In those circumstances, the percentage interest specified in the joint venture agreement should be used with appropriate disclosures.

Conforming the Accounting Principles of the Venture

3.42 The accounts of a venture may reflect accounting practices (such as those used to prepare tax basis data for investors) that vary from U.S. generally accepted accounting principles (GAAP). If the financial statements of the investor are to be prepared in conformity with GAAP, such variances that are material should be identified and conformed to.

Losses in Excess of a Venturer's Investment, Loans, and Advances

3.43 A venturer should record its share of joint venture losses in excess of its investment, loans, and advances in accordance with paragraphs 19–30, and "Pending Content" of paragraphs 19–30, of FASB ASC 323-10-35. An investor's share of losses of an investee may equal or exceed the carrying amount of an investment accounted for by the equity method plus advances made by the investor. An equity method investor should continue to report losses up to the investor's investment carrying amount, including any additional financial support made or committed to by the investor. Additional financial support made or committed to by the investor may take the form of any of the following:

- Capital contributions to the investee
- Investments in additional common stock of the investee
- Investments in preferred stock of the investee
- Loans to the investee
- Investments in debt securities (including mandatorily redeemable preferred stock) of the investee
- Advances to the investee

The investor ordinarily should discontinue applying the equity method if the investment (and net advances) is reduced to zero and should not provide for additional losses unless the investor has guaranteed obligations of the investee or is otherwise committed to provide further financial support for the investee.

An investor should, however, provide for additional losses if the imminent return to profitable operations by an investee appears to be assured. For example, a material, nonrecurring loss of an isolated nature may reduce an investment below zero even though the underlying profitable operating pattern of an investee is unimpaired. If the investee subsequently reports net income, the investor should resume applying the equity method only after its share of that net income equals the share of net losses not recognized during the period the equity method was suspended. For additional guidance, refer to FASB ASC 323-10.

Disclosures in a Venturer's Financial Statements

3.44 In addition to the presentation of the basic financial statements and required disclosures in those statements, paragraphs 1–3 of FASB ASC 323-10-50 describe additional disclosures relating to investments accounted for using the equity method of accounting. All of the following disclosure requirements generally apply to the equity method of accounting for investments in common stock:

- Financial statements of an investor should parenthetically disclose, in the notes to financial statements or in separate statements or schedules,
  - — the name of each investee and percentage of ownership of common stock.
  - — the accounting policies of the investor with respect to investments in common stock. Disclosure should include the names of any significant investee entities in which the investor holds 20 percent or more of the voting stock, but for which the common stock is not accounted for using the equity method, together with the reasons why the equity method is not considered appropriate, and the names of any significant investee corporations in which the investor holds less than 20 percent of the voting stock and the common stock is accounted for using the equity method, together with the reasons why the equity method is considered appropriate.
  - — the difference, if any, between the amount at which an investment is carried and the amount of underlying equity in net assets and the accounting treatment of the difference.
- For those investments in common stock for which a quoted market price is available, the aggregate value of each identified investment based on the quoted market price usually should be disclosed. This disclosure is not required for investments in common stock of subsidiaries.
- If investments in common stock of corporate joint ventures or other investments accounted for under the equity method are, in the aggregate, material in relation to the financial position or results of operations of an investor, it may be necessary for summarized information about assets, liabilities, and results of

operations of the investees to be presented in the notes or in separate statements, either individually or in groups, as appropriate.

- Conversion of outstanding convertible securities, exercise of outstanding options and warrants, and other contingent issuances of an investee may have a significant effect on an investor's share of reported earnings or losses. Accordingly, material effects of possible conversions, exercises, or contingent issuances should be disclosed in notes to financial statements of an investor.

  For disclosures related to consolidated financial statements and VIEs, readers should refer to the guidance in FASB ASC 810-10-50, which also specifies the required disclosures under the available private company accounting alternative. When presenting financial statements that include cost-method investments, readers should refer to the guidance in FASB ASC 325-20-50.

3.45 Additional items that a venturer should consider for disclosure include the following:

- Any important provisions of the joint venture agreement
- If the joint venture's financial statements are not fully consolidated with those of the venturer, separate or combined financial statements of the ventures in summary form, including disclosure of accounting principles of the ventures that differ significantly from those of the venturer
- Intercompany transactions during the period and the basis of intercompany billings and charges
- Liabilities and contingent liabilities arising from the joint venture arrangement, including venturer's obligations under guarantees

Chapter 4

Financial Reporting by Affiliated Entities

4.01 Nonaccounting considerations, including taxation and exposure to legal liability, dictate the organizational structure and operating arrangements of many entities in the construction industry. As a result, many construction operations, when viewed as economic units, include several affiliated entities that are *related parties*, which, as defined in the FASB *Accounting Standards Codification* (ASC) glossary, includes affiliates of the entity. Related parties include

- entities for which investments in their equity securities would be required, absent the election of the fair value option in FASB ASC 825-10-15, to be accounted for by the equity method by the investing entity.
- trusts for the benefit of employees, such as pension and profit-sharing trusts that are managed by or under the trusteeship of management.
- principal owners of the entity and members of their immediate families.
- management of the entity and members of their immediate families.
- other parties with which the entity may enter into transactions if one party controls or can significantly influence the management or operating policies of the other to an extent that one of the transacting parties might be prevented from fully pursuing its own separate interests.
- other parties that can significantly influence the management or operating policies of the transacting parties or that have an ownership interest in one of the transacting parties and can significantly influence the other to an extent that one or more of the transacting parties might be prevented from fully pursuing its own separate interests.

An *affiliated entity*, as defined by the FASB ASC glossary, is an entity that directly or indirectly controls, is controlled by, or is under common control with another entity. The definition also includes a party with which the entity may deal if one party has the ability to exercise significant influence over the other's operating and financial policies.

4.02 The owners of closely held construction contractors may establish separate legal entities to acquire equipment or real estate that are then leased to the contractor. The separate financial statements of the members of the group usually cannot stand on their own because they may not reflect appropriate contract revenue, costs, or overhead allocations and because transactions may be unduly influenced by controlling related parties. A presumption exists that consolidated financial statements are more meaningful than separate financial statements and that they are usually necessary for a fair presentation when one of the entities in the consolidated group directly or indirectly has a controlling financial interest in the other entities.

4.03 FASB ASC 810, *Consolidation*, provides guidance for determining whether and how to consolidate another entity and the basis of presentation. FASB ASC 810-10-10-1 states that the purpose of consolidated statements is to present, primarily for the benefit of the owners and creditors of the parent, the results of operations and the financial position of a parent and all its subsidiaries essentially as if the consolidated group were a single economic entity. Among other types of investments by a reporting entity in an affiliated entity, FASB ASC 810 provides guidance and establishes requirements on the financial statement presentations of the following common types of investments that a reporting entity may have in another entity:

- Investments by a parent that constitute a controlling financial interest through direct or indirect ownership of a majority voting interest in a subsidiary
- Investments by a reporting entity in another entity that is not determined to be a variable interest entity (VIE) that constitute a controlling financial interest
- Investments by a reporting entity in another entity that is not determined to be a VIE that constitute a noncontrolling financial interest
- Investments by a reporting entity in a partnership or similar entity that is not determined to be a VIE
- Investments by a reporting entity in another entity that is determined to be a VIE[1]

Combined Financial Statements

4.04 For the purpose of presenting financial condition, results of operations, and cash flows of a group of commonly controlled entities that generally conduct their construction operations as, in effect, a single economic entity, FASB ASC 810-10-55-1B establishes that combined financial statements (as distinguished from consolidated financial statements) are likely to be more meaningful. The FASB ASC glossary defines *combined financial statements* as financial statements of a combined group of commonly controlled entities or commonly managed entities presented as those of a single economic unit. The combined group does not include the parent. Examples of circumstances in which combined financial statements may be useful, as provided in FASB ASC 810-10-55-1B, include the existence of several entities that are related in their operations or the existence of entities that are under common management.

4.05 FASB ASC 810-10-45-10 establishes, in the presentation of combined financial statements for a group of related entities, such as a group of commonly controlled entities, that intraentity transactions and profits or losses should be eliminated and that noncontrolling interests, foreign operations, different fiscal

---

[1] For additional discussion of variable interest entities (VIEs), see the preceding chapter. Several technical practice aids issued by the AICPA provide additional guidance in the form of nonauthoritative questions and answers that address various topics relevant to VIEs, including (*a*) combined versus consolidated financial statements, (*b*) presenting stand-alone financial statements of a VIE, and (*c*) implications for the auditor's report if the reporting entity does not consolidate the VIE. Readers should refer to Technical Questions and Answers sections 1400.29–.31 (*Technical Questions and Answers*).

periods, or income taxes should be treated in the same manner as consolidated financial statements.

4.06 The disclosures required in consolidated financial statements should be made, as well as disclosures relating specifically to combined financial statements. These include

- a statement to the effect that combined financial statements are not those of a separate legal entity.
- the names and year-ends of the major entities included in the combined group.
- the nature of the relationship between the entities.

The capital of each entity should be disclosed on the face of the financial statements or in a note, either in detail by entity if the number of entities is small or, if detailed disclosure is not practicable, in condensed form with an explanation of how the information was accumulated.

Presentation of Separate Financial Statements of Members of an Affiliated Group

4.07 Consolidated or combined financial statements of affiliated entities as the primary financial statements of an economic unit are normally recommended, but the needs of specific users may sometimes necessitate the presentation of separate financial statements for individual members of an affiliated group. The issuer of separate financial statements for a member of an affiliated group should make appropriate disclosures of related parties.

4.08 As provided in FASB ASC 850-10-05-3, examples of related party transactions include transactions between a parent entity and its subsidiaries, subsidiaries of a common parent, an entity and trusts for the benefit of employees, an entity and its principal owners, management, or members of their immediate families, and affiliates. FASB ASC defines *affiliate* as a party that, directly or indirectly through one or more intermediaries, controls, is controlled by, or is under common control with an entity.

4.09 In accordance with FASB ASC 850-10-50-1, financial statements of a reporting entity that has participated in material related party transactions should disclose, individually or in the aggregate, the following:

- The nature of the relationship(s) involved[2]
- A description of the transactions, including transactions to which no amounts or nominal amounts were ascribed, for each of the periods for which income statements are presented, and such other information deemed necessary to an understanding of the effects of the transactions on the financial statements
- The dollar amounts of transactions for each of the periods for which income statements are presented and the effects of any

[2] As established by FASB *Accounting Standards Codification* 850-10-50-6, if the reporting entity and one or more other entities are under common ownership or management control and the existence of that control could result in operating results or financial position of the reporting entity significantly different from those that would have been obtained if the entities were autonomous, the nature of the control relationship should be disclosed even though there are no transactions between the entities.

change in the method of establishing the terms from that used in the preceding period

- Amounts due from or to related parties as of the date of each balance sheet presented and, if not otherwise apparent, the terms and manner of settlement
- The information required by FASB ASC 740-10-50-17 related to deferred taxes

4.10 Additionally, FASB ASC 850-10-50-2 requires notes or accounts receivable from affiliated entities to be shown separately and not included under a general heading, such as notes receivable or accounts receivable.

Presentation of Separate Financial Statements of Members of an Affiliated Group That Constitute an Economic Unit

4.11 Presentation in a note to the financial statements of the condensed consolidated or combined balance sheet and statement of income of the members of the affiliated group that constitute the economic unit is also recommended.

Chapter 5

Other Accounting Considerations

Gray shaded text in this chapter reflects guidance issued but not yet effective as of the date of this guide, July 1, 2018, but becoming effective on or prior to December 31, 2018, exclusive of any option to early adopt ahead of the mandatory effective date. Unless otherwise indicated, all unshaded text reflects guidance that was already effective as of the date of this guide.

Definition of a *Public Business Entity*[1]

5.01 The FASB *Accounting Standards Codification* (ASC) Master Glossary defines *public business entity* as a business entity meeting any one of the following criteria:

- It is required by the SEC to file or furnish financial statements, or does file or furnish financial statements (including voluntary filers), with the SEC (including other entities whose financial statements or financial information are required to be or are included in a filing).
- It is required by the Securities Exchange Act of 1934, as amended, or rules or regulations promulgated under the act, to file or furnish financial statements with a regulatory agency other than the SEC.
- It is required to file or furnish financial statements with a foreign or domestic regulatory agency in preparation for the sale of or for purposes of issuing securities that are not subject to contractual restrictions on transfer.
- It has issued, or is a conduit bond obligor for, securities that are traded, listed, or quoted on an exchange or an over-the-counter market.
- It has one or more securities that are not subject to contractual restrictions on transfer, and it is required by law, contract, or regulation to prepare generally accepted accounting principles (U.S. GAAP) financial statements (including footnotes) and make them publicly available on a periodic basis (for example, interim or annual periods). An entity must meet both of these conditions to meet this criterion.

An entity may meet the definition of a public business entity solely because its financial statements or financial information is included in another entity's filing with the SEC. In that case, the entity is only a public business entity for purposes of financial statements that are filed or furnished with the SEC.

[1] *Technical Questions and Answers* provides significant additional nonauthoritative guidance to help preparers and practitioners determine if their organization or client is a public business entity (PBE) under the updated definition.

Fair Value Measurements

5.02 The fair value measurement provisions in FASB ASC 820 and FASB ASC 825, *Financial Instruments*, set forth many considerations affecting the way construction contractors determine the fair value of their financial assets and financial liabilities, including investments in debt and equity securities and derivative instruments, transferred receivables, and financial assets and financial liabilities acquired in a business combination. In addition, this statement affects the definition of fair values used to measure nonfinancial assets and liabilities, including the following:

- Certain impaired assets and liabilities
- Goodwill and intangible assets
- Assets retirement obligations
- Nonmonetary transactions
- Assets and liabilities acquired in a business combination

5.03 FASB ASC 820 defines *fair value*, establishes a framework for measuring fair value, and requires disclosures about fair value measurements. The following paragraphs summarize FASB ASC 820 but are not intended as a substitute for reading FASB ASC 820 in its entirety.

5.04 FASB ASC 820-10-15 states that, with certain exceptions, the guidance in FASB ASC 820 applies when GAAP require or permit fair value measurements or disclosures about fair value measurements. It also applies to measurements, such as fair value less costs to sell, based on fair value or disclosures about those measurements.

Definition of *Fair Value*

5.05 The FASB ASC glossary defines *fair value* as "the price that would be received to sell an asset or paid to transfer a liability in an orderly transaction between market participants at the measurement date." FASB ASC 820-10-35-5 states that a fair value measurement assumes that the transaction to sell the asset or transfer the liability occurs in the principal market for the asset or liability or, in the absence of a principal market, the most advantageous market for the asset or liability. The FASB ASC glossary defines the *principal market* as the market with the greatest volume and level of activity for the asset or liability and the *most advantageous market* as the market that maximizes the amount that would be received to sell the asset or minimizes the amount that would be paid to transfer the liability, after taking into account transaction costs and transportation costs. Although an entity must be able to access the market, it does not need to be able to sell the particular asset or transfer the particular liability on the measurement date to be able to measure fair value on the basis of the price in that market.

5.06 FASB ASC 820-10-35-6C states that even when there is no observable market to provide pricing information about the sale of an asset or the transfer of a liability at the measurement date, a fair value measurement assumes that a transaction takes place at that date, considered from the perspective of a market participant that holds the asset or owes the liability. That assumed transaction establishes a basis for estimating the price to sell the asset or to transfer the liability.

5.07 The definition of fair value focuses on the price that would be received to sell the asset or paid to transfer the liability (an exit price), not the price that would be paid to acquire the asset or received to assume the liability (an entry price). Conceptually, entry prices and exit prices are different, however, FASB ASC 820-10-30-3 explains that, in many cases, a transaction price will equal the fair value. Even with that said, when determining whether fair value equals the transaction price, an entity should take into account factors specific to the transactions. FASB ASC 820-10-30-3A provides conditions for which a transaction price might not represent the fair value of an asset or a liability.

5.08 One such condition is if the transaction price includes transaction costs (costs that result directly from and are essential to a transaction and that would not have been incurred by the entity had it not decided to sell the asset or transfer the liability). FASB ASC 820-10-35-9B provides that the price in the principal (or most advantageous) market should not be adjusted for transaction costs. Transaction costs are not a characteristic of the asset or liability measured. However, as noted in FASB ASC 820-10-35-9C, if location is a characteristic of the asset (as might be the case, for example, for a commodity), the price in the principal (or most advantageous) market should be adjusted for the costs, if any, that would be incurred to transport the asset from its current location to that market. That is, transaction costs do not include costs that would be incurred to transport an asset from its current location to its principal (or most advantageous) market as the price will be adjusted by these costs.

Fair Value of Nonfinancial Assets

5.09 Paragraphs 10A–10E, 11A, and 14 of FASB ASC 820-10-35 provide guidance for the fair value measurement of nonfinancial assets. A fair value measurement of a nonfinancial asset takes into account a market participant's ability to generate economic benefits by using the asset in its highest and best use or by selling it to another market participant that would use the asset in its highest and best use, considering the use of the asset that is physically possible, legally permissible, and financially feasible at the measurement date. An entity may not intend to use the nonfinancial asset according to its highest and best use; nevertheless, the entity should measure the fair value of a nonfinancial asset assuming its highest and best use by market participants.

5.10 More specifically, FASB ASC 820-10-35-10E provides that the highest and best use for an asset is established by one of two valuation premises. A nonfinancial asset might provide maximum value to market participants through its use in combination with other assets as a group (as installed or otherwise configured for use) or in combination with other assets and liabilities (for example, a business). If so, a nonfinancial asset's fair value should be based on the price that would be received in a current transaction to sell the asset assuming that the asset would be used with other assets or with other assets and liabilities and that those assets and liabilities (that is, its complementary assets and the associated liabilities) would be available to market participants. Alternatively, a nonfinancial asset might provide maximum value to market participants on a standalone basis. If the highest and best use of the asset is to use it on a standalone basis, the fair value of the asset is the price that would be received in a current transaction to sell the asset to market participants that would use the asset on a standalone basis.

Fair Value of Liabilities

5.11 Paragraphs 16–16B, and "Pending Content" in 16BB, 16D, and 16H–18C, of FASB ASC 820-10-35 provide guidance for the fair value measurement of liabilities. The fair value of a liability reflects the effect of nonperformance risk (the risk that an entity will not fulfill an obligation). Nonperformance risk is assumed to be the same before and after the transfer of the liability. Because nonperformance risk includes (but may not be limited to), a reporting entity's own credit risk, an entity should take into account the effect of its credit standing and any other factors that might influence the likelihood that the obligation will or will not be fulfilled when measuring the fair value of a liability. If the fair value option is elected for a liability issued with an inseparable third-party credit enhancement (for example, debt that is issued with a contractual third-party guarantee), FASB ASC 825-10-25-13 states the unit of accounting for the liability does not include the effects of the third-party credit enhancement when the issuer of the liability measures or discloses the fair value of the liability.

5.12 When a quoted price for the transfer of an identical or a similar liability is not available and the identical item is held by another party as an asset, an entity should measure the fair value of the liability from the perspective of a market participant that holds the identical item as an asset at the measurement date. An entity should adjust the quoted price of the liability held by another party as an asset only if there are factors specific to the asset that are not applicable to the fair value measurement of the liability. An entity should ensure that the price of the asset does not reflect the effect of a restriction preventing the sale of that asset. FASB ASC 820-10-35-16D includes some factors, including a third-party credit enhancement, that may indicate that the quoted price of the asset should be adjusted.

Valuation Techniques

5.13 Paragraphs 24, and "Pending Content" in 24A and 24B–27, of FASB ASC 820-10-35 describe the acceptable valuation techniques that can be used to measure fair value. The objective of using a valuation technique is to estimate the price at which an orderly transaction to sell the asset or to transfer the liability would take place between market participants at the measurement date under current market conditions. To measure fair value, an entity should use acceptable valuation techniques that are appropriate in the circumstances and for which sufficient data are available, maximizing the use of relevant observable inputs and minimizing the use of unobservable inputs. Three widely used valuation techniques are the market approach, cost approach, and income approach. Paragraphs 3A–3G of FASB ASC 820-10-55 describe those valuation techniques as follows:

- The market approach uses prices and other relevant information generated by market transactions involving identical or comparable (that is, similar) assets, liabilities, or a group of assets and liabilities, such as a business. Valuation techniques consistent with the market approach include matrix pricing and often use market multiples derived from a set of comparables.
- The income approach converts future amounts (for example, cash flows or income and expenses) to a single current (that is, discounted) amount. When the income approach is used, the fair value measurement reflects current market expectations about those future amounts. Valuation techniques consistent with the

income approach include present value techniques, option-pricing models, and the multiperiod excess earnings method.

- The cost approach reflects the amount that would be required currently to replace the service capacity of an asset (often referred to as current replacement cost). Fair value is determined based on the cost to a market participant (buyer) to acquire or construct a substitute asset of comparable utility, adjusted for obsolescence.

5.14 FASB ASC 820-10-35-24B explains that in some cases, a single valuation technique will be appropriate (for example, when valuing an asset or a liability using quoted prices in an active market for identical assets or liabilities). In other cases, multiple valuation techniques will be appropriate (for example, that might be the case when valuing a reporting unit). If multiple valuation techniques are used to measure fair value, the results (that is, respective indications of fair value) should be evaluated considering the reasonableness of the range of values indicated by those results. A fair value measurement is the point within that range that is most representative of fair value in the circumstances. Example 3 ("Pending Content" in paragraph 35 and paragraphs 36–41) in FASB ASC 820-10-55 illustrates the use of multiple valuation techniques.

5.15 As explained in paragraphs 25–26 of FASB ASC 820-10-35, valuation techniques used to measure fair value should be applied consistently. However, a change in a valuation technique or its application is appropriate if the change results in a measurement that is equally or more representative of fair value in the circumstances. Such a change would be accounted for as a change in accounting estimate in accordance with the provisions of FASB ASC 250, *Accounting Changes and Error Corrections*. However, as explained in FASB ASC 250-10-50-5, the disclosures in FASB ASC 250 for a change in accounting estimate are not required for revisions resulting from a change in a valuation technique or its application.

Present Value Techniques

5.16 Paragraphs 4–20 of FASB ASC 820-10-55 provide guidance on present value techniques, however, these paragraphs neither prescribe the use of one specific present value technique nor limit the use of present value techniques discussed therein. These paragraphs state that a fair value measurement of an asset or liability using present value techniques should capture all of the following elements from the perspective of market participants as of the measurement date:

- An estimate of future cash flows
- Expectations about possible variations in the amount and timing of the cash flows
- The time value of money
- The price for bearing the uncertainty inherent in the cash flows (risk premium)
- Other factors market participants would take into account in the circumstance
- In the case of a liability, the nonperformance risk relating to that liability, including the reporting entity's (obligor's) own credit risk

5.17 FASB ASC 820-10-55-6 provides the general principles that govern any present value technique, as follows:

- Cash flows and discount rates should reflect assumptions that market participants would use in pricing the asset or liability.
- Cash flows and discount rates should consider only factors attributed to the asset (or liability) being measured.
- To avoid double counting or omitting the effects of risk factors, discount rates should reflect assumptions that are consistent with those inherent in the cash flows. For example, a discount rate that reflects expectations about future defaults is appropriate if using the contractual cash flows of a loan but is not appropriate if the cash flows themselves are adjusted to reflect possible defaults.
- Assumptions about cash flows and discount rates should be internally consistent. For example, nominal cash flows (that include the effects of inflation) should be discounted at a rate that includes the effects of inflation.
- Discount rates should be consistent with the underlying economic factors of the currency in which the cash flows are denominated.

5.18 FASB ASC 820-10-55-9 describes how present value techniques differ in how they adjust for risk and in the type of cash flows they use. For example, the discount rate adjustment technique (also called the traditional present value technique) uses a risk-adjusted discount rate and contractual, promised, or most likely cash flows. In contrast, expected present value techniques use the probability-weighted average of all possible cash flows (referred to as expected cash flows). The traditional present value technique and two methods of expected present value techniques are discussed more fully in paragraphs 4–20 of FASB ASC 820-10-55.

The Fair Value Hierarchy

5.19 FASB ASC 820 emphasizes that fair value is a market-based measurement, not an entity-specific measurement. FASB ASC 820-10-35-9 states that fair value should be measured using the assumptions that market participants would use in pricing the asset or liability (referred to as inputs), assuming that market participants act in their economic best interest. The FASB ASC glossary defines *inputs* as assumptions that market participants would use when pricing the asset or liability, including assumptions about risk, such as the risk inherent in a particular valuation technique used to measure fair value (such as a pricing model) or the risk inherent in the inputs to the valuation technique. Inputs may be observable or unobservable:

- Observable inputs are developed using market data, such as publicly available information about actual events or transactions, and reflect the assumptions that market participants would use when pricing the asset or liability.
- Unobservable inputs are inputs for which market data are not available and are developed using the best information available about the assumptions that market participants would use when pricing the asset or liability.

Paragraphs 37–54B, exclusive of paragraphs previously superseded, of FASB ASC 820-10-35 establish a fair value hierarchy that distinguishes between observable and unobservable inputs. Valuation techniques used to measure fair value should maximize the use of observable inputs and minimize the use of unobservable inputs.

5.20 The fair value hierarchy in FASB ASC 820 characterizes into three levels the inputs to valuation techniques used to measure fair value. The three levels, which are described in paragraphs 40–54A, exclusive of paragraphs previously superseded, of FASB ASC 820-10-35, are as follows:

- *Level 1 inputs.* Paragraphs 40–46, exclusive of paragraphs previously superseded, of FASB ASC 820-10-35 state that level 1 inputs are quoted prices (unadjusted) in active markets for identical assets or liabilities that the reporting entity has the ability to access at the measurement date. An *active market* is a market in which transactions for the asset or liability take place with sufficient frequency and volume to provide pricing information on an ongoing basis. A quoted price in an active market provides the most reliable evidence of fair value and should be used without adjustment to measure fair value whenever available, except as discussed in FASB ASC 820-10-35-41C.
- *Level 2 inputs.* Paragraphs 47–51, exclusive of paragraphs previously superseded, of FASB ASC 820-10-35 state that level 2 inputs are inputs other than quoted prices included within level 1 that are observable for the asset or liability, either directly or indirectly. If the asset or liability has a specified (contractual) term, a level 2 input must be observable for substantially the full term of the asset or liability. Level 2 inputs include the following:
  — quoted prices for similar assets or liabilities in active markets.
  — quoted prices for identical or similar assets or liabilities in markets that are not active.
  — inputs other than quoted prices that are observable for the asset or liability (for example, interest rates and yield curves observable at commonly quoted intervals, volatilities, and credit spreads).
  — inputs that are derived principally from or corroborated by observable market data by correlation or other means (market-corroborated inputs).

  Adjustments to level 2 inputs will vary depending on factors specific to the asset or liability. Those factors include the condition or location of the asset, the extent to which inputs relate to items that are comparable to the asset (including those factors described in FASB ASC 820-10-35-16D), and the volume or level of activity in the markets within which the inputs are observed. An adjustment to a level 2 input that is significant to the entire measurement might result in a fair value measurement categorized within level 3 of the fair value hierarchy if the adjustment uses significant unobservable inputs.
- *Level 3 inputs.* Paragraphs 52–54A of FASB ASC 820-10-35 state that level 3 inputs are unobservable inputs for the asset or liability. Unobservable inputs should be used to measure fair value

to the extent that relevant observable inputs are not available, thereby allowing for situations in which there is little, if any, market activity for the asset or liability at the measurement date. A reporting entity should develop unobservable inputs using the best information available in the circumstances, which might include the entity's own data. In developing unobservable inputs, a reporting entity may begin with its own data, but it should adjust those data if reasonably available information indicates that other market participants would use different data or there is something particular to the reporting entity that is not available to other market participants (for example, an entity-specific synergy). A reporting entity need not undertake exhaustive efforts to obtain information about market participant assumptions. Unobservable inputs should reflect the assumptions that market participants would use when pricing the asset or liability, including assumptions about risk. Assumptions about risk include the risk inherent in a particular valuation technique and the risk inherent in the inputs to the valuation technique. A measurement that does not include an adjustment for risk would not represent a fair value measurement if market participants would include one when pricing the asset or liability. The reporting entity should take into account all information about market participant assumptions that is reasonably available. Unobservable inputs are developed using the best information available about the assumptions that market participants would use when pricing the asset or liability.

5.21 As explained in FASB ASC 820-10-35-37A, in some cases, the inputs used to measure the fair value of an asset or a liability might be categorized within different levels of the fair value hierarchy. In those cases, FASB ASC 820-10-35-37A states that the fair value measurement is categorized in its entirety in the same level of the fair value hierarchy as the lowest level input that is significant to the entire measurement. Adjustments to arrive at measurements based on fair value, such as costs to sell when measuring fair value less costs to sell, should not be taken into account when determining the level of the fair value hierarchy within which a fair value measurement is categorized.

5.22 As discussed in FASB ASC 820-10-35-38, the availability of relevant inputs and their relative subjectivity might affect the selection of appropriate valuation techniques. However, the fair value hierarchy prioritizes the inputs to valuation techniques, not the valuation techniques used to measure fair value. For example, a fair value measurement developed using a present value technique might be categorized within level 2 or level 3, depending on the inputs that are significant to the entire measurement and the level of the fair value hierarchy within which those inputs are categorized. As stated in FASB ASC 820-10-35-2C, the effect on the measurement arising from a particular characteristic will differ depending on how that characteristic would be taken into account by market participants. FASB ASC 820-10-55-51 illustrates a restriction's effect on fair value measurement.

Application of Fair Value Measurements

5.23 FASB ASC 820-10-35-10A provides that a fair value measurement of a nonfinancial asset takes into account a market participant's ability to generate economic benefits by using the asset in its highest and best use or by selling it to another market participant that would use the asset in its highest and best use. The FASB ASC glossary defines *highest and best use* as the use of a nonfinancial asset by market participants that would maximize the value of the asset or the group of assets and liabilities (for example, a business) within which the asset would be used. Further, FASB ASC 820-10-35-11A states that the fair value measurement of a nonfinancial asset assumes that the asset is sold consistent with the unit of account (which may be an individual asset). That is the case even when that fair value measurement assumes that the highest and best use of the asset is to use it in combination with other assets or with other assets and liabilities because a fair value measurement assumes that the market participant already holds the complementary assets and associate liabilities.

5.24 Paragraphs 16 and 16A of FASB ASC 820-10-35 state that fair value measurement assumes that a financial or nonfinancial liability or an instrument classified in a reporting entity's shareholders' equity is transferred to a market participant at the measurement date. The transfer of a liability or an instrument classified in a reporting entity's shareholders' equity assumes that (*a*) a liability would remain outstanding and the market participant transferee would be required to fulfill the obligation and (*b*) an instrument classified in a reporting entity's shareholders' equity would remain outstanding and the market participant transferee would take on the rights and responsibilities associated with the instrument. It is also assumed the liability or instrument would not be settled with the counterparty, cancelled, or otherwise extinguished on the measurement date. Even when there is no observable market to provide pricing information about the transfer of a liability or an instrument classified in a reporting entity's shareholders' equity (for example, because contractual or other legal restrictions prevent the transfer of such items), there might be an observable market for such items if they are held by other parties as assets (for example, a corporate bond or a call option on a reporting entity's shares).

5.25 Paragraphs 16B–16BB of FASB ASC 820-10-35 state that when a quoted price for the transfer of an identical or a similar liability or instrument classified in a reporting entity's shareholders' equity is not available and the identical item is held by another party as an asset, a reporting entity should measure the fair value from the perspective of a market participant that holds the identical item as an asset at the measurement date. In such cases, a reporting entity should measure the fair value of the liability or equity instrument as follows:

a. Using the quoted price in an active market for the identical item held by another party as an asset, if that price is available

b. If that price is not available, using other observable inputs, such as the quoted price in a market that is not active for the identical item held by another party as an asset

c. If the observable prices in items *a–b* are not available, using another valuation approach, such as an income approach or a market approach[2]

5.26 According to FASB ASC 820-10-35-16D, a reporting entity should adjust the quoted price of a liability or an instrument classified in a reporting entity's shareholders' equity held by another party as an asset only if there are factors specific to the asset that are not applicable to the fair value measurement of the liability or equity instrument. A reporting entity should determine

[2] Technical correction due to FASB Accounting Standards Update (ASU) No. 2016-19, *Technical Corrections and Improvements*.

that the price of the asset does not reflect the effect of a restriction preventing the sale of that asset. Some factors that may indicate that the quoted price of the asset should be adjusted include (*a*) the quoted price for the asset relates to a similar, but not identical, liability or equity instrument held by another party as an asset, or (*b*) the unit of account for the asset is not be the same as for the liability or equity instrument.

5.27 FASB ASC 820-10-35-16H explains that when a quoted price for the transfer of an identical or a similar liability or instrument classified in a reporting entity's shareholders' equity is not available and the identical item is not held by another party as an asset, a reporting entity should measure the fair value of the liability or equity instrument using a valuation technique from the perspective of a market participant that owes the liability or has issued the claim on equity.

5.28 When measuring the fair value of a liability or an instrument classified in a reporting entity's shareholders' equity, FASB ASC 820-10-35-18B states that a reporting entity should not include a separate input or an adjustment to other inputs relating to the existence of a restriction that prevents the transfer of the item because the effect of that restriction is either implicitly or explicitly included in the other inputs to the fair value measurement. Refer to FASB ASC 820-10-35-18C for an example of the fair value measurement of a liability with such a restriction.

5.29 Paragraphs 17–18 of FASB ASC 820-10-35 provide that the fair value of a liability should reflect the effect of nonperformance risk (which includes, but is not limited to, a reporting entity's own credit risk). Nonperformance risk is assumed to be the same before and after the transfer of the liability. When measuring the fair value of a liability, a reporting entity should take into account the effect of its credit risk (credit standing) and any other factors that might influence the likelihood that the obligation will or will not be fulfilled.

5.30 FASB ASC 820-10-35-18A discusses fair value measurement of a liability that has an inseparable third-party credit enhancement (for example, debt that is issued with a financial guarantee from a third party that guarantees the issuer's payment obligation). The fair value of a liability reflects the effect of nonperformance risk on the basis of its unit of account. In accordance with FASB ASC 825, the issuer of a liability issued with an inseparable third-party credit enhancement that is accounted for separately from the liability should not include the effect of the credit enhancement (for example, the third-party guarantee of debt) in the fair value measurement of the liability. If the credit enhancement is accounted for separately from the liability, the issuer would take into account its own credit standing and not that of the third party guarantor when measuring the fair value of the liability.

5.31 FASB ASC 820-10-35-36B notes that reporting entity should select inputs that are consistent with the characteristics of the asset or liability that market participants would take into account in a transaction for the asset or liability. In some cases, those characteristics result in the application of an adjustment, such as a premium or discount (for example, a control premium or noncontrolling interest discount). However, a fair value measurement should not incorporate a premium or discount that is inconsistent with the unit of account in FASB ASC 820 that requires or permits the fair value measurement. Premiums or discounts that reflect size as a characteristic of the reporting entity's holding rather than as a characteristic of the asset or liability (for example, a control premium when measuring the fair value of a controlling interest) are not permitted in a fair value measurement. In all cases, if there is a quoted price in an active market (that is, a level 1 input) for an asset or a liability, a reporting entity should use that quoted price without adjustment when measuring fair value, except as specified in FASB ASC 820-10-35-41C.

Additional Guidance For Fair Value Measurement in Special Circumstances

5.32 FASB ASC 820-10-35 provides additional guidance for fair value measurements in the following circumstances:

- Measuring fair value of liabilities held by other parties as assets (paragraphs 16B–16D, exclusive of paragraphs previously superseded and inclusive of "Pending Content" when applicable, of FASB ASC 820-10-35)
- Measuring fair value when the volume or level of activity for an asset or a liability has significantly decreased (paragraphs 54C–54H of FASB ASC 820-10-35)
- Identifying transactions that are not orderly (paragraphs 54I–54J of FASB ASC 820-10-35)
- Using quoted prices provided by third parties (paragraphs 54K–54M of FASB ASC 820-10-35)
- Measuring the fair value of investments in certain entities that calculate net asset value per share or its equivalent (paragraphs 59–62 of FASB ASC 820-10-35)

Decrease in Market Activity

5.33 FASB ASC 820-10-35-44 affirms the requirement that the fair value of a position in a single asset or liability (including a position comprising a large number of identical assets or liabilities, such as a holding of financial instruments) that trades in an active market should be measured within level 1 as the product of the quoted price for the individual asset or liability and the quantity held by the reporting entity. That is the case even if a market's normal daily trading volume is not sufficient to absorb the quantity held, and placing orders to sell the position in a single transaction might affect the quoted price. If there has been a significant decrease in the volume or level of activity for the asset or liability in relation to normal market activity for the asset or liability (or similar assets or liabilities), further analysis of the transactions or quoted prices is needed. A decrease in the volume or level of activity on its own may not indicate that a transaction price or quoted price does not represent fair value. However, if a reporting entity determines that a transaction or quoted price does not represent fair value (for example, there may be transactions that are not orderly), an adjustment will be necessary if the reporting entity uses those transactions or prices as a basis for measuring fair value. That adjustment may be significant to the fair value measurement in its entirety. Adjustments also may be necessary in other circumstances (for example, when a price for a similar asset requires significant adjustment to make it comparable to the asset being measured or when the price is stale). Further, if there has been a significant decrease in the volume or level of activity for the asset or liability, a change in valuation technique or the use of multiple valuation techniques may be appropriate (for example, the use of a market approach and a present value technique).

Transactions That Are Not Orderly

5.34 When measuring fair value, an entity should take into account transaction prices for orderly transactions. If evidence indicates that a transaction is not orderly, an entity should place little, if any, weight (compared with other indications of fair value) on that transaction price. When an entity does not have sufficient information to conclude whether particular transactions are orderly, it should place less weight on those transactions when compared with other transactions that are known to be orderly.

Quoted Prices Provided by Third Parties

5.35 An entity may use quoted prices provided by third parties, such as pricing services or brokers, if it has determined that those prices are developed in accordance with FASB ASC 820. More weight should be given to quotes provided by third parties that represent binding offers than to quotes that are indicative prices. Less weight (when compared with other indications of fair value that reflect the results of transactions) should be placed on quotes that do not reflect the result of transactions.

Investments in Entities That Calculate Net Asset Value per Share

5.36 An investment within the scope of paragraphs 4–5 of FASB ASC 820-10-15 for which fair value is measured using net asset value per share (or its equivalent) as a practical expedient, should not be categorized within the fair value hierarchy. In addition, the disclosure requirements in FASB ASC 820-10-50-2 do not apply to that investment.

Disclosures required for an investment for which fair value is measured using net asset value per share (or its equivalent) as a practical expedient are described in FASB ASC 820-10-50-6A. Although the investment is not categorized within the fair value hierarchy, the entity should provide the amount measured using the net asset value per share (or its equivalent) practical expedient to permit reconciliation of the fair value of investments included in the fair value hierarchy to the line items presented in the statement of financial position.

In order to measure the fair value of investments in certain entities that calculate net asset value per share (or its equivalent), FASB ASC 820-10-35-59 states that an entity is permitted, as a practical expedient, to estimate the fair value of an investment within the scope of paragraphs 4–5 of FASB ASC 820-10-15 using the net asset value per share (or its equivalent, such as member units or an ownership interest in partners' capital to which a proportionate share of net assets is attributed) of the investment, if the net asset value per share of the investment (or its equivalent) is calculated in a manner consistent with the measurement principles of FASB ASC 946, *Financial Services—Investment Companies*, as of the reporting entity's measurement date. FASB ASC 820-10-15-4 explains that this guidance applies only to an investment that meets both of the following criteria as of the reporting entity's measurement date:

- The investment does not have a readily determinable fair value.
- The investment is in an entity that has all the attributes specified in FASB ASC 946-10-15-2 (investment activity, unit ownership,

pooling of funds, and reporting entity) or, if one or more of the attributes specified in FASB ASC 946-10-15-2 are not present, is in an entity for which it is industry practice to issue financial statements using guidance that is consistent with the measurement principles in FASB ASC 946.

Disclosures

5.37 Paragraphs 1–8, exclusive of paragraphs previously superseded and inclusive of "Pending Content" when applicable, of FASB ASC 820-10-50 require disclosures about assets and liabilities measured at fair value on a recurring or nonrecurring basis on the balance sheet after initial recognition. The quantitative disclosures required should be presented in a tabular format. The disclosures do not apply to the initial measurement of an asset or liability at fair value. For assets and liabilities that are measured at fair value on the balance sheet after initial recognition, an entity should disclose information to help users of its financial statements assess the valuation techniques and inputs used to develop those measurements. For recurring fair value measurements using significant unobservable inputs (level 3), an entity should disclose information to help users assess the effects of the measurements on earnings. FASB ASC 820-10-50-1A lists the following items that are required to be considered when addressing disclosure objectives in FASB ASC 820-10-50-1. To meet those objectives an entity should consider all of the following, and disclose additional information necessary to meet the objectives:

- The level of detail necessary to satisfy the disclosure requirements
- How much emphasis to place on each of the various requirements
- How much aggregation or disaggregation to undertake
- Whether users of financial statements need additional information to evaluate the quantitative information disclosed

5.38 FASB ASC 820-10-55-104 builds on this guidance, adding that a reporting entity might disclose some or all of the following:

- The nature of the item being measured at fair value, including the characteristics of the item being measured that are taken into account in the determination of relevant inputs
- How third-party information such as broker quotes, pricing services, net asset values, and relevant market data was taken into account when measuring fair value

5.39 FASB ASC 820-10-50-2 requires a reporting entity to disclose, at a minimum, the following information for each class of assets and liabilities (see paragraph 820-10-50-2B for information on determining appropriate classes of assets and liabilities) measured at fair value in the statement of financial position after initial recognition:

1. For recurring fair value measurements, the fair value measurement at the end of the reporting period, and for nonrecurring fair value measurements, the fair value measurement at the relevant measurement date and the reasons for the measurement. Recurring fair value measurements of assets or liabilities are those that other FASB ASC topics require or permit in the statement of financial position at the end of each reporting period. Nonrecurring

fair value measurements of assets or liabilities are those that other FASB ASC topics require or permit in the statement of financial position in particular circumstances (for example, when a reporting entity measures a long-lived asset or disposal group classified as held for sale at fair value less costs to sell in accordance with FASB ASC 360, *Property, Plant and Equipment*, because the asset's fair value less costs to sell is lower than its carrying value). For nonrecurring measurements estimated at a date during the reporting period other than the end of the reporting period, a reporting entity shall clearly indicate that the fair value information presented is not as of the period's end as well as the date or period that the measurement was taken.

2. For recurring and nonrecurring fair value measurements, the level within the fair value hierarchy in which the fair value measurements are categorized in their entirety (level 1, 2, or 3).

3. For assets and liabilities held at the end of the reporting period that are measured at fair value on a recurring basis, the amounts of any transfers between level 1 and level 2 of the fair value hierarchy, the reasons for the transfers, and the reporting entity's policy for determining when transfers between levels are deemed to have occurred. Transfers into each level should be disclosed separately from transfers out of each level. FASB ASC 820-10-50-2C explains that a reporting entity should disclose and consistently follow its policy for determining when transfers between levels of the fair value hierarchy are deemed to have occurred. The policy about the timing of recognizing transfers should be the same for transfers into the levels as that for transfers out of the levels. Examples of policies for determining the timing of transfers include the following: the date of the event or change in circumstances that caused the transfer, the beginning of the reporting period, and the end of the reporting period.

4. The information should include

   a. for recurring and nonrecurring fair value measurements categorized within level 2 and level 3 of the fair value hierarchy, a description of the valuation technique(s) and the inputs used in the fair value measurement. If there has been a change in valuation technique (for example, changing from a market approach to an income approach or the use of an additional valuation technique), the reporting entity should disclose that change and the reason(s) for making it.

   a. for recurring and nonrecurring fair value measurements categorized within level 2 and level 3 of the fair value hierarchy, a description of the valuation technique(s) and the inputs used in the fair value measurement. If there has been a change in either or both a valuation approach and a valuation technique (for example, changing from matrix pricing to the binomial model or the use of an additional valuation technique), the reporting entity shall disclose that change and the reason(s) for making it.[3]

b. for fair value measurements categorized within level 3 of the fair value hierarchy, a reporting entity should provide quantitative information about the significant unobservable inputs used in the fair value measurement. A reporting entity is not required to create quantitative information to comply with this disclosure requirement if quantitative unobservable inputs are not developed by the reporting entity when measuring fair value (for example, when a reporting entity uses prices from prior transactions or third-party pricing information without adjustment). However, when providing this disclosure, a reporting entity cannot ignore quantitative unobservable inputs that are significant to the fair value measurement and are reasonably available to the reporting entity.

5. For recurring fair value measurements categorized within level 3 of the fair value hierarchy, a reconciliation from the opening balances to the closing balances, disclosing separately changes during the period attributable to any of the following:

   a. Total gains or losses for the period recognized in earnings, and the line items(s) in the statement of income (or activities) in which those gains or losses are recognized.

   b. Total gains or losses recognized in other comprehensive income, and the line item(s) in other comprehensive income in which those gains or losses are recognized.

   c. Purchases, sales, issuances, and settlements (each of those types of changes disclosed separately).

---

[3] FASB ASU No. 2016-01, *Financial Instruments—Overall (Subtopic 825-10): Recognition and Measurement of Financial Assets and Financial Liabilities*, was issued in January 2016. For PBEs, the amendments in this ASU are effective for fiscal years beginning after December 15, 2017, including interim periods within those fiscal years. For all other entities including not-for-profit entities and employee benefit plans within the scope of FASB *Accounting Standards Codification* (ASC) 960 through 965 on plan accounting, the amendments in this ASU are effective for fiscal years beginning after December 15, 2018, and interim periods within fiscal years beginning after December 15, 2019. All entities that are not PBEs may adopt the amendments in this ASU earlier as of the fiscal years beginning after December 15, 2017, including interim periods within those fiscal years. Early application by PBEs to financial statements of fiscal years or interim periods that have not yet been issued or, by all other entities, that have not yet been made available for issuance of the following amendments in this ASU are permitted as of the beginning of the fiscal year of adoption:

1. An entity should present separately in other comprehensive income the portion of the total change in the fair value of a liability resulting from a change in the instrument-specific credit risk if the entity has elected to measure the liability at fair value in accordance with the fair value option for financial instruments.
2. Entities that are not public business entities are not required to apply the fair value of financial instruments disclosure guidance in the General Subsection of FASB ASC 825-10-50.

Except for the early application guidance discussed previously, early adoption of the amendments in this ASU is not permitted.

Readers are encouraged to read the full text of the ASU, available at www.fasb.org. Readers should apply the appropriate guidance based on their facts and circumstances.

d. The amounts of any transfers into or out of level 3 of the fair value hierarchy, the reasons for those transfers, and the reporting entity's policy for determining when transfers between levels are deemed to have occurred. Transfers into level 3 should be disclosed and discussed separately from transfers out of level 3.

6. For recurring fair value measurements categorized within level 3 of the fair value hierarchy, the amount of the total gains or losses for the period in item 5(*a*) included in earnings that is attributable to the change in unrealized gains or losses relating to those assets and liabilities still held at the end of the reporting period, and the line item(s) in the statement of income (or activities) in which those unrealized gains or losses are recognized.

7. For recurring and nonrecurring fair value measurements categorized within level 3 of the fair value hierarchy, a description of the valuation processes used by the reporting entity (including, for example, how an entity decides its valuation policies and procedures and analyzes changes in fair value measurements from period to period). See paragraph 105 of FASB ASC 820-10-55 for further guidance.

8. For recurring fair value measurements categorized within level 3 of the fair value hierarchy, a narrative description of the sensitivity of the fair value measurement to changes in unobservable inputs if a change in those inputs to a different amount might result in a significantly higher or lower fair value measurement. If there are interrelationships between those inputs and other unobservable inputs used in the fair value measurement, a reporting entity should also provide a description of those interrelationships and how they magnify or mitigate the effect of changes in the unobservable inputs of the fair value measurement. To comply with that disclosure requirement, the narrative description of the sensitivity to changes in unobservable inputs should include, at a minimum, the unobservable inputs disclosed.

9. For recurring and nonrecurring fair value measurements, if the highest and best use of a nonfinancial asset differs from its current use, a reporting entity should disclose that fact and why the nonfinancial asset is being used in a manner that differs from its highest and best use.

5.40 When implementing the disclosure requirement related to valuation processes, consider disclosing the following items set forth in FASB ASC 820-10-55-105:

- For the group within the reporting entity that decides the reporting entity's valuation policies and procedures, (*a*) its description, (*b*) to whom that group reports, and (*c*) the internal reporting procedures in place (for example, whether and, if so, how pricing, risk management, or audit committees discuss and assess the fair value measurements)
- The frequency and methods for calibration, back testing, and other testing procedures of pricing models

- The process for analyzing changes in fair value measurements from period to period
- How the reporting entity determined that third-party information, such as broker quotes or pricing services, used in the fair value measurement was developed in accordance with FASB ASC 820
- The methods used to develop and substantiate the unobservable inputs used in a fair value measurement

5.41 FASB ASC 820-10-50-2B explains that a reporting entity should determine appropriate classes of assets and liabilities on the basis of the nature, characteristics, and risks of the asset or liability, and the level of the fair value hierarchy within which the fair value measurement is categorized. Further, the number of classes may need to be greater for fair value measurements within level 3 of the fair value hierarchy because those measurements have a greater degree of uncertainty and subjectivity. A class of assets and liabilities will often require greater disaggregation than the line items presented in the statement of financial position.

5.42 Certain of the disclosures in FASB ASC 820-10-50 apply only to public entities, including entities that are conduit bond obligors for conduit debt securities that are traded in a public market (a domestic or foreign stock exchange or an over-the-counter market, including local or regional markets).

5.43 "Pending Content" in FASB ASC 820-10-50-6A states that for investments in certain entities that calculate net asset value per share (investments that are within the scope of paragraphs 4–5 of FASB ASC 820-10-15) and measured at fair value on a recurring or nonrecurring basis during the period, a reporting entity should disclose information that help users of financial statements to understand the nature and risks of the investments and whether the investments are probable of being sold at amounts different from net asset value per share (or its equivalent).

5.44 These disclosures are required, regardless of whether the practical expedient in FASB ASC 820-10-35-59 has been applied. These disclosures, to the extent applicable, are required for each class of investment. The required disclosures, according to FASB ASC 820-10-50-6A, to the extent applicable, are required for each class of investment. The required disclosures, according to FASB ASC 820-10-50-6A, at a minimum, are as follows:

a. The fair value measurement (as determined by applying paragraphs 59–62 of FASB ASC 820-10-35) of the investments in the class at the reporting date and a description of the significant investment strategies of the investee(s) in the class.

b. For each class of investment that includes investments that can never be redeemed with the investees, but the reporting entity receives distributions through the liquidation of the underlying assets of the investees, the reporting entity's estimate of the period of time over which the underlying assets are expected to be liquidated by the investees.

c. The amount of the reporting entity's unfunded commitments related to investments in the class.

d. A general description of the terms and conditions upon which the investor may redeem investments in the class (for example, quarterly redemption with 60 days' notice).

e. The circumstances in which an otherwise redeemable investment in the class (or a portion thereof) might not be redeemable (for example, investments subject to a lockup or gate). Also, for those otherwise redeemable investments that are restricted from redemption as of the reporting entity's measurement date, the reporting entity should disclose its estimate of when the restriction from redemption might lapse. If an estimate cannot be made, the reporting entity should disclose that fact and how long the restriction has been in effect.

f. Any other significant restriction on the ability to sell investments in the class at the measurement date.

g. Superseded by FASB Accounting Standards Update (ASU) No. 2015-07, *Fair Value Measurement (Topic 820): Disclosures for Investments in Certain Entities That Calculate Net Asset Value per Share (or Its Equivalent) (a consensus of the Emerging Issues Task Force)*.

h. If a group of investments would otherwise meet the criteria in FASB ASC 820-10-35-62, but the individual investments to be sold have not been identified (for example, if a reporting entity decides to sell 20 percent of its investments in private equity funds, but the individual investments to be sold have not been identified), so the investments continue to qualify for the practical expedient in FASB ASC 820-10-35-59, the reporting entity should disclose its plans to sell and any remaining actions required to complete the sale(s).

5.45 "Pending Content" in FASB ASC 820-10-55-107 provides an example of the disclosures required by FASB ASC 820-10-50-6A.

5.46 FASB ASC 820-10-50-2E provides disclosure requirements for those classes of assets and liabilities not measured at fair value in the statement of financial position but for which the fair value is disclosed. Specifically, for those classes of assets and liabilities, a reporting entity should disclose the information required. No other disclosures in FASB ASC 820-10-50 (summarized in paragraph 5.36) are required for those classes of assets and liabilities. Paragraphs 3–4 of FASB ASC 825-10-55 list examples of financial instruments that a financial entity and nonfinancial entity, respectively, would include in their disclosures about the fair value of financial instruments, including the following:

- Cash and short-term investments
- Investment securities and trading account assets
- Long-term investments
- Loan receivables
- Deposit liabilities
- Long-term debt

- Commitments to extend credit
- Standby letters of credit
- Written financial guarantees

Other examples may include, but would not be limited to, the following: tender option bonds, reverse repurchase agreements, lines of credit, and variable-rate demand preferred shares.

FASB ASC 820-10-50-2E provides disclosure requirements for those classes of assets and liabilities not measured at fair value in the statement of financial position but for which the fair value is disclosed. Specifically, for those classes of assets and liabilities, a reporting entity should disclose the information required. No other disclosures in FASB ASC 820-10-50 (summarized in paragraph 5.36) are required for those classes of assets and liabilities.[4]

Fair Value Option

5.47 The "Fair Value Option" subsections of FASB ASC 825-10 permit an entity to irrevocably elect fair value as the initial and subsequent measure for many financial instruments and certain other items, with changes in fair value recognized in the income statement as those changes occur. FASB ASC 825-10-35-4 explains that a business entity should report unrealized gains and losses on items for which the fair value option has been elected in earnings at each subsequent reporting date. Paragraphs 4–6 of FASB ASC 815-15-25 similarly permit an elective fair value remeasurement for any hybrid financial instrument that contains an embedded derivative, if that embedded derivative would otherwise have to be separated from its debt host contract in conformity with FASB ASC 815-15. An election is made on an instrument-by-instrument basis (with certain exceptions), generally when an instrument is initially recognized in the financial statements.

The "Fair Value Option" subsections of FASB ASC 825-10 permit an entity to irrevocably elect fair value as the initial and subsequent measure for many financial instruments and certain other items, with changes in fair value recognized in the income statement as those changes occur. "Pending Content" in paragraphs 4–6 of FASB ASC 815-15-25 similarly permit an elective fair value remeasurement for any hybrid financial instrument that contains an embedded derivative, if that embedded derivative would otherwise have to be separated from its debt host contract in conformity with FASB ASC 815-15. An election is made on an instrument-by-instrument basis (with certain exceptions), generally when an instrument is initially recognized in the financial statements.[5]

5.48 The "Fair Value Option" subsection of FASB ASC 825-10-15 describes the financial assets and liabilities for which the option is available. The fair value option need not be applied to all identical items, except as required by FASB ASC 825-10-25-7. Most financial assets and financial liabilities are

---

[4] See footnote 3.
[5] See footnote 3.

eligible to be recognized using the fair value option, as are firm commitments for financial instruments and certain nonfinancial contracts.

5.49 Specifically excluded from eligibility are investments in other entities that are required to be consolidated (which includes an interest in a VIE that a reporting entity is required to consolidate) employer's and plan's obligations for pension benefits, other postretirement benefits (including health care and life insurance benefits), postemployment benefits, employee stock option and stock purchase plans, and other deferred compensation arrangements (or assets representing overfunded positions in those plans), financial assets and liabilities recognized under leases (this does not apply to a guarantee of a third-party lease obligation or contingent obligation arising from a cancelled lease), deposit liabilities of depository institutions, and financial instruments that are, in whole or in part, classified by the issuer as a component of shareholder's equity (including temporary equity) (for example, a convertible debt security with a noncontingent beneficial conversion feature). Additionally, the election cannot be made for most nonfinancial assets and liabilities or for current or deferred income taxes.

5.50 FASB ASC 825-10-45 and FASB ASC 825-10-50 establish presentation and disclosure requirements designed to facilitate comparisons between entities that choose different measurement attributes for similar types of assets and liabilities. Paragraphs 1–2 of FASB ASC 825-10-45 state that entities should report assets and liabilities that are measured at fair value pursuant to the fair value option in a manner that separates those reported fair values from the carrying amounts of similar assets and liabilities measured using another measurement attribute. To accomplish that, an entity should either (*a*) report the aggregate carrying amount for both fair value and non-fair-value items on a single line, with the fair value amount parenthetically disclosed or (*b*) present separate lines for the fair value carrying amounts and the non-fair-value carrying amounts. As discussed in FASB ASC 825-10-25-3, upfront costs and fees related to items for which the fair value option is elected should be recognized in earnings as incurred and not deferred.

FASB ASC 825-10-45 and FASB ASC 825-10-50 establish presentation and disclosure requirements designed to facilitate comparisons between entities that choose different measurement attributes for similar types of assets and liabilities. "Pending Content" in paragraphs 1B–2 of FASB ASC 825-10-45 state that entities should report assets and liabilities that are measured at fair value pursuant to the fair value option in a manner that separates those reported fair values from the carrying amounts of similar assets and liabilities measured using another measurement attribute. To accomplish that, an entity should either (*a*) report the aggregate carrying amount for both fair value and non-fair-value items on a single line, with the fair value amount parenthetically disclosed or (*b*) present separate lines for the fair value carrying amounts and the non-fair-value carrying amounts. As discussed in FASB ASC 825-10-25-3, upfront costs and fees related to items for which the fair value option is elected should be recognized in earnings as incurred and not deferred.[6]

---

[6] See footnote 3.

Accounting for Certain Receive-Variable, Pay-Fixed Interest Rate Swaps

5.51 FASB ASC 815, *Derivatives and Hedging* addresses the accounting for certain receive-variable, pay-fixed interest rate swaps. The following paragraphs summarize some of the major provisions of FASB ASC 815 but are not intended as a substitute for reviewing relevant sections of FASB ASC 815 in their entirety.

5.52 As stated in FASB ASC 815-10-35-1A, as a practical expedient, a receive-variable, pay-fixed interest rate swap for which the simplified hedge accounting approach is applied may be measured subsequently at settlement value (that is, where nonperformance risk is not considered) instead of fair value.

5.53 Provided all of the conditions in FASB ASC 815-20-25-131D are met, the simplified hedge accounting approach may be applied by a private company, that is, an entity that does not meet the definition of a *public business entity* contained in the FASB ASC Master Glossary. The entity may elect the simplified hedge accounting approach for any receive-variable, pay-fixed interest rate swap, provided that all of the conditions for applying the simplified hedge accounting approach specified in that paragraph are met.

5.54 The conditions for the simplified hedge accounting approach determine which cash flow hedging relationships qualify for a simplified version of hedge accounting. If all of the conditions in paragraphs 131B–131D of FASB ASC 815-20-25 are met, an entity may assume that there is no ineffectiveness in a cash flow hedging relationship involving a variable-rate borrowing and a receive-variable, pay-fixed interest rate swap. The conditions of paragraph 131D of FASB ASC 815-20-25 include

- the variable rate on both the swap and the borrowing is based on the same index and reset period. For example, arrangements in which the variable rate on both the swap and debt is based on three-month LIBOR would meet this condition, unlike arrangements in which the rate on the swap is based on three-month LIBOR and the rate on the debt is based on one-month LIBOR.
- the swap is a "plain-vanilla" interest rate swap that does not include a cap or floor on the variable interest rate, unless the debt has a comparable cap or floor.
- the repricing and settlement dates of the swap and the debt either match or differ by no more than a few days.
- the swap's fair value at inception is at or near zero.
- the notional amount of the swap matches the hedged principal amount of the debt.
- all interest payments on the debt are designated as hedged during the term of the swap, or during the effective term of a forward starting swap, either in total or in proportion to the hedged principal amount of the debt.

Disclosure

5.55 If the simplified hedge accounting approach is applied in accounting for a qualifying receive-variable, pay-fixed interest rate swap, the settlement value of that swap may be used in place of fair value when disclosing the information FASB ASC 815-10-50 or in providing other fair value disclosures, such as those required under FASB ASC 820, on fair value. For the purposes of complying with these disclosure requirements, amounts disclosed at settlement value are subject to all of the same disclosure requirements as amounts disclosed at fair value. Any amounts disclosed at settlement value should be clearly stated as such and disclosed separately from amounts disclosed at fair value.

Service Concession Arrangements

5.56 FASB ASC 853, *Service Concession Arrangements*, and "Pending Content" therein addresses the accounting for service concessions. The following paragraphs summarize some of the major provisions of FASB ASC 853 but are not intended as a substitute for reviewing relevant sections of FASB ASC 853 in their entirety.

5.57 Service concession arrangements can take many different forms. A service concession arrangement is an arrangement between a grantor and an operating entity for which the terms provide that the operating entity will operate the grantor's infrastructure (for example, airports, roads, bridges, tunnels, prisons, and hospitals) for a specified period of time. The operating entity may also maintain the infrastructure. The infrastructure already may exist or may be constructed by the operating entity during the period of the service concession arrangement. If the infrastructure already exists, the operating entity may be required to provide significant upgrades as part of the arrangement.

5.58 In a typical service concession arrangement, an operating entity operates and maintains for a period of time the infrastructure of the grantor that will be used to provide a public service. In exchange, the operating entity may receive payments from the grantor to perform those services. Those payments may be paid as the services are performed or over an extended period of time.

5.59 In addition to payments from the grantor, the operating entity may be given a right to charge third-party users to use the infrastructure (for example, an hourly fee charged to an individual to use a parking structure). The arrangement may contain an unconditional guarantee from the grantor under which the grantor provides a guaranteed minimum payment if the fees collected from the third-party users do not reach a specified minimum threshold.

5.60 FASB ASC 853 applies to the accounting by operating entities of a service concession arrangement under which a public-sector entity grantor enters into a contract with an operating entity to operate the grantor's infrastructure. A public-sector entity includes a governmental body or an entity to which the responsibility to provide public service has been delegated.

5.61 In a service concession arrangement, both of the following conditions exist:

- The grantor controls or has the ability to modify or approve the services that the operating entity must provide with the infrastructure, to whom it must provide them, and at what price.
- The grantor controls, through ownership, beneficial entitlement, or otherwise, any residual interest in the infrastructure at the end of the term of the arrangement.

The grantor's infrastructure is not recognized as property, plant, and equipment of the operating entity.

Discontinued Operations

5.62 FASB ASC 205-20 addresses the presentation of discontinued operations. The following paragraphs summarize some of the major provisions of FASB ASC 205-20 but are not intended as a substitute for reviewing relevant sections of FASB ASC 205-20 in their entirety.

5.63 Per FASB ASC 205-20-45-1B a disposal of a component of an entity or a group of components of an entity should be reported in discontinued operations if the disposal represents a strategic shift that has (or will have) a major effect on an entity's operations and financial results and when the component of an entity or group of components of an entity meets the criteria to be classified as held for sale, is disposed of by sale or is disposed of other than by sale in accordance with FASB ASC 360-10-45-15 (for example, by abandonment or in a distribution to owners in a spinoff).

5.64 Examples of a strategic shift that has (or will have) a major effect on an entity's operations and financial results could include a disposal of a major geographical area, a major line of business, a major equity method investment, or other major parts of an entity.

5.65 FASB ASC 205-20-45-1E discussed the criteria that a component of an entity or a group of components of an entity, or a business or nonprofit activity (the entity to be sold), must meet to be classified as held for sale. At any point that this criteria is no longer met, except as permitted by FASB ASC 205-20-45-1G, an entity to be sold that is classified as held for sale should be reclassified as held and used and measured in accordance with the applicable guidance in FASB ASC 360.

Disposal Group Classified as Held for Sale

5.66 In the period or periods that a discontinued operation is classified as held for sale and for all prior periods presented, the assets and liabilities of the discontinued operation should be presented separately (not offset) in the asset and liability sections, respectively, of the statement of financial position.

5.67 If a discontinued operation is part of a disposal group that includes other assets and liabilities that are not part of the discontinued operation, the entity may present the assets and liabilities of the disposal group separately in the asset and liability sections, respectively, of the statement of financial position.

5.68 If a discontinued operation is disposed of before meeting the criteria in FASB ASC 205-20-45-1E to be classified as held for sale, an entity should present the assets and liabilities of the discontinued operation separately in the asset and liability sections, respectively, of the statement of financial position for the periods presented in the statement of financial position before the period that includes the disposal.

For any discontinued operation initially classified as held for sale in the current period, the entity should present the major classes of assets and liabilities of the discontinued operation classified as held for sale for all periods presented in the statement of financial position either by

- presentation on the face of the statement of financial position or
- disclosure in the notes to financial statements.

Disclosure

5.69 FASB ASC 205-20-50-1 prescribes that the following should be disclosed in the notes to financial statements that cover the period in which a discontinued operation either has been disposed of or is classified as held for sale under the requirements of FASB ASC 205-20-45-1E:

a. A description of both of the following:

  i. The facts and circumstances leading to the disposal or expected disposal

  ii. The expected manner and timing of that disposal

b. If not separately presented on the face of the statement where net income is reported as part of discontinued operations, the gain or loss recognized

c. If applicable, the segment or segments in which the discontinued operation is reported under FASB ASC 280, *Segment Reporting*

5.70 FASB ASC 205-20-50-3 notes that any changes to the plan of sale, any adjustments to previously reported amounts and any significant continuing involvement with a discontinued operation after the disposal date should be disclosed in the notes to financial statements.

Impairment of Long-Lived Assets

Property, Plant, and Equipment

5.71 Many construction contractors have considerable amounts of owned equipment on their books that need to be routinely tested for impairment. FASB ASC 360-10 addresses financial accounting and reporting for the impairment or disposal of long-lived assets. The FASB ASC glossary defines *impairment* as the condition that exists when the carrying amount of a long-lived asset (asset group) exceeds its fair value. The FASB ASC glossary defines an *asset group* as the unit of accounting for a long-lived asset or assets to be held and used, which represents the lowest level for which identifiable cash flows are largely independent of the cash flows of other groups of assets and liabilities.

5.72 FASB ASC 360-10-35-21 establishes that a long-lived asset (asset group) should be tested for recoverability whenever events or changes in circumstances indicate that its carrying amount may not be recoverable. The following are examples of such events or changes in circumstances:

- A significant decrease in the market price of a long-lived asset (asset group).
- A significant adverse change in the extent or manner in which a long-lived asset (asset group) is being used or in its physical condition.
- A significant adverse change in legal factors or in the business climate that could affect the value of a long-lived asset (asset group), including an adverse action or assessment by a regulator.

- An accumulation of costs significantly in excess of the amount originally expected for the acquisition or construction of a long-lived asset (asset group).
- A current-period operating or cash flow loss combined with a history of operating or cash flow losses or a projection or forecast that demonstrates continuing losses associated with the use of a long-lived asset (asset group).
- A current expectation that, more likely than not, a long-lived asset (asset group) will be sold or otherwise disposed of significantly before the end of its previously estimated useful life. The term *more likely than not* refers to a level of likelihood that is more than 50 percent.

5.73 FASB ASC 360-10-35-17 provides that an impairment loss should be recognized only if the carrying amount of a long-lived asset (asset group) is not recoverable and exceeds its fair value. The carrying amount of a long-lived asset (asset group) is not recoverable if it exceeds the sum of the undiscounted cash flows expected to result from the use and eventual disposition of the asset (asset group). That assessment should be based on the carrying amount of the asset (asset group) at the date it is tested for recoverability, whether in use or under development. An impairment loss should be measured as the amount by which the carrying amount of a long-lived asset (asset group) exceeds its fair value. FASB ASC 820, discussed earlier in this chapter, provides guidance on fair value measurements.

5.74 As explained in FASB ASC 360-10-35-22, when a long-lived asset (asset group) is tested for recoverability, it also may be necessary to review depreciation estimates and methods as required by FASB ASC 250 or the amortization period as required by FASB ASC 350, *Intangibles—Goodwill and Other*. Any revision to the remaining useful life of a long-lived asset resulting from that review also should be considered in developing estimates of future cash flows used to test the asset (asset group) for recoverability. However, any change in the accounting method for the asset resulting from that review should be made only after applying the provisions of FASB ASC 360-10.

5.75 FASB ASC 360 provides guidance on the circumstances in which long-lived assets may be disposed of other than by sale. FASB ASC 360-10-35-47 explains that a long-lived asset to be abandoned is disposed of when it ceases to be used. If an entity commits to a plan to abandon a long-lived asset before the end of its previously estimated useful life, depreciation estimates should be revised in accordance with paragraphs 17–20 of FASB ASC 250-10-45 and FASB ASC 250-10-50-4 to reflect the use of the asset over its shortened useful life. FASB ASC 360-10-40-4 states that a long-lived asset to be disposed of in an exchange measured based on the recorded amount of the nonmonetary asset relinquished or to be distributed to owners in a spinoff is disposed of when it is exchanged or distributed.

5.76 In accordance with FASB ASC 360-10-35-43, a long-lived asset (disposal group) classified as held for sale should be measured at the lower of its carrying amount or fair value less cost to sell. If the asset (disposal group) is newly acquired, the carrying amount of the asset (disposal group) should be established based on its fair value less cost to sell at the acquisition date. A long-lived asset should not be depreciated (amortized) while it is classified as held for sale. Interest and other expenses attributable to the liabilities of a disposal group classified as held for sale should continue to be accrued.

Intangibles—Goodwill

> **© Update 5-1 *Accounting and Reporting*: Financial Instruments**
>
> FASB ASU No. 2017-04, *Intangibles—Goodwill and Other (Topic 350): Simplifying the Test for Goodwill Impairment*, was issued in January 2017. An entity should apply the amendments in this ASU on a prospective basis. An entity is required to disclose the nature of and reason for the change in accounting principle upon transition. That disclosure should be provided in the first annual period and in the interim period within the first annual period when the entity initially adopts the amendments in this ASU.
>
> A public business entity that is an SEC filer should adopt the amendments in this ASU for its annual or any interim goodwill impairment tests in fiscal years beginning after December 15, 2019. A public business entity that is not an SEC filer should adopt the amendments in this ASU for its annual or any interim goodwill impairment tests in fiscal years beginning after December 15, 2020. All other entities, including not-for-profit entities, that are adopting the amendments in this ASU should do so for their annual or any interim goodwill impairment tests in fiscal years beginning after December 15, 2021.
>
> Early adoption is permitted for interim or annual goodwill impairment tests performed on testing dates after January 1, 2017.
>
> The amendments in this ASU modify the concept of impairment from the condition that exists when the carrying amount of goodwill exceeds its implied fair value to the condition that exists when the carrying amount of a reporting unit exceeds its fair value. An entity no longer will determine goodwill impairment by calculating the implied fair value of goodwill by assigning the fair value of a reporting unit to all of its assets and liabilities as if that reporting unit had been acquired in a business combination. Because these amendments eliminate step 2 from the goodwill impairment test, they should reduce the cost and complexity of evaluating goodwill for impairment.

5.77 FASB ASC 350-20 addresses financial accounting and reporting for goodwill subsequent to its acquisition and for the cost of internally developing goodwill. The following paragraphs summarize some of the major provisions of FASB ASC 350-20 but are not intended as a substitute for reviewing FASB ASC 350-20 in its entirety.

5.78 *Goodwill*, as defined in the FASB ASC glossary, is the excess of the cost of an acquired entity over the net of the amounts assigned to assets acquired and liabilities assumed. The amount recognized as goodwill includes acquired intangible assets that do not meet the criteria in FASB ASC 805, *Business Combinations* for recognition as an asset apart from goodwill. Paragraphs 1–2 of FASB ASC 350-20-35 explain that goodwill should not be amortized. Instead, goodwill should be tested for impairment at a level of reporting referred to as a reporting unit. The FASB ASC glossary defines *reporting unit* as an operating segment or one level below an operating segment (also known as a component). Impairment is the condition that exists when the carrying amount of goodwill exceeds its implied fair value. The fair value of goodwill can be measured only as a residual and cannot be measured directly. Therefore, FASB ASC

350-20-35 sets forth a methodology for determining a reasonable estimate of the value of goodwill for purposes of measuring an impairment loss.

5.79 Goodwill of a reporting unit should be tested for impairment on an annual basis and between annual tests if an event occurs or circumstances change that would more likely than not reduce the fair value of a reporting unit below its carrying amount. The annual goodwill impairment test may be performed any time during the fiscal year provided the test is performed at the same time every year. Different reporting units may be tested for impairment at different times.

5.80 The entity may first assess qualitative factors to determine whether it is necessary to perform the two-step goodwill impairment test described in paragraphs 4–19 of FASB ASC 350-20-35. If it is determined to be necessary to perform the two-step impairment test, this test will be used to identify potential goodwill impairment and to measure the amount of a goodwill impairment loss to be recognized, if any. Note that the entity has an unconditional option to bypass the qualitative assessment for any reporting unit in any period and proceed directly to performing the first step in the two-step impairment test.

5.81 The entity should assess relevant events and circumstance when assessing the qualitative factors to determine where it is more likely than not (that is, a likelihood greater than 50 percent) that the fair value of a reporting unit is less than its carrying amount, including goodwill. Item (c) of FASB ASC 350-30-35-3 lists example events and circumstances.

5.82 The fair value of a reporting unit refers to the price that would be received to sell the unit as a whole in an orderly transaction between market participants at the measurement date. Quoted market prices in active markets are the best evidence of fair value and should be used as the basis for the measurement, if available. However, the market price of an individual equity security (and thus the market capitalization of a reporting unit with publicly traded equity securities) may not be representative of the fair value of the reporting unit as a whole.

5.83 If, after assessing the totality of events or circumstances such as those described in the preceding paragraph, an entity determines that it is not more likely than not that the fair value of a reporting unit is less than its carrying amount, then the first and second steps of the goodwill impairment test are unnecessary. However, if, after assessing the totality of events or circumstances the entity determines that it is more likely than not that the fair value of a reporting unit is less than its carrying amount, then the entity must perform the first step of the two-step goodwill impairment test.

5.84 The first step of the goodwill impairment test used to identify potential impairment compares the fair value of a reporting unit with its carrying amount, including goodwill. If the carrying amount of a reporting unit is greater than zero and its fair value exceeds its carrying amount, goodwill of the reporting unit is considered not impaired; thus, the second step of the impairment test is unnecessary. If the carrying amount of a reporting unit exceeds its fair value, the second step of the goodwill impairment test should be performed to measure the amount of impairment loss, if any.

5.85 The second step of the goodwill impairment test, used to measure the amount of impairment loss, compares the implied fair value of reporting unit goodwill with the carrying amount of that goodwill. If the carrying amount of reporting unit goodwill exceeds the implied fair value of that goodwill, an impairment loss should be recognized in an amount equal to that excess. The loss recognized cannot exceed the carrying amount of goodwill.

5.86 After a goodwill impairment loss is recognized, the adjusted carrying amount of goodwill should be its new accounting basis. Subsequent reversal of a previously recognized goodwill impairment loss is prohibited once that loss has been recognized.

Accounting Alternative

5.87 FASB ASC 350-20 addresses the accounting alternative for goodwill. The following paragraphs summarize some of the major provisions of FASB ASC 350-20 but are not intended as a substitute for reviewing relevant sections of FASB ASC 350-20 in their entirety.

5.88 Per FASB ASC 350-20-15-4, a private company, that is, an entity that does not meet the definition of a *public business entity* contained in the FASB Master Glossary, may make an accounting policy election and apply guidance in the Accounting Alternative subsections of FASB ASC 350-20 to the following transactions or activities:

a. Goodwill that an entity recognizes in a business combination in accordance with FASB ASC 805-30 after it has been initially recognized and measured

b. Amounts recognized as goodwill in applying the equity method of accounting in accordance with FASB ASC 323, *Investments—Equity Method and Joint Ventures*, and to the excess reorganization value recognized by entities that adopt fresh-start reporting in accordance with FASB ASC 852, *Reorganizations*

5.89 Once an entity elects this accounting alternative it should apply the guidance to existing goodwill and to all additions to goodwill recognized in future transactions within the scope of the accounting alternative.

Amortization of Goodwill

5.90 FASB ASC 350-20-35-63 states that under the accounting alternative, goodwill relating to each business combination or reorganization event resulting in fresh-start reporting (amortizable unit of goodwill) should be amortized on a straight-line basis over 10 years, or less than 10 years if the entity demonstrates that another useful life is more appropriate.

5.91 The entity may revise the remaining useful life of goodwill upon the occurrence of events and changes in circumstances that warrant a revision to the remaining period of amortization. However, the cumulative amortization period for any amortizable unit of goodwill cannot exceed 10 years.

5.92 If the estimate of the remaining useful life of goodwill is revised, the remaining carrying amount of goodwill should be amortized prospectively on a straight-line basis over that revised remaining useful life.

Testing Goodwill for Impairment

5.93 In accordance with FASB ASC 350-20-35-65, upon adoption, the entity should make an accounting policy election to test goodwill for impairment at the entity level or the reporting unit level. The entity that elects to perform its impairment tests at the reporting unit level should follow the guidance in paragraphs 33–38 of FASB ASC 350-20-35 to determine the reporting units.

5.94 Goodwill should be tested for impairment if an event occurs or circumstances change that indicate that the fair value of the entity (or the reporting unit) may be below its carrying amount (a triggering event). If an entity determines that there are no triggering events, then further testing is unnecessary.

5.95 Upon the occurrence of a triggering event, the entity may assess qualitative factors to determine whether it is more likely than not (that is, a likelihood of more than 50 percent) that the fair value of the entity (or the reporting unit) is less than its carrying amount, including goodwill.

5.96 The entity has an unconditional option to bypass the qualitative assessment described in paragraphs 67–69 of FASB ASC 350-20-35 and proceed directly to a quantitative calculation by comparing the entity's (or the reporting unit's) fair value with its carrying amount. The entity may resume performing the qualitative assessment upon the occurrence of any subsequent triggering events.

5.97 The entity should consider relevant events and circumstances that affect the fair value or carrying amount of the entity (or of the reporting unit) in determining whether to perform the quantitative goodwill impairment test. The entity should consider the extent to which each of the adverse events and circumstances identified could affect the comparison of its fair value with its carrying amount. The entity also should consider positive and mitigating events and circumstances that may affect its determination of whether it is more likely than not that its fair value is less than its carrying amount. However, the existence of positive and mitigating events and circumstances is not intended to represent a rebuttable presumption that the entity should not perform the quantitative goodwill impairment test.

5.98 The entity should evaluate, on the basis of the weight of evidence, the significance of all identified events and circumstances in the context of determining whether it is more likely than not that the fair value of the entity (or the reporting unit) is less than its carrying amount. If, after assessing the totality of events or circumstances the entity determines that it is not more likely than not that the fair value of the entity (or the reporting unit) is less than its carrying amount, further testing is unnecessary.

5.99 If an entity determines that it is more likely than not that the fair value of the entity (or the reporting unit) is less than its carrying amount or if the entity elected to bypass the qualitative assessment, the entity should determine the fair value of the entity (or the reporting unit) and compare the fair value of the entity (or the reporting unit) with its carrying amount, including goodwill. A goodwill impairment loss shall be recognized if the carrying amount of the entity (or the reporting unit) exceeds its fair value.

5.100 Any goodwill impairment loss should be measured as the amount by which the carrying amount of an entity (or a reporting unit) including goodwill exceeds its fair value. The loss recognized cannot exceed the carrying amount of goodwill and should be allocated to individual amortizable units of goodwill of the entity (or the reporting unit) on a pro rata basis using their relative carrying amounts or using another reasonable and rational basis.

5.101 After a goodwill impairment loss is recognized, the adjusted carrying amount of goodwill should be its new accounting basis. Subsequent reversal of a previously recognized goodwill impairment loss is prohibited once that loss has been recognized.

Intangibles—Other

5.102 FASB ASC 350-30 addresses financial accounting and reporting for intangible assets (other than goodwill) acquired individually or with a group of other assets. The following paragraphs summarize some of the major provisions of FASB ASC 350-30 but are not intended as a substitute for reviewing FASB ASC 350-30 in its entirety.

5.103 The FASB ASC glossary defines *intangibles* as assets (not including financial assets) that lack physical substance. The term *intangible assets* is used to refer to intangible assets other than goodwill. FASB ASC 350-30-35-1 states that the accounting for a recognized intangible asset is based on its useful life to the reporting entity. An intangible asset with a finite useful life should be amortized; an intangible asset with an indefinite useful life should not be amortized. Paragraphs 18–20 of FASB ASC 350-30-35 explain that an intangible asset that is not subject to amortization should be tested for impairment annually, or more frequently if events or changes in circumstances indicate that the asset might be impaired. FASB ASC 360-10-35-21 includes examples of impairment indicators. The impairment test should consist of a comparison of the fair value of an intangible asset with its carrying amount. If the carrying amount of an intangible asset exceeds its fair value, an impairment loss should be recognized in an amount equal to that excess. After an impairment loss is recognized, the adjusted carrying amount of the intangible asset should be its new accounting basis. Subsequent reversal of a previously recognized impairment loss is prohibited.

5.104 FASB ASC 350-30-35-14 explains that an intangible asset that is subject to amortization should be reviewed for impairment in accordance with the impairment provisions applicable to long-lived assets in FASB ASC 360. In accordance with the recognition and measurement provisions in FASB ASC 360-10, an impairment loss should be recognized if the carrying amount of an intangible asset is not recoverable and if its carrying amount exceeds its fair value. After an impairment loss is recognized, the adjusted carrying amount of the intangible asset should be its new accounting basis. Subsequent reversal of a previously recognized impairment loss is prohibited.

Accounting for Identifiable Intangible Assets in a Business Combination

Accounting Alternative

5.105 Under the accounting alternative, as discussed in paragraphs 25–33 of FASB ASC 805-20-25, a private company, within the scope of FASB ASC 805-20-15-2, as discussed in paragraph 5.107, should not recognize, separately from goodwill, the following intangible assets:

- Customer-related intangible assets unless they are capable of being sold or licensed independently from other assets of a business
- Noncompetition agreements

5.106 Paragraph 31 of FASB ASC 805-20-25 states that customer-related intangible assets that would meet the criterion for recognition under this accounting alternative are those that are capable of being sold or licensed independently from the other assets of a business.

5.107 FASB ASC 805-20-15-2 states that a private company may make an accounting policy election to apply an accounting alternative for the recognition of identifiable intangible assets acquired in a business combination when the private company is required to recognize or otherwise consider the fair value of intangible assets as a result of any one of the following transactions:

- Applying the acquisition method in accordance with FASB ASC 805
- Assessing the nature of the difference between the carrying amount of an investment and the amount of underlying equity in net assets of an investee when applying the equity method of accounting in accordance with FASB ASC 323
- Adopting fresh-start reporting in accordance with FASB ASC 852 on reorganizations

5.108 FASB ASC 805-20-15-3 states that when the entity elects the accounting alternative it should apply all of the related recognition requirements upon election and should apply all of the related recognition requirements to all future transactions fall under the transactions within the scope of the election.

5.109 If the entity elects the accounting alternative, according to FASB ASC 805-20-15-4, it must also adopt the accounting alternative for amortizing goodwill. If the accounting alternative for amortizing goodwill was not adopted previously, it should be adopted on a prospective basis as of the adoption of the accounting alternative for intangible assets.

Business Combinations—Pushdown Accounting

5.110 FASB ASC 805-50 establishes accounting standards for pushdown accounting when an entity obtains control of an acquiree through one of several ways outlined in FASB ASC 805-50-25-4. The following paragraphs summarize some of the major provisions of FASB ASC 805-50 but are not intended as a substitute for reviewing FASB ASC 805-50 in its entirety.

5.111 An entity has the option to apply pushdown accounting in its separate financial statements when it obtains control of an acquiree, or each time there is a change-in-control event in which the entity obtains control of the acquiree and the election must be made before the financial statements are issued or available to be issued for the reporting period in which the change-in-control event occurred.

5.112 Per FASB ASC 805-50-25-7, if the entity does not elect to apply pushdown accounting upon a change-in-control event, it can elect to apply pushdown accounting to its most recent change-in-control event in a subsequent reporting period as a change in accounting principle in accordance with FASB ASC 250. Pushdown accounting should be applied as of the acquisition date of the change-in-control event. Note that this election to apply pushdown accounting to a specific change-in-control event if elected by an acquiree is irrevocable.

5.113 If the entity elects the option to apply pushdown accounting, the entity should reflect in its separate financial statements the new basis of accounting established by the acquirer for the individual assets and liabilities of the acquiree by applying the guidance in other related guidance in FASB ASC 805. The entity should also recognize any goodwill that arises because of the application of pushdown accounting in those separate financial statements.

5.114 FASB ASC 805-50-50-5 states that the entity should disclose information in the period in which the pushdown accounting was applied (or in the current reporting period if the acquiree recognizes adjustments that relate to pushdown accounting) that enables users of financial statements to evaluate the effect of pushdown accounting. FASB ASC 805-50-50-6 provides disclosures that the entity may include to help financial statement users to evaluate the effect of pushdown accounting.

5.115 After the initial measurement, the entity should follow the general subsequent measurement guidance contained in FASB ASC 805 as well as other applicable guidance to subsequently measure and account for its assets, liabilities, and equity instruments.

Asset Retirement Obligations

5.116 FASB ASC 410-20 establishes accounting standards for recognition and measurement of a liability for an asset retirement obligation and the associated asset retirement cost. The following paragraphs summarize some of the major provisions of FASB ASC 410-20 but are not intended as a substitute for reviewing FASB ASC 410-20 in its entirety.

5.117 Many construction contractors have mining operations or asphalt or concrete plants that have significant dismantling and restoration costs associated with retirement of the assets. FASB ASC 410-20 addresses financial accounting and reporting for *asset retirement obligations*, which are defined by the FASB ASC Master Glossary as obligations associated with the retirement of a tangible long-lived asset. The FASB ASC Master Glossary defines *retirement* as the other-than-temporary removal of a long-lived asset from service. That term encompasses sales, abandonments or disposals in some other manner. However, it does not encompass the temporary idling of a long-lived asset. The guidance in FASB ASC 410-20 applies to the following:

- Legal obligations associated with the retirement of a tangible long-lived asset that result from the acquisition, construction, development or the normal operation of a long-lived asset, including any legal obligations that require disposal of a replaced part that is a component of a tangible long-lived asset. The FASB ASC glossary defines a *legal obligation* as an obligation that a party is required to settle as a result of an existing or enacted law, statute, ordinance, or written or oral contract or by legal construction of a contract under the doctrine of promissory estoppel.
- An environmental remediation liability that results from the normal operation of a long-lived asset and that is associated with the retirement of that asset.
- A conditional obligation to perform a retirement activity. The FASB ASC glossary defines a *conditional asset retirement obligation* as a legal obligation to perform an asset retirement activity in which the timing and method of settlement are conditional on a future event that may or may not be within the control of the

entity. Uncertainty about the timing of settlement of the asset retirement obligation does not remove that obligation from the scope of FASB ASC 410-20 but will affect the measurement of a liability for that obligation.

- Obligations of a lessor in connection with leased property that meet the provisions in the preceding first list item.
- The costs associated with the retirement of a specified asset that qualifies as historical waste equipment as defined by EU Directive 2002/96/EC.

5.118 Exclusions to the guidance in FASB ASC 410-20-15 include

- obligations that arise solely from a plan to sell or otherwise dispose of a long-lived assed covered by FASB ASC 360-10.
- an environmental remediation liability that results from the improper operation of a long-lived asset as covered by FASB ASC 410-30.
- activities necessary to prepare an asset for an alternative use as they are not associated with the retirement of the asset.
- obligations associated with maintenance, rather than retirement, of a long-lived asset
- the cost of a replacement part that is a component of a long-lived asset.

FASB ASC 410-20-15-3 provides additional exclusions to which the preceding guidance on asset retirement obligations does not apply.

5.119 Paragraphs 4–6 of FASB ASC 410-20-25 establish that the entity should recognize the fair value of a liability for an asset retirement obligation in the period in which it is incurred if a reasonable estimate of fair value can be made. If a reasonable estimate of fair value cannot be made in the period the asset retirement obligation is incurred, the liability should be recognized when a reasonable estimate of fair value can be made. Upon initial recognition of a liability for an asset retirement obligation, an entity should capitalize an asset retirement cost by increasing the carrying amount of the related long-lived asset by the same amount as the liability. The FASB ASC glossary defines *asset retirement cost* as the amount capitalized that increases the carrying amount of the long-lived asset when a liability for an asset retirement obligation is recognized.

5.120 FASB ASC 410-20-25-6 states that an entity should identify all its asset retirement obligations. An entity has sufficient information to reasonably estimate the fair value of an asset retirement obligation if any of the following conditions exist:

- It is evident that the fair value of the obligation is embodied in the acquisition price of the asset.
- An active market exists for the transfer of the obligation.
- Sufficient information exists to apply an expected present value technique.

5.121 FASB ASC 410-20-30-1 explains that an expected present value technique will usually be the only appropriate technique with which to estimate the fair value of a liability for an asset retirement obligation. Paragraphs

2–5 of FASB ASC 410-20-35 provide that an entity should subsequently allocate that asset retirement cost to expense using a systematic and rational method over its useful life. In periods subsequent to initial measurement, an entity should recognize period-to-period changes in the liability for an asset retirement obligation resulting from the following:

- The passage of time
- Revisions to either the timing or the amount of the original estimate of undiscounted cash flows

5.122 An entity should measure and incorporate changes due to the passage of time into the carrying amount of the liability before measuring changes resulting from a revision to either the timing or the amount of estimated cash flows. An entity should measure changes in the liability for an asset retirement obligation due to passage of time by applying an interest method of allocation to the amount of the liability at the beginning of the period. The interest rate used to measure that change should be the credit-adjusted risk-free rate that existed when the liability, or portion thereof, was initially measured. That amount should be recognized as an increase in the carrying amount of the liability and as an expense classified as accretion expense. The FASB ASC glossary defines *accretion expense* as an amount recognized as an expense classified as an operating item in the statement of income resulting from the increase in the carrying amount of the liability associated with the asset retirement obligation.

Mandatorily Redeemable Stock[7]

5.123 FASB ASC 480, *Distinguishing Liabilities from Equity*, establishes standards for how an issuer classifies and measures in its statement of financial position certain financial instruments with characteristics of both liabilities and equity. FASB ASC 480-10-25-8 requires that an issuer classify a financial instrument that is within its scope as a liability (or an asset in some circumstances) because that financial instrument embodies an obligation of the issuer. "Pending Content" in FASB ASC 480-10-25-4 states that a mandatorily redeemable financial instrument should be classified as a liability unless the redemption is required to occur only upon the liquidation or termination of the reporting entity. "Pending Content" in the FASB ASC glossary defines a *mandatorily redeemable financial instrument* as any of various financial instruments issued in the form of shares that embody an unconditional obligation requiring the issuer to redeem the instrument by transferring its assets at a specified or determinable date (or dates) or upon an event that is certain to occur. "Pending

---

[7] FASB ASC 480-10-65-1 states that the effective date of FASB ASC 480, *Distinguishing Liabilities from Equity*, is deferred for mandatorily redeemable financial instruments issued by nonpublic entities that are not SEC registrants, as follows:

- For instruments that are mandatorily redeemable on fixed dates for amounts that either are fixed or are determined by reference to an interest rate index, currency index, or another external index, the classification, measurement, and disclosure provisions of FASB ASC 480 were effective for fiscal periods beginning after December 15, 2004.
- For all other financial instruments that are mandatorily redeemable, the classification, measurement, and disclosure provisions of FASB ASC 480 are deferred indefinitely pending further FASB action.
- Mandatorily redeemable financial instruments issued by SEC registrants are not eligible for either of those deferrals.

Other deferral provisions apply. Refer to FASB ASC, available on the FASB website at www.fasb.org, for the full text of the accounting standards.

Content" in FASB ASC 480-10-55-4 states that an example of a mandatorily redeemable financial instrument is a stock that must be redeemed upon the death or termination of the individual who holds it, which is an event that is certain to occur. Moreover, "Pending Content" in FASB ASC 480-10-30-1 states that mandatorily redeemable financial instruments should be measured initially at fair value.

5.124 FASB ASC 480 may have a significant impact on the financial statements of construction contractors. Many contractors are closely held, and many of them have buy-sell agreements requiring the entity to redeem the shares of the owners in the event of death or disability or other leave of employment. It is possible that such buy-sell agreements for share redemption would meet the definition of *mandatorily redeemable financial instruments* under FASB ASC 480. The application of the requirements of FASB ASC 480 may have significant effects on financial information and financial ratios of construction contractors, which could affect compliance with existing requirements of loan agreements, surety bonds, and other agreements.

Presentation of an Unrecognized Tax Benefit When a Tax Carryforward Exists

5.125 FASB ASC 740, *Income Taxes*, and "Pending Content" therein addresses the presentation of an unrecognized tax benefit when a tax carryforward exists. The following paragraphs summarize some of the major provisions of FASB ASC 740 but are not intended as a substitute for reviewing relevant sections of FASB ASC 740 in their entirety.

5.126 As presented in paragraphs 10A–12 in FASB ASC 740-10-45, the presentation of an unrecognized tax benefit when a net operating loss carryforward, a similar tax loss, or a tax credit carryforward exists:

- Except as indicated in paragraphs 10B and 12 in FASB ASC 740-10-45, an unrecognized tax benefit, or a portion of an unrecognized tax benefit, shall be presented in the financial statements as a reduction to a deferred tax asset for a net operating loss carryforward, a similar tax loss, or a tax credit carryforward.
- To the extent a net operating loss carryforward, a similar tax loss, or a tax credit carryforward is not available at the reporting date under the tax law of the applicable jurisdiction to settle any additional income taxes that would result from the disallowance of a tax position or the tax law of the applicable jurisdiction does not require the entity to use, and the entity does not intend to use, the deferred tax asset for such purpose, the unrecognized tax benefit shall be presented in the financial statements as a liability and shall not be combined with deferred tax assets. The assessment of whether a deferred tax asset is available is based on the unrecognized tax benefit and deferred tax asset that exist at the reporting date and shall be made presuming disallowance of the tax position at the reporting date.
- An entity that presents a classified statement of financial position shall classify an unrecognized tax benefit that is presented as a liability in accordance with "Pending Content" in paragraphs 10A–10B of FASB ASC 740-10-45 to the extent the entity

anticipates payment (or receipt) of cash within one year or the operating cycle, if longer.

- An unrecognized tax benefit presented as a liability shall not be classified as a deferred tax liability unless it arises from a taxable temporary difference. Paragraph 17 of FASB ASC 740-10-25 explains how the recognition and measurement of a tax position may affect the calculation of a temporary difference.

Differences Between Financial Accounting and Income Tax Accounting

5.127 Differing and often conflicting objectives and needs in determining income for current income tax reporting and for financial reporting have led to the practice, common in the construction industry, of measuring income for income tax purposes by methods different from those used for financial reporting purposes.

5.128 As previously discussed, income determination in the construction contracting industry involves many varied and changing conditions over which a contractor may have little control. Under most contracts, cash payments, which frequently represent amounts in excess of contract profit, are withheld by the owner until final acceptance of the project and are paid to the contractor in a period or periods different from those in which the income is earned. Those conditions have led contractors to adopt acceptable income tax reporting policies that defer income recognition for tax purposes until contracts are completed or that report income from contracts on a cash basis or on the basis of billings.

5.129 Despite the acceptability and appropriateness of such methods for determining current tax payments, it is essential that the contractor, when measuring current financial status for financial reporting purposes, take into account all known factors regarding contract performance. The financial reports serve as the basis for management planning and control. The reports also provide bonding companies and lenders with information on the current contract and financial status.

5.130 The differences between the periodic amounts of contract income reported during the term of a contract for financial reporting and income tax purposes result in temporary differences. FASB ASC 740 is the primary FASB ASC topic for financial statement accounting for income taxes.

5.131 FASB ASC 740-10-15-2AA clarifies that the sections of FASB ASC 740-10 relating to accounting for uncertain tax positions are applicable to all entities, including tax-exempt not-for-profit entities, pass-through entities, and entities that are taxed in a manner similar to pass-through entities such as real estate investment trusts and registered investment companies. *Tax position*, as defined by the FASB ASC glossary, is a position in a previously filed tax return or a position expected to be taken in a future tax return that is reflected in measuring current or deferred income tax assets and liabilities for interim or annual periods. A tax position can result in a permanent reduction of income taxes payable, a deferral of income taxes otherwise currently payable to future years, or a change in the expected realizability of deferred tax assets. The term tax position also encompasses, but is not limited to

- a decision not to file a tax return.
- an allocation or a shift of income between jurisdictions.
- the characterization of income or a decision to exclude reporting taxable income in a tax return.
- a decision to classify a transaction, entity, or other position in a tax return as tax exempt.
- an entity's status, including its status as a pass-through entity or a tax-exempt not-for-profit entity.

5.132 FASB ASC 740 establishes financial accounting and reporting standards for the effects of income taxes that result from an entity's activities during the current and preceding years. It requires an asset and liability approach for financial accounting and reporting for income taxes. FASB ASC 740-10-05-7 states deferred tax assets and liabilities represent the future effects on income taxes that result from temporary differences and carryforwards that exist at the end of a period. FASB ASC 740-10-05-7 states the tax effects of transactions are measured using enacted tax rates and provisions of the enacted tax law and are not discounted to reflect the time-value of money. As established in FASB ASC 740-10-25-47, the effects of changes in tax rates or tax laws should be recognized at the date of enactment. When deferred tax accounts are adjusted for the effect of a change in tax laws or rates, the effect should be included in income from continuing operations for the period that includes the enactment date. FASB ASC 740-10-25-32 clarifies that the recognition of deferred tax assets and liabilities may have limited application to a nontaxable entity (for example, a partnership) that may not pay income taxes at the entity level.

5.133 Many of the various types of temporary differences are the same for contractors as they are for other business enterprises. In addition, the following operating and financial reporting characteristics in the construction industry affect the nature and types of temporary differences in the industry:

- For reasons previously discussed, it is often not desirable for contractors to use, for income tax purposes, the method of accounting for contracts that is appropriate for financial reporting purposes.
- Joint performance of contracts under formal venture agreements is often necessary, and this creates a separate tax accounting entity with its own contract accounting methods and tax accounting policies. Also, taxable periods and accounting methods of such an entity may not coincide with those of the venturers.
- When current estimates of contract performance indicate an ultimate loss, accounting principles require a current loss provision, which is not deductible currently for income tax purposes.

5.134 Long-term construction contractors are generally required to use the percentage-of-completion method for computing long-term contract revenue for financial reporting purposes, rather than the completed-contract method. The use of the completed-contract method may result in an income materially different from the percentage-of-completion method which will result in a timing difference for tax purposes. This timing difference will reverse in later years.

Accounting Methods Acceptable for Income Tax Purposes

5.135 In addition to the percentage-of-completion and completed-contract methods, contractors ordinarily have available to them the cash method (normally very small contractors) and *accrual* methods (billings and costs) of accounting, among other methods, for determining taxable income. Certain conditions of eligibility for these different methods may apply. Contractors, like other taxpayers, are not ordinarily required to use the same method for both financial reporting and tax purposes. Effective tax planning may dictate the use of a different method for tax purposes.

Cash Method

5.136 The cash method has a potential tax advantage for a contractor because careful year-end scheduling of controllable receipts and disbursements can be used in tax planning. Under the cash method of computing taxable income, all items that represent gross income—whether in the form of cash, property, or services—are included in income for the taxable year in which they are received or constructively received. Expenditures are generally deducted as expenses in the taxable year in which they are paid. Income is constructively received in the taxable year in which it is credited to the taxpayer's account or set apart for him so that he may draw on it at any time. However, income is not constructively received if the taxpayer's control of its receipt is subject to substantial limitations or restrictions. A contractor using the cash method who intentionally defers or postpones billings to shift income from one period to another may be deemed to have constructively received as income amounts of billings deferred or postponed. The provisions of the contract and the actual performance on the project are the factors that determine when income is taxable. Although taxable income is affected by normal lags between billings and payments, a taxpayer reporting on a cash basis cannot arbitrarily determine the period in which income on a contract will be reported by arbitrarily selecting a billing date.

5.137 Under the cash method, contract costs are deductible in the year in which they are paid, even though the contract income has not been earned or received. For tax purposes, contract costs are deferred charges, not inventories. Although the cash basis method of reporting income cannot be applied to inventories, carrying minor amounts of inventories does not preclude a taxpayer from using that method. However, the cash method cannot be applied to inventories of large quantities of materials purchased and stored for future use without assignment for a specific contract. As provided in the Internal Revenue Code, a taxpayer in the home building business who builds speculative homes for resale must accumulate construction costs and deduct them in the year in which the sale of the property is reported, even though he may use the cash basis for tax purposes. Under those circumstances, construction costs are treated as work in progress. Also, an expenditure may be deductible only in part for the taxable year in which it is made if the expenditure is for an asset (for example, a depreciable asset or a three-year insurance policy) having a useful life that extends substantially beyond the close of the taxable year.

Accrual Method

5.138 An entity using an accrual method for income tax purposes reports as revenue amounts billed on contracts and as cost of earned revenue contract costs incurred to the date of the most recently rendered contract billing. Other expenditures are deductible as incurred. The accrual method may accelerate tax liabilities if gross margins on early billings are greater than gross margins on billings in the later stages of the contract. A contractor may elect to exclude retentions from income until they are received (modified accrual method); otherwise, they are recognized when billed, which may create a cash flow disadvantage because retentions normally are not collected until after contract completion.

Chapter 6

Financial Statement Presentation

Gray shaded text in this chapter reflects guidance issued but not yet effective as of the date of this guide, July 1, 2017, but becoming effective on or prior to December 31, 2017, exclusive of any option to early adopt ahead of the mandatory effective date. Unless otherwise indicated, all unshaded text reflects guidance that was already effective as of the date of this guide.

Balance Sheet Classification

6.01 The predominant practice in the construction industry is to present balance sheets with assets and liabilities classified as current and noncurrent, in accordance with FASB ASC 210, *Balance Sheet*, on the basis of one year or the operating cycle (if it exceeds one year). According to FASB ASC 210-10-05-4, the balance sheets of most entities show separate classifications of current assets and current liabilities (commonly referred to as *classified balance sheets*) permitting ready determination of working capital.

6.02 Construction contractors may use either a classified or unclassified balance sheet:

- A classified balance sheet is preferable for entities whose operating cycle is one year or less. An entity whose operating cycle for most of its contracts is one year or less, but that periodically obtains some contracts that are significantly longer than normal, may use a classified balance sheet with a separate classification and disclosure for items that relate to contracts that deviate from its normal operating cycle. For example, if an entity with a normal cycle of one year obtains a substantial contract that greatly exceeds one year, it may still use a classified balance sheet if it excludes from current assets and liabilities the assets and liabilities related to the contract that are expected to be realized or liquidated after one year and discloses in the financial statements information on the realization and maturity of those items. The one-year basis of classification, where appropriate, presents information in a form preferred by many sureties and credit grantors as one of the many tools that they use to make analyses of a contractor's operations and financial statements.
- Typically, an unclassified balance sheet is preferable for entities whose operating cycle exceeds one year, however, some banks prefer a classified balance sheet even if the operating cycle exceeds 1 year. An entity whose operating cycle exceeds one year may also use a classified balance sheet with assets and liabilities classified as current on the basis of the operating cycle if, in management's opinion, an unclassified balance sheet would not result in a meaningful presentation.

6.03 FASB ASC 910-235-50-2 states an entity should disclose liquidity characteristics of specific assets and liabilities if either of the following conditions is met:

- The entity's operating cycle exceeds one year.
- The entity uses an unclassified balance sheet.

6.04 If receivables include amounts representing balances billed but not paid by customers under contract retainage provisions, FASB ASC 910-310-50-4 states that a contractor should disclose, either in the balance sheet or in a note to the financial statements, all of the following:

- The amounts
- The portion, if any, expected to be collected after one year
- If practicable, the years in which the amounts are expected to be collected

6.05 Regarding certain liabilities common to construction contractors, FASB ASC 910-405-50-1 states information relating to accounts and retentions payable should be disclosed, including the amounts of retentions to be paid after one year and, if practicable, the year in which the amounts are expected to be paid.

Guidelines for Classified Balance Sheets

6.06 A classified balance sheet should be prepared in accordance with FASB ASC 210 and the guidelines discussed in the following paragraphs.

General Guidance

6.07 For most construction contractors, the operating cycle is difficult to measure with precision because it is determined by contracts of varying durations. The FASB ASC glossary defines the *operating cycle* as the average time intervening between the acquisition of materials or services and the final cash realization. The operating cycle of a contractor is determined by a composite of many individual contracts in various stages of completion. Thus, the operating cycle of a contractor is measured by the duration of contracts, that is, the average time intervening between the inception of contracts and the substantial completion of contracts.

6.08 According to the FASB ASC glossary, the term *current assets* is used to designate cash and other assets and resources commonly identified as those that are reasonably expected to be realized in cash or sold or consumed during the normal operating cycle of the business. FASB ASC 210-10-45-1 states current assets generally include all of the following:

- Cash available for current operations and items that are cash equivalents
- Inventories of merchandise, raw materials, goods in process, finished goods, operating supplies, and ordinary maintenance material and parts
- Trade accounts, notes, and acceptances receivable
- Receivables from officers, employees, affiliates, and others, if collectible in the ordinary course of business within a year
- Installment or deferred accounts and notes receivable if they conform generally to normal trade practices and terms within the business

- Marketable securities representing the investment of cash available for current operations, including investments in debt and equity securities classified as trading securities under FASB ASC 320-10
- Prepaid expenses, such as insurance, interest, rents, taxes, unused royalties, current paid advertising services not yet received, and operating supplies

According to the FASB ASC glossary, the term *current assets* is used to designate cash and other assets and resources commonly identified as those that are reasonably expected to be realized in cash or sold or consumed during the normal operating cycle of the business. FASB ASC 210-10-45-1 states current assets generally include all of the following:

- Cash available for current operations and items that are cash equivalents
- Inventories of merchandise, raw materials, goods in process, finished goods, operating supplies, and ordinary maintenance material and parts
- Trade accounts, notes, and acceptances receivable
- Receivables from officers, employees, affiliates, and others, if collectible in the ordinary course of business within a year
- Installment or deferred accounts and notes receivable if they conform generally to normal trade practices and terms within the business
- Marketable securities representing the investment of cash available for current operations
- Prepaid expenses, such as insurance, interest, rents, taxes, unused royalties, current paid advertising services not yet received, and operating supplies[1]

---

[1] FASB Accounting Standards Update (ASU) No. 2016-01, *Financial Instruments—Overall (Subtopic 825-10): Recognition and Measurement of Financial Assets and Financial Liabilities*, was issued in January 2016. For public business entities, the amendments in this ASU are effective for fiscal years beginning after December 15, 2017, including interim periods within those fiscal years. For all other entities including not-for-profit entities and employee benefit plans within the scope of FASB *Accounting Standards Codification* (ASC) 960 through 965 on plan accounting, the amendments in this ASU are effective for fiscal years beginning after December 15, 2018, and interim periods within fiscal years beginning after December 15, 2019. All entities that are not public business entities may adopt the amendments in this ASU earlier as of the fiscal years beginning after December 15, 2017, including interim periods within those fiscal years. Early application by public business entities to financial statements of fiscal years or interim periods that have not yet been issued or, by all other entities, that have not yet been made available for issuance of the following amendments in this ASU are permitted as of the beginning of the fiscal year of adoption:

1. An entity should present separately in other comprehensive income the portion of the total change in the fair value of a liability resulting from a change in the instrument-specific credit risk if the entity has elected to measure the liability at fair value in accordance with the fair value option for financial instruments.
2. Entities that are not public business entities are not required to apply the fair value of financial instruments disclosure guidance in the General Subsection of FASB ASC 825-10-50.

Except for the early application guidance discussed previously, early adoption of the amendments in this ASU is not permitted.

Readers are encouraged to read the full text of the ASU, available at www.fasb.org. Readers should apply the appropriate guidance based on their facts and circumstances.

6.09 According to the FASB ASC glossary, the term *current liabilities* is used principally to designate obligations whose liquidation is reasonably expected to require the use of existing resources properly classifiable as current assets, or the creation of other current liabilities. Moreover, paragraphs 8–9 of FASB ASC 210-10-45 explain that, as a balance sheet category, the classification of current liabilities generally includes obligations for items that have entered into the operating cycle, such as the following:

- Payables incurred in the acquisition of materials and supplies to be used in the production of goods or in providing services to be offered for sale
- Collections received in advance of the delivery of goods or performance of services
- Debts that arise from operations directly related to the operating cycle, such as accruals for wages, salaries, commissions, rentals, royalties, and income and other taxes
- Other liabilities whose regular and ordinary liquidation is expected to occur within a relatively short period of time, usually 12 months, such as the following:
  - — Short term debts arising from the acquisition of capital assets
  - — Serial maturities of long term obligations
  - — Amounts required to be expended within one year under sinking fund provisions
  - — Agency obligations arising from the collection or acceptance of cash or other assets for the account of third persons

FASB ASC 470-10-45 includes guidance on various debt transactions that may result in current liability classification. These transactions include due on demand loan agreements, callable debt agreements, short term obligations expected to be refinanced, and debt in default and debt which may cause a failure to meet established covenants.

6.10 In applying the foregoing definitions, the predominant practice in the construction industry for contractors whose operating cycle exceeds one year is to classify all contract-related assets and liabilities as current under the operating cycle concept and to follow other, more specific guidance in classifying other assets and liabilities. Following those general rules promotes uniformity of presentation and narrows the range of variations in practice. The following is a list of types of assets and liabilities that are generally considered to be contract related and that should generally be classified as current under the operating cycle concept:

a. Contract-related assets include

i. accounts receivable on contracts (including retentions);

ii. unbilled contract receivables;

iii. costs and estimated earnings in excess of billings;

iv. other deferred contract costs; and

v. equipment and small tools specifically purchased for, or expected to be used solely on, an individual contract.

b. Contract-related liabilities include

i. accounts payable on contracts (including retentions);

ii. accrued contract costs;

iii. billings in excess of costs and estimated earnings;

iv. deferred taxes resulting from the use of a method of income recognition for tax purposes different from the method used for financial reporting purposes;

v. advanced payments on contracts for mobilization or other purposes;

vi. obligations for equipment specifically purchased for, or expected to be used solely on, an individual contract regardless of the payment terms of the obligations; and

vii. provision for losses on contracts in accordance with paragraphs 1–2 of FASB ASC 605-35-45.

6.11 Following the foregoing guidance in preparing classified balance sheets will promote consistency in practice and facilitate consolidation of construction contracting segments of an entity with segments not engaged in construction contracting.

Retentions Receivable and Payable

6.12 Circumstances may be such that retentions receivable may not be collected within one year (for example, the existence of special arrangements with owners). FASB ASC 910-310-45-1 states that the portion of retainages not collectible within one year, or within the operating cycle if it is longer than one year, should be classified as noncurrent in a classified balance sheet.

6.13 Similarly, circumstances may be such that retentions payable will not be paid within an entity's normal operating cycle (for example, the existence of special arrangements with subcontractors or vendors), and these payables should be classified as noncurrent in a classified balance sheet.

6.14 In practice, many contractors opt not to present retentions receivable or retentions payable as noncurrent and commonly disclose this presentation election in a note to the financial statements.[2]

Investments in Construction Joint Ventures

6.15 Chapter 3, "Accounting for and Reporting Investments in Construction Joint Ventures," of this guide provides guidance for investors on acceptable financial statement presentation of investments in construction joint ventures. If a joint venture investment is presented on the cost or equity basis, the investment should be classified as noncurrent unless the venture is expected to be completed and liquidated during the current operating cycle of the investor. Losses in excess of an investment should be presented as a liability, and the classification principle for assets should apply.

---

[2] An example of such a note to the financial statements may be as follows:

> ***BALANCE SHEET CLASSIFICATIONS***
>
> The Company includes in current assets and liabilities amounts receivable and payable under construction contracts which may extend beyond one year. A one-year time period is used as the basis for classifying all other current assets and liabilities.

Equipment

6.16 The cost of equipment that is acquired for a specific contract, that will be used only on that contract, and that will be consumed during the life of the contract or disposed of at the conclusion of the contract should be classified as a contract cost.

Liabilities

6.17 For an entity with an operating cycle in excess of one year, liabilities related to contracts should be classified as current on the basis of the operating cycle. For example, if a classified balance sheet is prepared using an operating cycle longer than one year, all contract-related liabilities maturing within that cycle should be classified as current. Other liabilities should be classified on the basis of the specific guidance in FASB ASC 210-10.

Deferred Income Taxes

6.18 A deferred tax liability or asset represents the increase or decrease in taxes payable or refundable in future years as a result of temporary differences and carryforwards at the end of the current year. "Pending Content" in FASB ASC 740-10-45-4 states that in a classified statement of financial position, an entity shall classify deferred tax liabilities and assets as noncurrent amounts. Paragraphs 77–222 of FASB ASC 740-10-55 provide illustrations of the balance sheet classification of certain types of deferred income taxes, including methods of reporting construction contracts.[3]

Offsetting or Netting Amounts

6.19 A basic principle of accounting is that assets and liabilities should not be offset unless a right of offset exists. Thus, the net debit balances for certain contracts should not ordinarily be offset against net credit balances relating to others unless the balances relate to contracts that meet the criteria for combining in paragraphs 5–9 in FASB ASC 605-35-25.

The preceding heading and paragraph will be deleted upon the effective date of FASB Accounting Standards Update (ASU) No. 2014-09, *Revenue from Contracts with Customers (Topic 606)*.[4]

---

[3] Please refer to chapter 5, "Other Accounting Considerations," for further discussion of accounting for income taxes.

[4] FASB ASU No. 2014-09, *Revenue from Contracts with Customers (Topic 606)*, was issued in May 2014. Public business entities, certain not-for-profit entities, and certain employee benefit plans should apply the guidance in ASU No. 2014-09 as amended by FASB ASU No. 2015-14, *Revenue from Contracts with Customers (Topic 606): Deferral of the Effective Date*, to annual reporting periods beginning after December 15, 2017, including interim reporting periods within that reporting period. Earlier application is permitted only as of annual reporting periods beginning after December 15, 2016, including interim reporting periods within that reporting period.

All other entities should apply the guidance in ASU No. 2014-09 to annual reporting periods beginning after December 15, 2018, and interim reporting periods within annual reporting periods beginning after December 15, 2019. All other entities may apply the guidance in ASU No. 2014-09 earlier as of an annual reporting period beginning after December 15, 2016, including interim reporting periods within that reporting period. All other entities also may apply the guidance in ASU No. 2014-09 earlier as of an annual reporting period beginning after December 15, 2016, and interim reporting periods within annual reporting periods beginning one year after the annual reporting period in which the entity first applies the guidance in ASU No. 2014-09.

Readers are encouraged to read the full text of the FASB ASU, available at www.fasb.org. Readers should apply the appropriate guidance based on their facts and circumstances.

6.20 Paragraphs 3–4 of FASB ASC 605-35-45 recognize the principle of offsetting in discussing the two accepted methods of accounting for long term construction-type contracts. For the percentage-of-completion method, current assets may include costs and recognized income not yet billed with respect to certain contracts. Liabilities (in most cases current liabilities) may include billings in excess of costs and recognized income with respect to other contracts. For the completed-contract method, an excess of accumulated costs over related billings should be shown in the balance sheet as a current asset, and an excess of accumulated billings over related costs should be shown among the liabilities (in most cases as a current liability). If costs exceed billings on some contracts, and billings exceed costs on others, the contracts should ordinarily be segregated so that the amounts on the asset side include only those contracts on which costs exceed billings, and those on the liability side include only those on which billings exceed costs.

The preceding paragraph will be deleted upon the effective date of FASB ASU No. 2014-09.

6.21 Offsetting should be applied in the same way under the percentage-of-completion method.

The preceding paragraph will be deleted upon the effective date of FASB ASU No. 2014-09.

6.22 Although the suggested mechanics of segregating contracts between those on which costs exceed billings and those on which billings exceed costs do not indicate whether billings and related costs should be presented separately or combined (netted), separate disclosure in comparative financial statements is preferable because it shows the dollar volume of billings and costs (but not an indication of future profit or loss). In addition, grantors of credit, such as banks and insurance companies, have expressed a preference for separate disclosure. Disclosure may be made by short extension of the amounts on the balance sheet or in the notes to the financial statements. Thus, under the percentage-of-completion method, the current assets may disclose separately total costs and total recognized income not yet billed for certain contracts, and current liabilities may disclose separately total billings and total costs and recognized income for other contracts. The separate disclosure of revenue and costs in statements of income is the generally accepted practice. Only through comparable presentation of such data in the balance sheet can the reader adequately evaluate the contractor's comparative position.

The preceding paragraph will be deleted upon the effective date of FASB ASU No. 2014-09.

6.23 In accordance with paragraphs 1–2 of FASB ASC 910-405-45, an advance received on a cost-plus contract should not offset against accumulated costs unless it is a payment on account of work in progress. Such advances are made to provide a revolving fund and are not applied as partial payment until the contract is nearly or fully completed. However, advances that are payments on account of work in progress should be shown as a deduction from the related asset. FASB ASC 910-405-50-2 states that the amounts of advances that are payments on account of work in progress should be disclosed.

The preceding paragraph will be deleted upon the effective date of FASB ASU No. 2014-09.

6.24 For advance payments on a terminated government contract, FASB ASC 912-405-45-5 states the financial statements of the contractor issued before final collection of the claim should reflect any balance of those advances as deductions from the claim receivable.

The preceding paragraph will be relocated to chapter 5, "Other Accounting Considerations," under the heading "Fixed-Price Contract Terminations" upon the effective date of FASB ASU No. 2014-09.

Disclosures in Financial Statements

6.25 In addition to the financial statement disclosures generally required in an entity's financial statements, the following disclosures should be made in the notes to the financial statements of contractors if they are not disclosed in the body of the financial statements.

Significant Accounting Policies

6.26 In accordance with the disclosure sections of FASB ASC 323, *Investments—Equity Method and Joint Ventures*; FASB ASC 605; and FASB ASC 910, significant accounting policy disclosures should include the following:

- *a.* *Method of reporting affiliated entities.* Information relating to the method of reporting by affiliated entities should be disclosed, along with the disclosures recommended in chapter 4, "Financial Reporting by Affiliated Entities."
- *b.* *Operating cycle.* If the operating cycle exceeds one year, the range of contract durations should be disclosed. In addition, balance sheet classification disclosures consistent with ASC 210-10-05-4 and construction specific items consistent with ASC 910-235-50 should be disclosed.
- *c.* *Revenue recognition.* The method of recognizing income (percentage of completion or completed contract) should be disclosed:
  - i. If the percentage-of-completion method is used, the method or methods of measuring extent of progress toward completion (for example, cost to cost, labor hours) should be disclosed.
  - ii. If the completed-contract method is used, the reason for selecting that method should be indicated (for example, numerous short term contracts for which financial position and results of operations reported on the completed-contract basis would not vary materially from those resulting from use of the percentage-of-completion method; inherent hazards or undependable estimates that cause forecasts to be doubtful).

Item *c* will be deleted upon the effective date of FASB ASU No. 2014-09.

d. *Method of reporting joint venture investments.* The method of reporting joint ventures should be disclosed, along with other joint venture disclosures.

e. *Contract costs.*

   i. The aggregate amount included in contract costs representing unapproved change orders, claims, or similar items subject to uncertainty concerning their determination or ultimate realization, plus a description of the nature and status of the principal items comprising such aggregate amounts and the basis on which such items are recorded (for example, cost or realizable value).

   ii. The amount of progress payments netted against contract costs at the date of the balance sheet.

f. *Deferred costs.* For costs deferred either in anticipation of future sales (precontract costs that are not within the scope of FASB ASC 720-15) or as a result of an unapproved change order, the policy of deferral and the amounts involved should be disclosed.

Revised Estimates

6.27 Revisions in estimates of the percentage of completion are changes in accounting estimates as defined in FASB ASC 250, *Accounting Changes and Error Corrections*. FASB ASC 605-35-50-9 states that although estimating is a continuous and normal process for contractors, FASB ASC 250-10-50-4 requires disclosure of the effect of revisions if the effect is material. The effect on income from continuing operations, net income (or other appropriate captions of changes in the applicable net assets or performance indicator), and any related per-share amounts of the current period should be disclosed for a change in estimate that affects several future periods. Additionally, if a change in estimate does not have a material effect in the period of change but is reasonably certain to have a material effect in later periods, a description of that change in estimate should be disclosed whenever the financial statements of the period of change are presented.

The preceding paragraph will be deleted upon the effective date of FASB ASU No. 2014-09.

Backlog on Existing Contracts

6.28 In the construction industry, one of the most important indexes is the amount of backlog on uncompleted contracts at the end of the current year as compared with the backlog at the end of the prior year. Contractors are encouraged, but not required, to present backlog information for signed contracts on hand whose cancellation is not anticipated because many surety and bank underwriters utilize and rely on this disclosure when considering providing credit to the contractor. Backlog can be reported by industry or type of facility and by location (domestic or foreign). Additional disclosures that an entity may want to make include backlog on letters of intent and a schedule showing backlog at the beginning of the year, new contract awards, revenue recognized for the year, and backlog at the end of the year. The presentation of backlog information is desirable only if a reasonably dependable determination of total revenue and a reasonably dependable estimate of total cost under signed contracts or letters of intent can be made. Information on contracts should be segregated if signed contracts, letters of intent, and unsigned, but substantially agreed upon, contracts are all presented.

Receivables

6.29 If receivables include billed or unbilled amounts under contracts representing unapproved change orders, claims, or similar items subject to uncertainty concerning their determination or ultimate realization, the balance sheet, or a note to the financial statements, should disclose the amount, a description of the nature and status of the principal items comprising the amount, and the portion, if any, expected to be collected after one year. Paragraphs 25–31 of FASB ASC 605-35-25 discuss accounting for change orders and claims.

The preceding paragraph will be deleted upon the effective date of FASB ASU No. 2014-09.

6.30 If receivables include other amounts representing the recognized sales value of performance under contracts that have not been billed and were not billable to customers at the date of the balance sheet, these amounts, a general description of the prerequisites for billings, and the portion, if any, expected to be collected after one year should be disclosed.

The preceding paragraph will be deleted upon the effective date of FASB ASU No. 2014-09.

6.31 FASB ASC 605-35-50-8 states a contract claim receivable should be disclosed as a contingent asset in accordance with FASB ASC 450-30-50-1 if at least one of the following conditions exist:

- It is not probable that the claim will result in additional contract revenue.
- The claim amount cannot be reliably estimated.
- It is probable that a claim will result in additional contract revenue and that the claim amount can be reliably estimated, but the claim exceeds the recorded contract costs.

As provided by FASB ASC 450-30-50-1, adequate disclosure should be made of contingencies that might result in gains, but care should be exercised to avoid misleading implications about the likelihood of realization.

The preceding paragraph will be deleted upon the effective date of FASB ASU No. 2014-09.

6.32 FASB ASC 910-310-50-3 states that if receivables include amounts maturing after one year, the following should be disclosed:

- The amount maturing after one year and, if practicable, the amounts maturing in each year
- Interest rates on major receivable items, or on classes of receivables, maturing after one year or an indication of the average interest rate or the range of rates on all receivables

6.33 In accordance with FASB ASC 910-310-50-4, if receivables include amounts representing balances billed, but not paid by customers under contract retainage provisions, a contractor should disclose, either in the balance sheet or in a note to the financial statements, all of the following:

- The amounts
- The portion (if any) expected to be collected after one year
- If practicable, the years in which the amounts are expected to be collected

FASB ASC 910-310-45-1 states the portion of retainages not collectible within one year, or within the operating cycle if it is longer than one year, should be classified as noncurrent in a classified balance sheet.

6.34 Related party receivables are common in the construction industry. Refer to chapter 4 for the definition of *related parties*. In accordance with FASB ASC 210-10-45-4, the concept of the nature of current assets contemplates the exclusion from current assets of loans or advances to affiliates, officers, and employees that are not expected to be collected within 12 months. FASB ASC 850-10-50-2 states notes or accounts receivable from officers, employees, or affiliated entities must be shown separately and not included under a general heading such as "notes receivable" or "accounts receivable." If the reporting entity and 1 or more other entities are under common ownership or management control, and if the existence of that control could result in operating results or financial position of the reporting entity significantly different from those that would have been obtained if the entities were autonomous, the nature of the control relationship should be disclosed even though no transactions exist between the entities. This guidance specific to control relationships is found in FASB ASC 850-10-50-6.

6.35 As provided in FASB ASC 850-10-50-1, financial statements should include disclosures of material related party transactions, other than compensation arrangements, expense allowances, and other similar items in the ordinary course of business. However, disclosure of transactions that are eliminated in the preparation of consolidated or combined financial statements is not required in those statements. The disclosures should include the following:

- The nature of the relationship(s) involved
- A description of the transactions, including transactions to which no amounts or nominal amounts were ascribed, for each of the periods for which income statements are presented, and such other information deemed necessary to an understanding of the effects of the transactions on the financial statements
- The dollar amounts of transactions for each of the periods for which income statements are presented and the effects of any change in the method of establishing the terms from that used in the preceding period
- Amounts due from or to related parties as of the date of each balance sheet presented and, if not otherwise apparent, the terms and manner of settlement
- When a contractor is a member of a consolidated tax return but issues separate financial statements, disclosures in those statements should include the following in accordance with FASB ASC 740-10-50-17:

- The aggregate amount of current and deferred tax expense for each income statement presented and the amount of any tax-related balances due to or from affiliates as of the date of each balance sheet presented
- The principal provisions of the method by which the consolidated amount of current and deferred tax expense is allocated to members of the group and the nature and effect of any changes in that method (and in determining related balances to or from affiliates) during the years for which the preceding disclosures are presented

Going Concern[5]

6.36 "Pending Content" in FASB ASC 205-40-05-1 states that continuation of an entity as a going concern is presumed as the basis for financial reporting unless and until the entity's liquidation becomes imminent. Preparation of financial statements under this presumption is commonly referred to as the *going concern basis of accounting*. If and when an entity's liquidation becomes imminent, financial statements are prepared under the liquidation basis of accounting.

6.37 Even if an entity's liquidation is not imminent, there may be conditions and events, considered in the aggregate, that raise substantial doubt about the entity's ability to continue as a going concern. In those situations, financial statements continue to be prepared under the going concern basis of accounting, but the guidance in this subtopic should be followed to determine whether to disclose information about the relevant conditions or events.

6.38 The FASB ASC Master Glossary, as "Pending Content," defines *substantial doubt about the entity's ability to continue as a going concern* as existing when conditions and events, considered in the aggregate, indicate that it is probable that the entity will be unable to meet its obligations as they become due within one year after the date that the financial statements are issued (or within one year after the date that the financial statements are available to be issued when applicable).

6.39 In connection with preparing financial statements for each annual and interim reporting period, an entity's management should evaluate whether there are conditions and events, considered in the aggregate, that raise substantial doubt about an entity's ability to continue as a going concern within one year after the date that the financial statements are issued (or within one year after the date that the financial statements are available to be issued when applicable).

6.40 Ordinarily, conditions or events that raise substantial doubt about an entity's ability to continue as a going concern relate to the entity's ability to meet its obligations as they become due. Management's evaluation shall be based on relevant conditions and events that are known and reasonably knowable at the date that the financial statements are issued and management should consider both quantitative and qualitative information.

6.41 When relevant conditions or events, considered in the aggregate, initially indicate that it is probable that an entity will be unable to meet its

[5] Auditor requirements prescribed by AICPA *Professional Standards* are discussed in chapter 11, "Other Audit Considerations."

obligations as they become due within one year after the date that the financial statements are issued (and therefore they raise substantial doubt about the entity's ability to continue as a going concern), management should evaluate whether its plans that are intended to mitigate those conditions and events, when implemented, will alleviate substantial doubt about the entity's ability to continue as a going concern. This evaluation should be based on the feasibility of implementation of management's plans in light of an entity's specific facts and circumstances.

6.42 If, after considering management's plans, substantial doubt about an entity's ability to continue as a going concern is alleviated as a result of consideration of management's plans, an entity should disclose, as required by "Pending Content" in FASB ASC 205-40-50, in the footnotes information that enables users of the financial statements to understand all of the following (or refer to similar information disclosed elsewhere in the footnotes):

- Principal conditions or events that raised substantial doubt about the entity's ability to continue as a going concern (before consideration of management's plans)
- Management's evaluation of the significance of those conditions or events in relation to the entity's ability to meet its obligations
- Management's plans that alleviated substantial doubt about the entity's ability to continue as a going concern

6.43 If, after considering management's plans, substantial doubt about an entity's ability to continue as a going concern is not alleviated, the entity should include a statement in the footnotes indicating that there is substantial doubt about the entity's ability to continue as a going concern within one year after the date that the financial statements are issued. Additionally, the entity should disclose information that enables users of the financial statements to understand all of the following:

- Principal conditions or events that raise substantial doubt about the entity's ability to continue as a going concern
- Management's evaluation of the significance of those conditions or events in relation to the entity's ability to meet its obligations
- Management's plans that are intended to mitigate the conditions or events that raise substantial doubt about the entity's ability to continue as a going concern

6.44 If conditions or events continue to raise substantial doubt about an entity's ability to continue as a going concern in subsequent annual or interim reporting periods, the entity should continue to provide the required disclosures in those subsequent periods.

6.45 Disclosures should become more extensive as additional information becomes available about the relevant conditions or events and about management's plans. The entity should provide appropriate context and continuity in explaining how conditions or events have changed between reporting periods.

6.46 For the period in which substantial doubt no longer exists (before or after consideration of management's plans), the entity should disclose how the relevant conditions or events that raised substantial doubt were resolved.

Disclosures of Certain Significant Risks and Uncertainties

6.47 In accordance with FASB ASC 275-10-50-1, reporting entities should include in their financial statements disclosures about the risks and uncertainties existing as of the date of those statements in the following areas:

- Nature of their operations
- Use of estimates in the preparation of financial statements
- Certain significant estimates
- Current vulnerability due to certain concentrations

These four areas of disclosure are not mutually exclusive. The information required by some may overlap. Accordingly, the disclosures required by FASB ASC 275-10 may be combined in various ways, grouped together, placed in diverse parts of the financial statements, or included as part of the disclosures made pursuant to the other requirements within generally accepted accounting principles. Although the guidance in FASB ASC 275, *Risks and Uncertainties*, applies to complete interim financial statements, it does not apply to condensed or summarized interim financial statements. If comparative financial statements are presented, the disclosure requirements apply only to the financial statements for the most recent fiscal period presented. Paragraphs 1–19 of FASB ASC 275-10-55 provide examples of disclosures, and paragraphs 2–10 of FASB ASC 605-35-55 provide examples of disclosures required by FASB ASC 275 as they specifically pertain to the effects of possible near term changes in contract estimates.

These four areas of disclosure are not mutually exclusive. The information required by some may overlap. Accordingly, the disclosures required by FASB ASC 275-10 may be combined in various ways, grouped together, placed in diverse parts of the financial statements, or included as part of the disclosures made pursuant to the other requirements within generally accepted accounting principles. Although the guidance in FASB ASC 275, *Risks and Uncertainties*, applies to complete interim financial statements, it does not apply to condensed or summarized interim financial statements. If comparative financial statements are presented, the disclosure requirements apply only to the financial statements for the most recent fiscal period presented. Paragraphs 1–19 of FASB ASC 275-10-55 provide examples of these disclosures.[6]

6.48 Certain loan products have contractual terms that expose entities to risks and uncertainties described in the preceding paragraph. FASB ASC 825-10-55-1 states that certain loan products may increase a reporting entity's exposure to credit risk and thereby may result in a concentration of credit risk as that term is used in FASB ASC 825-10, either as an individual product type or as a group of products with similar features. Among other required disclosures about each significant concentration, FASB ASC 825-10-50-21 states that information about the (shared) activity, region, or economic characteristic that identifies the concentration should be disclosed, except for certain financial instruments identified in FASB ASC 825-10-50-22. According to paragraphs 1–2

---

[6] See footnote 4.

of FASB ASC 825-10-55, possible shared characteristics on which significant concentrations may be determined include, but are not limited to

- borrowers subject to significant payment increases,
- loans with terms that permit negative amortization, and
- loans with high loan-to-value ratios.

Judgment is required to determine whether loan products have terms that give rise to a concentration of credit risk.

Accounting for Weather Derivatives

6.49 FASB ASC 815-45 prescribes the accounting treatment, establishes disclosure requirements, and provides implementation guidance and illustrations for weather derivatives (that is, contracts indexed to climactic or geological variables).

Disclosures of Multiemployer Pension Plans

6.50 Multiemployer pension plans have become commonplace in the construction industry due to the heavily unionized workforce, amongst other reasons. Because of the nature of the industry, it is common for a construction contractor to pay employment benefits into several different plans that cover various states and jurisdictions.

Multiemployer Plans That Provide Pension Benefits

6.51 FASB ASC 715-80-50-2 states that an employer is required to apply the provisions of FASB ASC 450, *Contingencies*, if it is either probable or reasonably possible that either of the following would occur:

a. An employer would withdraw from the plan under circumstances that would give rise to an obligation.

b. An employer's contribution to the fund would be increased during the remainder of the contract period to make up a shortfall in the funds necessary to maintain the negotiated level of benefit coverage (a maintenance of benefits clause).

6.52 FASB ASC 715-80-50-3 states that an employer is required to provide the disclosures required by paragraphs 4–10 of FASB ASC 715-80-50 in annual financial statements. These disclosures of the employer's contributions made to the plan include all items recognized as net pension costs. The disclosures based on *the most recently available* information should be the most recently available through the date at which the employer has evaluated subsequent events.

6.53 Per FASB ASC 715-80-50-4, an employer that participates in a multiemployer plan that provides pension benefits is required to provide a narrative description both of the general nature of the multiemployer plans that provide pension benefits and of the employer's participation in the plans that would indicate how the risks of participating in these plans are different from single-employer plans.

6.54 FASB ASC 715-80-50-5 states that for each individually significant[7] multiemployer plan that provides pension benefits, an employer's disclosures should include the following:

a. Legal name of the plan

b. The plan's Employer Identification Number and, if available, its plan number

c. For each statement of financial position presented, the most recently available certified zone status provided by the plan, as currently defined by the Pension Protection Act of 2006 or a subsequent amendment of that act. The disclosure should specify the date of the plan's year-end to which the zone status relates and whether the plan has utilized any extended amortization provisions that affect the calculation of the zone status. If the zone status is not available, an employer should disclose, as of the most recent date available, on the basis of the financial statements provided by the plan, the total plan assets and accumulated benefit obligations, whether the plan was

   i. less than 65 percent funded.

   ii. between 65 percent and 80 percent funded.

   iii. at least 80 percent funded.

d. The expiration date(s) of the collective-bargaining agreement(s) requiring contributions to the plan, if any. If more than one collective-bargaining agreement applies to the plan, the employer should provide a range of the expiration dates of those agreements, supplemented with a qualitative description that identifies the significant collective-bargaining agreements within that range as well as other information to help investors understand the significance of the collective-bargaining agreements and when they expire (for example, the portion of employees covered by each agreement or the portion of contributions required by each agreement).

e. For each period that a statement of income (statement of activities nonpublic entities) is presented

   i. the employer's contributions made to the plan.

   ii. whether the employer's contributions represent more than 5 percent of total contributions to the plan as indicated in the plan's most recently available annual report (Form 5500 for U.S. plans). The disclosure should specify the year-end date of the plan to which the annual report relates.

f. As of the end of the most recent annual period presented

   i. whether a funding improvement plan or rehabilitation plan (for example, as those terms are defined by the Employment Retirement Security Act of 1974) had been implemented or was pending.

   ii. whether the employer paid a surcharge to the plan.

---

[7] The determination of what is an individually significant plan is not defined in the standards; however it is noted in FASB ASC 715-80-50-5 that factors other than the amount of the contribution should be considered when determining if a plan is individually significant. For instance, the severity of the underfunded status of the plan may be a consideration in this determination.

iii. a description of any minimum contribution(s), required for future periods by the collective-bargaining agreement(s), statutory obligations, or other contractual obligations, if applicable.

Factors other than the amount of the employer's contribution to a plan, for example, the severity of the underfunded status of the plan, may need to be considered when determining whether a plan is significant. When feasible, this information should be provided in a tabular format. Information that requires greater narrative description may be provided outside the table.

6.55 As discussed in FASB ASC 715-80-50-6, an employer is required to provide a description of the nature and effect of any significant changes that affect comparability of total employer contributions from period to period, such as a

a. business combination or a divestiture.

b. change in the contractual employer contribution rate.

c. change in the number of employees covered by the plan during each year.

6.56 The requirements in FASB ASC 715-80-50-5, as discussed in paragraph 6.54, assume that the other information about the plan is available in the public domain. For example, for U.S. plans, the plan information in Form 5500 is publicly available. In circumstances in which plan level information is *not* available in the public domain, an employer is required to disclose, in addition to the requirements of paragraphs 5–6 of FASB ASC 715-80-50, the following information about each significant plan:

a. A description of the nature of the plan benefits

b. A qualitative description of the extent to which the employer could be responsible for the obligations of the plan, including benefits earned by employees during employment with another employer

c. Other quantitative information, to the extent available, as of the most recent date available, to help users understand the financial information about the plan, such as total plan assets, actuarial present value of accumulated plan benefits, and total contributions received by the plan

6.57 If the quantitative information in FASB ASC 715-80-50-5(c), FASB ASC 715-80-50-5(e)(2), or FASB ASC 715-80-50-7(c), as discussed in paragraph 6.54, cannot be obtained without undue cost and effort, that quantitative information may be omitted and the employer should describe what information has been omitted and why. In that circumstance, the employer also is required to provide any qualitative information as of the most recent date available that would help users understand the financial information that otherwise is required to be disclosed about the plan. This information should be included in a separate section of the tabular disclosure required by FASB ASC 715-80-50-5.

6.58 In addition to the information about the significant multiemployer plans that provide pension benefits required by paragraphs 5 and 7 of FASB ASC 715-80-50, an employer is required by paragraph 9 of FASB ASC 715-80-50 to disclose, in a tabular format for each annual period for which a statement of income or statement of activities is presented, both of the following:

a. Its total contributions made to all plans that are not individually significant

b. Its total contributions made to all plans

Multiemployer Plans That Provide Postretirement Benefits Other Than Pensions

6.59 FASB ASC 715-80-50-11 requires an employer to disclose the amount of contributions to multiemployer plans that provide postretirement benefits other than pensions each annual period for which a statement of income or statement of activities is presented. The disclosures should include a description of the nature and effect of any changes that affect comparability of total employer contributions from period to period, such as

a. A business combination or a divestiture

b. A change in the contractual employer contribution rate

c. A change in the number of employees covered by the plan during each year

The disclosures also should include a description of the nature of the benefits and the types of employees covered by these benefits, such as medical benefits provided to active employees and retirees.

Sample Disclosure for Plans That Provide Pension Benefits

6.60 Paragraphs 6–8 FASB ASC 715-80-55 present the following example disclosure:

> Entity A contributes to a number of multiemployer defined benefit pension plans under the terms of collective-bargaining agreements that cover its union-represented employees. The risks of participating in these multiemployer plans are different from single-employer plans in the following aspects:
>
> a. Assets contributed to the multiemployer plan by one employer may be used to provide benefits to employees of other participating employers.
>
> b. If a participating employer stops contributing to the plan, the unfunded obligations of the plan may be borne by the remaining participating employers.
>
> c. If Entity A chooses to stop participating in some of its multiemployer plans, Entity A may be required to pay those plans an amount based on the underfunded status of the plan, referred to as a withdrawal liability.
>
> Entity A's participation in these plans for the annual period ended December 31, 20X0, is outlined in the following table. The "EIN/Pension Plan Number" column provides the Employer Identification Number (EIN) and the three-digit plan number, if applicable. Unless otherwise noted, the most recent Pension Protection Act (PPA) zone status available in 20X0 and 20X9 is for the plan's year-end at December 31, 20X9, and December 31, 20X8, respectively. The zone status is based on information that Entity A received from the plan and is certified by the plan's actuary. Among other factors, plans in the red zone are generally less than 65 percent funded, plans in the yellow zone are less than 80 percent funded, and plans in the green zone are at least 80 percent funded. The "FIP/RP Status Pending/Implemented" column indicates plans for which a financial improvement plan (FIP) or a rehabilitation plan (RP) is either pending or has been implemented. The last column

Pension Fund	EIN/Pension Plan Number	Pension Protection Act Zone Status		FIP/RP Status Pending/ Implemented	Contributions of Entity A			Surcharge Imposed	Expiration Date of Collective-Bargaining Agreement
		20X0	20X9		20X0	20X9	20X8		
ABC Fund 34	32-1899999	Red as of 9/30/2009	Yellow as of 9/30/2008	Pending	$1,883,000	$2,309,000	$2,226,000	Yes	12/31/20X3
ABC Fund 37	52-5599999-002	Green	Yellow	No	3,342,000	3,609,000	3,586,000	No	12/31/20X2 to[(a)] 12/31/20X3
ABC Fund 40	92-3499999	Yellow	Yellow	No	5,798,000	6,435,000	6,374,000	No	12/31/20X5
ABC Fund 43	82-4299999	Red	Red	Pending	3,539,000	3,234,000	3,218,000	Yes	12/31/20X4
ABC Fund 46[(b)]	82-6899999	Green	Green	No	778,000	816,000	833,000	No	12/31/20X3
ABC Fund 49	52-6199999	Yellow	Yellow	No	534,000	547,000	491,000	No	12/31/20X2
ABC Fund 52	72-8599999-001	Red	Green	Implemented	1,349,000	1,134,000	1,050,000	No	12/31/20X5
ABC Fund 55	82-2999999	Green	Green	No	1,224,000	1,046,000	1,151,000	No	12/31/20X4
Plans for which plan financial information is not publicly available outside Entity A's financial statements.									
ABC Fund 61[(c)]	N/A	N/A	N/A	N/A	418,000	482,000	491,000	N/A	12/31/20X2
ABC Fund 73[(d)]	N/A	N/A	N/A	N/A	1,872,000	1,764,000	1,693,000	N/A	12/31/20X2
Other funds					147,000	160,000	169,000		
				Total contributions:	$20,884,000	$21,536,000	$21,282,000		

(a) Entity A is party to two significant collective-bargaining agreements that require contributions to ABC Fund 37. Agreements D and E expire on 12/31/20X2, and 12/31/20X3, respectively. Of the two, Agreement D is more significant because 70 percent of Entity A's employee participants in ABC Fund 37 are covered by that agreement. Agreement E also is significant because its participants are involved in multiple projects that Entity A is scheduled to start in 20X4.

(b) ABC Fund 46 utilized the special 30-year amortization rules provided by Public Law 111-192, Section 211 to amortize its losses from 2008. The plan rectified its zone status after using the amortization provisions of that law.

(c) Plan information for ABC Fund is not publicly available. ABC Fund 61 provides fixed, monthly retirement payments on the basis of the credits earned by the participating employees. To the extent that the plan is underfunded, the future contributions to the plan may increase and may be used to fund retirement benefits for employees related to other employers who have ceased operations. Entity A could be assessed a withdrawal liability in the event that it decides to cease participating in the plan. ABC Fund 61's financial statements for the years ended June 30, 20X0 and 20X9 indicated total assets of $62,000,000 and $51,000,000, respectively; total actuarial present value of accumulated plan benefits of $120,000,000 and $110,000,000, respectively; and total contributions for all participating employers of $9,000,000 and $8,000,000, respectively. The plan's financial statements for the plan years ended June 30, 20X0 and 20X9 indicated that the plan was less than 65 percent funded in both years.

(d) Plan information for ABC Fund 73 is not publicly available. ABC Fund 73 provides fixed retirement payments on the basis of the credits earned by the participating employees. However, in the event that the plan is underfunded, the monthly benefit amount can be reduced by the trustees of the plan. Entity A is not responsible for the underfunded status of the plan because ABC Fund 73 operates in a jurisdiction that does not require withdrawing participants to pay a withdrawal liability or other penalty. Entity A is unable to provide additional quantitative information on the plan because Entity A is unable to obtain that information without undue cost and effort. The collective-bargaining agreement of ABC Fund 73 requires contributions on the basis of hours worked. The agreement also has a minimum contribution requirement of $1,000,000 each year.

lists the expiration date(s) of the collective-bargaining agreement(s) to which the plans are subject. Finally, the number of employees covered by Entity A's multiemployer plans decreased by 5 percent from 20X9 to 20X0, affecting the period-to-period comparability of the contributions for years 20X9 and 20X0. The significant reduction in covered employees corresponded to a reduction in overall business. There have been no significant changes that affect the comparability of 20X8 and 20X9 contributions.

Entity A was listed in its plans' Forms 5500 as providing more than 5 percent of the total contributions for the following plans and plan years:

Pension Fund	Year Contributions to Plan Exceeded More Than 5 Percent of Total Contributions (as of December 31 of the Plan's Year-End)
ABC Fund 34	20X9 and 20X8
ABC Fund 43	20X8
ABC Fund 52	20X8
ABC Fund 61	20X9

At the date the financial statements were issued, Forms 5500 were not available for the plan years ending in 20X0.

Chapter 7

Auditing Within the Construction Industry

7.01 The objective of the auditing section of the guide is to assist the independent auditor in auditing the financial statements of entities in the construction industry. Independent auditors often encounter a variety of complex problems in such engagements because of the nature of operations in the industry and because of the methods used in accounting for contracts.

Audit Focus

7.02 In audits of the financial statements of construction contractors, the primary focus is on the profit centers, usually individual contracts, for recognizing revenues, accumulating costs, and measuring income. Obtaining a thorough understanding of the contracts that underlie the financial statements is an important part of the audit plan that describes in detail the nature, timing, and extent of risk assessment and further audit procedures performed in the audit. Evaluation of the profitability of contracts or profit centers is also central to the total audit process and the determination of whether the information in the financial statements is presented in conformity with generally accepted accounting principles.

7.03 The methods and the bases of measurement used in accounting for contracts affects the independent auditor's procedures performed with respect to costs incurred to date, estimated contract costs to complete, measures of extent of progress toward completion, revenues, and gross profit to form a conclusion on the reasonableness of costs, revenue, and gross profit allocated to the period being audited. Thus, much of the independent auditor's work involves evaluating subjective estimates relating to future events. AU-C section 540, *Auditing Accounting Estimates, Including Fair Value Accounting Estimates, and Related Disclosures*,[1] provides guidance to auditors on obtaining and evaluating sufficient appropriate audit evidence to support significant accounting estimates. A contractor's work in progress schedule is based on a substantial amount of estimations of contract price and costs, and, as the nature and reliability of information available to management to support the making of such accounting estimate varies, affecting the degree of estimation uncertainty and the risk of material misstatement, including their susceptibility to unintentional or intentional management bias, the auditor of a construction entity must be thoroughly familiar with the criteria that must be applied to those estimates.

7.04 Paragraph .03 of AU-C section 315, *Understanding the Entity and Its Environment and Assessing the Risks of Material Misstatement*, states that "(t)he objective of the auditor is to identify and assess the risks of material misstatement, whether due to fraud or error, at the financial statement and relevant assertion levels through understanding the entity and its environment, including the entity's internal control, thereby providing a basis for designing and implementing responses to the assessed risks of material misstatement." In the audits of the financial statements of construction contractors, the areas that normally receive particular attention include an entity's internal control, its operating systems and procedures, its project management, the nature of

---

[1] All AU-C sections can be found in AICPA *Professional Standards*.

its contracting work, its history of performance and profitability, and other relevant accounting and operating factors. The auditor's primary consideration is to obtain a sufficient understanding of the entity to assess the risks of material misstatement at both the overall financial statement level and the assertion level.

7.05 AU-C section 315 addresses the auditor's responsibility to identify and assess the risks of material misstatement through understanding the entity and its environment, including its internal control. Paragraph .13 of AU-C section 315 notes that although most controls relevant to the audit are likely to relate to financial reporting, not all controls that relate to financial reporting are relevant to the audit. It is a matter of the auditor's professional judgment whether a control, individually or in combination with others, is relevant to the audit.

7.06 When obtaining an understanding of controls that are relevant to the audit, the auditor should evaluate the design of those controls and determine whether they have been implemented by performing procedures in addition to inquiry of the entity's personnel. Areas of focus in the construction industry are contract revenues, costs, gross profit or loss, and related contract receivables and payables.

7.07 To provide a basis for designing and performing further audit procedures, the auditor should identify and assess the risks of material misstatement at the financial statement level and the relevant assertion level for classes of transactions, account balances, and disclosures. In the construction industry, the significant measurement uncertainty associated with the application of the percentage-of-completion method of accounting for contracts, among other judgmental matters associated with construction contracts, may present significant risks that, in the auditor's professional judgment, require special audit consideration. For further discussion of the auditor's responsibilities toward significant risks, refer to chapter 9, "Planning the Audit, Assessing and Responding to Audit Risk, and Additional Auditing Considerations."

Scope of Auditing Guidance Included in This Guide

7.08 The auditing section of this guide deals primarily with auditing procedures typically performed during audits of the financial statements of construction contractors. It does not discuss auditing procedures that are not unique to such audits or that do not require special application in them; such procedures may be found in other sources of generally accepted auditing standards.

Chapter 8

Controls in the Construction Industry

8.01 The discussion of controls in this chapter is primarily from management's perspective and relates to management's responsibility to establish and maintain adequate internal control over financial reporting. As directed in Section 404(a) of the Sarbanes-Oxley Act of 2002, management of an issuer must assess the effectiveness of the entity's internal control over financial reporting and include in the entity's annual report to shareholders management's conclusion as a result of that assessment about whether the entity's internal control is effective. This publication is not intended to provide guidance to management of public construction contractors on how to comply with the requirements of Section 404(a) of the Sarbanes-Oxley Act of 2002.

8.02 This chapter is not intended to provide the auditor with comprehensive auditing guidance but may serve as an overview of factors that will enable the auditor to better understand the entity and its environment, including its internal control. AU-C section 315, *Understanding the Entity and Its Environment and Assessing the Risks of Material Misstatement*,[1] addresses the auditor's responsibility to identify and assess the risks of material misstatement through understanding the entity and its environment, including its internal control.

8.03 This chapter presents a general discussion of some of the desirable control activities in the construction industry. Although not all the controls identified are found in every construction entity, their discussion can serve as guidance concerning what might be considered adequate controls for a contractor. This discussion considers aspects of controls in the following areas:

- Estimating and bidding
- Project administration and contract evaluation
- Job site accounting and controls
- Billing procedures (including determination of reimbursable costs under cost-plus contracts)
- Contract costs
- Contract revenues
- Construction equipment
- Claims, extras, and back charges
- Joint ventures
- Internal audit function

Estimating and Bidding

8.04 Effective controls over the estimating and bidding functions provide reasonable assurance that contracts are bid or negotiated on the basis of data carefully compiled to take into account all factors that will affect the cost, revenue, and profitability of each contract. Unreliable estimates can obscure losses

---

[1] All AU-C sections can be found in AICPA *Professional Standards*.

on contracts in their early stages or can overstate or understate the estimated profitability of contracts.

8.05 Controls over estimating and bidding are necessary to provide for adequate documentation, clerical verification, overall review of estimated costs, and approval of all bids by the appropriate levels of management. Examples of control activities related to estimating and bidding include the following:

- Conducting an independent review of general contract cost estimates based on specifications, plans, and drawings and comparing with actual contract estimates in order to provide assurance that the estimates of contract costs reflect all relevant costs
- Verifying the clerical accuracy of final contract estimates
- Reviewing the completeness and reasonableness of the final estimate
- Establishing procedures to preclude arbitrary, undocumented management-level adjustments to estimated costs

8.06 Preparation and maintenance of the estimate of contract costs and the accounting records in a consistent manner will permit subsequent detailed comparison of actual costs with estimated costs. A record of the bids submitted by competing firms normally should be maintained, if those bids are available. Such cost and bid information is helpful to management and may provide them with evidence of the reliability of their estimating and bidding process.

8.07 Having assigned personnel to regularly perform monitoring procedures is necessary to ensure that controls over the estimating and bidding functions are operating effectively. For instance, a contractor might assign personnel to perform the following tasks:

- Review the quantities of material and hours of labor in bid estimates and compare them to the customers' specifications.
- Compare and relate estimated material costs to published vendor price lists, price quotations, subcontractors' bids, or other supporting documentation.
- Compare and relate estimated labor rates to union contracts and other documentation supporting labor rates, payroll taxes, and fringe benefits.
- Compare and relate estimated equipment costs to the rates charged by suppliers for rental or used by the contractor to allocate the cost of owned equipment to jobs.
- Verify the clerical accuracy of estimates.
- Determine that estimates are reviewed and approved by designated management personnel.
- Review contracts periodically to assess the extent and effect of management changes or revisions of bids without supporting data, such as revised cost estimates.
- Review estimates periodically after discussions with engineering personnel responsible for the project.

Project Administration and Contract Evaluation

8.08 The quality and extent of project management often determine whether a construction contract is profitable or unprofitable. Timely and reliable progress, cost, and status reports on each contract are essential for management to evaluate the status and profitability of each project and to identify problems at an early stage. Regularly scheduled meetings with project managers and periodic management visits to job sites may also enhance the effectiveness of project administration.

8.09 In order to estimate the profit or loss on a contract in progress, it is essential that management review and evaluate regularly the status of each contract in progress. That procedure provides information that enables management to take corrective action to improve performance on a given contract, and such an evaluation is an integral part of effective internal control. Normally, the review should include a comparison of the detailed actual contract costs and the current estimate of costs to complete all phases of the project with the details of the original estimate and the total contract price. Other information to be considered in the review includes the following items:

- Cost records, which may be used for a comparison of the principal components of actual costs with original estimates
- Open purchase orders and commitments
- Reports, such as engineering progress reports, field reports, and project managers' status reports
- Conferences with project engineers and independent architects
- Correspondence files
- Change orders, including unpriced and unsigned change orders

8.10 Generally, controls over subcontract costs should provide that payments to subcontractors are made only on the basis of work performed, that performance bonds are obtained, and that retentions are recorded and accounted for properly.

Job Site Accounting and Controls

8.11 The size and location of some construction projects may require a contractor to establish an accounting office at the job site, and all or part of the accounting function relating to that project — including payrolls, purchasing, disbursements, equipment control, and billings — may be performed at the job site. Establishing adequate internal control at job site accounting offices may be difficult because such offices are temporary and may be staffed with a limited number of trained accounting personnel. Therefore, it is essential that management pay particular attention to the areas discussed in the following paragraphs.

8.12 The temporary nature of the employment of most construction workers can make the establishment of controls difficult. Further, many job sites employ on-site payment of workers, with signing authority residing with an on-site employee, usually the project manager or project accountant, rather than a dedicated resource in a centrally located payroll department. Construction contractors ordinarily should consider having internal auditors, or corporate administrative personnel, periodically disburse or observe payrolls at job sites to strengthen controls over payrolls. Additionally, the contractor may consider periodic testing of payroll disbursements, for example, tying to supporting information such as timecards, attendance logs, or other documentation.

8.13 Established accounting procedures normally dictate that a designated level of management authorize all material purchases at job sites and clearly specify the types of acceptable documentation as evidence of receipt of materials. Additionally, effective accounting procedures prohibit making payments for materials without proper authorization and evidence of receipt.

8.14 Adequate physical controls over equipment, materials, and supplies at job sites help prevent loss by pilferage or unauthorized usage. Adequate internal control also includes taking an inventory of surplus materials at the completion of a contract and monitoring the subsequent disposition of such materials for adherence to company policy and appropriate accounting treatment. Maintaining effective supervision over job site offices, particularly if the size or nature of a contractor does not permit the establishment of an internal audit function, is also an important control.

Billing Procedures

8.15 Billing procedures in the construction industry differ from those in other industries. A typical manufacturing entity, for example, normally bills a customer upon the shipment of its product. In contrast, billing procedures in the construction industry vary widely among entities and are often not correlated with performance. Different types of contracts and different ways of measuring performance for billing purposes are prevalent. For example, billings may be based on various measures of performance, such as cubic yards excavated, architects' estimates of completion, costs incurred on cost-plus type contracts, or time schedules. Also, the data required to prepare a billing for a fixed-price contract differ from the data required for a cost-plus contract.

8.16 Adequate internal controls normally provide that personnel responsible for billing receive accurate, timely information from job sites and include billing procedures designed to recognize unique contract features. Because billing and payment terms often vary from contract to contract, the personnel responsible for billing normally should be familiar with the terms of the contracts. Billings that are not made in accordance with the terms of the contract generally should be approved by designated management personnel.

8.17 A contractor's receivables usually include retentions, that is, amounts that are not due until contracts are completed or until specified contract conditions or guarantees are met. Retentions are governed by contract provisions and are typically a fixed percentage (for example, 5 percent or 10 percent) of each billing. Some contracts provide for a reduction in the percentage retained on billings as the contract nears completion. Effective billing procedures and related internal control provide that a contractor bill retentions in accordance with the terms of a contract and that accounts are reviewed periodically to determine that retention payments are ultimately received. A contractor ordinarily would have a process in place to monitor past due receivables and related liens. Further, the contractor may consider an additional policy of re-filing expiring liens,[2] as necessary, within a prescribed period of their expiration, in order to provide assurance that lien rights are protected before they expire.

---

[2] Many states have very strict laws concerning construction contractor liens and the timing of filing and refilling those liens. Contractors and auditors should be aware of the specific laws in the states in which they operate to ensure compliance.

8.18 To provide continuing assurance that desirable internal control is maintained over the billing function, it is essential that assigned personnel regularly perform monitoring procedures. A contractor might assign personnel to perform the following tasks:

- Relate billings, including retentions, to the terms of the original contract and of approved change orders
- Trace support information, including costs incurred to date, engineers' estimates of completion, architects' certifications, and other pertinent information to billings to ensure the billings are in accordance with the terms of the billing arrangement

Contract Costs

8.19 A contractor uses information on contract costs incurred to control costs, evaluate the status and profitability of contracts, and prepare customer billings. Contract costs are also necessary in the determination of revenue when the percentage-of-completion approach is utilized. Thus, the importance of accurate cost information cannot be overemphasized.

8.20 Generally, contract cost records should facilitate detailed comparisons of actual costs with estimated costs and provide for the classification and summarization of costs into appropriate categories such as materials, subcontract charges, labor, labor-related costs, equipment costs, and overhead. It is essential that the accounting system be capable of producing detailed cost reports for management and project managers. Their review of the reports serves to identify potential problems on contracts, check on the reasonableness of the cost records, and minimize the possibility of having unauthorized costs charged to the contract.

8.21 Controls over the processes related to contract costs, including the manner in which they are applied and the assignment of responsibility to designated personnel, are essential mechanisms to achieving the aforementioned objectives. Control activities might include, for example, periodic agreement of the detailed contract cost records to the general ledger control records and ensuring that proper cutoffs are made at the close of each accounting period. Other control activities that assigned personnel might regularly perform include

- comparing and relating the quantities and prices of materials charged to contracts to vendors' invoices, purchase orders, and evidence of receipt of materials and, if applicable, the withdrawal and return of documents from central stores.
- comparing documented labor charged to contracts by reference to payroll records and related documents (such as time cards, union contracts or pay authorizations, authorized deductions, and cancelled payroll checks) and reviewing payroll distribution to individual contracts.
- relating subcontract costs charged to contracts to the terms specified in the subcontract agreements and supporting documents.
- reviewing performance, guarantee, and similar bonds of subcontractors to ensure proper ongoing compliance with terms.
- obtaining and reviewing, for adequacy, insurance certificates obtained from subcontractors.

- comparing and relating retentions payable to subcontractors to subcontract agreements.
- inspecting waivers of lien on completed work from subcontractors.
- approving back charges, extras, and claims.
- comparing and relating equipment rental costs charged to contracts
  - — to the contractor's standard rates for owned equipment and vendor invoices or rental agreements for leased equipment, and
  - — to delivery reports, production or maintenance records, or similar data.
- comparing equipment costs charged directly to a contract (purchased for exclusive use on a particular contract, such as a cement plant and related trucks) to vendor invoices and related documents, and control the disposition of such equipment.
- reviewing the accumulation and allocation of indirect costs to contracts.
- reviewing the accumulation and segregation of reimbursable costs under cost-plus contracts.
- reviewing contract costs to ensure they are being allocated to the proper contract.

A contractor's internal controls over contract costs provides reasonable assurance that contract costs are appropriately recognized. This includes monitoring by appropriate personnel of the design and operation of controls on a timely basis and responding to the results of that assessment.

Contract Revenues

8.22 It is important that controls over contract revenues be designed to provide reliable information on the amount and timing of contract revenue. The types of controls established depend on the method of revenue recognition used. Relevant considerations when designing these types of controls include the amount of revenue expected from contracts and the procedures and information used either in measuring progress toward completion (to determine the amount of earned revenue under the percentage-of-completion method) or in determining when a contract is substantially completed (under the completed-contract method).

8.23 Control activities that assigned personnel might regularly perform include

- reviewing current estimates of total revenue under each contract in process based on supporting billings.
- processing and approving change orders and informing personnel responsible for performance of contracts of those change orders.
- determining that revenue arising from unpriced change orders and claims does not exceed the related recoverable costs, and that only costs that are reimbursable in accordance with the terms of cost-plus contracts are included in revenue.

- selecting methods to measure progress that are suitable to the circumstances and apply the methods consistently.
- accumulating and verifying the information used to measure the extent of progress toward completion, such as total cost incurred, total labor hours incurred, and units of output, depending on the method used.
- verifying the accuracy of the computations of the percentage of completion, earned revenue, and the cost of earned revenue.
- reviewing and documenting contracts reported on the completed-contract basis for consistent application of completion criteria.
- evaluating periodically the profitability of contracts and providing for losses on loss contracts in full at the earliest date on which they are determinable.
- reconciling periodically the total earned revenue on a contract to total billings on the contract.

A contractor's monitoring of controls over contract revenues ensures that internal control continues to operate effectively.

Construction Equipment

8.24 Contractors frequently have substantial investments in construction equipment. The dollar amounts involved and the necessity of charging equipment costs to contracts make it necessary to maintain effective controls over equipment. Records normally should be maintained for all major equipment, including adequate cost information that is in agreement with the general accounting records; this information enables the contractor to charge each project with costs related to the equipment being used on it. Common controls include having reporting procedures in place to control and record the transfer of equipment between projects, having the project managers review periodic equipment reports that include the location of the equipment, and performing periodic inventories of field equipment at the completion of each project. During economic downturns, equipment frequently becomes idle; therefore, it is necessary to have procedures in place to ensure that such equipment is identified and its carrying amount is evaluated for recoverability in accordance with FASB *Accounting Standards Codification* (ASC) 360, *Property, Plant, and Equipment*, as discussed in chapter 2, "Accounting for Performance of Construction-Type Contracts."

8.25 Adequate controls to safeguard access to small equipment, such as power hand tools, at the job site prevent loss or pilferage. Purchases of such equipment is often charged directly to a contract.

Claims, Extras, and Back Charges

8.26 Controls over claims, extras, back charges, and similar items are necessary to provide reasonable assurance that such items are properly documented and provide for the accumulation of related revenues and costs. For example, validating that change orders for jobs have the appropriate written authorizations or approvals. Another effective control is to have procedures in place for identifying and evaluating the financial accounting and reporting implications of claims filed against the contractor pursuant to FASB ASC 450, *Contingencies*, including those arising from litigation and assessments.

Joint Ventures

8.27 Control over the operations of joint ventures is essential for the financial success of the venture and the participating contractors. Although the nature and extent of control over the operations and the accounting records of joint ventures varies with each venture, a joint venture participant should be satisfied that adequate accounting records and desirable controls are maintained.

Internal Audit Function

8.28 Contractors engaged in large, complex, and diverse operations especially benefit from internal auditing. An internal audit staff may conduct both operational and financial reviews at a contractor's administrative offices as well as at job sites. The reviews generally should cover the estimates of cost to complete and the methods used to measure performance on individual contracts. Internal auditors ordinarily should be involved in testing and evaluating every important control area discussed in this chapter. Their intimate involvement can provide management with continuous feedback on the effectiveness of internal control and the degree of compliance with company policies, and such involvement can enable the internal auditors to make recommendations for improvements in the entity's internal control.

8.29 One of the objectives of internal audits at job sites is to determine whether personnel at the sites are complying with the contractor's established policies and practices. Such audits may involve a physical inspection of equipment and review and testing of expenditures (including payroll disbursements) from a job site office, status reports to the home office, field equipment records, and contract billings to determine their appropriateness.

Chapter 9

Planning the Audit, Assessing and Responding to Audit Risk, and Additional Auditing Considerations

Scope of This Chapter

9.01 AU-C section 200, *Overall Objectives of the Independent Auditor and the Conduct of an Audit in Accordance With Generally Accepted Auditing Standards*,[1] addresses the independent auditor's overall responsibilities when conducting an audit of financial statements in accordance with generally accepted auditing standards (GAAS). Specifically, it sets out the overall objectives of the independent auditor (the auditor) and explains the nature and scope of an audit designed to enable the auditor to meet those objectives. It also explains the scope, authority, and structure of GAAS and includes requirements establishing the general responsibilities of the auditor applicable in all audits, including the obligation to comply with GAAS. Auditing standards provide a measure of audit quality and the objectives to be achieved in an audit. The preceding chapter discusses, from the perspective of management, the features of effective internal control that a contractor ordinarily should establish and maintain. This chapter provides guidance to the practitioner primarily on the application of certain standards. Specifically, this chapter provides guidance on the risk assessment process (which includes, among other things, obtaining an understanding of the entity and its environment, including its internal control) and some general auditing considerations for construction contractors.

9.02 In some instances, a practitioner may be engaged to examine and to express an opinion on the design and operating effectiveness of a nonissuer's internal control over financial reporting that is integrated with an audit of the nonissuer's financial statements. The auditor's responsibility in connection with this type of attest engagement is beyond the scope of this guide. This type of engagement is discussed in AU-C section 940, *An Audit of Internal Control Over Financial Reporting That Is Integrated With an Audit of Financial Statements*.

Planning and Other Auditing Considerations

9.03 The objective of an audit of a construction contractor's financial statements is to provide financial statement users with an opinion by the auditor on whether the financial statements are presented fairly, in all material respects, in accordance with an applicable financial reporting framework, which enhances the degree of confidence that intended users can place in the financial statements. As the basis for the auditor's opinion, GAAS require the auditor to obtain reasonable assurance about whether the financial statements as a whole are free from material misstatement, whether due to fraud or error. It is obtained when the auditor has obtained sufficient appropriate audit evidence

---

[1] All AU-C sections can be found in AICPA *Professional Standards*.

to reduce audit risk (that is, the risk that the auditor expresses an inappropriate opinion when the financial statements are materially misstated) to an acceptably low level. This section addresses general planning considerations and other auditing considerations relevant to construction contractors.

Planning the Audit

9.04 AU-C section 300, *Planning an Audit*, states that the objective of the auditor is to plan the audit so that it will be performed in an effective manner and addresses the auditor's responsibility to plan an audit of financial statements and notes that planning an audit involves establishing the overall audit strategy for the engagement and developing an audit plan. Adequate planning benefits the audit of financial statements in several ways, including the following:

- Helping the auditor identify and devote appropriate attention to important areas of the audit
- Helping the auditor identify and resolve potential problems on a timely basis
- Helping the auditor properly organize and manage the audit engagement so that it is performed in an effective and efficient manner
- Assisting in the selection of engagement team members with appropriate levels of capabilities and competence to respond to anticipated risks and allocating team member responsibilities
- Facilitating the direction and supervision of engagement team members and the review of their work
- Assisting, when applicable, in coordination of work done by auditors of components and specialists

9.05 AU-C section 300 establishes requirements and provides guidance on the considerations and activities applicable to planning and supervision of an audit conducted in accordance with GAAS, including the involvement of key engagement team members in planning; preliminary engagement activities; general planning activities, including establishing an overall audit strategy that sets the scope, timing and direction of the audit and that guides the development of the audit plan, which may include developing specific procedures for high risk audit areas; determining the extent of the involvement of professionals possessing specialized skills; additional considerations for initial audit engagements, including performing procedures required by AU-C section 220, *Quality Control for an Engagement Conducted in Accordance With Generally Accepted Auditing Standards*, and any necessary communications in accordance with AU-C section 210, *Terms of Engagement*; and documentation considerations.

9.06 The nature and extent of planning activities will vary according to the size and complexity of the entity, the key engagement team members' previous experience with the entity, and changes in circumstances that occur during the audit engagement. Planning is not a discrete phase of an audit but rather a continual and iterative process that often begins shortly after (or in connection with) the completion of the previous audit and continues until the completion of the current audit engagement. Planning, however, includes consideration of the timing of certain activities and audit procedures that need to be completed prior to the performance of further audit procedures.

Auditor's Communication With Those Charged With Governance

9.07 The objectives of the auditor's communication with those charged with governance, as prescribed in AU-C section 260, *The Auditor's Communication With Those Charged With Governance*, are to

a. communicate clearly with those charged with governance the responsibilities of the auditor regarding the financial statement audit and an overview of the planned scope and timing of the audit.

b. obtain from those charged with governance information relevant to the audit.

c. provide those charged with governance with timely observations arising from the audit that are significant and relevant to their responsibility to oversee the financial reporting process.

d. promote effective two-way communication between the auditor and those charged with governance.

9.08 AU-C section 260, recognizing the importance of effective two-way communication in an audit of financial statements, provides an overarching framework for the auditor's communication with those charged with governance and identifies some specific matters to be communicated.[2] Paragraph .06 of AU-C section 260 defines *those charged with governance* as the person(s) or organization(s) (for example, a corporate trustee) with responsibility for overseeing the strategic direction of the entity and the obligations related to the accountability of the entity. This includes overseeing the financial reporting process. Those charged with governance may include management personnel; for example, executive members of a governance board or an owner-manager. In most entities, governance is the collective responsibility of a governing body, such as a board of directors; a supervisory board; partners; proprietors; a committee of management; trustees; or equivalent persons. In some smaller entities, however, one person may be charged with governance, such as the owner-manager, when there are no other owners, or a sole trustee. When governance is a collective responsibility, a subgroup, such as an audit committee or even an individual, may be charged with specific tasks to assist the governing body in meeting its responsibilities.

9.09 AU-C section 260 notes that clear communication of the auditor's responsibilities, the planned scope and timing of the audit and the expected general content of communications help establish the basis of effective two-way communication. Matters that may also contribute to effective two-way communication include discussion of the

- purpose of communications. When the purpose is clear, the auditor and those charged with governance are in a better position to have a mutual understanding of relevant issues and the expected actions arising from the communication process.
- form in which communications will be made.

[2] Additional matters to be communicated are identified in other AU-C sections. In addition, AU-C section 265, *Communicating Internal Control Related Matters Identified in an Audit*, addresses the auditor's responsibility to appropriately communicate to those charged with governance and management deficiencies in internal control that the auditor has identified in an audit of financial statements. Further, matters not required by generally accepted auditing standards may be required to be communicated by agreement with those charged with governance or management or in accordance with external requirements.

- person(s) on the audit team and among those charged with governance who will communicate regarding particular matters.
- auditor's expectation that communication will be two-way and that those charged with governance will communicate with the auditor matters they consider relevant to the audit. Such matters might include (*a*) strategic decisions that may significantly affect the nature, timing, and extent of audit procedures; (*b*) the suspicion or the detection of fraud; or (*c*) concerns with the integrity or competence of senior management.
- process for taking action and reporting back on matters communicated by the auditor.
- process for taking action and reporting back on matters communicated by those charged with governance.

9.10 Paragraph .A42 of AU-C section 260 states that the appropriate timing for communications will vary with the circumstances of the engagement. Considerations include the significance and nature of the matter and the action expected to be taken by those charged with governance. The auditor may consider communicating

- planning matters early in the audit engagement and, for an initial engagement, as part of the terms of the engagement.
- significant difficulties encountered during the audit as soon as practicable if those charged with governance are able to assist the auditor in overcoming the difficulties or if the difficulties are likely to lead to a modified opinion.

9.11 Further, paragraph .A43 of AU-C section 260 notes other factors that may be relevant to the timing of communications include

- the size, operating structure, control environment, and legal structure of the entity being audited.
- any legal obligation to communicate certain matters within a specified timeframe.
- the expectations of those charged with governance, including arrangements made for periodic meetings or communications with the auditor.
- the time at which the auditor identifies certain matters (for example, timely communication of a material weakness to enable appropriate remedial action to be taken).
- whether the auditor is auditing both general purpose and special purpose financial statements.

9.12 Although AU-C section 260 applies regardless of an entity's governance structure or size, particular considerations apply when all of those charged with governance are involved in managing an entity. This section does not establish requirements regarding the auditor's communication with an entity's management or owners unless they are also charged with a governance role.

9.13 In some cases, all of those charged with governance are involved in managing the entity; for example, a small business in which a single owner manages the entity and no one else has a governance role. In these cases, if matters required by this section are communicated with a person(s) with management responsibilities and that person(s) also has governance responsibilities, the matters need not be communicated again with the same person(s) in that person's governance role. These matters are noted in paragraph .14 of AU-C section 260. The auditor should, nonetheless, be satisfied that communication with person(s) with management responsibilities adequately informs all of those with whom the auditor would otherwise communicate in their governance capacity.

9.14 The communication process will vary with the circumstances, including the size and governance structure of the entity, how those charged with governance operate, and the auditor's view of the significance of matters to be communicated. The importance of effective two-way communication is evidenced by the statement in paragraph .A36 of AU-C section 260 that difficulty in establishing effective two-way communication may indicate that the communication between the auditor and those charged with governance is not adequate for the purpose of the audit.

9.15 In fact, if the two-way communication between the auditor and those charged with governance is not adequate and the situation cannot be resolved, the auditor may take actions such as the following:

- Modifying the auditor's opinion on the basis of a scope limitation
- Obtaining legal advice about the consequences of different courses of action
- Communicating with third parties (for example, a regulator) or a higher authority in the governance structure that is outside the entity, such as the owners of a business (for example, shareholders in a general meeting), or the responsible government agency for certain governmental entities
- Withdrawing from the engagement when withdrawal is possible under applicable law or regulation

9.16 The auditor should communicate the auditor's responsibilities with regards to the financial statement audit and these communications should include that

a. the auditor is responsible for forming and expressing an opinion about whether the financial statements that have been prepared by management, with the oversight of those charged with governance, are prepared, in all material respects, in conformity with the applicable financial reporting framework.

b. the audit of the financial statements does not relieve management or those charged with governance of their responsibilities.

9.17 Paragraph .12 of AU-C section 260 identifies the following matters related to significant findings or issues in the audit that the auditor should communicate with those charged with governance:

a. The auditor's views about qualitative aspects of the entity's significant accounting practices, including accounting policies, accounting estimates, and financial statement disclosures. When applicable, the auditor should

i. explain to those charged with governance why the auditor considers a significant accounting practice that is acceptable under the applicable financial reporting framework not to be most appropriate to the particular circumstances of the entity and

ii. determine that those charged with governance are informed about the process used by management in formulating particularly sensitive accounting estimates, including fair value estimates, and about the basis for the auditor's conclusions regarding the reasonableness of those estimates.

b. Significant difficulties, if any, encountered during the audit.

c. Disagreements with management, if any.

d. Other findings or issues, if any, arising from the audit that are, in the auditor's professional judgment, significant and relevant to those charged with governance regarding their responsibility to oversee the financial reporting process.

9.18 Further, and more specifically, with respect to uncorrected misstatements in the audit, the auditor should communicate with those charged with governance uncorrected misstatements accumulated by the auditor and the effect that they, individually or in the aggregate, may have on the opinion in the auditor's report and the effect of uncorrected misstatements related to prior periods on the relevant classes of transactions, account balances or disclosures, and the financial statements as a whole. The auditor's communication should identify material uncorrected misstatements individually and should request that uncorrected misstatements be corrected.

9.19 In the case when not all of those charged with governance are involved in management, the auditor should also communicate

a. material, corrected misstatements that were brought to the attention of management as a result of audit procedures.

b. significant findings or issues, if any, arising from the audit that were discussed, or the subject of correspondence, with management.

c. the auditor's views about significant matters that were the subject of management's consultations with other accountants on accounting or auditing matters when the auditor is aware that such consultation has occurred.

d. written representations the auditor is requesting.

9.20 Readers can refer to AU-C section 265, *Communicating Internal Control Related Matters Identified in an Audit*, and chapter 11, "Other Audit Considerations," for guidance pertaining to the communication of internal control related matters. Readers can refer to AU-C section 240, *Consideration of Fraud in a Financial Statement Audit*, and chapter 12, "Consideration of Fraud in a Financial Statement Audit," for guidance pertaining to communication about possible fraud. For additional matters to be communicated to those charged with governance, readers can refer to the "Application and Other Explanatory Material" section of AU-C section 260.

9.21 Nothing in AU-C section 260 precludes the auditor from communicating any other matters to those charged with governance.

Audit Risk

9.22 AU-C section 200 states that *audit risk* is the risk that the auditor expresses an inappropriate audit opinion when the financial statements are materially misstated and is a function of the risks of material misstatement and detection risk. The auditor should obtain sufficient appropriate audit evidence to reduce audit risk to an acceptably low level and thereby enable the auditor to draw reasonable conclusions on which to base the auditor's opinion.

9.23 *Detection risk* is the risk that the procedures performed by the auditor to reduce audit risk to an acceptably low level will not detect a misstatement that exists and that could be material, either individually or when aggregated with other misstatements. The *risk of material misstatement* is the risk that the financial statements are materially misstated prior to the audit and consists of inherent risk and control risk, both at the assertion level.

9.24 GAAS does not ordinarily refer to inherent risk and control risk separately, but rather to a combined assessment of the risks of material misstatement. However, the auditor may make separate or combined assessments of inherent and control risk depending on preferred audit techniques or methodologies and practical considerations. The assessment of the risks of material misstatement may be expressed in quantitative terms, such as in percentages or in nonquantitative terms. In any case, the need for the auditor to make appropriate risk assessments is more important than the different approaches by which they may be made.

9.25 The auditor should, while establishing a basis for designing and performing further audit procedures, identify and assess the risks of material misstatement at the financial statement level and at the relevant assertion level for classes of transactions, account balances, and disclosures. Risks of material misstatement at the relevant assertion level for classes of transactions, account balances, and disclosures need to be considered because such consideration directly assists in determining the nature, timing, and extent of further audit procedures at the assertion level necessary to obtain sufficient appropriate audit evidence.

9.26 In identifying and assessing risks of material misstatement at the relevant assertion level, the auditor may conclude that the identified risks relate more pervasively to the financial statements as a whole and potentially affect many relevant assertions. Risks of this nature are not necessarily risks identifiable with specific assertions at the class of transactions, account balance, or disclosure level. Rather, they represent circumstances that may increase the risks of material misstatement at the assertion level (for example, through management override of internal control). For audits of construction contractors, a major area of risks of misstatements is in the area of contracts. Contracts have a pervasive effect at the account balance, class of transactions, and disclosure level. The factors in exhibit 9-1 indicate the effect of various aspects of construction contracts on audit risk.

Exhibit 9-1

Factor	*Characteristics That Normally Reduce Audit Risk*	*Characteristics That Normally Increase Audit Risk*
Percent of contract complete	• 0% to 10% • > 90%	• 10% to 90%
Size of project	• Relatively small job	• Relatively large job
Type of project	• Simple/routine • Within contractor's expertise	• Complex, one of a kind • Not within contractor's expertise
Timing and scheduling	• Short-term project • Work is on schedule • Comfortable time frame • No penalties for late completion	• Long-term project • Work is falling behind schedule • Accelerated time frame • Significant penalties for late completion
Location	• Established area with past successful projects • Materials and labor readily available	• New area • Remote area—materials and labor not readily available
Weather	• Low susceptibility to adverse weather	• High susceptibility to adverse weather
Owner/investor	• Many previous contracts with contractor • Solid financial position	• Very few previous contracts with contractor • Weak financial position
Subcontractors	• Large portion of work performed by subcontractors • Many previous contracts with contractor • Solid financial position • Majority of significant subcontract agreements finalized	• Small portion of work performed by subcontractors • Very few previous contracts with contractor • Weak financial position • Majority of significant subcontract agreements not finalized
Bid spread	• Narrow variances in bid amounts among competing contractors	• Significant variances in bid amounts among competing contractors
Profit fade	• No significant profit fade	• Significant profit fade

Factor	*Characteristics That Normally Reduce Audit Risk*	*Characteristics That Normally Increase Audit Risk*
Underbilling	• Nominal underbilling (cost and estimated earnings in excess of billings)	• Unusual/significant underbilling
Type of contract	• Cost-type, clear definition of reimbursable costs	• Fixed-price • Cost-type, difficult to determine reimbursable costs
Claims	• No claims	• Significant claims
Material costs	• Low susceptibility to price escalations during performance of contract	• High susceptibility to price escalations during performance of contract

Materiality

9.27 The concept of materiality is applied by the auditor both in planning and performing the audit; evaluating the effect of identified misstatements on the audit and the effect of uncorrected misstatements, if any, on the financial statements; and in forming the opinion in the auditor's report. In planning the audit, the auditor makes judgments about the size of misstatements that will be considered material. These judgments provide a basis for

a. determining the nature and extent of risk assessment procedures;

b. identifying and assessing the risks of material misstatement; and

c. determining the nature, timing, and extent of further audit procedures.

9.28 The auditor's determination of materiality is a matter of professional judgment and is affected by the auditor's perception of the financial information needs of users of the financial statements.

9.29 The materiality determined when planning the audit does not necessarily establish an amount below which uncorrected misstatements, individually or in the aggregate, will always be evaluated as immaterial. The circumstances related to some misstatements may cause the auditor to evaluate them as material even if they are below materiality. Although it is not practicable to design audit procedures to detect misstatements that could be material solely because of their nature (that is, qualitative considerations), the auditor considers not only the size but also the nature of uncorrected misstatements, and the particular circumstances of their occurrence, when evaluating their effect on the financial statements.

9.30 When establishing the overall audit strategy, the auditor should determine materiality for the financial statements as a whole. If, in the specific circumstances of the entity, one or more particular classes of transactions, account balances, or disclosures exist for which misstatements of lesser amounts than materiality for the financial statements as a whole could reasonably be expected to influence the economic decisions of users, then, taken on the basis of the financial statements, the auditor also should determine the materiality level or levels to be applied to those particular classes of transactions, account balances, or disclosures.

9.31 Once established during planning, materiality is not static throughout the audit. The auditor should revise materiality for the financial statements as a whole (and, if applicable, the materiality level or levels for particular classes of transactions, account balances, or disclosures) in the event of becoming aware of information during the audit that would have caused the auditor to have determined a different amount (or amounts) initially.

Performance Materiality

9.32 Planning the audit solely to detect individual material misstatements overlooks the fact that the aggregate of individually immaterial misstatements may cause the financial statements to be materially misstated and leaves no margin for possible undetected misstatements. To address this concern, performance materiality is considered. Performance materiality is the amount or amounts set by the auditor at less than materiality for the financial statements as a whole to reduce to an appropriately low level the probability that the aggregate of uncorrected and undetected misstatements exceeds materiality for the financial statements as a whole. If applicable, *performance materiality* also refers to the amount or amounts set by the auditor at less than the materiality level or levels for particular classes of transactions, account balances, or disclosures. Performance materiality is to be distinguished from *tolerable misstatement*, which is the application of performance materiality to a particular sampling procedure. AU-C section 530, *Audit Sampling*, defines tolerable misstatement and provides further application guidance about the concept.

Qualitative Aspects of Materiality

9.33 Determining whether a classification misstatement is material involves the evaluation of qualitative considerations, such as the effect of the classification misstatement on, for example, compliance with debt or other contractual covenants, individual line items or subtotals in the financial statements, or on key ratios) and whether those effects would be considered material by potential users of the financial statements.

9.34 The circumstances related to some misstatements may cause the auditor to evaluate them as material, individually or when considered together with other misstatements accumulated during the audit, even if they are lower than materiality for the financial statements as a whole. Paragraph .A23 of AU-C section 450, *Evaluation of Misstatements Identified During the Audit*, provides qualitative factors that the auditor may consider relevant in determining whether misstatements are material.

Use of Assertions in Obtaining Audit Evidence

9.35 Paragraphs .A113–.A115 of AU-C section 315, *Understanding the Entity and Its Environment and Assessing the Risks of Material Misstatement*, discuss the use of assertions in obtaining audit evidence. In representing that the financial statements are in accordance with the applicable financial reporting framework, management implicitly or explicitly makes assertions regarding the recognition, measurement, presentation, and disclosure of the various elements of financial statements and related disclosures. Assertions used by the auditor to consider the different types of potential misstatements that may occur fall into the following three categories and may take the following forms:

Categories of Assertions

	Description of Assertions		
	Classes of Transactions and Events During the Period Under Audit	*Account Balances at the End of the Period*	*Presentation and Disclosure*
Occurrence/ Existence	Transactions and events that have been recorded have occurred and pertain to the entity.	Assets, liabilities, and equity interests exist.	Disclosed events and transactions have occurred.
Rights and Obligations	—	The entity holds or controls the rights to assets, and liabilities are the obligations of the entity.	Disclosed events and transactions pertain to the entity.
Completeness	All transactions and events that should have been recorded have been recorded.	All assets, liabilities, and equity interests that should have been recorded have been recorded.	All disclosures that should have been included in the financial statements have been included.
Accuracy/ Valuation and Allocation	Amounts and other data relating to recorded transactions and events have been recorded appropriately.	Assets, liabilities, and equity interests are included in the financial statements at appropriate amounts, and any resulting valuation or allocation adjustments are recorded appropriately.	Financial and other information is disclosed fairly and at appropriate amounts.

(continued)

Categories of Assertions—*continued*

	Description of Assertions		
	Classes of Transactions and Events During the Period Under Audit	*Account Balances at the End of the Period*	*Presentation and Disclosure*
Cut-off	Transactions and events have been recorded in the correct accounting period.	Transactions and events have been recorded in the correct accounting period.	—
Classification and Understandability	Transactions and events have been recorded in the proper accounts.	—	Financial information is appropriately presented and described, and information in disclosures is expressed clearly.

9.36 The auditor should use relevant assertions for classes of transactions, account balances, and presentation and disclosures in sufficient detail to form a basis for the assessment of risks of material misstatement and the design and performance of further audit procedures. The auditor should use relevant assertions in assessing risks by the identified risks to what can go wrong at the relevant assertion, taking account of relevant controls that the auditor intends to test, and designing further audit procedures that are responsive to the assessed risks.

Understanding the Entity, Its Environment, and Its Internal Control

9.37 AU-C section 315 addresses the auditor's responsibility to identify and assess the risks of material misstatement in the financial statements through understanding the entity and its environment, including the entity's internal control.

9.38 Obtaining an understanding of the entity and its environment, including its internal control, is a continuous, dynamic process of gathering, updating, and analyzing information throughout the audit.

9.39 The auditor is required to exercise professional judgment[3] to determine the extent of the required understanding of the entity. The auditor's primary consideration is whether the understanding of the entity that has been

---

[3] Paragraph .18 of AU-C section 200, *Overall Objectives of the Independent Auditor and the Conduct of an Audit in Accordance With Generally Accepted Auditing Standards*, requires the auditor to exercise professional judgment in planning and performing an audit.

obtained is sufficient to meet the objective stated in this section. Note that the depth of the overall understanding that is required by the auditor is less than that possessed by management in managing the entity.

Risk Assessment Procedures

9.40 As described in AU-C section 315, audit procedures performed to obtain an understanding of the entity and its environment, including its internal control, to identify and assess the risks of material misstatement, whether due to fraud or error, at the financial statement and relevant assertion levels are referred to as *risk assessment procedures*. Paragraph .05 of AU-C section 315 states that the auditor should perform risk assessment procedures to provide a basis for the identification and assessment of risks of material misstatement at the financial statement and relevant assertion levels. Risk assessment procedures by themselves, however, do not provide sufficient appropriate audit evidence on which to base the audit.

9.41 In accordance with paragraph .06 of AU-C section 315, risk assessment procedures should include

- inquiries of management and others within the entity who, in the auditor's professional judgment, may have information that is likely to assist in identifying risks of material misstatement due to fraud or error.
- analytical procedures.
- observation and inspection.

Discussion Among the Audit Team

9.42 The engagement partner and other key engagement team members should discuss the susceptibility of the entity's financial statements to material misstatement and the application of the applicable financial reporting framework to the entity's facts and circumstances. The engagement partner should determine which matters are to be communicated to engagement team members not involved in the discussion. This discussion may be held concurrently with the discussion among the engagement team that is required by paragraph .15 of AU-C section 240 to discuss the susceptibility of the entity's financial statements to fraud. Readers can refer to chapter 12 for additional guidance pertaining to the requirements surrounding audit team planning discussions.

Understanding the Entity and Its Environment

9.43 The auditor should obtain an understanding of the following:

a. Relevant industry, regulatory, and other external factors, including the applicable financial reporting framework

b. The nature of the entity, including

  i. its operations;

  ii. its ownership and governance structures;

  iii. the types of investments that the entity is making and plans to make, including investments in entities formed to accomplish specific objectives; and

  iv. the way that the entity is structured and how it is financed, to enable the auditor to understand the classes of transactions, account balances, and disclosures to be expected in the financial statements

c. The entity's selection and application of accounting policies, including the reasons for changes thereto. The auditor should evaluate whether the entity's accounting policies are appropriate for its business and consistent with the applicable financial reporting framework and accounting policies used in the relevant industry

d. The entity's objectives and strategies and those related business risks that may result in risks of material misstatement

e. The measurement and review of the entity's financial performance

Refer to the "Application and Other Explanatory Material" section of AU-C section 315 for examples of matters that the auditor may consider in obtaining an understanding of the entity and its environment relating to categories (*a*)–(*e*).

Review of Contracts

9.44 As part of obtaining the required understanding described in the preceding paragraphs, the auditor would normally review the terms of a representative sample of the contractor's contracts applicable to the period under audit. This review includes both contracts with customers and contracts with subcontractors. Information that the auditor would expect to find is set forth in the following. This information can be used in the preliminary review of contracts and also in the other stages of the audit:

- Job number
- Type of contract
- Contract price
- Original cost estimate and related gross profit
- Billing and retention terms
- Provisions for changes in contract prices and terms, such as escalation, cancellation, and renegotiation
- Penalty or bonus features relating to completion dates and other performance criteria
- Bonding and insurance requirements
- Location and description of project

9.45 Contract files may indicate bids entered by other contractors. If these are available, the auditor would normally investigate significant differences between such bids and the related contracts to evaluate whether there may be inherent errors in the estimating and bidding process.

Understanding of Internal Control

9.46 AU-C section 315 defines *internal control* as "a process effected by those charged with governance, management, and other personnel that is designed to provide reasonable assurance about the achievement of the entity's objectives with regard to the reliability of financial reporting, effectiveness and efficiency of operations, and compliance with applicable laws and regulations."

9.47 The auditor should obtain an understanding of internal control relevant to the audit. Although most controls relevant to the audit are likely to relate to financial reporting, not all controls that relate to financial reporting are relevant to the audit. When obtaining an understanding of controls that are relevant to the audit, the auditor should evaluate the design of those controls and determine whether they have been implemented by performing procedures in addition to inquiry of the entity's personnel.

9.48 Evaluating the design of a control involves considering whether the control, individually or in combination with other controls, is capable of effectively preventing, or detecting and correcting, material misstatements. Implementation of a control means that the control exists and that the entity is using it. Assessing the implementation of a control that is not effectively designed is of little use, and so the design of a control is considered first. An improperly designed control may represent a significant deficiency or material weakness in the entity's internal control.

9.49 Risk assessment procedures to obtain audit evidence about the design and implementation of relevant controls may include

- inquiring of entity personnel.
- observing the application of specific controls.
- inspecting documents and reports.
- tracing transactions through the information system relevant to financial reporting.

Inquiry alone, however, is not sufficient for such purposes.

9.50 Obtaining an understanding of an entity's controls is not sufficient to test their operating effectiveness, unless some automation provides for the consistent operation of the controls Tests of the operating effectiveness of controls are further described in AU-C section 330, *Performing Audit Procedures in Response to Assessed Risks and Evaluating the Audit Evidence Obtained*.

9.51 Internal control consists of five interrelated components:

- The control environment
- The entity's risk assessment process
- The information system, including the related business processes relevant to financial reporting and communication
- Control activities
- Monitoring of controls

Refer paragraphs .15–.25 of AU-C section 315 for a detailed discussion of the internal control components.

Control Environment

9.52 The auditor should obtain an understanding of the control environment. As part of obtaining this understanding, the auditor should evaluate whether

a. management, with the oversight of those charged with governance, has created and maintained a culture of honesty and ethical behavior and

b. the strengths in the control environment elements collectively provide an appropriate foundation for the other components of internal control and whether those other components are not undermined by deficiencies in the control environment.

Risk Assessment Process

9.53 The auditor should obtain an understanding of whether the entity has a process for

a. identifying business risks relevant to financial reporting objectives,

b. estimating the significance of the risks,

c. assessing the likelihood of their occurrence, and

d. deciding about actions to address those risks.

9.54 If the entity has established a risk assessment process, the auditor should obtain an understanding of it and the results thereof. If the entity has not established such a process, or has an ad hoc process, the auditor should discuss with management whether business risks relevant to financial reporting objectives have been identified and how they have been addressed. The auditor should evaluate whether the absence of a documented risk assessment process is appropriate in the circumstances or determine whether it represents a significant deficiency or material weakness in the entity's internal control.

The Information System, Including the Related Business Processes Relevant to Financial Reporting and Communication

9.55 The auditor should obtain an understanding of the information system, including the related business processes relevant to financial reporting, including the following areas:

a. The classes of transactions in the entity's operations that are significant to the financial statements

b. The procedures within both IT and manual systems by which those transactions are initiated, authorized, recorded, processed, corrected as necessary, transferred to the general ledger, and reported in the financial statements

c. The related accounting records supporting information and specific accounts in the financial statements that are used to initiate, authorize, record, process, and report transactions. This includes the correction of incorrect information and how information is transferred to the general ledger. The records may be in either manual or electronic form

d. How the information system captures events and conditions, other than transactions, that are significant to the financial statements

e. The financial reporting process used to prepare the entity's financial statements, including significant accounting estimates and disclosures

f. Controls surrounding journal entries, including nonstandard journal entries used to record nonrecurring, unusual transactions, or adjustments

g. The way that the entity communicates financial reporting roles and responsibilities and significant matters relating to financial reporting, including communications between management and those charged with governance and external communications, such as those with regulatory authorities

Control Activities

9.56 The auditor should obtain an understanding of control activities relevant to the audit, which are those control activities the auditor judges necessary to understand in order to assess the risks of material misstatement at the assertion level and design further audit procedures responsive to assessed risks.

9.57 An audit does not require an understanding of all the control activities related to each significant class of transactions, account balance, and disclosure in the financial statements or to every assertion relevant to them. However, the auditor should obtain an understanding of the controls relevant to the audit; those over financial reporting necessary to assure the financial information is appropriately accumulated and reported.

9.58 Control activities that are relevant to the audit are those that are required to be treated as such, being control activities that relate to significant risks and those that relate to risks for which substantive procedures alone do not provide sufficient appropriate audit evidence or considered to be relevant in the professional judgment of the auditor.

9.59 Further, in understanding the entity's control activities, the auditor should obtain an understanding of how the entity has responded to risks arising from IT.

Monitoring of Controls

9.60 The auditor should obtain an understanding of the major activities that the entity uses to monitor internal control over financial reporting, including those related to those control activities relevant to the audit, and how the entity initiates remedial actions to deficiencies in its controls.

9.61 If the contractor has an internal audit function,[4] the auditor, to determine whether the internal audit function is likely to be relevant to the audit, should obtain an understanding of

- The nature of the internal audit function's responsibilities and how the internal audit function fits in the entity's organizational structure
- The activities performed or to be performed by the internal audit function

---

[4] AU-C section 610, *Using the Work of Internal Auditors*, addresses the external auditor's responsibilities if using the work of internal auditors. Using the work of internal auditors includes (*a*) using the work of the internal audit function in obtaining audit evidence and (*b*) using internal auditors to provide direct assistance under the direction, supervision, and review of the external auditor.

AU-C section 610 does not apply if the entity does not have an internal audit function. If the entity has an internal audit function, the requirements in AU-C section 610 relating to using the work of the internal audit function in obtaining audit evidence do not apply if

a. the responsibilities and activities of the function are not relevant to the audit, or

b. based on the external auditor's preliminary understanding of the function obtained as a result of procedures performed under AU-C section 315, *Understanding the Entity and Its Environment and Assessing the Risks of Material Misstatement*, the external auditor does not expect to use the work of the function in obtaining audit evidence.

Nothing in AU-C section 610 requires the external auditor to use the work of the internal audit function to modify the nature or timing, or reduce the extent, of audit procedures to be performed directly by the external auditor; it remains the external auditor's decision to establish the overall audit strategy. Furthermore, the requirements in AU-C section 610 relating to using internal auditors to provide direct assistance do not apply if the external auditor does not plan to use internal auditors to provide direct assistance.

9.62 The auditor should obtain an understanding of the sources of the information used in the entity's monitoring activities and the basis upon which management considers the information to be sufficiently reliable for the purpose.

Assessment of Risks of Material Misstatement and the Design of Further Audit Procedures

9.63 As discussed previously, risk assessment procedures allow the auditor to gather the information necessary to obtain an understanding of the entity and its environments, including its internal control. This knowledge provides a basis for assessing the risks of material misstatement of the financial statements. These risk assessments are then used to design further audit procedures, such as tests of controls, substantive tests, or both. This section provides guidance on assessing the risks of material misstatement and how to design further audit procedures that effectively respond to those risks.

Assessing the Risks of Material Misstatement

9.64 Paragraph .26 of AU-C section 315 states that the auditor should identify and assess the risks of material misstatement at the financial statement level and at the relevant assertion level related to classes of transactions, account balances, and disclosures. For this purpose, the auditor should

- identify risks throughout the process of obtaining an understanding of the entity and its environment, including relevant controls that relate to the risks, by considering the classes of transactions, account balances, and disclosures in the financial statements.
- assess the identified risks and evaluate whether they relate more pervasively to the financial statements as a whole and potentially affect many assertions.
- relate the identified risks to what can go wrong at the relevant assertion level, taking account of relevant controls that the auditor intends to test; and
- consider the likelihood of misstatement, including the possibility of multiple misstatements, and whether the potential misstatement is of a magnitude that could result in a material misstatement.

9.65 The auditor should use information gathered by performing risk assessment procedures, including the audit evidence obtained in evaluating the design of controls and determining whether they have been implemented, as audit evidence to support the risk assessment. The auditor should use the assessment of the risks of material misstatement at the relevant assertion level as the basis to determine the nature, timing, and extent of further audit procedures to be performed.

Identification of Significant Risks

9.66 As part of the assessment of the risks of material misstatement, the auditor should determine whether any of the risks identified are, in the auditor's professional judgment, a significant risk, those that require special audit consideration (such risks are defined as *significant risks*).

9.67 Significant risks often relate to significant nonroutine transactions and matters that require significant judgment. *Nonroutine transactions* are transactions that are unusual, either due to size or nature, and that, therefore, occur infrequently. Matters that require significant judgment, and are especially significant in the construction industry, may include the development of accounting estimates for which a significant measurement uncertainty exists.

9.68 In exercising professional judgment about which risks are significant risks, the auditor should consider at least

a. whether the risk is a risk of fraud;

b. whether the risk is related to recent significant economic, accounting, or other developments and, therefore, requires specific attention;

c. the complexity of transactions;

d. whether the risk involves significant transactions with related parties;

e. the degree of subjectivity in the measurement of financial information related to the risk, especially those measurements involving a wide range of measurement uncertainty; and

f. whether the risk involves significant transactions that are outside the normal course of business for the entity or that otherwise appears to be unusual.

9.69 In the construction industry, auditors may find that a significant risk exists with regards to the accuracy of management's estimates of costs to complete for contracts in progress. Another example of a significant risk area may include contract revenues due to the possible effects of unsigned or unpriced change orders and claims. The auditor's understanding of the contractor's controls for such significant risks includes, for example, whether control activities (such as a review of estimates and contract prices by senior management and the existence of formal processes for compiling estimates) have been implemented to address the significant risks.

Designing and Performing Further Audit Procedures

9.70 AU-C section 330 addresses the auditor's responsibility to design and implement responses to the risks of material misstatement identified and assessed by the auditor in accordance with AU-C section 315 and to evaluate the audit evidence obtained in an audit of financial statements. The objective, outlined by AU-C section 330, is for the auditor to obtain sufficient appropriate audit evidence regarding the assessed risks of material misstatement through designing and implementing appropriate responses to those risks.

9.71 To reduce audit risk to an acceptably low level, the auditor (*a*) should design and implement overall responses to address the assessed risks of material misstatement at the financial statement level and (*b*) should design and perform further audit procedures whose nature, timing, and extent are based on, and are responsive to, the assessed risks of material misstatement at the relevant assertion level.

Overall Responses

9.72 The auditor's overall responses to address the assessed risks of material misstatement at the financial statement level may include emphasizing to the audit team the need to maintain professional skepticism in gathering and evaluating audit evidence, assigning more experienced staff or those with specialized skills or using specialists, providing more supervision, or incorporating additional elements of unpredictability in the selection of further audit procedures to be performed. Additionally, the auditor may make general changes to the nature, timing, or extent of further audit procedures as an overall response, for example, by performing substantive procedures at period end instead of at an interim date.

Further Audit Procedures

9.73 The auditor should design and perform further audit procedures whose nature, timing, and extent are based on, and are responsive to, the assessed risks of material misstatement at the relevant assertion level.

9.74 In some cases, an auditor may determine that performing only substantive procedures is appropriate for particular assertions, and therefore, the auditor excludes the effect of controls from the relevant risk assessment. This may be because the auditor's risk assessment procedures have not identified any effective controls relevant to the assertion or because testing controls would be inefficient, and therefore, the auditor does not intend to rely on the operating effectiveness of controls in determining the nature, timing, and extent of substantive procedures.

9.75 However, the auditor may determine that in addition to the substantive procedures that are required for all relevant assertions, in accordance with paragraph .18 of AU-C section 330, an effective response to the assessed risk of material misstatement for a particular assertion can be achieved only by also performing tests of controls. The auditor often will determine that a combined audit approach using both tests of the operating effectiveness of controls and substantive procedures is an effective audit approach.

9.76 The auditor should design and perform tests of controls to obtain sufficient appropriate audit evidence about the operating effectiveness of relevant controls if the auditor's assessment of risks of material misstatement at the relevant assertion level includes an expectation that the controls are operating effectively (that is, the auditor intends to rely on the operating effectiveness of controls in determining the nature, timing, and extent of substantive procedures) or substantive procedures alone cannot provide sufficient appropriate audit evidence at the relevant assertion level.

9.77 Tests of the operating effectiveness of controls are performed only on those controls that the auditor has determined are suitably designed to prevent, or detect and correct, a material misstatement in a relevant assertion.

9.78 Testing the operating effectiveness of controls is different from obtaining an understanding of and evaluating the design and implementation of controls. However, the same types of audit procedures are used. The auditor may, therefore, decide it is efficient to test the operating effectiveness of controls at the same time the auditor is evaluating their design and determining that they have been implemented.

9.79 When performing tests of controls, the auditor should obtain audit evidence about the operating effectiveness of the controls. This includes obtaining audit evidence about how controls were applied at relevant times during the period under audit, the consistency with which they were applied, and by whom or by what means they were applied, including, when applicable, whether the person performing the control possesses the necessary authority and competence to perform the control effectively. If substantially different controls were used at different times during the period under audit, the auditor should consider each separately.

9.80 Further, in designing and performing tests of controls, the auditor should determine whether the controls to be tested depend upon other controls (indirect controls) and, if so, whether it is necessary to obtain audit evidence supporting the operating effectiveness of those indirect controls.

9.81 Although some risk assessment procedures that the auditor performs to evaluate the design of controls and determine that they have been implemented may not have been specifically designed as tests of controls, they may nevertheless provide audit evidence about the operating effectiveness of the controls and, consequently, serve as tests of controls.

9.82 The discussion of tests of controls relates only to those aspects of a contractor's internal control that relate to the relevant assertions that are likely to prevent or detect a material misstatement in the account balances, classes of transactions, and disclosure components of the financial statements. The preceding chapter outlines desirable components of internal control for, among other things, estimating and bidding, billings, contract costs, and contract revenues. Some of those controls may not be relevant to an audit and, therefore, need not be considered by the auditor. The auditor considers only those aspects of internal control that relate to the relevant assertions that are likely to prevent or detect a material misstatement in the account balances, classes of transactions, and disclosure components of the financial statements.

9.83 Tests of controls may consist of procedures such as inquires of appropriate entity personnel; observation of the application of the control; inspection of documents, reports, or electronic files indicating performance of the control; and reperformance of the application of the control by the auditor (such as tracing transactions through the information system). AU-C section 530[5] provides guidance on the use of audit sampling in audits conducted in accordance with GAAS. That guidance may be useful to auditors in determining the extent of tests of controls.

9.84 Substantive procedures are performed to detect material misstatements at the assertion level and include tests of details of classes of transactions, account balances, and disclosures and substantive analytical procedures.

9.85 Regardless of the assessed risks of material misstatement, the auditor should design and perform substantive procedures for all relevant assertions related to each material class of transactions, account balance, and disclosure. This requirement reflects the facts that (*a*) the auditor's assessment of risk is judgmental and may not identify all risks of material misstatement and (*b*) inherent limitations to internal control exist, including management override.

---

[5] Refer to the AICPA Audit Guide *Audit Sampling*, which provides guidance to help auditors apply audit sampling in accordance with AU-C section 530, *Audit Sampling*. This guide may be used both as a reference source for those who are knowledgeable about audit sampling and as initial background for those who are new to this area.

Evaluating Misstatements

9.86 Based on the results of substantive procedures, the auditor may identify misstatements in accounts or notes to the financial statements. Per paragraph .05 of AU-C section 450, the auditor should accumulate misstatements identified during the audit, other than those that are clearly trivial, and should communicate on a timely basis with the appropriate level of management all misstatements accumulated during the audit, as well as request management to correct those misstatements.

9.87 If management refuses to correct some or all of the misstatements communicated by the auditor, the auditor should obtain an understanding of management's reasons for not making the corrections and should take that understanding into account when evaluating whether the financial statements as a whole are free from material misstatement.

9.88 The auditor should determine whether uncorrected misstatements are material, individually or in the aggregate. In making this determination, the auditor should consider

a. the size and nature of the misstatements, both in relation to particular classes of transactions, account balances, or disclosures and the financial statements as a whole, and the particular circumstances of their occurrence and

b. the effect of uncorrected misstatements related to prior periods on the relevant classes of transactions, account balances, or disclosures and the financial statements as a whole.

Audit Documentation

9.89 Audit documentation that meets the requirements AU-C section 230, *Audit Documentation*, and the specific documentation requirements of other relevant AU-C sections provides evidence of the auditor's basis for a conclusion about the achievement of the overall objectives of the auditor and evidence that the audit was planned and performed in accordance with GAAS and applicable legal and regulatory requirements.

9.90 The objective of the auditor is to prepare documentation that provides a sufficient and appropriate record of the basis for the auditor's report and evidence that the audit was planned and performed in accordance with GAAS and applicable legal and regulatory requirements.

9.91 Audit documentation should be prepared on a timely basis and be sufficient to enable an experienced auditor, having no previous connection with the audit, to understand the nature, timing, extent and result of the procedures performed, the audit evidence obtained and the significant finding or issues which arose, the conclusions reached thereon and the significant professional judgments made in reaching those conclusions.

9.92 In documenting the nature, timing, and extent of audit procedures performed, the auditor should record the identifying characteristics of the specific items or matters tested, who performed the work and the date such work was completed, and who reviewed the audit work performed and the date and extent of such review.

9.93 With respect to construction contracts and agreements used in audit procedures related to the inspection of significant contracts or agreements, the auditor should include abstracts or copies of those contracts or agreements in the audit documentation.

9.94 The auditor should assemble the audit documentation in an audit file and complete the administrative process of assembling the final audit file on a timely basis, no later than 60 days following the report release date. Statutes, regulations, or the audit firm's quality control policies may specify a shorter period of time in which this assembly process should be completed. After the documentation completion date, the auditor should not delete or discard audit documentation before the end of the specified retention period. Such retention period should not be shorter than five years from the report release date. Statutes, regulations, or the audit firm's quality control policies may specify a retention period longer than five years.

9.95 In many cases, the report release date will be the date the auditor delivers the audit report to the entity. When there are delays in releasing the report, a fact may become known to the auditor that, had it been known to the auditor at the date of the auditor's report, may have caused the auditor to revise the auditor's report. AU-C section 560, *Subsequent Events and Subsequently Discovered Facts*, addresses the auditor's responsibilities in such circumstances, and paragraph .14 of AU-C section 230 addresses the documentation requirements in the rare circumstances in which the auditor performs new or additional audit procedures or draws new conclusions after the date of the auditor's report.

9.96 Paragraph .41 of AU-C section 700, *Forming an Opinion and Reporting on Financial Statements*, states that the auditor's report should not be dated earlier than the date on which the auditor has obtained sufficient appropriate audit evidence on which to base the auditor's opinion on the financial statements. Among other things, sufficient appropriate audit evidence includes evidence that the audit documentation has been reviewed and that the entity's financial statements, including the related notes, have been prepared and that management has asserted that it has taken responsibility for them.

9.97 Audit documentation is the property of the auditor, and some states recognize this right of ownership in their statutes. The auditor may make available to the entity at the auditor's discretion copies of the audit documentation, provided such disclosure does not undermine the effectiveness and integrity of the audit process.

9.98 Audit documentation requirements contained in other Statements on Auditing Standards can be found in the "Application and Other Explanatory Material" section of AU-C section 230.

Identifying and Evaluating Control Deficiencies

9.99 The auditor is required to obtain an understanding of internal control relevant to the audit when identifying and assessing the risks of material misstatement. In making those risk assessments, the auditor considers internal control in order to design audit procedures that are appropriate in the circumstances but not for the purpose of expressing an opinion on the effectiveness of internal control. The auditor may identify deficiencies in internal control not only during this risk assessment process but also at any other stage of the audit.

9.100 The auditor should determine whether, on the basis of the audit work performed, the auditor has identified one or more deficiencies in internal control. If the auditor has identified one or more deficiencies in internal control, the auditor should evaluate each deficiency to determine, on the basis of the audit work performed, whether, individually or in combination, they constitute significant deficiencies or material weaknesses. If the auditor determines that a deficiency, or a combination of deficiencies, in internal control is not a material weakness, the auditor should consider whether prudent officials, having knowledge of the same facts and circumstances, would likely reach the same conclusion.

9.101 The auditor should communicate in writing to those charged with governance on a timely basis significant deficiencies and material weaknesses identified during the audit, including those that were remediated during the audit.

9.102 The auditor also should communicate to management at an appropriate level of responsibility, on a timely basis in writing, significant deficiencies and material weaknesses that the auditor has communicated or intends to communicate to those charged with governance, unless it would be inappropriate to communicate directly to management in the circumstances. Further, the auditor should communicate to management at an appropriate level of responsibility, on a timely basis in writing or orally, other deficiencies in internal control identified during the audit that have not been communicated to management by other parties and that, in the auditor's professional judgment, are of sufficient importance to merit management's attention. If other deficiencies in internal control are communicated orally, the auditor should document the communication.

9.103 The auditor should not issue a written communication stating that no significant deficiencies were identified during the audit.

Chapter 10

Major Auditing Procedures for Contractors

Gray shaded text in this chapter reflects guidance issued but not yet effective as of the date of this guide, July 1, 2017, but becoming effective on or prior to December 31, 2017, exclusive of any option to early adopt ahead of the mandatory effective date. Unless otherwise indicated, all unshaded text reflects guidance that was already effective as of the date of this guide.

10.01 This chapter provides guidance on the major auditing procedures applicable to financial statement audits of construction contractors. The areas discussed are job site visits, accounts receivable, liabilities related to contracts, contract costs, income recognition, and review of backlog on existing contracts. As discussed in chapter 9, "Planning the Audit, Assessing and Responding to Audit Risk, and Additional Auditing Considerations," the nature, timing, and extent of these procedures should be responsive to the assessed risks of material misstatement at the relevant assertion level. In accordance with AU-C section 330, *Performing Audit Procedures in Response to Assessed Risks and Evaluating the Audit Evidence Obtained*,[1] certain substantive procedures should be performed on all engagements. These procedures include

- performing substantive procedures for all relevant assertions related to each material class of transactions, account balance, and disclosure;
- agreeing or reconciling the financial statements to the underlying accounting records; and
- examining material journal entries and other adjustments made during the course of preparing the financial statements.

Job Site Visits and Interim Audit Procedures

10.02 In certain situations, job site visits are essential for the auditor to understand the contractor's operations and to relate the internal accounting information to events that occur at the job sites. All or part of the accounting function relating to a given project may be performed at a temporary job site office staffed by a limited number of trained accounting personnel, and internal control at job sites may be ineffective. Observations and discussions with operating personnel at the job sites may also assist the auditor in assessing physical security, the status of projects, and the representations of management (for example, representations about the stage of completion and estimated costs to complete). The auditor should consider using specialists, such as outside engineering consultants, in performing job site audit procedures. AU-C section 620, *Using the Work of an Auditor's Specialist*, provides guidance and establishes requirements in this area. Job site visits assist the auditor in meeting the following objectives:

- Gaining an understanding of the contractor's method of operations

---

[1] All AU-C sections can be found in AICPA *Professional Standards*.

- Determining that the job actually exists
- Obtaining information from field employees to corroborate the information obtained from management, including whether employees at the job site are the same ones whose time is charged to the job
- Obtaining an understanding of those components of internal control maintained at the job site
- Obtaining information relating to job status, including whether materials charged to the job have been installed, and problems (if any) that may be useful in other phases of the audit
- Obtaining information of fixed assets, including equipment or company vehicles, obtaining the VIN or equipment numbers and physically confirming the existence

10.03 These objectives can usually be achieved during one visit to a job site. To do so, however, requires careful planning so that the information to be obtained or examined will be identified before the visit. Furthermore, to meet the third objective, it is usually desirable, before selecting the job sites to be visited, to consider (*a*) the contractor's internal control; (*b*) the size, nature, significance, and location of projects; and (*c*) projects that have unusual features or that appear to be troublesome. Unusual or troublesome contracts may include those accounted for under the percentage-of-completion method on the basis of estimates in ranges, or on the basis of zero profit estimates, those that are combined or segmented for accounting purposes, and those with significant unpriced change orders or unsatisfied claims, all of which are discussed in FASB *Accounting Standards Codification* (ASC) 605-35.

10.04 Other characteristics of troublesome contracts may include those that have significant profit fades from the prior interim or annual period, those that have a significant underbilling, those with significant liquidated damages, and those subject to unusual risks because of factors such as location, ability to complete turnkey projects satisfactorily, postponement or cancellation provisions, or disputes between the parties.

10.05 To accomplish audit objectives, job site visits may be made at any time during the year or at the end of the year. When considering obtaining audit evidence about the effectiveness of internal controls during an interim period, the auditor should determine what additional audit evidence should be obtained for the remaining period. In making this determination, the auditor should consider the significance of the assessed risks of material misstatement at the relevant assertion level. Factors that support the risk assessment may include the design, implementation, and effectiveness of internal control; the number, size, and significance of projects; the existence of projects with unusual or troublesome features; and the method of accounting for revenue. However, if the contractor's internal control is inadequate and if the contractor has in progress any large projects that individually have a material effect on the contractor's results of operations or any projects that have unusual features or that appear to be troublesome, the auditor should select those projects for visits at or near the year-end. The auditor should also consider the length of the remaining period, the extent to which the auditor intends to reduce further substantive procedures based on the reliance of controls, and the control environment. Further guidance concerning the timing of tests of controls in connection with the audit of financial statements is provided in paragraphs .11–.17 of AU-C section 330.

10.06 AU-C section 330 provides guidance and establishes requirements for applying substantive tests at an interim date. The higher the risk of material misstatement, the more likely it is that the auditor may decide it is more effective to perform substantive procedures nearer to, or at, the period end rather than at an earlier date, or to perform audit procedures unannounced or at unpredictable times (for example, performing audit procedures at selected locations on an unannounced basis). Further guidance concerning the timing of substantive procedures is also provided in paragraphs .23–.24 of AU-C section 330.

10.07 In addition to obtaining an understanding of the entity and its environment, including its internal control and performing tests of the accounting records, the independent auditor might consider performing the following procedures during a job site visit:

- Observation of uninstalled materials
- Observation and verification of subcontractors or other vendors to further substantiate contract costs
- Observation of work performed to date
- Observation of contractor-owned or rented equipment
- Discussions with project managers, superintendents, and other appropriate individuals, including if possible the independent architect, regarding the status of the contract and any significant problems, uninstalled materials, as it relates to financial statement presentation, or deferred costs

Job site visits facilitate the auditor's collection of information concerning the organization and management of the job, the accounting reports submitted to the general accounting office, the present status of the job, and unusual matters affecting the estimated costs to complete the project.

Accounts Receivable

10.08 Accounts receivable for a construction contractor may differ significantly from that of an industrial or commercial enterprise in that contract receivables do not have a direct correlation to revenue recognized on the completed contract or percentage-of-completion method as noted in paragraph 10.32; however, the basic approach to the auditing of receivables is similar.

10.09 AU-C section 505, *External Confirmations*, provides guidance about the confirmation process in audits performed in accordance the requirements of AU-C section 330 and AU-C section 500, *Audit Evidence*. The auditor confirms accounts receivable, including retentions.

10.10 The confirmation ordinarily contains other pertinent information, such as the contract price, payments made, and status of the contract. Exhibit 10-1 is a sample confirmation letter requiring positive confirmation. Although negative confirmations may also be used if the conditions described in paragraph .15 of AU-C section 505 exist, such conditions rarely exist in the audit of a construction contractor.

10.11 Certain characteristics of a construction contractor's accounts receivable, such as the following, may require special audit consideration:

- Unbilled receivables
- Retentions
- Unapproved change orders, extras, claims, and back charges
- Contract scope changes
- Contract guarantees and cancellation or postponement provisions
- Collectibility

Other characteristics that may require special audit consideration regarding the scope of the work to be performed include approved but unpriced change orders and government contracts under which the contractor proceeds with all phases of the contract even though government funding is approved piecemeal.

The auditor may elect to review management's receivables aging schedules to determine if there are any additional significant aged receivable balances, make inquiries about identified balances, and review those balances for subsequent collection.

Unbilled Receivables

10.12 Unbilled receivables arise when revenues have been recorded due to the performance of contract work being performed, but the amount cannot be billed under the terms of the contract until a later date. Specifically, such balances may represent (*a*) unbilled amounts, (*b*) incurred cost to be billed under cost-reimbursement-type contracts, or (*c*) amounts arising from routine lags in billing (for example, for work completed in one month but not billed until the next month). It may not be possible to confirm those amounts as receivables directly with the customer; consequently, the auditor should apply alternative audit procedures, such as the subsequent examination of the billing and collection of the receivables and evaluation of billing information on the basis of accumulated cost data.

Exhibit 10-1

Sample Confirmation Request to Owner, General Contractor, or Other Buyer[2]

Re: [*Description of Contract*]

Gentlemen:

Our independent auditors, [*name and address*], are engaged in an audit of our financial statements. For verification purposes only, would you kindly respond directly to them about the accuracy of the following information at [*date*]:

1. Original contract price $____________
2. Total approved change orders $____________
3. Total billings $____________
4. Total payments $____________
5. Total unpaid balance $________ including retentions of ________
6. Details of any claims, extras, back charges, or disputes concerning this contract (attach separate sheet if necessary)
7. Estimated completion date ____________
8. Estimated percent complete ____________

We have enclosed a self-addressed, stamped envelope for your convenience in replying directly to our auditors. Your prompt response will be greatly appreciated.

Very truly yours,

Enc.

The above information is:

( ) Correct

( ) Incorrect (please submit details of any differences)

By:

____________________ ____________________

Signature Date

____

Title

---

[2] AU-C section 505, *External Confirmations*, notes that when a confirmation allows for electronic responses or when an electronic confirmation process or system is used, the auditor's consideration of the following risks includes the consideration of risks that the electronic confirmation process is not secure or is improperly controlled:

- The information obtained may not be from an authentic source.
- A respondent may not be knowledgeable about the information to be confirmed.
- The integrity of the information may have been compromised.

Further, responses received electronically (for example, by fax or email) involve risks relating to reliability because proof of origin or identity of the confirming party may be difficult to establish, and alterations may be difficult to detect. The auditor may determine that it is appropriate to address such risks by utilizing a system or process that validates the respondent or by directly contacting the purported sender (for example, by telephone) to validate the identity of the sender of the response and to validate that the information received by the auditor corresponds to what was transmitted by the sender.

Retentions

10.13 The contractor's accounting records ordinarily should provide for separate control for retentions because they are generally withheld until the contract is completed and, in certain instances, for even longer periods. They may also be subject to restrictive conditions, such as fulfillment guarantees. The auditor should test retentions as part of performing further audit procedures whose nature, timing, and extent are responsive to the assessed risks of material misstatement at the relevant assertion level. Relevant assertions are assertions that have a meaningful bearing on whether the account is fairly stated. For example, the completeness assertion is relevant to retentions in that it relates to whether all retentions are recorded, but the valuation assertion may be less relevant.

10.14 Auditors may consider testing retentions via reviewing contract retentions percentages, typically 5 percent to 10 percent of the amounts billed. While the contract is in progress, retentions generally have a direct percentage relationship to billings to date or other specified performance criteria.

Unapproved Change Orders, Extras, Claims, and Back Charges

10.15 Unapproved change orders and claims are often significant and recurring in the construction industry, and receivables arising from those sources may require special audit consideration. Paragraphs 25–31 of FASB ASC 605-35-25 set forth the circumstances and conditions under which amounts may be recorded as revenue from unapproved change orders, extras, claims, and back charges. Because of the nature of those receivables, the auditor may encounter difficulties in evaluating their propriety or the collectibility of the related additional revenue. The auditor may be able to confirm the amounts of unapproved change orders, extras, claims, and back charges with customers or subcontractors; however, if confirmation is not possible or if the amounts are disputed, the auditor should obtain evidence to evaluate the likelihood of settlement on satisfactory terms and the collectibility of the recorded amounts. The auditor might consider how the contractor has historically collected on its unapproved change orders. For example, if historically the contractor does not get the ultimate approval for a change order, or if it is approved for an amount less than what is expected by management, the auditor should consider this when determining the reasonableness of the current and pending change orders. To determine whether the conditions specified in FASB ASC 605-35 to record a receivable have been met, the auditor should review the terms of the contract and should document the amounts by discussions with the contractor's legal counsel and with contractor personnel who are knowledgeable about the contract.

10.16 When unapproved change orders, extras, claims, or back charges are the basis for significant additional contract revenues, or are otherwise identified for testing as part of the auditor's consideration of substantive procedures to be performed, the auditor should evaluate the propriety of accumulated costs underlying the unapproved change orders, extras, claims, or back charges. The following are some of the procedures that may be used in auditing such accumulated costs:

- Tests of the accumulation of costs to underlying invoices, time records, and other supporting documentation. In some circumstances, confirmation of relevant data and related amounts with subcontractors and others may be feasible.

- Consideration of whether the work performed or costs incurred were authorized in writing by the customer. If not, additional contract revenues may not be billable, and the costs may not be recoverable.
- Evaluation of whether the costs relate to work within or outside the scope of the contract. If the costs relate to work within the scope of a lump-sum contract, no basis for additional contract revenues may exist, and the costs may not be recoverable.

10.17 The auditor might also evaluate the nature and reasonableness of claimed damages that are attributable to customer-caused delays, errors in specifications that caused incorrect bids, or various other reasons. In connection with such an evaluation, the auditor should consider the quality and extent of the documentary evidence supporting the claim and the extent to which management has pursued the claim; the auditor also should consider consultation with technical personnel. It may also be appropriate to obtain an opinion from legal counsel (*a*) on the contractor's legal right to file such a claim against the customer, and (*b*) on the contractor's likelihood of success in pursuing the claim.

10.18 A claim may be properly supported, but, nevertheless, may be uncollectible. Many factors influence collectibility, including the relationship between the contractor and the customer. For example, a contractor may be less likely to press for collection of a claim from a major customer. In evaluating a claim, the auditor may consider the contractor's past experience in settling similar claims. If, for example, the contractor has demonstrated a reasonable degree of success in negotiating and settling similar types of claims and if the documentation supporting a claim under review appears to be similar in scope, depth, and content, the auditor may consider such prior experience in evaluating the collectibility of the claim. The auditor's use of heightened skepticism is warranted toward claims for which the contractor cannot provide collaborative evidence to support but rather are recorded based solely on management's feel or estimate.

Contract Scope Changes

10.19 Scope changes on contracts, particularly cost-plus contracts, are often not well documented. Large cost-plus contracts frequently evolve through various stages of design and planning, with numerous starts and stops on the part of both the customer and the contractor. As a result, the final scope of the contract is not always clearly defined. The auditor should carefully examine costs designated to be passed through to the customer under such contracts and should determine whether the costs are reimbursable or whether they should be absorbed by the contractor as unreimbursable contract costs. If receivables arise from contract scope changes that are unapproved or disputed by customers, the previous discussion on claims applies.

Contract Guarantees and Cancellation or Postponement Provisions

10.20 Many contracts provide for contract guarantees, such as a guarantee that a power plant, when completed, will generate a specified number of kilowatt hours. A contract may specify a fixed completion date, which, if not met, may result in substantial penalties. For some contracts, retentions and their ultimate realization are related to the fulfillment of contract guarantees.

The auditor should carefully read the contracts to identify guarantees or contingencies associated with a project to determine whether the contractor has given adequate consideration to the cost of fulfilling contract guarantees.

10.21 In addition, the auditor should carefully read the contracts to identify cancellation and postponement provisions associated with a project. Effective internal procedures provide for the contractor's timely notification to subcontractors of contracts cancelled or postponed in order to minimize problems and the possibility of litigation.

10.22 Cancelled or postponed contracts may be identified in the contractor's records or may be disclosed in other ways during the audit. For example, the auditor's confirmation procedures may disclose cancelled or postponed contracts. The auditor should then satisfy himself or herself that the open balance of accounts receivable, which may in effect be a claim, is valid and collectible.

10.23 For a contract that has been cancelled, the auditor should evaluate the contractor's right and ability to recover costs and damages under the contract. If the amounts that the contractor seeks to recover under the contracts are in dispute, the auditor should evaluate them as claims in accordance with the previous discussion on claims.

10.24 For contracts that have been postponed, the auditor should evaluate whether the estimated cost to complete is documented and reflects inflationary factors that may cause costs to increase because of the delay in the performance of the contract. The auditor should consider the reason for postponement and its ultimate implications because a postponement could ultimately lead to a cancellation with attendant problems relating to the recoverability of costs. In this area of the audit, the auditor should consider consultation with legal counsel in evaluating the client's contractual rights.

Collectibility

10.25 As work progresses on the contract, construction contractors may experience problems relating to the collectibility of receivables that differ from those found in industrial and commercial entities. Problems may result from the long period of the contract, the size of the contract, the possibility for disputes, the type of financing the customer has arranged, or the current economic environment. The contractor ordinarily should evaluate whether the customer has financial substance or has made financing arrangements through a third party with financial substance. The auditor might review the contractor's determination and also consider performing such auditing procedures as a review of financial statements of the customer or a review of the financing arrangements entered into by the customer with a third party, even though there may be no apparent indication that the receivable might not be collectible.

10.26 In the evaluation of the ability of the customer to satisfy his obligations, the auditor should also consider the stage of completion of the contract, the past payment performance of the customer, and the amount of the contract price yet to be billed under the contract—not solely the customer's ability to remit the year-end outstanding balance. In the event of indications that a customer may be unable to pay the contractor, the auditor should consider the extent to which bonding arrangements and lien rights will limit possible losses by the contractor. The auditor should consider whether lien rights have been filed to protect the contractor's rights. Some of the information obtained in the evaluation of collectibility may be useful in the audit of amounts recognized as income on the contract.

Liabilities Related to Contracts

10.27 The auditor should be satisfied that liabilities include not only amounts currently due but also retained percentages that apply to both subcontractors and suppliers who bill the contractor in that manner. The auditor might request confirmation of balances, as well as other relevant information, from specific suppliers and subcontractors. Exhibit 10-2 is a suggested confirmation form for subcontractors.

Exhibit 10-2

Sample Confirmation Request to Subcontractor[3]

Gentlemen:

Our independent auditors, [*name and address*], are engaged in an audit of our financial statements. For verification purposes only, would you kindly submit directly to them the following information with respect to each (or specific) contract(s) in force at [*date*]:

1. Original contract price $
2. Total approved change orders $
3. Total billings $
4. Total payments $
5. Total unpaid balance, including retentions $
6. Total retentions included in total balance due $
7. Total amount and details of pending extras and claims in process of preparation, if any (attach separate sheet if necessary) $
8. Estimated completion date

We have enclosed a self-addressed, stamped envelope for your convenience in replying directly to our auditors. Your prompt response will be greatly appreciated.

Very truly yours,

Enc.

10.28 The auditor should satisfy himself or herself that the contractor has made a proper cutoff and that all costs, including charges from subcontractors, have been recorded in the correct period. The auditor should also perform audit procedures to test whether charges by subcontractors are in accordance with the terms of their contracts and the work performed by the subcontractor and are not simply advances that may be allowable under contract terms. The amounts billable by a subcontractor under the terms of a contract is the amount that should be recorded in accounts payable; however, the actual work performed on the job represents the amount that should be recorded as allowable cost in determining the extent of progress toward completion. In reviewing liabilities, it is essential that the auditor be alert for indications of claims and extras that may be billed by the subcontractor. The review may also disclose amounts that should be accounted for as back charges to the subcontractor under the terms of the contract.

10.29 Invoices for services rendered should ordinarily be recorded as accounts payable even though the amount may not be used in measuring the performance to date on the contract. The auditor should satisfy himself or herself that the contractor has not included amounts not used in measuring performance in both the cost incurred to date and the estimated cost to complete.

10.30 The auditor should review older invoices and retentions included in accounts payable for an indication of defective work, failure on performance

---

[3] See footnote 2.

guarantees, or other contingencies that may not have been recorded on the contractor's records or included in the estimated cost to complete.

10.31 Under the Uniform Commercial Code (UCC), financial institutions and other creditors often file a notice of a security interest in personal property on which they have advanced credit. Notices may be filed with both the state and county in which the property is located. The auditor should consider sending UCC inquiry forms to states and counties in which the contractor has significant jobs. Such inquiries may disclose unrecorded liabilities and security interests, as defined in the UCC.

Contract Costs

10.32 The auditing of contract costs involves two primary areas: the accumulated costs to date and the estimated cost to complete. The auditor is reminded that in the audit of a contractor, the emphasis is on the contract and the proper recording of contract revenues and costs. The determination of the accuracy of both the costs incurred to date and the estimated costs to complete is necessary for each contract in order to determine whether the gross profit on a contract is recognized in conformity with generally accepted accounting principles. Further, the auditor's consideration of the proper allocation of costs to individual contracts is crucial to mitigate a possible significant fraud risk.

10.33 Income for a contractor is determined by the ultimate profit or estimated profit on each contract and is not based on the billings to date or the cost incurred to date. Under the completed-contract method, profit recognition is deferred until the contract is substantially completed; therefore, the cost incurred to date on uncompleted contracts is not reflected in the determination of current income unless a loss on the contract is anticipated. Conversely, the percentage-of-completion method requires that projected gross profit on the contract be estimated before the gross profit for the period under audit can be determined.

10.34 The audit considerations concerning both the accumulated cost to date and the estimated cost to complete are discussed in this section.

Costs Incurred to Date

10.35 The auditor should satisfy himself or herself that the contractor has properly recorded costs incurred to date by contract. The auditor should satisfy himself or herself that the contractor has included in accumulated contract costs identifiable direct and indirect costs and an acceptable and consistent allocation of overhead to specific contracts. For cost-plus contracts, the auditor should satisfy himself or herself that the contractor has not recognized contract revenue based on unreimbursable contract costs. The extent of substantive testing will depend on the auditor's assessment of the risks of material misstatement, as discussed in chapter 9.

Estimated Cost to Complete

10.36 One of the most important phases of the audit of a construction contractor relates to estimated costs to complete contracts in process because that information is used in determining the estimated final gross profit or loss on contracts. Estimated costs to complete involve expectations about future performance, and the auditor should (*a*) critically review representations of management, (*b*) obtain explanations of apparent disparities between estimates and past performance on contracts, experience on other contracts, and information gained in other phases of the audit, and (*c*) document the results of work in these areas. Because of the direct effect on the estimated interim and final revenue and gross profit or loss on the contract, the auditor should evaluate whether the contractor's estimate of cost to complete is reasonable, including any special provisions, for example, guaranteed maximum price shared savings provisions. AU-C section 540, *Auditing Accounting Estimates, Including Fair Value Accounting Estimates, and Related Disclosures*, provides guidance to auditors on obtaining and evaluating sufficient appropriate audit evidence to support significant accounting estimates in an audit of financial statements in accordance with GAAS.

10.37 The information that the auditor should consider using in the review of estimated costs to complete includes the following:

- The auditor's knowledge of internal control, with particular emphasis on the auditor's assessment of the risks of material misstatement in areas such as estimating and bidding; project management and contract evaluation; contract costs; and claims, extras, and back charges, including a summary of the results of internal audits and a discussion of the contractor's historical experience.
- A comparison of costs incurred to date plus estimated cost to complete with the original bid estimate, along with explanations of unusual variances and changes in trends.
- A summary of work performed to determine that actual or expected contract price and estimated costs to complete include price and quantity increases, penalties for termination or late completion, warranties or contract guarantees, and related items.
- A review of project engineers' reports and interim financial data, including reports and data issued after the balance sheet date, with explanations for unusual variances or changes in projections. Of particular importance would be a review of revised or updated estimates of cost to complete and a comparison of the estimates with the actual costs incurred after the balance sheet date. Contracts with margin percentages below the normal percentage range for the year, or historically, may call for particular attention.
- A review of information received from customers or other third parties in confirmations and in conversations about disputes, contract guarantees, and so forth that could affect total contract revenue and estimated cost to complete.
- Discussions with the contractor's engineering personnel and project managers who are familiar with, and responsible for, the contract in process.
- A review of the reports of independent architects and engineers.
- A review of information received from the contractor's attorney that relates to disputes and contingencies.

- Analytical procedures,[4] including comparing prior year's estimates with subsequent actual results and determining the reasonableness of the estimated gross profit percentage as compared to jobs completed during the current fiscal period.

10.38 Not all of the previously listed types of evidence are available for all audits of all construction contractors. The auditor should consider the sufficiency and appropriateness of each type of evidence in forming an opinion. The auditor's objective is to test the overall reasonableness of the estimated cost to complete in the light of the information obtained from those and other available sources.

Income Recognition

10.39 The amount and timing of income recognized from contracts depend primarily on the methods and bases used to account for those contracts, including those contracts that may be combined or segmented in accordance with the paragraphs that follow. The auditor should satisfy himself or herself that contracts are accounted for in accordance with FASB ASC 605-35, and that the guidance is applied consistently to all like contracts and in all periods. To form an opinion on the reasonableness of the amount and timing of income recognized, the auditor should obtain an overview of costs and revenues by contract.

10.40 As a result of the technological complexity or the nature of the contractor's work, the auditor might use the work of independent specialists, such as engineers, architects, and attorneys, to obtain audit evidence in various phases of the audit. For example, on some complex contracts, the auditor might use a specialist to evaluate the percentage of completion or the estimated cost to complete. AU-C section 620 provides guidance in this area.

10.41 Anticipated losses on contracts, including contracts on which work has not started, should be recognized in full at the earliest date at which they are determinable. In addition, the contractor ordinarily should consider the need to recognize other contract costs or revenue adjustments, such as guarantees or warranties, penalties for late completion, bonuses for early completion, unreimbursable costs under cost-plus contracts, and foreseeable losses arising from terminated contracts.

Evaluating the Acceptability of Income Recognition Methods

10.42 Paragraphs 1–2 of FASB ASC 605-35-25 provide guidance for evaluating the acceptability of a contractor's basic policy for income recognition. The audit procedures described in this and the preceding chapter are closely interrelated, and together they assist the auditor in satisfying himself or herself in regard to the acceptability of the method of income recognition and the bases of applying that method. The procedures include all those previously discussed (review of contracts; understanding the entity and its environment, including its internal control, particularly as it relates to costs and contract revenues; job site visits; and procedures applied in the audit of receivables, liabilities related

[4] Refer to the AICPA Audit Guide *Analytical Procedures*, which provides guidance on the effective use of analytical procedures with an emphasis on analytical procedures as substantive tests. This includes a discussion of AU-C section 520, *Analytical Procedures*, and the underlying concepts and definitions, a series of questions and answers, an illustrative case study, and an appendix that includes useful financial ratios.

to contracts, and contract costs) and the procedures discussed in this section on income recognition.

10.43 In evaluating the acceptability of the accounting method used by a contractor, the auditor should satisfy himself or herself that the contractor has followed the guidance in FASB ASC 605-35-25-57, which states that the use of the percentage-of-completion method as the basic accounting policy is considered preferable when reasonably dependable estimates can be made, and the contracts meet all the conditions specified. If contracts meet those conditions, FASB ASC 605-35-25-58 states that the presumption is a contractor has the ability to make estimates that are sufficiently dependable to justify the use of the percentage-of-completion method of accounting. Normally, as provided in FASB ASC 605-35-25-60, estimates of total contract revenue and total contract cost in single amounts should be used as the basis of accounting for contracts under the percentage-of-completion method. However, estimates based on ranges of amounts or on a breakeven or zero-profit basis are acceptable in circumstances described in FASB ASC 605-35-25-60. The auditor should satisfy himself or herself that the aforementioned guidance has been reasonably applied.

10.44 Paragraphs 79–81 of FASB ASC 605-35-25 discuss the considerations that should underlie the selection of a method of measuring the extent of progress toward completion under the percentage-of-completion method. The auditor should evaluate the methods used by the contractor in accordance with those considerations.

10.45 In evaluating the acceptability of the percentage-of-completion method as a contractor's basic accounting policy, as well as the acceptability of the basis used to measure the extent of progress toward completion, the auditor should consider procedures such as the following:

- Performing a risk assessment of all of the contracts, measuring degrees of risk based on, but not limited to, the following risks:
  - Phase of contract (percent complete)
  - Contracts with significant or unusual costs and estimated earnings in excess of billings
  - Contracts with estimated losses
  - Contracts with significant declines in estimates from the prior year
- Reviewing a selected sample of contracts to evaluate whether the contracts meet the basic conditions in FASB ASC 605-35-25-57 for use of the percentage-of-completion method
- Obtaining, reviewing, and evaluating documentation of estimates of contract revenues, costs, and the extent of progress toward completion for the selected sample of contracts
- Consulting, if necessary, with independent engineers or independent architects
- Obtaining and reviewing a representative sample of completed contracts to evaluate the quality of the contractor's original and periodic estimates of profit on those contracts
- Obtaining a representation from management on the acceptability of the method

10.46 If the contractor applies the percentage-of-completion method on the basis of estimates in terms of ranges or in terms of zero profit for any contracts, the auditor should obtain separate schedules for contracts accounted for on each of those bases and for contracts initially reported on those bases but changed to the normal basis during the period. For contracts in each of those categories, the auditor should consider the following procedures in evaluating the acceptability of those approaches to applying the percentage-of-completion method:

- For a selected sample of such contracts, obtaining documentation from management of the circumstances justifying the approaches
- Discussing with management personnel and, if necessary, independent architects and engineers the reasonableness of the approaches used for the sample of contracts selected in each category
- Obtaining representation from management on the circumstances justifying each of the approaches

10.47 Paragraphs 90–93 of FASB ASC 605-35-25 describe the appropriate circumstances for use of the completed-contract method as the basic accounting policy. When the lack of dependable estimates or inherent hazards cause forecasts to be doubtful, the completed-contract method is preferable. The completed-contract method may also be used as an entity's basic accounting policy in circumstances in which financial position and results of operations would not vary materially from those resulting from use of the percentage-of-completion method (for example, in circumstances in which an entity has primarily short-term contracts).

10.48 In evaluating whether the circumstances in the preceding paragraph exist, the auditor should consider the use of procedures such as the following:

- Reviewing the nature of the contractor's contracts and the period required to perform them
- Obtaining a schedule of uncompleted contracts at the beginning and end of the period and evaluating whether the volume is significant in relation to the volume of contracts started and completed during the period
- Estimating the effect of reporting on the percentage-of-completion basis and evaluating whether the results would produce a material difference in financial position or results of operations

The Percentage-of-Completion Method

10.49 The auditor's objective in examining contracts accounted for by the percentage-of-completion method is to determine that the income recognized during the current period is based on (*a*) the total gross profit projected for the contract on completion and (*b*) the work performed to date. The total gross profit expected from each contract is derived from an estimate of the final contract price less the total of contract costs to date and estimated cost to complete. The auditor tests those components in connection with other auditing procedures previously discussed.

10.50 The auditor should satisfy himself or herself that, in relation to the nature of the contract, the method selected and used by the contractor to measure progress (such as measures based on architectural or engineering estimates, cost-to-cost, labor hours, machine hours, or units produced) produces a reasonable measurement of the work performed to date. Information obtained from job site visits may be particularly useful in reviewing costs incurred to date when the cost-to-cost method is used. Such information may point out the need to disregard certain costs (such as advance billings by subcontractors, cost of undelivered materials, or cost of uninstalled materials) in order to measure more accurately the work performed to date. Contract billings to customers may signify the percentage of completion if the contract provisions require that billings be associated with various stages of work performed on the contract.

10.51 The auditor should examine unbilled contract revenues to determine the reasons that they have not been billed. If such revenues relate to change orders or claims, the auditor should evaluate the collectibility of the change orders or claims.

The Completed-Contract Method

10.52 The objectives of the auditor in examining contracts accounted for by the completed-contract method are to determine (*a*) the proper amount and accounting period for recognition of the profit from completed contracts, (*b*) the amount of anticipated losses, if any, on uncompleted contracts to be recognized in the current period, and (*c*) consistency in application of the method of determining completion.

10.53 The auditor should review events, contract costs, and contract billings subsequent to the end of the accounting period to obtain additional assurance that all contract revenues and related costs are included in the period in which the contracts are deemed to be substantially completed for income recognition purposes. As established in FASB ASC 605-35-25-96, a contract may be regarded as substantially completed, as a general rule, if remaining cost and potential risks are insignificant in amount. The overriding accounting objectives are to maintain consistency in determining when contracts are substantially completed and to avoid arbitrary acceleration or deferral of income.

Combining and Segmenting

10.54 Income recognition in a given period may be significantly affected by the combining or segmenting of contracts. In the course of the audit, the auditor may find that contracts have been, or in his or her opinion should have been, combined or segmented. The auditor should, therefore, evaluate the propriety of combining contracts or, conversely, segmenting components of a contract or a group of contracts in accordance with the criteria in paragraphs 3–14 of FASB ASC 605-35-25. In evaluating the propriety of combining a group of contracts and the propriety of segmenting a contract or a group of contracts, the auditor should satisfy himself or herself that the criteria are applied consistently to contracts with similar characteristics in similar circumstances. The auditor should consider procedures such as the following:

- Reviewing combined contracts to determine whether they meet the aforementioned criteria and reviewing a representative sample of other contracts to determine if any other contracts meet those criteria

- Reviewing contracts or groups of contracts that are reported on a segmented basis to determine whether they meet the aforementioned criteria and whether the criteria are applied consistently

Review of Earned Revenue

10.55 For significant contracts, the auditor should obtain and review working paper schedules that summarize contract information from the contractor's books and records together with audit data arising from the audit of contract activity. The schedules are valuable because they permit an orderly analysis of the relationship of costs and revenues on a contract-by-contract basis. Illustrations of such schedules, prepared for fixed-price contracts accounted for by the percentage-of-completion method, are presented in exhibits 10-3–10-4.

10.56 The illustrations are based on the assumption that the contractor determines the stage of completion and adjusts his accounts accordingly. Even so, as demonstrated by the illustrations, the schedules enable the auditor to pinpoint the need for adjustments.

10.57 Similar, although less detailed, schedules should also be considered for significant cost-plus contracts in process and for significant contracts closed during the period.

Analysis of Gross Profit Margins

10.58 Finally, the auditor should consider analyzing gross profit margins on contracts and investigating and obtaining explanations for contracts with unusually high or low profit margins in the light of present and past experience on similar contracts. The auditor should consider a review of the original estimates of any contracts in question and a comparison of the results on those contracts for the current period with the results of prior periods. Audit procedures performed might include comparison of profit margins recognized on open contracts (with the final results on similar closed contracts) and comparison of the final profit on closed contracts (with the estimated profit on those contracts in the prior year). Similarly, at or near the date of the auditor's report, the auditor should obtain the contractor's most recent interim financial statements and work-in-process analysis to review, among other things, the contractor's most recent cost estimates on contracts not completed at the balance sheet date. Paragraph .11 of AU-C section 560, *Subsequent Events and Subsequently Discovered Facts*, states that if as a result of this review and the additional procedures performed as required by paragraphs .09–.10 of AU-C section 560, the auditor identifies subsequent events that require adjustment of, or disclosure in, the financial statements, the auditor should determine whether each such event is appropriately reflected in the financial statements in accordance with the applicable financial reporting framework.

10.59 The auditor should consider maintaining a summary of the historical information (the most recent four to five years, preferably) developed in the analysis for a reference in future audits. As provided in paragraph .A38 of AU-C section 330, in certain circumstances, audit evidence obtained from previous audits may provide audit evidence, provided that the auditor has determined whether changes have occurred since the previous audit that may affect its relevance to the current audit.

The preceding paragraphs, in the section titled "Income Recognition" and all subsections within, will be deleted upon the effective date of FASB Accounting Standards Update (ASU) No. 2014-09, *Revenue from Contracts with Customers (Topic 606)*, and replaced with the following under the same section heading.[5]

Income Recognition

The amount and timing of income recognized from contracts depend primarily on the methods and bases used to account for those contracts. The auditor should be satisfied that contracts are accounted for in accordance with FASB ASC 606, and that the guidance is applied consistently to all like contracts and in all periods. To form an opinion on the reasonableness of the amount and timing of income recognized, the auditor should obtain an overview of costs and revenues by contract.

As a result of the technological complexity or the nature of the contractor's work, the auditor might use the work of independent specialists, such as engineers, architects, and attorneys, to obtain audit evidence in various phases of the audit. For example, on some complex contracts, the auditor might use a specialist to evaluate the percentage of completion or the estimated cost to complete. AU-C section 620 provides guidance in this area.

Anticipated losses on contracts, including contracts on which work has not started, should be recognized in full at the earliest date at which they are determinable.

Evaluating the Acceptability of Income Recognition Methods

FASB ASC 606-25 provide guidance for evaluating the acceptability of a contractor's basic policy for income recognition. The audit procedures described in this and the preceding chapter are closely interrelated, and together they assist the auditor in assessing the acceptability of the method of income recognition and the bases of applying that method. The procedures include all those previously discussed (review of contracts; understanding the entity and its environment, including its internal control, particularly as it relates to costs and contract revenues; job site visits; and procedures applied in the audit of receivables, liabilities related to contracts, and contract costs) and the procedures discussed in this section on income recognition.

---

[5] FASB Accounting Standards Update (ASU) No. 2014-09, *Revenue from Contracts with Customers (Topic 606)*, was issued in May 2014. Public business entities, certain not-for-profit entities, and certain employee benefit plans should apply the guidance in ASU No. 2014-09 as amended by FASB ASU No. 2015-14, *Revenue from Contracts with Customers (Topic 606): Deferral of the Effective Date*, to annual reporting periods beginning after December 15, 2017, including interim reporting periods within that reporting period. Earlier application is permitted only as of annual reporting periods beginning after December 15, 2016, including interim reporting periods within that reporting period.

All other entities should apply the guidance in ASU No. 2014-09 to annual reporting periods beginning after December 15, 2018, and interim reporting periods within annual reporting periods beginning after December 15, 2019. All other entities may apply the guidance in ASU No. 2014-09 earlier as of an annual reporting period beginning after December 15, 2016, including interim reporting periods within that reporting period. All other entities also may apply the guidance in ASU No. 2014-09 earlier as of an annual reporting period beginning after December 15, 2016, and interim reporting periods within annual reporting periods beginning one year after the annual reporting period in which the entity first applies the guidance in ASU No. 2014-09.

Readers are encouraged to read the full text of the FASB ASU, available at www.fasb.org. Readers should apply the appropriate guidance based on their facts and circumstances.

Combining Contracts

Income recognition in a given period may be significantly affected by the combining of contracts. In the course of the audit, the auditor may find that contracts have been, or in his or her opinion should have been, combined. The auditor should, therefore, evaluate the propriety of combining contracts in accordance with the criteria in paragraph 9 of FASB ASC 606-10-25. In evaluating the propriety of combining a group of contracts, the auditor should be satisfied that the criteria are applied consistently to contracts with similar characteristics in similar circumstances. The auditor should consider reviewing combined contracts to determine whether they meet the aforementioned criteria and reviewing a representative sample of other contracts to determine if any other contracts meet those criteria.

Review of Earned Revenue

For significant contracts, the auditor should obtain and review schedules to be included in audit documentation that summarize contract information from the contractor's books and records together with audit data arising from the audit of contract activity. The schedules are important because they permit an orderly analysis of the relationship of costs and revenues on a contract-by-contract basis.

Analysis of Gross Profit Margins

Finally, the auditor should consider analyzing gross profit margins on contracts and investigating and obtaining explanations for contracts with unusually high or low profit margins in the light of present and past experience on similar contracts. The auditor should consider a review of the original estimates of any contracts in question and a comparison of the results on those contracts for the current period with the results of prior periods. Audit procedures performed might include comparison of profit margins recognized on open contracts (with the final results on similar closed contracts) and comparison of the final profit on closed contracts (with the estimated profit on those contracts in the prior year). Similarly, at or near the date of the auditor's report, the auditor should obtain the contractor's most recent interim financial statements and work-in-process analysis to review, among other things, the contractor's most recent cost estimates on contracts not completed at the balance sheet date. Paragraph .11 of AU-C section 560, *Subsequent Events and Subsequently Discovered Facts*, states that if as a result of this review and the additional procedures performed as required by paragraphs .09–.10 of AU-C section 560, the auditor identifies subsequent events that require adjustment of, or disclosure in, the financial statements, the auditor should determine whether each such event is appropriately reflected in the financial statements in accordance with the applicable financial reporting framework.

The auditor should consider maintaining a summary of the historical information (the most recent four to five years, preferably) developed in the analysis for a reference in future audits. As provided in paragraph .A38 of AU-C section 330, in certain circumstances, audit evidence obtained from previous audits may provide audit evidence in the current period under audit, provided that the auditor has determined whether changes have occurred since the previous audit that may affect its relevance to the current audit.

Exhibit 10-3

This exhibit will be revised upon the effective date of FASB ASU No. 2014-09. As industry practice develops, updated presentation or guidance, as appropriate, will be included in a future edition of this guide.

XYZ Company, Inc.
Fixed-Price Contracts in Process
Summary of Original and Revised Contract Estimates
As of Balance Sheet Date

Contract Identification	*Original Contract Price*	*Original Estimate of Contract Costs*	*Original Estimate of Gross Profit*		*Net Changes in Contract Price*	*Revised Contract Price*	*Revised Estimate of Contract Costs*			*Revised Estimate of Gross Profit*		*% of Completion Measured by*
			Amount	*%*			*Costs to Date*	*Estimated Costs to Complete*	*Revised Total Costs*	*Amount*	*%*	
	(1)	(2)	(2)	(2)	(3)		(4)	(5)				(6)
A	$100,000	$55,000	$45,000	45 %	0	$100,000	$42,000	$18,000	$60,000	$40,000	40 %	Cost to cost
B	130,000	110,000	20,000	15.4%	20,000	150,000	80,000	40,000	120,000	30,000	20 %	Cu.Yds.Completed
C	175,000	125,000	50,000	28.6%	25,000	200,000	125,000	75,000	200,000	0	—	Labor hours
D	250,000	200,000	50,000	20%	150,000	400,000	270,000	330,000	600,000	(200,000)	—	Cost to cost

(1) Per original contract.
(2) Per original bid.
(3) Supported by change orders or claims, or both, meeting accounting criteria for inclusion.
(4) Per audit of contract costs.
(5) Per audit of estimated costs to complete.
(6) Reviewed for appropriateness and consistency.

Exhibit 10-4

This exhibit will be revised, as appropriate, upon the effective date of FASB ASU No.2014-09. As industry practice develops, updated presentation or guidance,as appropriate, will be included in a future edition of this guide.

XYZ Company, Inc.
Fixed-Price Contracts in Process
Analysis of Contract Status
As of Balance Sheet Date

	Per Contractor's Books and Records						*Auditor's Adjustment*				*Adjusted Gross Profit*					
					Gross Profit to Date						*To Date*		*Prior Periods*		*Current Period*	
Contract Identification	*Contract Billings to Date*	*Costs Incurred to Date*	*% Completed*	*Revenue Earned to Date*	*Amount*	*%*	*Revised % Completed*	*Revised Earned Revenue to Date*	*Revenue Adjustments*	*Provision for Projected Loss Adjustments*	*Amount*	*%*	*Amount*	*%*	*Amount*	*%*
	(1)	(2)	(3)	(4)			(5)	(6)	(7)	(7)	(8)	(8)	(9)	(8)	(8)	(8)
A	$80,000	$42,000	70%	$80,000	$38,000	47.5%	70%	70,000	($10,000) (A)		$28,000	40%	$20,250	45%	$7,750	31%
B	82,500	80,000	65%	97,500	17,500	17.9%	67%	100,500	3,000 (B)		20,500	20%	8,500	18.9%	12,000	21.6%
C	150,000	125,000	55%	110,000	(15,000)	—	62.5%	125,000	15,000 (C)		0	—	28600	28.6%	(28,600)	—
D	300,000	270,000	45%	300,000	30,000	10 %	45%	180,000	(120,000) (A)	110,000 (D)	(200,000)	—	—	—	(200,000)	—

(1) Per audit of contract billings.
(2) Per audit of contract costs.
(3) Management's estimate of completion.
(4) Per contract revenue accounts on books.
(5) Per auditor—based on review and analysis of costs, billings, management's estimate, of completion, job site visits.
(6) Result of applying revised percentage of completion to revised contract price.
(7) Adjustments to be reviewed with and accepted by management.
(8) Should be compared with prior periods and with similar contracts.
(9) Per audit of prior periods.
(A) Adjustment necessary to reduce recorded earned revenue and recognize excess billings.
(B) Adjustment necessary to increase recorded earned revenue and recognize unbilled revenue.
(C) Adjustment necessary to increase recorded earned revenue and reduce recorded excess billings in order to reflect projected "break-even" on contract. Remaining revenue ($75,000) now equals estimated costs to complete.
(D) Adjustment necessary to provide for balance of the total projected loss on contract. Remaining revenue ($220,000) now equals estimated costs to complete ($330,000) less provision for projected loss ($110,000).

Review of Backlog Information on Signed Contracts and Letters of Intent

10.60 The accounting section of this guide encourages contractors to present in the basic financial statements backlog information for signed contracts whose cancellation is not expected, and it suggests that contractors may include additional backlog information on letters of intent and a schedule showing backlog at the beginning of the year, new contracts awarded during the year, revenue recognized during the year, and backlog at the end of the year (see the section "Backlog on Existing Contracts" in chapter 6, "Financial Statement Presentation"). The presentation of such information helps users of the contractor's financial statements assess the contractor's current level of activity and prospects for maintaining that level of activity in future periods.

10.61 Information on signed contracts whose cancellation by the parties is not expected is within the scope of an audit of the contractor's financial statements. If a contractor elects to present backlog information on signed contracts outside of the basic financial statements, in an auditor-submitted document (that is, rather than as a note to the financial statements), paragraph .09 of AU-C section 725, *Supplementary Information in Relation to the Financial Statements as a Whole*,[6] states that the auditor should report on the supplementary information in either (*a*) an other-matter paragraph in accordance with AU-C section 706, *Emphasis-of-Matter Paragraphs and Other-Matter Paragraphs in the Independent Auditor's Report*, or (*b*) in a separate report on the supplementary information.

10.62 Although an auditor has no obligation to apply auditing procedures to supplementary information presented outside the basic financial statements, the auditor may choose to modify or redirect certain of the procedures to be applied in the audit of the basic financial statements so that the auditor may express an opinion on the supplementary information in relation to the financial statements as a whole. Such procedures should include a review of the information and an evaluation of its completeness in light of other audit procedures for contract receivables, contract-related liabilities, contract costs, and contract revenues. For that purpose, the auditor should obtain a schedule of all uncompleted signed contracts showing for each contract total estimated revenue, total estimated cost, earned revenue to date, costs incurred to date, and cost of earned revenue.

10.63 If a contractor elects to present backlog information for both signed contracts and letters of intent and the auditor intends to express an opinion on this accompanying information, the auditor's responsibility for the information is less clear because letters of intent are not normally within the scope of the audit of a contractor's financial statements. The auditor may, however, be able to satisfy himself or herself regarding the completeness and reliability of the information on letters of intent. The auditor should consider obtaining a schedule of signed letters of intent, confirming the letters with customers, and reviewing their terms with the contractor's legal counsel.

---

[6] Refer to chapter 11, "Other Auditing Considerations," for a detailed discussion of auditing supplementary information in relation to the financial statements as a whole and appendix I, "Reporting on Supplementary Information in Relation to the Financial Statements as a Whole," for a detailed discussion of reporting on supplementary information in relation to the financial statements as a whole.

10.64 As indicated in chapter 6, the presentation of backlog information by a contractor is desirable only if a reasonably dependable determination of total revenue and a reasonably dependable estimate of total cost under signed contracts or letters of intent can be made, and the information on signed contracts should be segregated from the information on letters of intent.

Management Representations

10.65 The auditor must obtain written representations from management in accordance with the requirements of AU-C section 580, *Written Representations*. Written representations from management should be obtained for all financial statements and periods covered by the auditor's report.[7] The specific written representations to be obtained depend on the circumstances of the engagement and the nature and basis of the presentation of the financial statements. AU-C section 580 lists matters ordinarily included in management's representation letter. Additional representations specific to construction contractors that may be obtained include the following:

- Method of income recognition used
- Provisions for anticipated losses on contracts
- Unapproved change orders, extras, claims, and back charges, as well as contract postponements or cancellations
- Backlog information if presented in the financial statements
- Contracts completed during the year and in process as of the balance sheet date if presented in the financial statements
- Joint venture participations and other related party transactions

In addition to the foregoing items, the auditor should obtain specific management representations relating to all the types of matters suggested in AU-C section 580 that are relevant to the engagement.

---

[7] Technical Questions and Answers (Q&A) section 8900.11, "Management Representations Regarding Prior Periods Presented That Were Audited by Predecessor Auditor" (*Technical Questions and Answers*), addresses a situation where the prior period financial statements were audited by a predecessor auditor, and the predecessor auditor's report on the prior period's financial statements is not reissued. The auditor's report will express an opinion on the current period's financial statements and will include an other-matter paragraph in accordance with paragraph .54 of AU-C section 700, *Forming an Opinion and Reporting on Financial Statements*. The Q&A addresses whether the auditor is required to obtain a representation letter covering the prior period financial statements.

Chapter 11

Other Audit Considerations

11.01 This chapter addresses additional audit considerations that may be relevant in audits of construction contractors. They include affiliated entities, capitalization and cash flow, types of auditor's reports, and legal and regulatory requirements.

Affiliated Entities

11.02 In the construction industry, contractors frequently participate in joint ventures or have a direct or indirect affiliation with other entities and, as a consequence, are frequently involved in related party transactions as the term *related parties* is defined in FASB *Accounting Standards Codification* (ASC) 850, *Related Party Disclosures*. The prevalence of such arrangements in the industry can be attributed to factors such as legal liability, taxation, competition, ownership and operating arrangements, labor and labor union considerations, and regulatory requirements. Auditing and reporting considerations appropriate in the circumstances are discussed in this section.

Participation in Joint Ventures

11.03 The auditor reviews a contractor's participations in joint ventures to evaluate whether investments in joint ventures are reported in accordance with the recommendations in chapter 3, "Accounting for and Reporting Investments in Construction Joint Ventures," of this guide. The following are among the factors that may influence the auditor's evaluation:

- The method or methods of reporting joint venture investments
- The nature of capital contributions and the methods of recording capital contributions
- The timeliness of the available financial statements of joint ventures in relation to those of the reporting investor
- The appropriateness of the accounting for joint venture losses that exceed a contractor's loans and investments
- The adequacy of joint venture related disclosures in the contractor's financial statements

11.04 The auditor should review joint venture agreements and document a contractor's participation. Information that the auditor might consider documenting includes the following:

- Capital contributions and funding requirements of the venture participants
- Ownership percentages
- Profit or loss participation ratios
- Duration of the venture
- Performance requirements of the venture participants
- Financial guarantees or recourse, or both, between the parties and to outside parties

11.05 The audit considerations for a contractor's participation in a partnership (for example, in a real estate partnership) are similar to those for participation in corporate joint ventures. They may differ primarily in relation to the contractor's unlimited liability as a general partner for partnership obligations.

11.06 For partnership interests, the auditor might document the following information:

- The extent and nature of fees and other amounts to be paid by the partnership to the contractor and the conditions and events that would require such payments
- The contractor's obligations to the partnership for capital contributions and other funding
- Performance and other requirements of the contractor as a general partner and specified penalties for nonperformance, if any
- Profit participation ratios of the partners and events or conditions that change such ratios
- The duration of the partnership

11.07 The auditor should assess the economic and tax incentives underlying the creation of the partnership, the events requiring capital contribution installments by limited partners, and temporary and permanent financing arrangements and related costs. The auditor should also assess the extent of actual and contingent obligations that arise from the contractor's role as a general partner. To that end, the auditor should review the financial condition of the other general partners and their ability to participate in the funding of required capital contributions, partnership obligations, and partnership losses, if any. The inability of other general partners to provide their share of such funding may require the contractor to recognize additional obligations based on the contractor's legal liability as a general partner for all partnership obligations.

11.08 For any type of venture, the auditor should evaluate the nature of the venture, the scope of its operations, and the extent of involvement of each participant. To further the auditor's understanding, the auditor should obtain financial statements of the venture entity for the period under review. AU-C section 600, *Special Considerations—Audits of Group Financial Statements (Including the Work of Component Auditors)*,[1] provides guidance and establishes requirements for audit engagements in which the financial statements of the venture are audited by another independent auditor. In most situations, the joint venture entity will be deemed as a component under AU-C section 600.

11.09 If the venture's financial statements are unaudited, the principal auditor should perform such procedures as he or she deems necessary in the circumstances to obtain sufficient appropriate audit evidence. For determining what procedures to perform, AU-C section 501, *Audit Evidence—Specific Considerations for Selected Items*, provides guidance and establishes requirements on auditing investments in debt and equity securities and investments accounted for under FASB ASC 323, *Investments—Equity Method and Joint Ventures*. When such procedures cannot be performed, and the resulting effect is a restriction on the scope of the audit, AU-C section 705, *Modifications to the Opinion in the Independent Auditor's Report*, provide applicable guidance.

---

[1] All AU-C sections can be found in AICPA *Professional Standards*.

Auditing Affiliated Entities and Related Party Transactions

11.10 An auditor engaged to audit one of a group of affiliated entities that comprises an economic unit may find that an examination of the records of that entity does not satisfy him in regard to such aspects as substance, nature, business purpose, and transfer prices of significant transactions between the parties. AU-C section 550, *Related Parties*, provides guidance and establishes requirements for identifying and reporting on related party transactions, including a consideration of fraud. The auditor should be aware of the possible existence of material related party transactions that could affect the financial statements and of common ownership or management control relationships, even though no transactions exist. The auditing of affiliated entities and related party transactions will often necessitate the consideration of the applicability of accounting, presentation and disclosure requirements for variable interest entities. Consolidated or combined financial statements in place of, or supplementary to, the separate financial statements of the entity being audited may sometimes be necessary to present the financial position, results of operations, and cash flows of the entity being audited in accordance with the recommendations in chapter 4, "Financial Reporting by Affiliated Entities," of this guide.

11.11 In addition, an understanding of the entity's related party relationships and transactions is relevant to the auditor's evaluation of whether one or more fraud risk factors are present, as required by AU-C section 240, *Consideration of Fraud in a Financial Statement Audit*, because fraud may be more easily committed through related parties.

Participation in a Group Audit[2]

11.12 AU-C section 600 identifies a *group audit* as the audit of group financial statements, that is, financial statements that include the financial information of more than one component. A group audit exists, for example, when management prepares financial information that is included in the group financial statements related to a function, process, product or service, or geographical location (subsidiary in a foreign country).

11.13 A group audit engagement includes the following entities and actors:

- The *component* is an entity or business activity for which group or component management prepares financial information that is required by the applicable financial reporting framework to be included in the group financial statements.
- The *component auditor* is the auditor who performs work on the financial information of a component that will be used as audit evidence for the group audit. A component auditor may be part of the group engagement partner's firm, a network firm of the group engagement partner's firm, or another firm.
- The *group engagement partner* is the partner or other person in the firm who is responsible for the group audit engagement and its performance and for the auditor's report on the group financial

---

[2] For more information on AU-C section 600, *Special Considerations—Audits of Group Financial Statements (Including the Work of Component Auditors)*, see Audit Risk Alert *Understanding the Responsibilities of Auditors for Audits of Group Financial Statements*.

statements that is issued on behalf of the firm. When joint auditors conduct the group audit, the joint engagement partners and their engagement teams collectively constitute the group engagement partner and the group engagement team.

11.14 Auditors of construction contractors, due to the potential for the involvement of component auditors in audit processes such as job site visits, inventory considerations and joint venture audits, should carefully consider the requirements of AU-C section 600 when planning and performing their audits.

Capitalization and Cash Flow

11.15 Contractors often follow practices that accelerate the cash collections to be generated from a contract. The practices include the use of unbalanced bids and other front-end loading procedures that allocate a relatively larger portion of the total contract price to phases of work likely to be completed in early stages of the contract than to phases likely to be completed later. Also, overestimating the percentage of work completed in computing billings on contracts may have a similar effect on cash collections and may result in a potential misstatement of the financial statements.

11.16 If a contractor incurs substantial losses on contracts that have been front-end loaded, a cash deficiency toward the end of those contracts may be experienced. The deficiency may prevent the contractor from meeting current obligations, and the contractor may have to front-end load new contracts to generate funds to meet those obligations. The necessity to generate cash may cause the contractor to accept jobs that are only marginally profitable.

11.17 Therefore, the auditor should review uncompleted contracts not only to assess the adequacy of provisions for anticipated losses in the current period but also to determine the effect of projected cash receipts and payments on the contractor's cash position and ability to meet current obligations.

Types of Auditor's Reports on Financial Statements[3]

11.18 The auditor's conclusion to issue an unmodified opinion on the financial statements may be expressed only when the auditor has formed such an opinion on the basis of an audit performed in accordance with generally accepted auditing standards (GAAS). When evaluating the quantity and quality of audit evidence, and thus its sufficiency and appropriateness, to support the audit opinion, AU-C section 500, *Audit Evidence*, provides applicable guidance. Restrictions on the scope of the audit, the inability to obtain sufficient competent audit evidence, or an inadequacy in the accounting records may require the auditor to qualify his or her opinion or to disclaim an opinion as appropriate in the circumstances. The following are examples of situations that may cause the auditor to modify his or her standard report on the financial statements:

- The auditor is unable to evaluate the propriety or collectibility of significant amounts of contract revenue related to claims. Those circumstances may require the auditor to issue a qualified opinion or disclaim an opinion, depending on the particular circumstances.

---

[3] See appendix K, "The Auditor's Report," for further discussion and illustrative examples of auditor's reports meeting the requirements of AU-C section 700, *Forming an Opinion and Reporting on Financial Statements*.

- A contractor does not maintain detailed cost records by contract, and the auditor is unable to perform extended auditing procedures to obtain sufficient appropriate audit evidence that the data purporting to represent accumulated costs to date are reasonably correct. In this situation, a modified opinion may be appropriate.
- An entity has cash problems because of undercapitalization or because losses have eroded its net worth and threaten its ability to continue to operate as a viable entity. When, in such a situation, the auditor has evaluated management's plans and concludes that substantial doubt about the entity's ability to continue as a going concern for a reasonable period of time exists, the auditor should (*a*) consider the adequacy of disclosure about the entity's possible inability to continue as a going concern for a reasonable period of time, and (*b*) include an emphasis-of-matter paragraph in the audit report to reflect his or her conclusion in accordance with AU-C section 570, *The Auditor's Consideration of an Entity's Ability to Continue as a Going Concern*.

Going Concern Considerations

11.19 AU-C section 570 addresses the auditor's responsibilities in the audit of financial statements relating to the entity's ability to continue as a going concern and the implications for the auditor's report and applies to all audits of a complete set of financial statements, regardless of whether the financial statements are prepared in accordance with a general purpose or a special purpose framework.

11.20 The following paragraphs summarize some of the major provisions of AU-C section 570 but are not intended as a substitute for reviewing relevant sections of AU-C section 570 in their entirety.
The objectives of the auditor are to

a. obtain sufficient appropriate audit evidence regarding, and to conclude on, the appropriateness of management's use of the going concern basis of accounting, when relevant, in the preparation of the financial statements.

b. conclude, based on the audit evidence obtained, whether substantial doubt about an entity's ability to continue as a going concern for a reasonable period of time exists.

c. evaluate the possible financial statement effects, including the adequacy of disclosure regarding the entity's ability to continue as a going concern for a reasonable period of time.

d. report in accordance with this AU-C section 570.

11.21 Additional care should be given when management's plans, regarding the entity's ability to continue as a going concern, include financial support by third parties or the entity's owner-manager and such support is necessary in supporting management's assertions about the entity's ability to continue as a going concern for a reasonable period of time. In this situation, the auditor should obtain sufficient appropriate audit evidence about the following:

a. The intent of such supporting parties to provide the necessary financial support, including written evidence of such intent, and *b.* The ability of such supporting parties to provide the necessary financial support.

The failure to obtain the written evidence required by item *a* constitutes a lack of sufficient appropriate audit evidence regarding the intent of the supporting parties to provide financial support. Therefore, the auditor should conclude that management's plans are insufficient to alleviate the determination that substantial doubt exists about the entity's ability to continue as a going concern for a reasonable period of time.

11.22 AU-C section 570 defines a *reasonable period of time* as the period of time required by the applicable financial reporting framework or, if no such requirement exists, within one year after the date that the financial statements are issued (or within one year after the date that the financial statements are available to be issued, when applicable).

11.23 Based on the audit evidence obtained, the auditor should conclude whether, in the auditor's judgment, there are conditions or events, considered in the aggregate, that raise substantial doubt about an entity's ability to continue as a going concern for a reasonable period of time.

11.24 If the financial statements have been prepared using the going concern basis of accounting but, in the auditor's judgment, management's use of the going concern basis of accounting in the preparation of the financial statements is inappropriate, the auditor should express an adverse opinion.

11.25 If, after considering identified conditions or events and management's plans, the auditor concludes that substantial doubt about the entity's ability to continue as a going concern for a reasonable period of time remains, the auditor should include an emphasis-of-matter paragraph in the auditor's report.

11.26 The emphasis-of-matter paragraph about the entity's ability to continue as a going concern for a reasonable period of time should be expressed through the use of terms consistent with those included in the applicable financial reporting framework. In a going concern emphasis-of-matter paragraph, the auditor should not use conditional language concerning the existence of substantial doubt about the entity's ability to continue as a going concern for a reasonable period of time.

11.27 If adequate disclosure about an entity's ability to continue as a going concern for a reasonable period of time is not made in the financial statements, the auditor should express a qualified opinion or adverse opinion, as appropriate, in accordance with AU-C section 705.

Supplementary Information in Relation to the Financial Statements as a Whole[4]

11.28 AU-C section 725, *Supplementary Information in Relation to the Financial Statements as a Whole*, defines *supplementary information* as information presented outside the basic financial statements, excluding required

[4] See appendix I, "Reporting on Supplementary Information in Relation to the Financial Statements as a Whole," for a discussion of reporting on supplementary information in relation to the financial statements as a whole, including example supplementary information and an illustrative auditor's report example.

supplementary information that is not considered necessary for the financial statements to be fairly presented in accordance with the applicable financial reporting framework. Such information may be presented in a document containing the audited financial statements or separate from the financial statements.

11.29 The objective of the auditor, when engaged to report on supplementary information in relation to the financial statements as a whole, is to evaluate the presentation of the supplementary information in relation to the financial statements as a whole and to report on whether the supplementary information is fairly stated, in all material respects, in relation to the financial statements as a whole.

11.30 In order to opine on whether supplementary information is fairly stated, in all material respects, in relation to the financial statements as a whole, the auditor should determine that the supplementary information was derived from, and relates directly to, the underlying accounting and other records used to prepare the financial statements and relates to the same period as the financial statements. Further, the auditor must have issued an audit report on the financial statements that contained neither an adverse opinion nor a disclaimer of opinion and the supplementary information will accompany those audited financial statements, or such audited financial statements will be made readily available by the entity.

11.31 The auditor should obtain the agreement of management that it acknowledges and understands its responsibility for the preparation of the supplementary information in accordance with the applicable criteria. Management must also acknowledge that it will include the auditor's report on the supplementary information in any document that contains the supplementary information and that indicates that the auditor has reported on such supplementary information.

11.32 The auditor should also obtain the agreement of management that management will present the supplementary information with the audited financial statements or, if the supplementary information will not be presented with the audited financial statements, to make the audited financial statements readily available to the intended users of the supplementary information no later than the date of issuance by the entity of the supplementary information and the auditor's report thereon.

11.33 In addition to the procedures performed during the audit of the financial statements, in order to opine on whether supplementary information is fairly stated, in all material respects, in relation to the financial statements as a whole, the auditor should perform the following procedures using the same materiality level used in the audit of the financial statements:

a. Inquire of management about the purpose of the supplementary information and the criteria used by management to prepare the supplementary information, such as an applicable financial reporting framework, criteria established by a regulator, a contractual agreement, or other requirements.

b. Determine whether the form and content of the supplementary information complies with the applicable criteria.

c. Obtain an understanding about the methods of preparing the supplementary information and determine whether the methods of preparing the supplementary information have changed from those used in the prior period and, if the methods have changed, the reasons for such changes.

d. Inquire of management about any significant assumptions or interpretations underlying the measurement or presentation of the supplementary information.

e. Compare and reconcile the supplementary information to the underlying accounting and other records used in preparing the financial statements or to the financial statements themselves.

f. Evaluate the appropriateness and completeness of the supplementary information, considering the results of the procedures performed and other knowledge obtained during the audit of the financial statements.

g. Obtain written representations from management

i. that it acknowledges its responsibility for the presentation of the supplementary information in accordance with the applicable criteria;

ii. that it believes the supplementary information, including its form and content, is fairly presented in accordance with the applicable criteria;

iii. that the methods of measurement or presentation have not changed from those used in the prior period or, if the methods of measurement or presentation have changed, the reasons for such changes;

iv. about any significant assumptions or interpretations underlying the measurement or presentation of the supplementary information; and

v. that when the supplementary information is not presented with the audited financial statements, management will make the audited financial statements readily available to the intended users of the supplementary information no later than the date of issuance by the entity of the supplementary information and the auditor's report thereon.

11.34 The auditor has no responsibility for the consideration of subsequent events with respect to the supplementary information. However, if information comes to the auditor's attention prior to the release of the auditor's report on the financial statements regarding subsequent events that affect the financial statements, or subsequent to the release of the auditor's report on the financial statements regarding facts that, had they been known to the auditor at the date of the auditor's report, may have caused the auditor to revise the auditor's report, the auditor should apply the relevant requirements in AU-C section 560, *Subsequent Events and Subsequently Discovered Facts*.

11.35 In accordance with paragraph .09 of AU-C section 725, the other-matter paragraph or separate report should include the following elements:

- A statement that the audit was conducted for the purpose of forming an opinion on the financial statements as a whole
- A statement that the supplementary information is presented for purposes of additional analysis and is not a required part of the financial statements

- A statement that the supplementary information is the responsibility of management and was derived from, and relates directly to, the underlying accounting and other records used to prepare the financial statements
- A statement that the supplementary information has been subjected to the auditing procedures applied in the audit of the financial statements and certain additional procedures, including comparing and reconciling such information directly to the underlying accounting and other records used to prepare the financial statements or to the financial statements themselves and other additional procedures, in accordance with auditing standards generally accepted in the United States of America
- If the auditor issues an unmodified opinion on the financial statements and the auditor has concluded that the supplementary information is fairly stated, in all material respects, in relation to the financial statements as a whole, a statement that, in the auditor's opinion, the supplementary information is fairly stated, in all material respects, in relation to the financial statements as a whole
- If the auditor issues a qualified opinion on the financial statements and the qualification has an effect on the supplementary information, a statement that, in the auditor's opinion, except for the effects on the supplementary information of (refer to the paragraph in the auditor's report explaining the qualification), such information is fairly stated, in all material respects, in relation to the financial statements as a whole

11.36 The date of the auditor's report on the supplementary information in relation to the financial statements as a whole should not be earlier than the date on which the auditor completed the procedures required in paragraph 11.23.

Additional Considerations

11.37 When the auditor's report on the audited financial statements contains an adverse opinion or a disclaimer of opinion and the auditor has been engaged to report on whether supplementary information is fairly stated, in all material respects, in relation to such financial statements as a whole, the auditor is precluded from expressing an opinion on the supplementary information. When permitted by law or regulation, the auditor may withdraw from the engagement to report on the supplementary information. If the auditor does not withdraw, the auditor's report on the supplementary information should state that because of the significance of the matter disclosed in the auditor's report, it is inappropriate to, and the auditor does not, express an opinion on the supplementary information.

11.38 If the auditor concludes, on the basis of the procedures performed, that the supplementary information is materially misstated in relation to the financial statements as a whole, the auditor should discuss the matter with management and propose appropriate revision of the supplementary information. If management does not revise the supplementary information, the auditor should either

- modify the auditor's opinion on the supplementary information and describe the misstatement in the auditor's report, or
- if a separate report is being issued on the supplementary information, withhold the auditor's report on the supplementary information.

Auditor's Communications Related to Internal Control Matters

11.39 Whenever an auditor expresses an opinion (including a disclaimer of opinion) on the financial statements of a nonissuer, AU-C section 265, *Communicating Internal Control Related Matters Identified in an Audit*, states that the auditor must communicate, in writing, to those charged with governance, significant deficiencies or material weaknesses identified during the audit, including those that were remediated during the audit. The communication required by AU-C section 265 includes significant deficiencies and material weaknesses identified and communicated to management and those charged with governance in prior audits but not yet remediated. The written communication should be made no later than 60 days following the report release date. Nothing precludes the auditor from communicating to management and those charged with governance other matters that the auditor believes to be of potential benefit to the entity or that the auditor has been requested to communicate, which may include, for example, control deficiencies that are not significant deficiencies or material weaknesses. The auditor should not issue a written communication stating that no significant deficiencies were identified during the audit because of the potential for misinterpretation of the limited degree of assurance provided by such a communication. See paragraphs 9.07–.19 of this guide for additional guidance regarding auditor communication, including considerations under AU-C section 260, *The Auditor's Communication With Those Charged With Governance*.

Legal and Regulatory Considerations

State Statutes Affecting Construction Contractors

11.40 The auditor should be aware of the existence in some states of *lien* laws. Those laws vary from state to state but generally provide that funds received or receivable by a contractor constitute trust funds that may only be used to pay specified contract-related costs. The auditor should review with the contractor and the contractor's counsel the applicable statute in each state in which the contractor operates to evaluate whether amounts that constitute trust funds under those statutes have been properly applied. Other state statutes may also have audit or disclosure requirements. The auditor should consider such statutes in the performance of an audit and in the evaluation of the adequacy of financial statement disclosures.

The Auditor's Consideration of Compliance With Laws and Regulations

11.41 As part of obtaining an understanding of the entity and its environment, in accordance with AU-C section 315, *Understanding the Entity and Its Environment and Assessing the Risks of Material Misstatement*, the auditor should obtain a general understanding of the legal and regulatory framework applicable to the entity and the industry or sector in which the entity operates, as well as how the entity is complying with that framework.

11.42 The auditor should perform inquiry of management and, when appropriate, those charged with governance about whether the entity is in compliance with such laws and regulations and should inspect correspondence, if any, with relevant licensing or regulatory authorities. For example, issues of noncompliance in the construction industry may include instances of nonadherence to competitive bidding rules, illegal payments to government officials to obtain favorable status, or falsifying employment records or documentation. These audit procedures may identify instances of noncompliance with other laws and regulations that may have a material effect on the financial statements.

11.43 During the audit, the auditor should remain alert to the possibility that other audit procedures applied may bring instances of noncompliance or suspected noncompliance with laws and regulations to the auditor's attention.

Reporting of Identified or Suspected Noncompliance

11.44 Unless all of those charged with governance are involved in management of the entity and aware of matters involving identified or suspected noncompliance already communicated by the auditor, the auditor should communicate with those charged with governance matters involving noncompliance with laws and regulations that come to the auditor's attention during the course of the audit, other than when the matters are clearly inconsequential. If, in the auditor's professional judgment, this noncompliance is believed to be intentional and material, the auditor should communicate the matter to those charged with governance as soon as practicable.

11.45 If the auditor suspects that management or those charged with governance are involved in noncompliance, the auditor should communicate the matter to the next higher level of authority at the entity, if it exists. When no higher authority exists, or if the auditor believes that the communication may not be acted upon or is unsure about the person to whom to report, the auditor should consider the need to obtain legal advice.

11.46 If the auditor concludes that the noncompliance has a material effect on the financial statements, and it has not been adequately reflected in the financial statements, the auditor should, in accordance with AU-C section 705, express a qualified or adverse opinion on the financial statements.

11.47 The auditor should include in the audit documentation a description of the identified or suspected noncompliance with laws and regulations and the results of discussion with management and, when applicable, those charged with governance and other parties inside or outside the entity.

Governmental Prequalification Reporting

11.48 Contractors are often required to file reports with agencies of the federal, state, or county governments in order to qualify for bidding on or performing work for such agencies. The report format required by the regulatory agencies may include preprinted auditors' reports, which differ from reports issued in conformity with GAAS.

11.49 If the auditor is required by law or regulation to use a specific layout, form, or wording of the auditor's report, the auditor's report should refer to GAAS only if the auditor's report includes, at a minimum, each of the following elements:

a. A title

b. An addressee

c. An introductory paragraph that identifies the special purpose financial statements audited

d. A description of the responsibility of management for the preparation and fair presentation of the special purpose financial statements

e. A reference to management's responsibility for determining that the applicable financial reporting framework is acceptable in the circumstances when required by paragraph .18*a* of AU-C section 800, *Special Considerations—Audits of Financial Statements Prepared in Accordance With Special Purpose Frameworks*

f. A description of the purpose for which the financial statements are prepared when required by paragraph .18*b* of AU-C section 800

g. A description of the auditor's responsibility to express an opinion on the special purpose financial statements and the scope of the audit, that includes

  i. A reference to GAAS and, if applicable, the law or regulation

  ii. A description of an audit in accordance with those standards

h. An opinion paragraph containing an expression of opinion on the special purpose financial statements and a reference to the special purpose framework used to prepare the financial statements (including identifying the origin of the framework) and, if applicable, an opinion on whether the special purpose financial statements are presented fairly, in all material respects, in accordance with U.S. generally accepted accounting principles when required by paragraph .21 of AU-C section 800

i. An *emphasis-of-matter* paragraph that indicates that the financial statements are prepared in accordance with a special purpose framework when required by paragraph .19 of AU-C section 800

j. An *other-matter* paragraph that restricts the use of the auditor's report when required by paragraph .20 of AU-C section 800

k. The auditor's signature

l. The auditor's city and state

m. The date of the auditor's report

11.50 If the prescribed specific layout, form, or wording of the auditor's report is not acceptable or would cause an auditor to make a statement that the auditor has no basis to make, the auditor should reword the printed forms or schedules of report or attach an appropriately worded separate report.

Chapter 12

Consideration of Fraud in a Financial Statement

12.01 AU-C section 240, *Consideration of Fraud in a Financial Statement Audit*,[1] is the primary source of authoritative guidance about an auditor's responsibilities concerning the consideration of fraud in a financial statement audit. AU-C section 240 establishes standards and provides guidance to auditors in fulfilling their responsibility to plan and perform the audit to obtain reasonable assurance about whether the financial statements are free of material misstatement, whether caused by error or fraud, as stated in AU-C section 200, *Overall Objectives of the Independent Auditors and the Conduct of an Audit in Accordance With Generally Accepted Auditing Standards*.

12.02 Two types of misstatements that are relevant to the auditor's consideration of fraud in a financial statement audit are misstatements arising from fraudulent financial reporting and misstatements arising from misappropriation of assets. Additionally, three conditions generally are present when fraud occurs. First, management or other employees have an *incentive* or are under *pressure,* which provides a reason to commit fraud. Second, circumstances exist — for example, the absence of controls, ineffective controls, or the ability of management to override controls — that provide a perceived *opportunity* for a fraud to be perpetrated. Third, those involved are able to *rationalize* committing a fraudulent act.

The Importance of Exercising Professional Skepticism

12.03 Because of the characteristics of fraud, the auditor's exercise of professional skepticism is important when considering the risk of material misstatement due to fraud. Professional skepticism is an attitude that includes a questioning mind and a critical assessment of audit evidence. The auditor should conduct the engagement with a mindset recognizing the possibility that a material misstatement due to fraud could exist, notwithstanding the auditor's past experience of the honesty and integrity of the entity's management and those charged with governance. Furthermore, professional skepticism requires an ongoing questioning of whether the information and audit evidence obtained suggests that a material misstatement due to fraud may exist.

Discussion Among Engagement Personnel Regarding the Risks of Material Misstatement Due to Fraud

12.04 AU-C section 315, *Understanding the Entity and Its Environment and Assessing the Risks of Material Misstatement*, requires a discussion among the key engagement team members, including the engagement partner, and a determination by the engagement partner of which matters are to be communicated to those team members not involved in the discussion. This discussion should include an exchange of ideas or brainstorming among the engagement team members about how and where the entity's financial statements might

[1] All AU-C sections can be found in AICPA *Professional Standards*.

be susceptible to material misstatement due to fraud, how management could perpetrate and conceal fraudulent financial reporting, and how assets of the entity could be misappropriated.

12.05 The discussion should occur setting aside beliefs that the engagement team members may have that management and those charged with governance are honest and have integrity, and should, in particular, also address

a. known external and internal factors affecting the entity that may create an incentive or pressure for management or others to commit fraud, provide the opportunity for fraud to be perpetrated, and indicate a culture or environment that enables management or others to rationalize committing fraud;

b. the risk of management override of controls;

c. consideration of circumstances that might be indicative of earnings management or manipulation of other financial measures and the practices that might be followed by management to manage earnings or other financial measures that could lead to fraudulent financial reporting;

d. the importance of maintaining professional skepticism throughout the audit regarding the potential for material misstatement due to fraud; and

e. how the auditor might respond to the susceptibility of the entity's financial statements to material misstatement due to fraud.

Communication among the engagement team members about the risks of material misstatement due to fraud should continue throughout the audit, particularly upon discovery of new facts during the audit.

12.06 Although there certainly are a number of large national and international construction contractors, some of which are public entities, the vast majority of contractors are privately owned businesses. The latter group within the construction industry tends to be dominated by a large number of family-owned contractors whose operations are conducted through various forms of organizations including corporations, partnerships, and limited liability entities. Those organizations, in turn, enter into joint ventures of all forms. It is common for construction contractors to own or control more than one operating entity. The term *double-breasting* refers to simultaneous operation of both a union contractor and a nonunion contractor. This is done to enable bidding on jobs regardless of the contract-mandated labor requirements.

12.07 In certain regions of the country, especially those that are highly unionized, the construction industry has historically experienced corruption. Despite the absence of any existing evidence of corruption, and regardless of any past experience with the industry, the entity, or management, the discussion among the auditing team should emphasize the need to maintain a questioning mind and to exercise professional skepticism in gathering and evaluating evidence throughout the audit.

12.08 Although every commercial transaction may be subject to the risk of fraud, the construction industry has been especially affected by frauds resulting from, among other factors

- dependence on consultants or government officials, or both, for obtaining regulatory approvals.

- noncompliance with labor laws and collective bargaining agreements.
- high-dollar value of many of the contracts.
- requirements to accept lowest bidders.
- dependence on consultants, including development managers, architects, and engineers for good-faith exercise of discretion.

12.09 Certain aspects of the construction industry can create a higher risk of the presence of fraud occurring at a construction entity. These items are discussed in the following list:

- *Incentives and Pressures*
  - — The percentage of completion method requires that loss contacts be accrued. A strong incentive exists for contractors to avoid such recognition by charging costs on jobs that are likely to result in losses to more profitable jobs to prevent the loss accrual or the contractor may allocate additional costs to a job that is already showing a loss, while underallocating costs to profitable jobs in order to make those jobs reflect more profits.
  - — Bonding generally is a requirement to bid on most large and nearly all government contracts. Bonding companies go through a working capital type calculation to determine *bonding capacity*. That calculation assigns differing weights by category of assets and generally excludes prepaid amounts, amounts due from related parties, and aged receivables (generally over 90 days) and provides credit for only half of the inventory. Knowing the formula behind the calculation provides the contractor an incentive to mask amounts due from related parties and allocate inventory and prepaid amounts to current job costs, thus reclassifying those costs on the balance sheet by either increasing underbillings or decreasing overbillings (and, as a further consequence of the abuse, accelerating revenue recognition on the jobs to which they are charged).
  - — Profit fade (the reduction of the estimated gross profit over the life of a contract) is recognized as evidence of a contractor's inability to effectively estimate or manage a job, or both. In order to prevent profit fade from appearing on an older job, contractors may attempt to inappropriately charge costs on those older jobs to newer ones.
  - — Very few bidders on a job and very high gross profit margins on jobs both may be signs that the bidding process is influenced by corruption.
  - — Depending on the nature of the employee-employer relationship and the construction contract, some employees may feel little loyalty to the projects they work on and have no inclination to complete work on time. Line employees may steal materials or intentionally create time and cost overruns to extend their own employment. As

material and labor costs soar during the construction phase, support personnel in accounting or purchasing departments may concoct inventory or accounts payable schemes to defraud their employers or customers.

— Pressure to meet covenants required by financial institutions for lines of credit or borrowings.

— Incentives due to management or employee, or both, bonus arrangements, based on job profitability.

- *Opportunities*

— Completed jobs often have unused materials left over. A scheme used by some contractors is to commingle those materials with recently purchased ones. In the year-end physical inventory, those with no cost are not identified as such, and the "recycled" inventory is repriced at historical cost along with the other items counted. And the book to physical inventory adjustment masks the reintroduction of the "recycled" materials into inventory.

— Most job costs are for materials and labor, which are costs that are not always project-specific. It is not unheard of for a contractor to charge personal costs to a job. Vehicle costs are not uncommon for construction contracts, and the cost of personal vehicles leased for family members do not stand out as unusual job costs. It is not unheard of for contractors to have built personal residences for themselves, family members, government and union officials and to charge those costs to a job or to a series of jobs. Similarly, "favors" in the form of repaving driveways, excavating a lot, or building a stonewall are some of the inappropriate items that sometimes may be charged to contracts.

— Significant equipment purchases are charged directly to contract job costs. Some contractors may inappropriately charge to a job the entire cost of capitalizable construction equipment all at once instead of capitalizing this equipment, depreciating it over its useful life, and allocating to the job only an applicable portion of depreciation expense. When a contractor uses the percentage of completion method, this will accelerate the revenue recognition process by increasing costs incurred to date. In an effort to further improve its profitability, the construction contractor may also attempt to charge its client for equipment that may be used on several jobs by either submitting change orders for fixed-price contracts or by simply including this equipment among costs for time-and-materials contracts.

— Because the percentage of completion method of accounting for long-term construction-type contracts is required whenever contractors have the ability to make reasonably dependable estimates, the estimate of total contract costs (incurred and to be incurred) is uniquely critical to the revenue recognition process in this industry. Underestimation of total contract cost would present the contract as more complete than it is and, as a consequence, would result in excess gross profit on the job and overstated operating results for the entity. Because of the subjective nature inherent in estimating total costs and costs to complete, the contractor is in a unique position to influence those estimates and, as a direct consequence, the operating results for the period.

- *Attitudes and Rationalizations*
  - — Many construction contractors will do whatever it takes to get the job. Financial reporting is considered merely a requirement to get the necessary loans and bonding to be able to effectively participate in the industry. The industry is a tough one in which to participate, and those who have been successful have had to apply good business judgment to overcome the constant challenges to their integrity.

Obtaining the Information Needed to Identify the Risks of Material Misstatement Due to Fraud

12.10 AU-C section 315 establishes requirements and provides guidance about how the auditor obtains an understanding of the entity and its environment, including its internal control for the purpose of assessing the risks of material misstatement. In performing that work, information may come to the auditor's attention that should be considered in identifying risks of material misstatement due to fraud. As part of this work, the auditor should perform the following procedures to obtain information that is used to identify the risks of material misstatement due to fraud:

a. Make inquiries of management and others within the entity to obtain their views about the risks of fraud and how they are addressed.

b. Consider any unusual or unexpected relationships that have been identified in performing analytical procedures in planning the audit.

c. Consider whether one or more fraud risk factors exist.

d. Consider other information that may be helpful in the identification of risks of material misstatement due to fraud.

12.11 In planning the audit, the auditor also should perform analytical procedures, including those related to revenue, with the objective of identifying unusual or unexpected relationships that may indicate a material misstatement due to fraudulent financial reporting. For example, in the construction industry, the following unusual or unexpected relationships may indicate a material misstatement due to fraud:

- Underbillings on uncompleted contracts that exceed 20 percent of equity or 25 percent of working capital, the explanation for which may include the masking losses or costs unrelated to a job being charged to that job

- Continually increasing underbillings, which may indicate that potential losses are being capitalized
- Overbillings that are not represented by cash, the explanation for which may include the use of excess cash collections to finance other possible loss contracts
- A higher gross profit on uncompleted contracts than on closed jobs, which may indicate an overly optimistic estimate of profitability on open jobs
- Inability to reconcile total costs incurred on open jobs and closed jobs to the total costs presented on the statement of operations, which may suggest that closed jobs may have been charged for current costs

Considering Fraud Risk Factors

12.12 The auditor may identify events or conditions that indicate incentives or pressures to perpetrate fraud, opportunities to carry out the fraud, or attitudes and rationalizations to justify a fraudulent action. Such events or conditions are referred to as *fraud risk factors*. Fraud risk factors do not necessarily indicate the existence of fraud; however, they have often been present in circumstances in which frauds have occurred and, therefore, may indicate risks of material misstatement due to fraud.

12.13 AU-C section 240 provides fraud risk factor examples that have been written to apply to most enterprises. Paragraph 12.09 provides a list of fraud risk factors specific to the construction industry. Remember that fraud risk factors are only one of several sources of information an auditor considers when identifying and assessing risk of material misstatement due to fraud.

Identifying Risks That May Result in a Material Misstatement Due to Fraud

12.14 In identifying risks of material misstatement due to fraud, it is helpful for the auditor to consider the information that has been gathered in accordance with the requirements of AU-C section 240. The auditor's identification of fraud risks may be influenced by characteristics such as the size, complexity, and ownership attributes of the entity. In addition, the auditor should identify and assess the risks of material misstatement due to fraud at the financial statement level and at the assertion level for classes of transactions, account balances, and disclosures. Certain accounts, classes of transactions, and assertions that have high inherent risk because they involve a high degree of management judgment and subjectivity also may present risks of material misstatement due to fraud because they are susceptible to manipulation by management.

12.15 As discussed, due to the nature of the construction industry, a number of accounts can be subject to fraudulent activities including underbillings and overbillings, inventory, prepaid expenses, and fixed assets. In addition, from a standpoint of potential manipulation of financial results, a few of the areas that involve the most judgment and, therefore, present the greatest risk of manipulation are described as follows:

- *Penalty clauses.* Municipal contracts, especially school contracts, very often contain penalty clauses for late completion of jobs. Those penalties are usually assessed on a daily basis, and they can become substantial. Often, contractors neglect to charge such costs to jobs as they are incurred in the hope that somehow those penalty amounts will be waived. Because they are contract costs, penalties should be accrued and charged to job costs as incurred. These penalty clauses may come in the form of liquidated damages (per the terms of the contract), actual damages assessed by the owner, or back charges.
- *Davis-Bacon Act consideration.* Contracts entered into by nonunion contractors covered by the Davis-Bacon Act require that contractors pay for nonunion labor at the prevailing wage of union workers. The differential between the prevailing union wage and the actual wage often is not paid directly to the worker but to a supplemental benefit plan that benefits the worker. Such payments are made less often than payroll payments. It is not uncommon to discover that such unpaid costs have not been accrued and charged to the job on a contemporaneous basis.

A Presumption That Improper Revenue Recognition Is a Fraud Risk

12.16 Material misstatements due to fraudulent financial reporting often result from an overstatement of revenues (for example, through premature revenue recognition or recording fictitious revenues) or an understatement of revenues (for example, through improperly shifting revenues to a later period). Therefore, when identifying and assessing the risks of material misstatement due to fraud, the auditor should, based on a presumption that risks of fraud exist in revenue recognition, evaluate which types of revenue, revenue transactions, or assertions give rise to such risks.

12.17 As discussed previously, revenue recognition process for construction contractors using the percentage of completion method is often based on an estimate of total cost. Underestimation of total contract cost would present the contract as more complete than it really is and, as a consequence, would result in excess gross profit on the job and acceleration of the revenue recognition process. Preparation of accurate work in process schedules is essential for proper revenue recognition. Care needs to be exercised to ensure that the costs incurred to date schedule includes all costs that actually have been incurred through the period-end and that no significant unrecorded liabilities exist. Then, the actual costs and the estimate of costs to be incurred are a meaningful estimate of total costs to use in estimating revenue. If the costs incurred to date schedule is incomplete, then total costs will most likely be understated, which will result in inaccurate revenue recognition, regardless of the revenue recognition method used by the contractor.

12.18 A popular misconception is that unrecorded liabilities only increase revenue in percentage of completion accounting. That would be so only if unrecorded liabilities excluded from the costs incurred to date were picked up in the estimate of costs to complete. However, this will not be the case if a contractor relies on an engineering assessment instead of the accounting system to estimate costs to complete by observing what has been done and what remains to be done. Auditors should select certain job sites for observation and discussion of stage of completion with engineering personnel. Contracts under 10 percent complete and over 90 percent complete generally present less risk to the auditor. This is simply because those under 10 percent complete have relatively little revenue recognized based on the estimates. Those over 90 percent complete are at a stage at which most of the costs have been incurred; therefore, the risk of revenue manipulation is minimized at this point.

12.19 Revenue recognition may be accelerated if a contractor reclassifies inventory and prepaid amounts to current job costs to satisfy working capital requirements of bonding companies.

12.20 Contractors also may accelerate revenue recognition by inappropriately charging to a job the entire cost of capitalizable construction equipment all at once instead of capitalizing this equipment, depreciating it over its useful life, and allocating to the job only an applicable portion of depreciation expense. When a contractor uses the percentage of completion method, this will accelerate the revenue recognition process by increasing costs incurred to date. In an effort to further increase its revenues, the construction contractor may also attempt to charge its client for equipment that may be used on several jobs by either submitting change orders for fixed-price contracts or by simply including this equipment among costs for time-and-materials contracts.

12.21 If the contractor has adopted the accounting policy that allows for total costs recognition on claims receivable, then the amount to be recognized should be limited to the actual costs incurred deemed to be realizable. Often, claims information is based on estimates prepared by outside consultants who are preparing for litigation. Those estimates generally include costs that are not recognizable under FASB *Accounting Standards Codification* (ASC) 605-35, and care needs to be exercised to ensure that amounts recognized are limited to the actual costs incurred.

12.22 Some construction contractors may assert the inability to estimate costs in an attempt to justify continued use of the completed contract method allowed in FASB ASC 605-35 under such circumstances. Such claims may have had some validity decades ago when estimates were done by hand; however, the abundance of off-the-shelf software that assists in making estimates and tracking costs on contracts renders most of such claims invalid.

Key Estimates

12.23 Key estimates in the construction industry involve the following items:

- Cost to complete
- Contract penalties and incentives
- Profit from change orders
- Revenue from claims
- Allocation of equipment costs
- Stage of completion

- Accounts receivable allowance
- Assumptions regarding impairments of long-lived assets
- Assumptions regarding deferred tax valuation allowances and effective tax rates

Assessing the Identified Risks After Taking Into Account an Evaluation of the Entity's Programs and Controls That Address the Risks

12.24 Paragraph .27 of AU-C section 240 provides that the auditor should treat those assessed risks of material misstatement due to fraud as significant risks and, accordingly, to the extent not already done so, the auditor should obtain an understanding of the entity's related controls, including control activities, relevant to such risks, including the evaluation of whether such controls have been suitably designed and implemented to mitigate such fraud risks. The following are examples of programs and controls that can be found in construction entities:

- Contractors have extensive systems for the identification and recognition of costs by job.
- Contractors have sophisticated systems to assist engineering personnel in making cost to complete estimates.
- Construction contractors generally are hands-on managers with intimate knowledge of the job, the progress on the job, and the expected completion of the job.
- Many privately owned construction entities are owned and managed by someone who has participated in the trades at many levels and therefore has intimate knowledge of the complexities of the trade and what can go wrong.
- Contractors have corporate policies, particularly in the areas of employee relations and enforcement, to establish an environment that minimizes the risk of fraud. Both management and lower level employees are less likely to engage in fraud, commercial crime, or destructive acts if they believe they have a stake in the entity and
  - — they are being fairly treated, for example, with respect to compensation.
  - — any employee will be severely dealt with for any breach of the law or the entity's policies.
- Construction contractors have physical access restrictions, for example, with respect to construction materials and supplies at the entity's premises and at work sites, will deter theft or sabotage.
- Contractors have supervisory performance, quality control, and independence checks to ensure that the entity's work is up to contract standards and minimize the potential for materials substitution or other quality problems.
- Contractors carry adequate insurance (for example, fidelity, liability, and theft).

Responding to the Results of the Assessment[2]

12.25 AU-C section 240 provides requirements and guidance about an auditor's response to the results of the assessment of the risks of material misstatement due to fraud.

12.26 The auditor should determine overall responses to address the assessed risks of material misstatement due to fraud at the financial statement level. In determining overall responses to address the assessed risks of material misstatement due to fraud at the financial statement level, the auditor should

a. assign and supervise personnel, taking into account the knowledge, skill, and ability of the individuals to be given significant engagement responsibilities and the auditor's assessment of the risks of material misstatement due to fraud for the engagement;

b. evaluate whether the selection and application of accounting policies by the entity, particularly those related to subjective measurements and complex transactions, may be indicative of fraudulent financial reporting resulting from management's effort to manage earnings, or a bias that may create a material misstatement; and

c. incorporate an element of unpredictability in the selection of the nature, timing, and extent of audit procedures.

12.27 The auditor should design and perform further audit procedures whose nature, timing, and extent are responsive to the assessed risks of material misstatement due to fraud at the assertion level. Construction audit procedures may include the following:

- Holding regular meetings with owners and project managers.
- Reviewing monthly internal financial reports with appropriate contractor personnel to include detailed review of work in process job schedule.
- Performing testing of the contractor's internal controls over job costing and contracts receivable.
- Reviewing analytical review procedures used by the contractor to identify fraudulent actions and understand the results of these analyses. Depending on the results, additional procedures may be necessary.
- Scheduling job site visits at or near year end and discuss progress on job to date with on-site personnel, especially those not directly involved in the preparation of the estimate of costs to complete.
- Inquiring with employees of various levels regarding their understanding of fraud risk factors, controls in place, and any known illegal acts or fraud.

12.28 Even if specific risks of material misstatement due to fraud are not identified by the auditor, a possibility exists that management override of controls could occur. Accordingly, the auditor should address the risk of management override of controls apart from any conclusions regarding the existence

---

[2] Paragraph .06 of AU-C section 330, *Performing Audit Procedures in Response to Assessed Risks and Evaluating the Audit Evidence Obtained*, states that the auditor should design and perform further audit procedures whose nature, timing, and extent are based on, and are responsive to, the assessed risks of material misstatement at the relevant assertion level.

of more specifically identifiable risks by designing and performing audit procedures to

a. test the appropriateness of journal entries recorded in the general ledger and other adjustments made in the preparation of the financial statements, including entries posted directly to financial statement drafts. In designing and performing audit procedures for such tests, the auditor should

   i. obtain an understanding of the entity's financial reporting process and controls over journal entries and other adjustments, and the suitability of design and implementation of such controls;

   ii. make inquiries of individuals involved in the financial reporting process about inappropriate or unusual activity relating to the processing of journal entries and other adjustments;

   iii. consider fraud risk indicators, the nature and complexity of accounts, and entries processed outside the normal course of business;

   iv. select journal entries and other adjustments made at the end of a reporting period; and

   v. consider the need to test journal entries and other adjustments throughout the period.

b. review accounting estimates for biases and evaluate whether the circumstances producing the bias, if any, represent a risk of material misstatement due to fraud. In performing this review, the auditor should

   i. evaluate whether the judgments and decisions made by management in making the accounting estimates included in the financial statements, even if they are individually reasonable, indicate a possible bias on the part of the entity's management that may represent a risk of material misstatement due to fraud. If so, the auditor should reevaluate the accounting estimates taken as a whole, and

   ii. perform a retrospective review of management judgments and assumptions related to significant accounting estimates reflected in the financial statements of the prior year. Estimates selected for review should include those that are based on highly sensitive assumptions or are otherwise significantly affected by judgments made by management.

c. evaluate, for significant transactions that are outside the normal course of business for the entity or that otherwise appear to be unusual given the auditor's understanding of the entity and its environment and other information obtained during the audit, whether the business rationale (or the lack thereof) of the transactions suggests that they may have been entered into to engage in fraudulent financial reporting or to conceal misappropriation of assets.

Evaluating Audit Evidence

12.29 The auditor should evaluate, at or near the end of the audit, whether the accumulated results of auditing procedures (including analytical procedures[3] that were performed as substantive tests or when forming an overall conclusion) affect the assessment of the risks of material misstatement due to fraud made earlier in the audit or indicate a previously unrecognized risk of material misstatement due to fraud.

12.30 The auditor also should consider whether responses to inquiries of management, those charged with governance, or others are inconsistent or otherwise unsatisfactory (for example, vague or implausible), and, if determined to be so, the auditor should further investigate the inconsistencies or unsatisfactory responses.

Responding to Misstatements That May Be the Result of Fraud

12.31 When audit test results identify misstatements in the financial statements, the auditor should consider whether such misstatements may be indicative of fraud. If such an indication exists, the auditor should evaluate the implications of the misstatement with regard to other aspects of the audit, particularly the auditor's evaluation of materiality, management and employee integrity, and the reliability of management representations, recognizing that an instance of fraud is unlikely to be an isolated occurrence.

12.32 If the auditor identifies a misstatement, whether material or not, and the auditor has reason to believe that it is, or may be, the result of fraud and that management (in particular, senior management) is involved, the auditor should reevaluate the assessment of the risks of material misstatement due to fraud and its resulting effect on the nature, timing, and extent of audit procedures to respond to the assessed risks. The auditor should also consider whether circumstances or conditions indicate possible collusion involving employees, management, or third parties when reconsidering the reliability of evidence previously obtained.

12.33 If the auditor concludes that, or is unable to conclude whether, the financial statements are materially misstated as a result of fraud, the auditor should evaluate the implications for the audit.

12.34 If, as a result of identified fraud or suspected fraud, the auditor encounters circumstances that bring into question the auditor's ability to continue performing the audit, the auditor should

a. determine the professional and legal responsibilities applicable in the circumstances, including whether a requirement exists for the auditor to report to the person or persons who engaged the auditor or, in some cases, to regulatory authorities;

---

[3] Refer to the AICPA Audit Guide *Analytical Procedures* for guidance on the effective use of analytical procedures with an emphasis on analytical procedures as substantive tests. This includes a discussion of AU-C section 520, *Analytical Procedures*, and the underlying concepts and definitions, a series of questions and answers, an illustrative case study, and an appendix that includes useful financial ratios.

b. consider whether it is appropriate to withdraw from the engagement, when withdrawal is possible under applicable law or regulation; and

c. if the auditor withdraws

   i. discuss with the appropriate level of management and those charged with governance the auditor's withdrawal from the engagement and the reasons for the withdrawal, and

   ii. determine whether a professional or legal requirement exists to report to the person or persons who engaged the auditor or, in some cases, to regulatory authorities, the auditor's withdrawal from the engagement and the reasons for the withdrawal.

Communicating About Possible Fraud to Management, Those Charged With Governance, and Others

12.35 Whenever the auditor has determined that there is evidence that fraud may exist, that matter should be brought to the attention of an appropriate level of management. See paragraphs .39–.41 of AU-C section 240 for further requirements and guidance about communications with management, those charged with governance, and others.

Documenting the Auditor's Consideration of Fraud

12.36 In order to document the auditor's consideration of fraud, the auditor should include the auditor's understanding of the entity and its environment and the assessment of the risks of material misstatements by documenting

- the significant decisions reached during the discussion among the engagement team regarding the susceptibility of the entity's financial statements to material misstatement due to fraud, and how and when the discussion occurred and the audit team members who participated

- the identified and assessed risks of material misstatement due to fraud at the financial statement level and at the assertion level

The auditor should also include the communications about fraud made to management, those charged with governance, regulators and other, in addition to the communications within the audit team.

12.37 In addition, the auditor should include the audit documentation of the auditor's responses to the assessed risks of material misstatement the overall responses to the assessed risks of material misstatement due to fraud at the financial statement level and the nature, timing, and extent of audit procedures, and the linkage of those procedures with the assessed risks of material misstatement due to fraud at the assertion level, as well as the results of the audit procedures, including those designed to address the risk of management override of controls.

12.38 Lastly, if the auditor has concluded that the presumption that there is a risk of material misstatement due to fraud related to revenue recognition is overcome in the circumstances of the engagement, the auditor should include in the audit documentation the reasons for that conclusion.

Appendix A

The New Revenue Recognition Standard: FASB ASC 606

This appendix is nonauthoritative and is included for informational purposes only.

Overview

On May 28, 2014, the International Accounting Standards Board (IASB) and FASB issued a joint accounting standard on revenue recognition to address a number of concerns regarding the complexity and lack of consistency surrounding the accounting for revenue transactions. Consistent with each board's policy, FASB issued Accounting Standards Update (ASU) No. 2014-09, *Revenue from Contracts with Customers (Topic 606)*, and the IASB issued International Financial Reporting Standard (IFRS) 15, *Revenue from Contracts with Customers*. FASB ASU No. 2014-09 will amend the FASB *Accounting Standards Codification®* (ASC) by creating a new Topic 606, *Revenue from Contracts with Customers*, and a new subtopic 340-40, *Other Assets and Deferred Costs—Contracts with Customers*. The guidance in FASB ASU No. 2014-09 provides what FASB describes as a framework for revenue recognition and supersedes or amends several of the revenue recognition requirements in FASB ASC 605, *Revenue Recognition*, as well as guidance within the 900 series of industry-specific topics.

As part of the boards' efforts to converge U.S. generally accepted accounting principles (GAAP) and IFRSs, the standard eliminates the transaction- and industry-specific revenue recognition guidance under current GAAP and replaces it with a principles-based approach for revenue recognition. The intent is to avoid inconsistencies of accounting treatment across different geographies and industries. In addition to improving comparability of revenue recognition practices, the new guidance provides more useful information to financial statement users through enhanced disclosure requirements. FASB and the IASB have essentially achieved convergence with these standards, with some minor differences related to the collectibility threshold, interim disclosure requirements, early application and effective date, impairment loss reversal, and nonpublic entity requirements.

The standard applies to any entity that either enters into contracts with customers to transfer goods or services or enters into contracts for the transfer of nonfinancial assets, unless those contracts are within the scope of other standards (for example, insurance or lease contracts).

Effective or Applicability Date

The guidance in ASU No. 2014-09 was originally effective for annual reporting periods of public entities beginning after December 15, 2016, including interim periods within that reporting period. Early application was not permitted for public entities, including not-for-profit entities (NFPs) that have issued, or are conduit bond obligors for, securities that are traded, listed, or quoted on an exchange or an over-the-counter market and for employee benefit plans that file or furnish financial statements to the SEC.

For nonpublic entities, the amendments in the new guidance were originally effective for annual reporting periods beginning after December 15, 2017, and interim periods within annual periods beginning after December 15, 2018.

On August 12, 2015, FASB issued ASU No. 2015-14, *Revenue from Contracts with Customers (Topic 606): Deferral of the Effective Date*, to allow entities additional time to implement systems, gather data, and resolve implementation questions. This update allows for public business entities, certain NFPs, and certain employee benefit plans to apply the new requirements to annual reporting periods beginning after December 15, 2017, including interim reporting periods within that reporting period. Earlier application is permitted only as of annual reporting periods beginning after December 15, 2016, including interim reporting periods within that reporting period.

All other entities will now apply the guidance in ASU No. 2014-09 to annual reporting periods beginning after December 15, 2018, and interim reporting periods within annual reporting periods beginning after December 15, 2019. Application is permitted earlier only as of an annual reporting period beginning after December 15, 2016, including interim reporting periods within that reporting period, or an annual reporting period beginning after December 15, 2016, and interim reporting periods within annual reporting periods beginning one year after the annual reporting period in which an entity first applies the guidance in ASU No. 2014-09.

Overview of the New Guidance

The core principle of the revised revenue recognition standard is that an entity should recognize revenue to depict the transfer of goods or services to customers in an amount that reflects the consideration to which the entity expects to be entitled in exchange for those good or services.

To apply the proposed revenue recognition standard, ASU No. 2014-09 states that an entity should follow these five steps:

1. Identify the contract(s) with a customer.
2. Identify the performance obligations in the contract.
3. Determine the transaction price.
4. Allocate the transaction price to the performance obligations in the contract.
5. Recognize revenue when (or as) the entity satisfies a performance obligation.

Under the new standard, revenue is recognized when a company satisfies a performance obligation by transferring a promised good or service to a customer (which is when the customer obtains control of that good or service). See the following discussion of the five steps involved when recognizing revenue under the new guidance.

Understanding the Five-Step Process

Step 1: Identify the Contract(s) With a Customer

ASU No. 2014-09 defines a *contract* as "an agreement between two or more parties that creates enforceable rights and obligations." The new standard affects contracts with a customer that meet the following criteria:

- Approval (in writing, orally, or in accordance with other customary business practices) and commitment of the parties
- Identification of the rights of the parties
- Identification of the payment terms
- Contract has commercial substance
- Probable that the entity will collect substantially all the consideration to which it will be entitled in exchange for the goods or services that will be transferred to the customer

A contract does not exist if each party to the contract has the unilateral enforceable right to terminate a wholly unperformed contract without compensating the other party (parties).

Step 2: Identify the Performance Obligations in the Contract

A *performance obligation* is a promise in a contract with a customer to transfer a good or service to the customer.

At contract inception, an entity should assess the goods or services promised in a contract with a customer and identify as a performance obligation (possibly multiple performance obligations) each promise to transfer to the customer either

- a good or service (or bundle of goods or services) that is distinct, or
- a series of distinct goods or services that are substantially the same and that have the same pattern of transfer to the customer.

A good or service that is not distinct should be combined with other promised goods or services until the entity identifies a bundle of goods or services that is distinct. In some cases, that would result in the entity accounting for all the goods or services promised in a contract as a single performance obligation.

Step 3: Determine the Transaction Price

The *transaction price* is the amount of consideration (fixed or variable) the entity expects to receive in exchange for transferring promised goods or services to a customer, excluding amounts collected on behalf of third parties. To determine the transaction price, an entity should consider the effects of

- variable consideration,
- constraining estimates of variable consideration,
- the existence of a significant financing component,
- noncash considerations, and
- consideration payable to the customer.

If the consideration promised in a contract includes a variable amount, then an entity should estimate the amount of consideration to which the entity will be entitled in exchange for transferring the promised goods or services to a customer. An entity would then include in the transaction price some or all of an amount of variable consideration only to the extent that it is probable that a significant reversal in the amount of cumulative revenue recognized will not occur when the uncertainty associated with the variable consideration is subsequently resolved.

An entity should consider the terms of the contract and its customary business practices to determine the transaction price.

Step 4: Allocate the Transaction Price to the Performance Obligations in the Contract

The transaction price is allocated to separate performance obligations in proportion to the standalone selling price of the promised goods or services. If a standalone selling price is not directly observable, then an entity should estimate it. Reallocation of the transaction price for changes in the standalone selling price is not permitted. When estimating the standalone selling price, entities can use various methods, including the adjusted market assessment approach, expected cost plus a margin approach, and residual approach (only if the selling price is highly variable and uncertain).

Sometimes, the transaction price includes a discount or a variable amount of consideration that relates entirely to one of the performance obligations in a contract. Guidance under the new standard specifies when an entity should allocate the discount or variable consideration to one (or some) performance obligation(s), rather than to all the performance obligations in the contract.

Step 5: Recognize Revenue When (or as) the Entity Satisfies a Performance Obligation

The amount of revenue recognized when transferring the promised good or service to a customer is equal to the amount allocated to the satisfied performance obligation, which may be satisfied at a point in time or over time. *Control of an asset* refers to the ability to direct the use of, and obtain substantially all the remaining benefits from, the asset. Control also includes the ability to prevent *other entities* from directing the use of, and obtaining the benefits from, an asset.

When performance obligations are satisfied over time, the entity should select an appropriate method for measuring its progress toward complete satisfaction of that performance obligation. The standard discusses methods of measuring progress, including input and output methods, and how to determine which method is appropriate.

Additional Guidance Under the New Standard

In addition to the five-step process for recognizing revenue, ASU No. 2014-09 also addresses the following areas:

- Accounting for incremental costs of obtaining a contract, as well as costs incurred to fulfill a contract
- Licenses
- Warranties

Lastly, the new guidance enhances disclosure requirements to include more information about specific revenue contracts entered into by the entity, including performance obligations and the transaction price.

Subsequent Developments

Subsequent to the issuance of ASU No. 2014-09, FASB issued updates to clarify guidance on performance obligations, licensing, principal versus agent considerations, and other narrow-scope improvements and practical expedients.

ASU No. 2016-08, *Revenue from Contracts with Customers (Topic 606): Principle versus Agent Considerations (Reporting Revenue Gross versus Net)*, was issued in March 2016 to clarify the guidance in FASB ASC 606 with respect to principal versus agent. There is little disagreement that an entity who is a principal recognizes revenue in the gross amount of consideration when a performance obligation is satisfied. An entity who is an agent (collecting revenue on behalf of the principal) recognizes revenue only to the extent of the commission or fee that the agent collects. This ASU hopes to eliminate the potential diversity in practice when determining whether an entity is a principal or an agent by clarifying the following:

- An entity determines whether it is a principal or an agent for each distinct good or service.
- An entity determines the nature of each specified good or service (including whether it is a right to a good or service)
- When an entity is a principal, it obtains control of
  - — a good or another asset from the other party that it then transfers to the customer;
  - — a right to a service that will be performed by another party, which gives the entity the ability to direct that party to provide the service to the customer on the entity's behalf; or
  - — a good or service from the other party that it combines with other goods or services to provide the specified good or service to the customer.
- Indicators in the assessment of control may be more or less relevant or persuasive, or both, to the control assessment, depending on the facts and circumstances.

Additional illustrative examples are also provided in ASU No. 2016-08 to further assist practitioners in applying this guidance. The effective date of this update is in line with the guidance in ASU No. 2014-09, as amended by ASU No. 2015-14.

ASU No. 2016-10, *Revenue from Contracts with Customers (Topic 606): Identifying Performance Obligations and Licensing*, was issued in April 2016 to reduce potential for diversity in practice at initial application of FASB ASC 606, as well as the cost and complexity of applying FASB ASC 606 at transition and on an ongoing basis. When identifying promised goods and services in a contract, this ASU states that entities

- are not required to assess whether promised goods or services are performance obligations if they are immaterial to the contract.

- can elect to account for shipping and handling activities as an activity to fulfill promises within the contract, rather than as an additional promised service.

When assessing whether promised goods or services are distinct, this ASU emphasizes the need to determine whether the nature of the promise is to transfer

- each of the goods or services, or
- a combined item (or items) to which the promised goods or services are inputs.

With regards to licensing, ASU No. 2016-10 clarifies whether revenue should be recognized at a point in time or over time, based on whether the license provides a right to use an entity's intellectual property or a right to access the entity's intellectual property. Specifically,

- if the intellectual property has significant standalone functionality, the license does not include supporting or maintaining that intellectual property during the license period. Therefore, the performance obligation would be considered satisfied at a point in time. Examples of this type of intellectual property include software, biological compounds or drug formulas, and media.
- licenses for symbolic intellectual property include supporting or maintaining that intellectual property during the license period and, therefore, are considered to be satisfied over time. Examples of symbolic intellectual property include brands, team or trade names, logos, and franchise rights.

Lastly, ASU No. 2016-10 provides clarification on implementation guidance on recognizing revenue for sales-based or usage-based royalty promised in exchange for a license of intellectual property. The effective date of this ASU is in line with the guidance in ASU No. 2014-09, as amended by ASU No. 2015-14.

FASB ASU No. 2016-12, *Revenue from Contracts with Customers (Topic 606): Narrow-Scope Improvements and Practical Expedients*, was issued in May 2016. Topics covered in this ASU include

- clarification on contract modifications. This amendment permits an entity to determine and allocate the transaction price on the basis of all satisfied and unsatisfied performance obligations in a modified contract as of the beginning of the earliest period presented in accordance with the guidance in FASB ASC 606. An entity would not be required to separately evaluate the effects of each contract modification. An entity that chooses to apply this practical expedient would apply the expedient consistently to similar types of contracts.
- how to assess the collectibility criterion. The amendment introduces new criteria to meet the collectibility requirement. An entity should assess the collectibility of the consideration promised in a contract for the goods or services that will be transferred to the customer, rather than assessing the collectibility of the consideration promised in the contract for all the promised goods or services.
- how to report sales taxes and similar taxes. This amendment states that an entity may make an accounting policy election to exclude from the measurement of the transaction price all taxes

assessed by a governmental authority that are both imposed on and concurrent with a specific revenue-producing transaction and collected by the entity from a customer (for example, sales, use, value added, and some excise taxes). Taxes assessed on an entity's total gross receipts or imposed during the inventory procurement process should be excluded from the scope of the election. An entity that makes this election should exclude from the transaction price all taxes in the scope of the election and should comply with the applicable accounting policy guidance, including disclosure requirements.

- when to measure noncash consideration. This amendment clarifies that the measurement date for noncash consideration is contract inception. If the fair value of the noncash consideration varies because of the form of the consideration and for reasons other than the form of the consideration, an entity should apply the guidance on variable consideration only to the variability resulting from reasons other than the form of the consideration.
- how to apply transition guidance. This amendment clarifies that a completed contract for purposes of transition is a contract for which all (or substantially all) the revenue was recognized under legacy GAAP before the date of initial application. Accounting for elements of a contract that do not affect revenue under legacy GAAP are irrelevant to the assessment of whether a contract is complete. In addition, the amendment permits an entity to apply the modified retrospective transition method either to all contracts or only to contracts that are not completed contracts.

The effective date of this ASU is in line with the guidance in ASU No. 2014-09, as amended by ASU No. 2015-14.

FASB also issued ASU No. 2016-20, *Technical Corrections and Improvements to Topic 606, Revenue from Contracts with Customers*, in December 2016. These amendments affect narrow aspects of guidance issued in ASU No. 2014-09, including but not limited to, guidance on

- impairment testing. When performing impairment testing, an entity should consider expected contract renewals and extensions. In addition, the assessment should include both the amount of consideration it already has received but has not yet recognized as revenue, and the amount it expects to receive in the future.
- additional scope exceptions. The term "insurance" is removed from the scope exceptions of Topic 606 to clarify that all contracts within the scope of Topic 944, *Financial Services – Insurance*, are excluded.
- provisions for losses on construction-type and production-type contracts. Such provisions should be determined at least at the contract level; however, an entity can make an accounting policy election to determine the provision for losses at the performance obligation level.
- disclosure of remaining performance obligations. Optional exemptions from the disclosure requirement are provided for remaining performance obligations when an entity is not required to estimate variable consideration to recognize revenue.

Consistent with the other ASUs, the effective date of ASU No. 2016-20 is in line with the guidance in ASU No. 2014-09, as amended by ASU No. 2015-14.

In February 2017, FASB issued ASU No. 2017-05, *Other Income—Gains and Losses from the Derecognition of Nonfinancial Assets (Subtopic 610-20): Clarifying the Scope of Asset Derecognition Guidance and Accounting for Partial Sales of Nonfinancial Assets*. The amendments in this ASU include, but are not limited to

- a definition of the term *in substance nonfinancial asset*, to clarify the scope of FASB ASC 610-20. An in substance nonfinancial asset is, in part, a financial asset promised to a counterparty in a contract if substantially all of the fair value of the assets (recognized and unrecognized) that are promised to the counterparty in the contract is concentrated in nonfinancial assets. An in substance nonfinancial asset also includes a financial asset that is held in an individual consolidated subsidiary within a contract if substantially all the fair value of the assets (recognized and unrecognized) that are promised to the counterparty in that subsidiary is concentrated in nonfinancial assets.
- a clarification that nonfinancial assets within the scope of FASB ASC 610-20 may include nonfinancial assets transferred within a legal entity to a counterparty. For example, a parent may transfer control of nonfinancial assets by transferring ownership interests in a consolidated subsidiary. A contract that includes the transfer of ownership interests in one or more consolidated subsidiaries is within the scope of Subtopic 610-20 if substantially all of the fair value of the assets that are promised to the counterparty in a contract is concentrated in nonfinancial assets.
- removal of the scope exception for transfers of equity method investment that were considered in substance nonfinancial assets. All transfers of equity method investments will be accounted for in accordance with FASB ASC 860, *Transfers and Servicing*.
- derecognition of each distinct nonfinancial asset or in substance nonfinancial asset promised to a counterparty. Each asset will be derecognized when a counterparty obtains control of it. The amendments also clarify that an entity should allocate consideration to each distinct asset by applying the guidance in FASB ASC 606 on allocating the transaction price to performance obligations.
- partial sales transactions. An entity will derecognize a distinct nonfinancial asset or distinct in substance nonfinancial asset in a partial sale transaction when it (1) does not have (or ceases to have) a controlling financial interest in the legal entity that holds the asset in accordance with FASB ASC 810, *Consolidation*, and (2) transfers control of the asset in accordance with FASB ASC 606. Once an entity transfers control of a distinct nonfinancial asset or distinct in substance nonfinancial asset, it is required to measure any noncontrolling interest it receives (or retains) at fair value. If an entity transfers ownership interests in a consolidated subsidiary and continues to have a controlling financial interest in that subsidiary, it does not derecognize the assets and liabilities of the subsidiary and accounts for the transaction as an equity transaction. Therefore, no gain or loss is recognized.

- contributions of nonfinancial assets to a joint venture or other non-controlled investee. These contributions will be within the scope of FASB ASC 610-20, and an entity will recognize a full gain or loss on transfers of nonfinancial assets to equity method investees.

Consistent with the other ASUs, the effective date of ASU No. 2017-05 is in line with the guidance in ASU No. 2014-09, as amended by ASU No. 2015-14.

FASB also issued ASU No. 2017-13, *Revenue Recognition (Topic 605), Revenue from Contracts with Customers (Topic 606), Leases (Topic 840), and Leases (Topic 842): Amendments to SEC Paragraphs Pursuant to the Staff Announcement at the July 20, 2017 EITF Meeting and Rescission of Prior SEC Staff Announcements and Observer Comments*, in September 2017. The amendments in this ASU state that public entities that do not meet the definition of a public business entity except for a requirement to include or the inclusion of its financial statements or financial information in another entity's filing with the SEC may adopt the effective date for nonpublic entities.

Conclusion

Upon implementation of the new standard, consistency of revenue recognition principles across geography and industry will be enhanced, and financial statement users will be provided better insight through improved disclosure requirements. To provide CPAs with guidance during this time of transition, the AICPA's Financial Reporting Center (FRC) offers invaluable resources on the topic, including a roadmap to ensure that companies take the necessary steps to prepare themselves for the new standard. In addition, the FRC includes a list of conferences, webcasts, and other products to keep you informed on upcoming changes in revenue recognition. Refer to https://www.aicpa.org/interestareas/frc/accountingfinancialreporting/revenuerecognition.html to stay updated on the latest information available on revenue recognition.

In addition, the AICPA continues to update the Revenue Recognition – Audit and Accounting Guide to include key accounting implementation issues across 16 industry task forces. Although the implementation issues have not all been finalized across the 16 task forces, this guide is currently available for purchase at https://www.aicpastore.com/accounting/revenue-recognition—audit-and-accounting-guide/prdovr~pc-012516/pc-012516.jsp, including updates to the guide as they become available.

Appendix B

The New Leases Standard: FASB ASC 842

This appendix is nonauthoritative and is included for informational purposes only.

Overview

Issuance and Objective

On February 25, 2016, FASB issued Accounting Standards Update (ASU) No. 2016-02, *Leases (Topic 842)*. The objective of the ASU is to increase transparency and comparability in financial reporting by requiring balance sheet recognition of leases and note disclosure of certain information about lease arrangements. This ASU codifies the new FASB ASC topic 842, *Leases*, and makes conforming amendments to other FASB ASC topics.

The new FASB ASC topic on leases consists of these subtopics:

a. Overall

b. Lessee

c. Lessor

d. Sale and leaseback transactions

e. Leveraged lease arrangements

Applicability and Effective Date

ASU No. 2016-02 is applicable to any entity that enters into a lease and is effective as follows:

	Fiscal Years Beginning After	*Interim Periods Within Fiscal Years Beginning After*
Public business entities, certain not-for-profit entities with conduit financing arrangements, and employee benefit plans	December 15, 2018	December 15, 2018
All other entities	December 15, 2019	December 15, 2020

FASB ASC 842 applies to all leases and subleases of property, plant, and equipment; it specifically does not apply to the following nondepreciable assets accounted for under other FASB ASC topics:

a. Leases of intangible assets

b. Leases to explore for or use nonregenerative resources such as minerals, oil, and natural gas

c. Leases of biological assets, such as timber

d. Leases of inventory

e. Leases of assets under construction

Main Provisions

Overall

Identifying a Lease

Key changes in the guidance are illustrated by comparing the definition of a lease in FASB ASC 840 (extant GAAP) and FASB ASC 842.

FASB ASC 840	*FASB ASC 842*
An agreement conveying the right to use property, plant, or equipment (land and/or depreciable assets) usually for a stated period of time.	A contract, or part of a contract, that conveys the right to control the use of identified property, plant, or equipment (an identified asset) for a period of time in exchange for consideration.

The identification of a lease under FASB ASC 842 should be based on the presence of key elements in the definition.

Separating Components of a Lease Contract

Under FASB ASC 842, a contract that contains a lease should be separated into lease and nonlease components. Separation should be based on the right to use; each underlying asset should be considered to be separate from other lease components when both of the following criteria are met:

a. The lessee can benefit from the right-of-use of the asset (either alone or with other readily available resources)

b. The right-of-use is neither highly dependent on or highly interrelated with other underlying assets in the contract

The consideration in the contract should be allocated to the separate lease and nonlease components in accordance with provisions of FASB ASC 842.

Lessees can make an accounting policy election to treat both lease and nonlease elements as a single lease component.

Lease Classification

When a lease meets any of the following specified criteria at commencement, the lease should be classified by the lessee and lessor as a finance lease and a sales-type lease, respectively. These criteria can be summarized as follows:

a. Transfers ownership to lessee

b. Purchase option reasonably certain to be exercised

c. Lease term for major portion of asset's remaining economic life

d. Present value of lease payments and residual value exceeds substantially all of the fair value of the underlying asset

e. Specialized nature of underlying asset results in no expectation of alternative use after the lease term

If none of the above criteria are met, the lease should be classified as follows:

Lessee—classify as an operating lease

Lessor—classify as an operating lease unless (1) the present value of the lease payments and any residual value guarantee that equals or exceeds substantially all of the fair value of the underlying asset and (2) it is probable that the lessor will collect the lease payments plus any residual value guarantee. If both of these summarized criteria from FASB ASC 842-10-25-3 are met, the lessor should classify the lease as a direct financing lease.

Lease Term and Measurement

The lease term is the noncancellable period of the lease together with all of the following:

a. Period covered by the option for the lessee to extend the lease if the option is reasonably certain to be exercised

b. Period covered by option for lessee to terminate the lease if reasonably certain not to be exercised

c. Period covered by option for lessor to extend or not terminate the lease if option is controlled by lessor.

Lease Payments

Lease payments relating to use of the underlying asset during the lease term include the following at the commencement date:

a. Fixed payments less incentives payable to lessee

b. Variable lease payments based on an index or other rate

c. Exercise price of an option to purchase the underlying asset if it is reasonably certain to be exercised

d. Payments for penalties for terminating a lease if the lease term reflects exercise of lessee option

e. Fees paid by the lessee to the owners of a special purpose entity for structuring the lease

f. For lessee only, amounts probable of being owed under residual value guarantees

Lease payments specifically exclude the following:

a. Certain other variable lease payments

b. Any guarantee by the lessee of the lessor's debt

c. Certain amounts allocated to nonlease components

Reassessment of the lease term and purchase options, and subsequent remeasurement by either the lessee or lessor are limited to certain specified circumstances.

Lessee

Recognition and Measurement

Commencement Date

At the commencement date of the lease, a lessee should recognize a right-of-use asset and a lease liability; for short term leases, an alternative accounting policy election is available.

The lease liability should be measured at the present value of the unpaid lease payments. The right-of-use asset should consist of the following: the amount of the initial lease liability; any lease payments made to lessor at or before the commencement date minus any incentives received; and initial direct costs.

A short term lease is defined by the FASB ASC master glossary as a lease that, at the commencement date has a lease term of 12 months or less and does not include an option to purchase the underlying asset that the lessee is reasonably certain to exercise. The accounting policy election for short term leases should be made by class of underlying asset. The election provides for recognition of the lease payments in profit or loss on a straight-line basis over the lease term and variable lease payments in the period in which the obligation for those payments is incurred.

After the Commencement Date

After the commencement date, the lessee should recognize in profit or loss (unless costs are included in the carrying amount of another asset) the following:

- Finance leases:
    - *a.* Amortization of the right-of-use asset and interest on the lease liability
    - *b.* Variable lease payments not included in the lease liability in the period obligation incurred
    - *c.* Any impairment
- Operating leases:
    - *a.* A single lease cost calculated such that the remaining cost is allocated on a straight line basis over the remaining lease term (unless another allocation is more representative of the benefit from use of the asset)
    - *b.* Variable lease payments not included in the lease liability in the period in which the obligation is incurred
    - *c.* Any impairment

Subsequent Measurement

FASB ASC 842-20-35 provides guidance for subsequent measurement.

Presentation and Disclosure

Key presentation matters include the following:

- Statement of financial position.
    - — Separate presentation of right-of-use assets and lease liabilities from finance leases and operating leases.
- Statement of comprehensive income.
    - — Finance leases—interest expense on the lease liability and amortization of right-of-use asset in a manner consistent with how the entity presents other interest expense and depreciation or amortization of similar assets.
    - — Operating leases—expense to be included in the lessee's income from continuing operations.

- Statement of cash flows.
  - Presentation within financing activities—the repayment of the principal portion of the lease liability arising from finance leases.
  - Presentation within operating activities—payments arising from operating leases; interest payments on the lease liability; variable lease payments and short term lease payments not included in lease liability.

Disclosure requirements include qualitative and quantitative information for leases, significant judgements, and amounts recognized in the financial statements, including certain specified information and amounts.

Lessor

Recognition and Measurement

FASB ASC 842 provides recognition guidance for sales-type leases, direct financing leases, and operating leases. The following table summarizes the guidance:

Sales-Type Leases	
At the Commencement Date	**After the Commencement Date**
Lessor should derecognize the underlying asset and recognize the following: *a.* Net investment in the lease (lease receivable and unguaranteed residual asset) *b.* Selling profit or loss arising from the lease *c.* Initial direct costs as an expense	Lessor should recognize all of the following: *a.* Interest income on the net investment in the lease *b.* Certain variable lease payments *c.* Impairment
Direct Financing Leases	
At the Commencement Date	**After the Commencement Date**
Lessor should derecognize the underlying asset and recognize the following: *a.* Net investment in the lease (lease receivable and unguaranteed residual asset reduced by selling profit) *b.* Selling loss arising from the lease, if applicable	Lessor should recognize all of the following: *a.* Interest income on the net investment in the lease *b.* Certain variable lease payments *c.* Impairment

(continued)

Operating Leases	
At the Commencement Date	**After the Commencement Date**
Lessor should defer initial direct costs.	Lessor should recognize all of the following: *a*. The lease payments as income in profit or loss over the lease term on a straight line basis (unless another method in more representative of the benefit received) *b*. Certain variable lease payments as income in profit or loss *c*. Initial direct costs as an expense over the lease term on the same basis as lease income

FASB ASC 842-30-35 provides guidance for subsequent measurement.

Presentation and Disclosure

Key presentation matters include the following:

For sales-type and direct financing leases:

- Statement of financial position
  - Separate presentation of lease assets (that is, aggregate of lessor's net investment in sales-type leases and direct financing leases) from other assets.
  - Classified as current or noncurrent based on same considerations as other assets.
- Statement of comprehensive income
  - Presentation of income from leases in the statement of comprehensive income or disclosure of income from leases in the notes with a reference to the corresponding line in the statement of comprehensive income.
  - Presentation of profit or loss recognized at commencement date in a manner appropriate to lessor's business model.
- Statement of cash flows
  - Presentation within operating activities—cash receipts from leases.

For operating leases:

- Statement of financial position
  - Presentation of an underlying asset subject to an operating leases in accordance with other FASB ASC topics.
- Statement of cash flows
  - Presentation within operating activities—cash receipts from leases.

Disclosure requirements include qualitative and quantitative information for leases, significant judgements, and amounts recognized in the financial statements, including certain specified information and amounts.

Sale and Leaseback Transactions

FASB ASC 842 provides guidance for both the transfer contract and the lease in a sale and leaseback transaction (a transaction in which a seller-lessee transfers an asset to a buyer-lessor and leases that asset back). Determination of whether the transfer is a sale should be based on provisions of FASB ASC 606, *Revenue from Contracts with Customers*. FASB ASC 842-40-25 provides measurement guidance for a transfer that is either determined to be a sale or determined not to be a sale.

FASB ASC 842-40 provides guidance for subsequent measurement, financial statement presentation, and disclosures.

Leveraged Lease Arrangements

The legacy accounting model for leveraged leases continues to apply to those leveraged leases that commenced before the effective date of FASB ASC 842. There is no separate accounting model for leveraged leases that commence after the effective date of FASB ASC 842.

Subsequent Developments

In January 2018, FASB issued ASU No. 2018-01, *Leases (Topic 842): Land Easement Practical Expedient for Transition to Topic 842*. This ASU permits an entity to elect an optional transition practical expedient to not evaluate under FASB ASC 842 existing or expired land easements not previously accounted for as leases under FASB ASC 840. The effective date of FASB ASU No. 2018-01 is in line with the guidance in ASU No. 2016-02.

Appendix C

Overview of Statements on Quality Control Standards

This appendix is nonauthoritative and is included for informational purposes only.

This appendix is a partial reproduction of chapter 1 of the AICPA practice aid *Establishing and Maintaining a System of Quality Control for a CPA Firm's Accounting and Auditing Practice*, available at www.aicpa.org/interestareas/frc/pages/enhancingauditqualitypracticeaid.aspx.

This appendix highlights certain aspects of the quality control standards issued by the AICPA. If appropriate, readers should also refer to the quality control standards issued by the PCAOB, available at www.pcaobus.org/standards/qc/pages/default.aspx.

1.01 The objectives of a system of quality control are to provide a CPA firm with reasonable assurance[1] that the firm and its personnel comply with professional standards and applicable regulatory and legal requirements, and that the firm or engagement partners issue reports that are appropriate in the circumstances. QC section 10, *A Firm's System of Quality Control* (AICPA, *Professional Standards*), addresses a CPA firm's responsibilities for its system of quality control for its accounting and auditing practice. That section is to be read in conjunction with the AICPA Code of Professional Conduct and other relevant ethical requirements.

1.02 A system of quality control consists of policies designed to achieve the objectives of the system and the procedures necessary to implement and monitor compliance with those policies. The nature, extent, and formality of a firm's quality control policies and procedures will depend on various factors such as the firm's size; the number and operating characteristics of its offices; the degree of authority allowed to, and the knowledge and experience possessed by, firm personnel; and the nature and complexity of the firm's practice.

Communication of Quality Control Policies and Procedures

1.03 The firm should communicate its quality control policies and procedures to its personnel. Most firms will find it appropriate to communicate their policies and procedures in writing and distribute them, or make them available electronically, to all professional personnel. Effective communication includes the following:

- A description of quality control policies and procedures and the objectives they are designed to achieve
- The message that each individual has a personal responsibility for quality
- A requirement for each individual to be familiar with and to comply with these policies and procedures

[1] The term *reasonable assurance*, which is defined as a high, but not absolute, level of assurance, is used because absolute assurance cannot be attained. Paragraph .53 of QC section 10, *A Firm's System of Quality Control* (AICPA, *Professional Standards*), states, "Any system of quality control has inherent limitations that can reduce its effectiveness."

Effective communication also includes procedures for personnel to communicate their views or concerns on quality control matters to the firm's management.

Elements of a System of Quality Control

1.04 A firm must establish and maintain a system of quality control. The firm's system of quality control should include policies and procedures that address each of the following elements of quality control identified in paragraph .17 of QC section 10:

- Leadership responsibilities for quality within the firm (the "tone at the top")
- Relevant ethical requirements
- Acceptance and continuance of client relationships and specific engagements
- Human resources
- Engagement performance
- Monitoring

1.05 The elements of quality control are interrelated. For example, a firm continually assesses client relationships to comply with relevant ethical requirements, including independence, integrity, and objectivity, and policies and procedures related to the acceptance and continuance of client relationships and specific engagements. Similarly, the human resources element of quality control encompasses criteria related to professional development, hiring, advancement, and assignment of firm personnel to engagements, all of which affect policies and procedures related to engagement performance. In addition, policies and procedures related to the monitoring element of quality control enable a firm to evaluate whether its policies and procedures for each of the other five elements of quality control are suitably designed and effectively applied.

1.06 Policies and procedures established by the firm related to each element are designed to achieve reasonable assurance with respect to the purpose of that element. Deficiencies in policies and procedures for an element may result in not achieving reasonable assurance with respect to the purpose of that element; however, the system of quality control, as a whole, may still be effective in providing the firm with reasonable assurance that the firm and its personnel comply with professional standards and applicable regulatory and legal requirements and that the firm or engagement partners issue reports that are appropriate in the circumstances.

1.07 If a firm merges, acquires, sells, or otherwise changes a portion of its practice, the surviving firm evaluates and, as necessary, revises, implements, and maintains firm-wide quality control policies and procedures that are appropriate for the changed circumstances.

Leadership Responsibilities for Quality Within the Firm (the "Tone at the Top")

1.08 The purpose of the leadership responsibilities element of a system of quality control is to promote an internal culture based on the recognition that quality is essential in performing engagements. The firm should establish and maintain the following policies and procedures to achieve this purpose:

- Require the firm's leadership (managing partner, board of managing partners, CEO, or equivalent) to assume ultimate responsibility for the firm's system of quality control.
- Provide the firm with reasonable assurance that personnel assigned operational responsibility for the firm's quality control system have sufficient and appropriate experience and ability to identify and understand quality control issues and develop appropriate policies and procedures, as well as the necessary authority to implement those policies and procedures.

1.09 Establishing and maintaining the following policies and procedures assists firms in recognizing that the firm's business strategy is subject to the overarching requirement for the firm to achieve the objectives of the system of quality control in all the engagements that the firm performs:

- Assign management responsibilities so that commercial considerations do not override the quality of the work performed.
- Design policies and procedures addressing performance evaluation, compensation, and advancement (including incentive systems) with regard to personnel to demonstrate the firm's overarching commitment to the objectives of the system of quality control.
- Devote sufficient and appropriate resources for the development, communication, and support of its quality control policies and procedures.

Relevant Ethical Requirements

1.10 The purpose of the relevant ethical requirements element of a system of quality control is to provide the firm with reasonable assurance that the firm and its personnel comply with relevant ethical requirements when discharging professional responsibilities. Relevant ethical requirements include independence, integrity, and objectivity. Establishing and maintaining policies such as the following assist the firm in obtaining this assurance:

- Require that personnel adhere to relevant ethical requirements such as those in regulations, interpretations, and rules of the AICPA, state CPA societies, state boards of accountancy, state statutes, the U.S. Government Accountability Office, and any other applicable regulators.
- Establish procedures to communicate independence requirements to firm personnel and, where applicable, others subject to them.
- Establish procedures to identify and evaluate possible threats to independence and objectivity, including the familiarity threat that may be created by using the same senior personnel on an audit or attest engagement over a long period of time, and to take appropriate action to eliminate those threats or reduce them to an acceptable level by applying safeguards.
- Require that the firm withdraw from the engagement if effective safeguards to reduce threats to independence to an acceptable level cannot be applied.

- Require written confirmation, at least annually, of compliance with the firm's policies and procedures on independence from all firm personnel required to be independent by relevant requirements.
- Establish procedures for confirming the independence of another firm or firm personnel in associated member firms who perform part of the engagement. This would apply to national firm personnel, foreign firm personnel, and foreign-associated firms.[2]
- Require the rotation of personnel for audit or attest engagements where regulatory or other authorities require such rotation after a specified period.

Acceptance and Continuance of Client Relationships and Specific Engagements

1.11 The purpose of the quality control element that addresses acceptance and continuance of client relationships and specific engagements is to establish criteria for deciding whether to accept or continue a client relationship and whether to perform a specific engagement for a client. A firm's client acceptance and continuance policies represent a key element in mitigating litigation and business risk. Accordingly, it is important that a firm be aware that the integrity and reputation of a client's management could reflect the reliability of the client's accounting records and financial representations and, therefore, affect the firm's reputation or involvement in litigation. A firm's policies and procedures related to the acceptance and continuance of client relationships and specific engagements should provide the firm with reasonable assurance that it will undertake or continue relationships and engagements only where it

- is competent to perform the engagement and has the capabilities, including the time and resources, to do so;
- can comply with legal and relevant ethical requirements;
- has considered the client's integrity and does not have information that would lead it to conclude that the client lacks integrity; and
- has reached an understanding with the client regarding the services to be performed.

1.12 This assurance should be obtained before accepting an engagement with a new client, when deciding whether to continue an existing engagement, and when considering acceptance of a new engagement with an existing client. Establishing and maintaining policies such as the following assist the firm in obtaining this assurance:

- Evaluate factors that have a bearing on management's integrity and consider the risk associated with providing professional services in particular circumstances.[3]

---

[2] A *foreign-associated firm* is a firm domiciled outside of the United States and its territories that is a member of, correspondent with, or similarly associated with an international firm or international association of firms.

[3] Such considerations would include the risk of providing professional services to significant clients or to other clients for which the practitioner's objectivity or the appearance of independence

(continued)

- Evaluate whether the engagement can be completed with professional competence; undertake only those engagements for which the firm has the capabilities, resources, and professional competence to complete; and evaluate, at the end of specific periods or upon occurrence of certain events, whether the relationship should be continued.
- Obtain an understanding, preferably in writing, with the client regarding the services to be performed.
- Establish procedures on continuing an engagement and the client relationship, including procedures for dealing with information that would have caused the firm to decline an engagement if the information had been available earlier.
- Require documentation of how issues relating to acceptance or continuance of client relationships and specific engagements were resolved.

Human Resources

1.13 The purpose of the human resources element of a system of quality control is to provide the firm with reasonable assurance that it has sufficient personnel with the capabilities, competence, and commitment to ethical principles necessary (*a*) to perform its engagements in accordance with professional standards and regulatory and legal requirements, and (*b*) to enable the firm to issue reports that are appropriate in the circumstances. Establishing and maintaining policies such as the following assist the firm in obtaining this assurance:

- Recruit and hire personnel of integrity who possess the characteristics that enable them to perform competently.
- Determine capabilities and competencies required for an engagement, especially for the engagement partner, based on the characteristics of the particular client, industry, and kind of service being performed. Specific competencies necessary for an engagement partner are discussed in paragraph .A27 of QC section 10.
- Determine the capabilities and competencies possessed by personnel.
- Assign the responsibility for each engagement to an engagement partner.
- Assign personnel based on the knowledge, skills, and abilities required in the circumstances and the nature and extent of supervision needed.
- Have personnel participate in general and industry-specific continuing professional education and professional development activities that enable them to accomplish assigned responsibilities

---

(footnote continued)

may be impaired. In broad terms, the significance of a client to a member or a firm refers to relationships that could diminish a practitioner's objectivity and independence in performing attest services. Examples of factors to consider in determining the significance of a client to an engagement partner, office, or practice unit include (*a*) the amount of time the partner, office, or practice unit devotes to the engagement, (*b*) the effect on the partner's stature within the firm as a result of his or her service to the client, (*c*) the manner in which the partner, office, or practice unit is compensated, or (*d*) the effect that losing the client would have on the partner, office, or practice unit.

and satisfy applicable continuing professional education requirements of the AICPA, state boards of accountancy, and other regulators.

- Select for advancement only those individuals who have the qualifications necessary to fulfill the responsibilities they will be called on to assume.

Engagement Performance

1.14 The purpose of the engagement performance element of quality control is to provide the firm with reasonable assurance (*a*) that engagements are consistently performed in accordance with applicable professional standards and regulatory and legal requirements, and (*b*) that the firm or the engagement partner issues reports that are appropriate in the circumstances. Policies and procedures for engagement performance should address all phases of the design and execution of the engagement, including engagement performance, supervision responsibilities, and review responsibilities. Policies and procedures also should require that consultation takes place when appropriate. In addition, a policy should establish criteria against which all engagements are to be evaluated to determine whether an engagement quality control review should be performed.

1.15 Establishing and maintaining policies such as the following assist the firm in obtaining the assurance required relating to the engagement performance element of quality control:

- Plan all engagements to meet professional, regulatory, and the firm's requirements.
- Perform work and issue reports and other communications that meet professional, regulatory, and the firm's requirements.
- Require that work performed by other team members be reviewed by qualified engagement team members, which may include the engagement partner, on a timely basis.
- Require the engagement team to complete the assembly of final engagement files on a timely basis.
- Establish procedures to maintain the confidentiality, safe custody, integrity, accessibility, and retrievability of engagement documentation.
- Require the retention of engagement documentation for a period of time sufficient to meet the needs of the firm, professional standards, laws, and regulations.
- Require that
    - — consultation take place when appropriate (for example, when dealing with complex, unusual, unfamiliar, difficult, or contentious issues);
    - — sufficient and appropriate resources be available to enable appropriate consultation to take place;
    - — all the relevant facts known to the engagement team be provided to those consulted;

- the nature, scope, and conclusions of such consultations be documented; and
- the conclusions resulting from such consultations be implemented.

- Require that
  - differences of opinion be dealt with and resolved;
  - conclusions reached are documented and implemented; and
  - the report not be released until the matter is resolved.
- Require that
  - all engagements be evaluated against the criteria for determining whether an engagement quality control review should be performed;
  - an engagement quality control review be performed for all engagements that meet the criteria; and
  - the review be completed before the report is released.
- Establish procedures addressing the nature, timing, extent, and documentation of the engagement quality control review.
- Establish criteria for the eligibility of engagement quality control reviewers.

Monitoring

1.16 The purpose of the monitoring element of a system of quality control is to provide the firm and its engagement partners with reasonable assurance that the policies and procedures related to the system of quality control are relevant, adequate, operating effectively, and complied with in practice. Monitoring involves an ongoing consideration and evaluation of the appropriateness of the design, the effectiveness of the operation of a firm's quality control system, and a firm's compliance with its quality control policies and procedures. The purpose of monitoring compliance with quality control policies and procedures is to provide an evaluation of the following:

- Adherence to professional standards and regulatory and legal requirements
- Whether the quality control system has been appropriately designed and effectively implemented
- Whether the firm's quality control policies and procedures have been operating effectively so that reports issued by the firm are appropriate in the circumstances

1.17 Establishing and maintaining policies such as the following assist the firm in obtaining the assurance required relating to the monitoring element of quality control:

- Assign responsibility for the monitoring process to a partner or partners or other persons with sufficient and appropriate experience and authority in the firm to assume that responsibility.

- Assign performance of the monitoring process to competent individuals.
- Require the performance of monitoring procedures that are sufficiently comprehensive to enable the firm to assess compliance with all applicable professional standards and the firm's quality control policies and procedures. Monitoring procedures consist of the following:
    - — Review of selected administrative and personnel records pertaining to the quality control elements.
    - — Review of engagement documentation, reports, and clients' financial statements.
    - — Summarization of the findings from the monitoring procedures, at least annually, and consideration of the systemic causes of findings that indicate that improvements are needed.
    - — Determination of any corrective actions to be taken or improvements to be made with respect to the specific engagements reviewed or the firm's quality control policies and procedures.
    - — Communication of the identified findings to appropriate firm management personnel.
    - — Consideration of findings by appropriate firm management personnel who should also determine that any actions necessary, including necessary modifications to the quality control system, are taken on a timely basis.
    - — Assessment of
        - the appropriateness of the firm's guidance materials and any practice aids;
        - new developments in professional standards and regulatory and legal requirements and how they are reflected in the firm's policies and procedures where appropriate;
        - compliance with policies and procedures on independence;
        - the effectiveness of continuing professional development, including training;
        - decisions related to acceptance and continuance of client relationships and specific engagements; and
        - firm personnel's understanding of the firm's quality control policies and procedures and implementation thereof.
- Communicate at least annually, to relevant engagement partners and other appropriate personnel, deficiencies noted as a result of the monitoring process and recommendations for appropriate remedial action.

- Communicate the results of the monitoring of its quality control system process to relevant firm personnel at least annually.
- Establish procedures designed to provide the firm with reasonable assurance that it deals appropriately with the following:
  - — Complaints and allegations that the work performed by the firm fails to comply with professional standards and regulatory and legal requirements.
  - — Allegations of noncompliance with the firm's system of quality control.
  - — Deficiencies in the design or operation of the firm's quality control policies and procedures, or noncompliance with the firm's system of quality control by an individual or individuals, as identified during the investigations into complaints and allegations.

    This includes establishing clearly defined channels for firm personnel to raise any concerns in a manner that enables them to come forward without fear of reprisal and documenting complaints and allegations and the responses to them.
- Require appropriate documentation to provide evidence of the operation of each element of its system of quality control. The form and content of documentation evidencing the operation of each of the elements of the system of quality control is a matter of judgment and depends on a number of factors, including the following, for example:
  - — The size of the firm and the number of offices.
  - — The nature and complexity of the firm's practice and organization.
- Require retention of documentation providing evidence of the operation of the system of quality control for a period of time sufficient to permit those performing monitoring procedures and peer review to evaluate the firm's compliance with its system of quality control, or for a longer period if required by law or regulation.

1.18 Some of the monitoring procedures discussed in the previous list may be accomplished through the performance of the following:

- Engagement quality control review
- Review of engagement documentation, reports, and clients' financial statements for selected engagements after the report release date
- Inspection[4] procedures

---

[4] *Inspection* is a retrospective evaluation of the adequacy of the firm's quality control policies and procedures, its personnel's understanding of those policies and procedures, and the extent of the firm's compliance with them. Although monitoring procedures are meant to be ongoing, they may include inspection procedures performed at a fixed point in time. Monitoring is a broad concept; inspection is one specific type of monitoring procedure.

Documentation of Quality Control Policies and Procedures

1.19 The firm should document each element of its system of quality control. The extent of the documentation will depend on the size, structure, and nature of the firm's practice. Documentation may be as simple as a checklist of the firm's policies and procedures or as extensive as practice manuals.

Appendix D

Illustrations of Segmenting Criteria

This appendix will be deleted upon the effective date of FASB Accounting Standards Update No. 2014-09, *Revenue from Contracts with Customers (Topic 606)*. As industry practice develops, updated guidance, as appropriate, will be included in a future edition of this guide.[1]

This appendix is nonauthoritative and is included for informational purposes only.

FASB *Accounting Standards Codification* (ASC) 605-35 provides revenue recognition guidance for contractors. Information relating to the segmenting of contracts for revenue recognition purposes and the criteria for segmenting are discussed in paragraphs 10–13 of FASB ASC 605-35-25. The following examples illustrate the application of those criteria in specific circumstances:

1. A design or build contractor, or both, negotiates a contract that provides for design engineering, procurement, and construction of a nuclear power plant. The contract specifies the separate phases of the work, and, for this type of project, the phases are frequently contracted separately. Moreover, the contractor has a significant history of providing similar services to other customers contracting for the phases separately. Such a history shows a relatively stable pricing policy. The contractor's normal fee on design engineering is 15 percent; on procurement, 2 percent; and on construction, 5 percent. These rates are commensurate with the different levels of risk attributable to the separate phases, and the aggregate of the values of the separate phases produced from such a fee structure is approximately equal to the overall contract price. The similarity of services and prices in the contract segments to services and the prices of such services to other customers contracted separately is documented and verifiable. The contract does not meet the first set of criteria in FASB ASC 605-35-25-12 but does meet the second set of criteria in FASB ASC 605-35-25-13 and, therefore, qualifies

[1] FASB Accounting Standards Update (ASU) No. 2014-09, *Revenue from Contracts with Customers (Topic 606)*, was issued in May 2014. Public business entities, certain not-for-profit entities, and certain employee benefit plans should apply the guidance in ASU No. 2014-09 as amended by FASB ASU No. 2015-14, *Revenue from Contracts with Customers (Topic 606): Deferral of the Effective Date*, to annual reporting periods beginning after December 15, 2017, including interim reporting periods within that reporting period. Earlier application is permitted only as of annual reporting periods beginning after December 15, 2016, including interim reporting periods within that reporting period.

All other entities should apply the guidance in ASU No. 2014-09 to annual reporting periods beginning after December 15, 2018, and interim reporting periods within annual reporting periods beginning after December 15, 2019. All other entities may apply the guidance in ASU No. 2014-09 earlier as of an annual reporting period beginning after December 15, 2016, including interim reporting periods within that reporting period. All other entities also may apply the guidance in ASU No. 2014-09 earlier as of an annual reporting period beginning after December 15, 2016, and interim reporting periods within annual reporting periods beginning one year after the annual reporting period in which the entity first applies the guidance in ASU No. 2014-09.

Readers are encouraged to read the full text of the FASB ASU, available at www.fasb.org. Readers should apply the appropriate guidance based on their facts and circumstances.

for segmenting. However, if any one of the required conditions in FASB ASC 605-35-25-13 is not met, segmenting would not be appropriate. For example, the contractor's significant history might have been with fossil fueled instead of nuclear powered generating plants. Or the different gross profit rates, even though supported by the contractor's history, might not be justified by different levels of risk or by disparities in the relationship of supply and demand for the segment services. Such circumstances could arise from an erratic or unusual labor market for a particular project.

2. A contract provides for construction of an apartment building, swimming pool, and other amenities. The contractor has a significant history of providing similar services to other customers who have contracted for such services separately. His or her significant history is one of a relatively stable pricing policy. He or she wishes to assign values to the segments on the basis of his or her normal historical prices and terms to such customers. On that basis, the aggregate of the segment values will approximate the total contract price. However, although this contractor performs the phases separately, the practice is unusual and is not done by other contractors in the industry. Also, the different gross profit rates that the contractor would ascribe to the segments based on his or her history cannot practicably be related to economic risk or supply and demand disparities. Because the facts do not meet the criteria in paragraphs 12–13 of FASB ASC 605-35-25, the contract should not be segmented.

3. A contractor is a road builder, performing alternately under contracts in which much of the work is subcontracted and under contracts in which he or she performs all the work himself or herself. Under contracts involving subcontractors, the contractor generally realizes a lower profit margin due to the spread of risk to subcontractors. He or she, therefore, wishes to segment his or her contract revenues between the subcontracted portions of the work and the portions that he or she performs himself or herself, assigning a greater amount of revenue to the latter and a lesser amount to the former. His or her history with both types of work is significant and is supported by a relatively stable pricing policy. However, it is not customary for the portions of the work to which the greater amounts of revenue are to be ascribed to be contracted separately from the other portions. The contract should not be segmented because the criteria in neither FASB ASC 605-35-25-12 nor FASB ASC 605-35-25-13 are met.

4. An electrical and mechanical subcontractor is awarded both the electrical and mechanical work based on separate, independent bids. Separate subcontracts are signed and become the profit centers for profit recognition purposes. Had the work been negotiated as a package, the contract might have been segmented only if the criteria in either FASB ASC 605-35-25-12 or FASB ASC 605-35-25-13 had been met.

5. A contractor is awarded a contract to construct three virtually identical generating power plants in different locations. His or her costs will vary because of differences in site work, transportation, labor conditions, and other factors at the three locations. He or she wishes

to segment contract revenues in response to cost differences. He or she has a significant history of constructing generating plants under separate contracts under a relatively stable pricing policy. However, segmenting contract revenues on this basis would not be commensurate with the different levels of risk or the supply or demand disparities of the three projects. The contract should not be segmented in these circumstances.

Appendix E

Computing Income Earned Under the Percentage-of-Completion Method

This appendix will be revised upon the effective date of FASB Accounting Standards Update No. 2014-09, *Revenue from Contracts with Customers (Topic 606)*. As industry practice develops, updated guidance, as appropriate, will be included in a future edition of this guide.[1]

This appendix is nonauthoritative and is included for informational purposes only.

Illustration of the Alternative A Procedure

The following hypothetical data are used to illustrate the computation of income earned under the alternative A procedure described in FASB ASC 605-35-25-83. A contracting company has a lump-sum contract for $9 million to build a bridge at a total estimated cost of approximately $8 million. The construction period covers 3 years. Financial data during the construction period are as follows.

	Year 1	*Year 2*	*Year 3*
		(in thousands of dollars)	
Total estimated revenue	$9,000	$9,100	$9,200
Cost recognized	$2,050	$6,100	$8,200
Estimated cost to complete	6,000	2,000	—
Total estimated cost	$8,050	$8,100	$8,200
Estimated gross profit	$950	$1,000	$1,000
Billings to date	$1,800	$5,500	$9,200
Collections to date	$1,500	$5,000	$9,200
Measure of progress	25%	75%	100%

[1] FASB Accounting Standards Update (ASU) No. 2014-09, *Revenue from Contracts with Customers (Topic 606)*, was issued in May 2014. Public business entities, certain not-for-profit entities, and certain employee benefit plans should apply the guidance in ASU No. 2014-09 as amended by FASB ASU No. 2015-14, *Revenue from Contracts with Customers (Topic 606): Deferral of the Effective Date*, to annual reporting periods beginning after December 15, 2017, including interim reporting periods within that reporting period. Earlier application is permitted only as of annual reporting periods beginning after December 15, 2016, including interim reporting periods within that reporting period.

All other entities should apply the guidance in ASU No. 2014-09 to annual reporting periods beginning after December 15, 2018, and interim reporting periods within annual reporting periods beginning after December 15, 2019. All other entities may apply the guidance in ASU No. 2014-09 earlier as of an annual reporting period beginning after December 15, 2016, including interim reporting periods within that reporting period. All other entities also may apply the guidance in ASU No. 2014-09 earlier as of an annual reporting period beginning after December 15, 2016, and interim reporting periods within annual reporting periods beginning one year after the annual reporting period in which the entity first applies the guidance in ASU No. 2014-09.

Readers are encouraged to read the full text of the FASB ASU, available at www.fasb.org. Readers should apply the appropriate guidance based on their facts and circumstances.

The amount of revenue, costs, and income recognized in the three periods would be as follows.

	To Date	*Recognized Prior Year(s)*	*Current Year*
Year 1			
Earned revenue			
($9,000 × .25)	$2,250		$2,250
Cost of earned revenue	2,050		2,050
Gross profit	$200		$200
Gross profit rate	8.8%		8.8%
Year 2			
Earned revenue			
($9,100 × .75)	$6,825	$2,250	$4,575
Cost of earned revenue	6,100	2,050	4,050
Gross profit	$725	$200	$525
Gross profit rate	10.6%	8.8%	11.5%
Year 3			
Earned revenue	$9,200	$6,825	$2,375
Cost of earned revenue	8,200	6,100	2,100
Gross profit	$1,000	$725	$275
Gross profit rate	10.9%	10.6%	11.6%

Comparison of Alternative A and Alternative B

The following hypothetical data are used to compare the income statement and balance sheet effects of alternative A described in FASB ASC 605-35-25-83 and alternative B described in FASB ASC 605-35-25-84.

Estimated Contract		
Revenues		$1,000,000
Cost		900,000
Gross profit		$100,000
Gross profit percentage		10%
Annual Information	*To Date*	*Current*
Year 1		
Billings	$200,000	$200,000
Cost incurred	300,000	300,000
% complete	25%	

Annual Information	To Date	Current
Year 2		
Billings	$750,000	$550,000
Cost incurred	650,000	350,000
% complete	75%	
Year 3		
Billings	$1,000,000	$250,000
Cost incurred	900,000	250,000
% complete	100%	

The results of measuring earned revenues, cost of earned revenues, and gross profit by alternative A and alternative B would be as follows.

	Alternative A	Alternative B
Income Statement		
Year 1		
Earned revenue	$250,000	$325,000
Cost of earned revenue	225,000	300,000
Gross profit	$25,000	$25,000
Gross profit percentage	10%	7.7%
Year 2		
Earned revenue	$500,000	$400,000
Cost of earned revenue	450,000	350,000
Gross profit	$50,000	$50,000
Gross profit percentage	10%	12.5%
Year 3		
Earned revenue	$250,000	$275,000
Cost of earned revenue	225,000	250,000
Gross profit	$25,000	$25,000
Gross profit percentage	10%	9.1%
Balance Sheet Debit (Credit)		
Alternative A		
Year 1		
Costs and estimated earnings in excess of billings on uncompleted contracts	$50,000	
Unbilled revenues		$50,000

(continued)

Balance Sheet Debit (Credit)

Alternative B		
Year 1		
Costs and estimated earnings in excess of billings on uncompleted contracts	$125,000	
Unbilled revenues		$125,000
Year 2		
Billings in excess of costs incurred and estimated earnings on uncompleted contracts	$(25,000)	
Excess billings		$(25,000)

Discussion of the Results Under the Two Methods

Under alternative A, earned revenue, cost of earned revenue, and gross profit are measured by the extent of progress toward completion. Under alternative B, only the amount of gross profit is measured by the extent of progress toward completion. Therefore, the same amount of gross profit is reported under either method. However, under alternative B, earned revenue is the amount of costs incurred during the period plus the amount of gross profit recognized based on the extent of progress toward completion, and the cost of earned revenue is the amount of costs incurred during the period. For that reason, earned revenue and cost of earned revenue under alternative B are not comparable to the measurement of extent of progress toward completion unless the extent of progress is measured by the cost-to-cost method.

Appendix F

Examples of Computation of Income Earned

This appendix will be revised upon the effective date of FASB Accounting Standards Update No. 2014-09, *Revenue from Contracts with Customers (Topic 606)*. As industry practice develops, up-dated guidance, as appropriate, will be included in a future edition of this guide.[1]

This appendix is nonauthoritative and is included for informational purposes only.

Exhibit Description	*Exhibit Number*
Cost-to-Cost Method	F-1
Labor-Hours Method	F-2
Construction Management	F-3
Units of Production	F-4
Zero Profit	F-5
Loss Contract	F-6
Combining	F-7
Segmenting	F-8

For convenience and consistency, all computations are based on the alternative A procedure described in FASB ASC 605-35-25-83.

Exhibit F-1 — Cost-to-Cost Method

A general contractor specializes in the construction of commercial and industrial buildings. The contractor is experienced in bidding long-term construction projects of this type, with the typical project lasting 15–24 months. The contractor uses the percentage-of-completion method of revenue recognition because, given the characteristics of the contractor's business and contracts, it is the

[1] FASB Accounting Standards Update (ASU) No. 2014-09, *Revenue from Contracts with Customers (Topic 606)*, was issued in May 2014. Public business entities, certain not-for-profit entities, and certain employee benefit plans should apply the guidance in ASU No. 2014-09 as amended by FASB ASU No. 2015-14, *Revenue from Contracts with Customers (Topic 606): Deferral of the Effective Date*, to annual reporting periods beginning after December 15, 2017, including interim reporting periods within that reporting period. Earlier application is permitted only as of annual reporting periods beginning after December 15, 2016, including interim reporting periods within that reporting period.

All other entities should apply the guidance in ASU No. 2014-09 to annual reporting periods beginning after December 15, 2018, and interim reporting periods within annual reporting periods beginning after December 15, 2019. All other entities may apply the guidance in ASU No. 2014-09 earlier as of an annual reporting period beginning after December 15, 2016, including interim reporting periods within that reporting period. All other entities also may apply the guidance in ASU No. 2014-09 earlier as of an annual reporting period beginning after December 15, 2016, and interim reporting periods within annual reporting periods beginning one year after the annual reporting period in which the entity first applies the guidance in ASU No. 2014-09.

Readers are encouraged to read the full text of the FASB ASU, available at www.fasb.org. Readers should apply the appropriate guidance based on their facts and circumstances.

most appropriate method. That is, the contracts entered into by the contractor normally specify clearly the rights of the parties regarding services to be provided and consideration, and the contractor has demonstrated the ability to provide dependable estimates of contract revenue, contract costs, and gross profit. Progress toward completion is measured on the basis of incurred costs to estimated total costs because, in the opinion of management, this basis of measurement is most appropriate in the circumstances.

The entity began work on a lump-sum contract at the beginning of year 1. As bid, the statistics were as follows:

Lump-sum price		$1,500,000
Estimated costs		
Labor	$300,000	
Materials and subcontractors	800,000	
Indirect costs	100,000	1,200,000
Estimated gross profit		$300,000

After construction began, a change order was negotiated, increasing the lump-sum price by $150,000 at an estimated additional contract cost of $120,000 (labor: $10,000, materials: $110,000).

At the end of the first year, the following was the status of the contract:

Billings to date		$800,000
Costs incurred to date		
Labor	$120,000	
Materials and subcontractors	478,000	
Indirect costs	50,000	648,000
Latest forecast total cost		1,320,000

Costs incurred to date include $40,000 for standard electrical and mechanical materials stored on the job site and $80,000 for steel in the fabricator's plant (including steel cost of $60,000 and labor cost of $20,000 based on 1,000 hours at $20 per hour). The steel is 100 percent complete and has been fabricated specifically to meet the unique requirements of this job.

Computations for the percentage-of-completion method follow:

$$\text{Measure of progress} = \frac{\text{Costs incurred to date}}{\text{Estimated total cost}}$$

$$= \frac{\$648{,}000 - \$40{,}000}{\$1{,}320{,}000}$$

$$= 46\% \text{ complete}$$

$$\text{Earned revenue} = 46\% \times (\$1{,}500{,}000 + \$150{,}000)$$

$$= \$759{,}000$$

$$\text{Cost of earned revenue} = 46\% \times (\$1{,}200{,}000 + \$120{,}000)$$

$$= \$608{,}000^{2}$$

[2] This may also be calculated as indirect costs incurred to date of $648,000 minus the stored standard electrical and mechanical materials stored on the job of $40,000.

The costs of the electrical and mechanical materials at the job site are excluded from "costs incurred to date" because the materials consist of stock items and have not yet become an integral part of the project; on the other hand, the $80,000 of steel is included in "costs incurred to date" because the steel is now specifically fabricated to meet the specifications of this project and, therefore, may be considered a part of the project at this point.

Therefore, an entry is required to reclassify the $40,000 cost of materials not installed from accumulated cost of contracts in progress to materials inventory. Also, an entry must be made to reflect earned revenue and related costs in the income and expense accounts. On the assumption that all costs related to the contract have been charged to the balance sheet account (the costs of contracts in progress), and all billings have been credited to the balance sheet account (progress billings), the following entry would be made:

	DR	*CR*
Balance Sheet		
Progress billings	$800,000	
Costs of contracts in progress		$608,000
Billings in excess of costs and estimated earnings on uncompleted contracts		$41,000
Income Statement		
Earned contract revenue		$759,000
Costs of earned contract revenue	$608,000	

Assuming the contract is completed in the next year with no change in price or cost, the results would appear in the income statement as follows:

	First Year	*Second Year*	*Total*
Progress measurement at end of year	46%	100%	
Contract operations			
Earned revenue	$759,000	$891,000	$1,650,000
Costs			
Labor	$120,000	$190,000	$310,000
Materials and subcontractors	438,000	472,000	910,000
Indirect costs	50,000	50,000	100,000
	$608,000	$712,000	$1,320,000
Gross profit	$151,000	$179,000	$330,000
Gross profit rate	20%	20%	20%

Exhibit F-2—Labor-Hours Method

A general contractor specializes in the construction of industrial plants for manufacturing businesses. The construction period of the typical manufacturing facility ranges from 13 to 24 months. Because of the nature of the construction contracts and the practices followed by the contractor, the contractor has determined that the percentage-of-completion method of revenue recognition is appropriate and that the labor-hours method is the best measure of progress toward completion.

Estimated labor hours must include the labor hours of the entity as well as the labor hours of its subcontractors that produce goods specifically for the project. For example, labor hours incurred by a steel entity in the production of standard items for the project are not included in total labor hours; however, labor hours incurred by a steel entity in fabricating standard items specifically for the project are included in total hours. If management is unable to obtain accurate estimates of its own or all appropriate subcontractors' labor hours at the beginning of the project and as work progresses, the labor-hours method would not be appropriate.

The assumptions and data used in this illustration are identical to those used in exhibit F-1 except that the contractor uses the labor-hours method instead of the cost-to-cost method.

At the end of the first year, the entity had incurred 6,000 labor hours, the steel fabricator 1,000 labor hours, and all other subcontractors 3,080 labor hours. Estimated total labor hours for the project are 21,000.

Computations under the percentage-of-completion method follow:

Measure of progress	=	Labor hours to date (10,080) / Estimated total labor hours (21,000)
Percentage complete	=	48%
Earned revenue	=	48% × ($1,500,000 + $150,000)
	=	$792,000
Cost of earned revenue	=	48% × ($1,200,000 + $120,000)
	=	$633,600

An entry is required to transfer the $40,000 cost of materials that have not entered into the revenue recognition process from accumulated cost of contracts in progress to materials inventory.

Materials inventory	$40,000	
Cost of contracts in progress		$40,000

After the adjustment, the balance in the cost-of-contracts-in-progress account is $608,000 ($648,000 – $40,000); however, because the cost of earned revenue is $633,600, an additional adjustment of $25,600 ($633,600 – $608,000 = $25,600) is required to properly state the cost associated with the revenue earned for the period.

Cost of contract in progress	$25,600	
Liability for contract work to be performed		$25,600

Assuming that the contract is completed in the next fiscal year with no change in price or cost, the results would appear in the income statement.

	First Year	*Second Year*	*Total*
Contract operations			
Earned revenue	$792,000	$858,000	$1,650,000
Cost of revenue earned	633,600	686,400	1,320,000
Gross profit	$158,400	$171,600	$330,000

Exhibit F-3—Construction Management

A construction entity enters into a construction management contract for the construction of a paper mill. The contract is a cost-plus contract in which the contractor acts solely in the capacity of an agent and has no risks associated with the costs managed. That is, the contractor is not responsible for the nature, type, characteristics, or specifications of materials or for the ultimate acceptance of the project; moreover, the contractor's fee was based on the lack of risk inherent in the negotiated contract.

Consistent with the "risk-free" nature of the management contract, the entity measures job progress based on the labor hours for which it has direct control. That is, only those labor hours incurred as a result of the actual management effort should be used to measure job progress. Thus, the hours incurred by the various contractors and subcontractors on the project do not enter into the measure of job progress from the construction manager's standpoint.

The contractor may accrue his or her fees as they become billable, assuming they are at a constant percentage of costs incurred. The following example, which assumes that the contractor employs the labor-hours method, gives the same results, because labor hours are the basis for fee reimbursement. Because he or she has no risks associated with subcontractors' work, their labor hours are excluded from the computation.

Assume the following:

Total estimated construction management hours	10,000	
Cost per hour (includes indirect costs)	$20	
Total estimated costs	$200,000	
Fee (15%)	30,000	
Total estimated revenue	$230,000	
At the end of the first year:		
Hours used	4,000	hrs.
Estimated total hours	10,000	hrs.
Measure of progress	40%	

If the contract is completed in the second year without any changes in contract revenues and costs, the results would appear in the income statement as follows.

	First Year	*Second Year*	*Total*
Contract revenues (hours used at $20 × 115%)	$92,000	$138,000	$230,000
Contract costs (includes indirect costs)	80,000	120,000	200,000
Gross profit (15%)	$12,000	$18,000	$30,000

Exhibit F-4—Units of Production

A road builder performs work primarily as a subcontractor on large highway projects. On those projects, the entity's work consists only of laying concrete. All site preparation and other work is performed by the general contractor or by other subcontractors to the general contractor. The cost elements include labor and related costs, cost of expansion and contraction joints, the cost of reinforcing steel, the cost of cement and other materials, and equipment costs. The entity reports its income on the percentage-of-completion basis and measures progress toward completion on the basis of units of work completed because all costs are incurred essentially equally as square yards of concrete are laid (with the exception of mobilization and demobilization costs, which are incurred at the beginning and end of the job).

A contract sets forth 10 separate pay items, which, when totaled and converted to price per square yard of concrete, equal $12 per square yard for concrete that is to be 9 inches thick. Estimated square yards of concrete to be laid approximate 450,000, and estimated total cost is $5,000,000. Costs incurred through the end of the first year on the contract, excluding mobilization costs, total $2,200,000, which includes $100,000 of materials not used. Mobilization costs incurred total $70,000, and projected demobilization costs total $30,000. Physical output as reported by the state engineer and confirmed by the entity engineer totals 200,000 square yards at the end of the first year.

Input information (square yards of concrete poured) should not be used for determination of revenue because the entity must lay the concrete in excess of 9 inches thick to meet state requirements that concrete not be less than 9 inches thick based on test borings; thus, input in terms of cubic yards poured would exceed billable output. Accordingly, the output measure (square yards laid) is the appropriate measure of progress.

The entity's earned revenue and costs of earned revenue for the first year are computed as follows:

$$\text{Measure of progress} = \frac{\text{Square yards laid}}{\text{Total square yards to be laid}}$$

$$= \frac{200{,}000}{450{,}000}$$

Percentage complete	=	44%
Earned revenue	=	44% × $5,400,000
	=	$2,376,000
Cost of earned revenue	=	44% × $5,000,000
	=	$2,200,000

Additional Considerations

If such a road builder served as the prime contractor and performed all site preparation, sewer, and other related work, no single unit would appropriately measure progress toward completion. Some other method, such as labor hours or cost to cost, would be preferable.

If the cost-to-cost method is used, it is necessary to include the mobilization costs and to exclude the cost of the materials not used from the cost incurred in the measure of progress calculation. The computation is as follows:

$$\text{Measure of progress} = \frac{\text{Cost incurred to date}}{\text{Estimated total cost}}$$

$$= \frac{\$2{,}200{,}000 + \$70{,}000 - \$100{,}000}{\$5{,}000{,}000}$$

Percentage complete = 43%

Exhibit F-5—Zero Profit

A contractor has been awarded a fixed-price contract with escalation clauses for the construction of a housing project in Saudi Arabia. The contractor has no construction experience in that part of the world, and various uncertainties involving mobilization, procurement costs, and labor costs make it difficult to determine the amount of total contract revenue and costs. However, although the contractor is unable to estimate total contract costs as either a single amount or range of amounts, the terms of the contract provide protection for the contractor from incurring a loss under any reasonable circumstances. The contract price is $460,000,000.

For purposes of this illustration, it is assumed that there are no changes in estimates of contract revenues for the duration of the contract. The contractor is consistently using an acceptable measure of progress, and at the end of the first year relating to this contract, the project is considered to be 12 percent complete. Costs incurred to date are $67,200,000. Since inception, there has been no improvement in the contractor's ability to estimate total costs in terms of a single amount or range of amounts.

Following is the status of the project for accounting purposes at the end of the first year:

Earned revenue (12% of $460,000,000)	$55,200,000
Cost of earned revenue	55,200,000
Gross profit	—
Deferred costs at end of year	$12,000,000

That portion of the cost incurred to date ($67,200,000) in excess of the cost of earned revenue ($55,200,000) is reported as a deferred cost in the balance sheet.

At the end of the second year, the contractor can estimate that the total contract costs will be between $410,000,000 and $440,000,000. The measure of work completed indicated that the project is 31 percent complete at that date. Costs incurred to date are $142,400,000.

Table 1 in this appendix gives the status of the project for accounting purposes at the end of the second year. The maximum estimated costs were used in accounting for the contract. The cumulative amount of earned revenue is $142,600,000 (31 percent of $460,000,000), and the cost of earned revenue is $136,400,000 (31 percent of $440,000,000). That portion of the cost incurred to date in excess of the cost of earned revenue is reported as a deferred cost in the balance sheet.

The change from the zero profit method is a change in estimate, and the effect of the change on the second year should be disclosed. In this illustration, the effect of the change is $1,200,000, computed as follows:

At the end of the first year, using revised estimates, the effects of change are as follows:

Earned revenue, 12% of $460,000,000	$55,200,000
Cost of earned revenue, 12% of $440,000,000	52,800,000
Gross profit	$2,400,000
Gross profit recognized to date	—
Effect of change in estimate, before tax effect	$2,400,000
Tax effect, at assumed 50% rate	1,200,000
Effect of change in estimate, after tax effect	$1,200,000

Table 2 in this appendix is a summary of the contract for the first and second years and the remaining years to completion. For this purpose, it is assumed there are no subsequent changes in estimates of contract costs from the $440,000,000 maximum estimate at the end of the second year.

Table 1

	First Year	*Second Year*	*Total*
Earned revenue	$55,200,000	$87,400,000	$142,600,000
Cost of earned revenue	55,200,000	81,200,000	136,400,000
Gross profit	$—	$6,200,000	$6,200,000
Deferred costs	$12,000,000	$6,000,000	

Table 2

	First Year	*Second Year*	*Remaining Years to Completion*	*Total*
Earned revenue	$55,200,000	$87,400,000	$317,400,000	$460,000,000
Cost of earned revenue	$55,200,000	$81,200,000	$303,600,000	$440,000,000
Gross profit	$—	$6,200,000	$13,800,000	$20,000,000
Deferred costs at end of year	$12,000,000	$6,000,000	$—	$—

Exhibit F-6—Loss Contract

A contractor specializes in underground construction work. As a rule, the projects on which the contractor works take from two to three years to complete. The contractor uses the percentage-of-completion method of revenue recognition because, given the contractor's ability to estimate contract costs, revenue, and progress, it is the most appropriate method. Furthermore, the contractor's standard contract normally includes provisions that specify the enforceable rights regarding the work to be performed, consideration, and terms of settlement. Taken in combination, these factors provide a sound basis for the use of percentage-of-completion.

In year 1, the contractor obtained a contract for $1,620,000 with an estimated total cost on the project of $1,377,000 leaving an estimated gross profit of $243,000. At December 31, year 1, $500,000 had been billed, costs of $510,000 had been incurred, and estimated costs to complete were projected to be $867,000, resulting in the projected profit of $243,000. The cost to complete was determined by the job superintendent and was checked against engineering estimates of units of work completed and units of work to be completed. During year 2, the entity encountered heavy rains, worse than anticipated soil conditions, and field supervision problems. As a result of this, a loss of $60,000 was projected at the completion of the project. At December 31, year 2, billings of $1,480,000 had been made, costs of $1,545,600 had been incurred, and costs to complete were estimated at $134,400. Work under the contract is completed in year 3, and there are no further changes in contract revenues and costs. As projected in year 2, a loss of $60,000 was incurred on the contract upon completion in year 3.

Using the foregoing information, the percentage of completion is computed in the following table for both years, using the cost-to-cost method to measure progress. The cost-to-cost method is used in this situation because management believes it provides the most accurate measure of job progress under the current contract conditions.

Year 1

$$\text{Measure of progress} = \frac{\text{costs incurred to date}}{\text{total estimated costs}}$$

$$= \frac{\$510{,}000}{\$1{,}377{,}000}$$

$$= 37\%$$

Year 2

$$\text{Measure of progress} = \frac{\$1{,}545{,}600}{\$1{,}680{,}000}$$

$$= 92\%$$

Year 3

$$\text{Measure of progress} = \frac{\$1{,}680{,}000}{\$1{,}680{,}000}$$

$$= 100\%$$

The computation of earned revenue, job costs, and gross profit for income statement purposes is shown in the following tables:

	Current Year		*Total-to-Date*
Year 1 (37% completed)			
Earned revenue			
($1,620,000 × 37%)	$599,400		$599,400
Actual cost of earned revenue	510,000		510,000
Gross profit	$89,400		$89,400
Gross profit rate	14.9%		14.9%
Year 2 (92% completed)			
Earned revenue			
($1,620,000 × 92%) – 599,400	$891,000	($1,620,000 × 92%)	$1,490,400
Cost of earned revenue (See note)	1,040,400		1,550,400
Gross profit	$(149,400)		$(60,000)
Gross profit rate	(16.8%)		(4.0%)
Year 3 (100% completed)			
Earned revenue			
($1,620,000 × 100%) – 1,490,400	$129,600	($1,620,000 × 100%)	$1,620,000
Cost of earned revenue			
($1,620,000 × 100%) – 1,490,400	129,600	($1,620,000 × 100%) + 60,000	1,680,000
Gross profit	$0		$(60,000)
Gross profit rate	—		(3.7%)

Note: The cost of earned revenue at the end of year 2, the year in which the estimated loss became known, is computed as follows:

Estimated total contract cost excluding estimated loss	$1,620,000
Measure of progress	× 92%
Actual cost of earned revenue before loss provision	$1,490,400
Add 100% of estimated total loss	$60,000
Cost of earned revenue at the end of year 2	$1,550,400
Less amount previously recognized	$510,000
Cost of earned revenue, year 2	$1,040,400

In accordance with paragraphs 45–50 of FASB ASC 605-35-25, a provision for the entire anticipated contract should be made in the period in which the loss becomes evident, which is year 2 in this example.[3]

FASB ASC 605-35-45-1 establishes that, unless the provision for loss is material in amount or unusual or infrequent in nature, it should be included in contract cost and not shown separately in the income statement; however, if the loss provision is material, it should be presented separately as a component of the cost included in the computation of gross profit, either on the face of the income statement or in the notes to the financial statements.

Exhibit F-7—Combining

A contractor who specializes in the construction of multifamily residential and commercial properties was approached by a prospective customer late in the fall to discuss the construction of a residential housing and shopping center project. They arrived at a general conceptual agreement about the nature of the work and appropriate timing and magnitude of cost estimates for the project. After the meeting, the project developer obtained the final members of the investment groups for the properties, and drawings and building specifications were then completed. The contractor was awarded the job, but under separate contracts for the apartment complex portion of the project and the shopping center portion. The developer explained that he or she needed separate contracts due to financing requirements and in order to maximize tax benefits for the investors.

[3] As an alternative to including the entirety of the anticipated loss in the normal calculation of the cost of earned revenues to date at the end of year 2, the contractor may record separately the balance of the total anticipated loss. Under this scenario, the cost of earned revenue in year 2 would be calculated normally by multiplying the total estimated contract cost by the percentage of completion on the contract: ($1,680,000) × 92% = $1,545,600. The journal entry to record the remainder of the anticipated loss would be calculated as the estimated total loss multiplied by the remaining percent complete on the contract, as follows:

	DR	*CR*
Income Statement	$4,800	
Provision for loss on uncompleted contract ($60,000 × 8%)		
Balance Sheet		$4,800
Accrued loss on uncompleted contract		

When presented the contracts, the contractor stated that the breakdown of price between the two sections of the project was not in agreement with his or her pricing structure. However, the contractor noted that the combined contract prices resulted in a gross profit that was satisfactory to him or her. Because of this and because the work on the separate phases would be performed in a relatively common time frame, he or she signed the contracts as they were prepared. Before signing the contracts, though, the contractor told the developer that it would not be practical to separate costs between the two projects because the same work crew and same machinery would be used jointly on the two phases. The contractor concluded that it would be appropriate to account for the two projects on a combined basis and report his or her financial results accordingly.

Estimated total contract revenues and costs for the two contracts are as follows:

	Apartment Project	*Shopping Center*	*Total*
Estimated contract revenue	$5,000,000	$2,000,000	$7,000,000
Estimated contract costs	4,000,000	1,800,000	5,800,000
Estimated gross profit	$1,000,000	$200,000	$1,200,000
Gross profit rate	20.00%	10.00%	17.14%

For purposes of this illustration, it is assumed that there are no changes in estimates of contract revenues or costs for the duration of the contracts and that the contractor uses the labor-hours method in determining percentage of completion. At the end of the first year relating to the two contracts, the following is their status:

	Apartment Project	*Shopping Center*	*Total*
Labor hours incurred to date	45,000	15,000	60,000
Estimated total contract labor hours	80,000	20,000	100,000
Measure of progress	56.25%	75.00%	60.00%
Actual contract costs	$2,250,000	$1,350,000	$3,480,000

Based on the foregoing, the recognized revenue, cost, and gross profit for the combined contract for the first fiscal year and for the second fiscal year of the contract is as follows:

	First Year	*Second Year*	*Total*
Year 1 (60% completed)			
Earned revenue			
(60% × $7,000,000)	$4,200,000		$4,200,000
Cost of earned revenue	3,480,000		3,480,000
Gross profit	$720,000		$720,000
Gross profit rate	17.14%		17.14%

	First Year	*Second Year*	*Total*
Year 2 (100% complete)			
Earned Revenue			
($7,000,000 × 100%)	$4,200,000	$2,800,000	$7,000,000
Cost of earned revenue	3,480,000	2,320,000	5,800,000
Gross profit	$720,000	$480,000	$1,200,000
Gross profit rate	17.14%	17.14%	17.14%

If the contracts had not been combined, the following differences would have occurred in the revenue, costs, and gross profit reported at the end of year 1.

	Earned Revenue	*Cost of Earned Revenue*	*Gross Profit*
Apartment project			
(56.25% complete)	$2,812,500	$2,250,000	$562,500
Shopping center			
(75% complete)	1,500,000	1,350,000	150,000
Total	$4,312,500	$3,600,000	$712,500
Amounts reported under combining	$4,200,000	$3,480,000	$720,000
Difference in amounts at end of first year if contracts had not been combined	$112,500	$120,000	$7,500

Exhibit F-8—Segmenting

An entity specializes in the engineering, procurement of materials, and construction of chemical processing plants. The entity has been awarded one such contract, which is priced at cost, plus 10 percent allowances for indirect costs on engineering and procurement phases and a fixed fee of $225,000. The scope of the contract calls for those separable phases of the work. Contract provisions state that the fixed fee was agreed to on the basis of the following rates:

	Base Cost	*Fee Rate*	*Fee*
Engineering	$176,000	25.00%	$44,000
Procurement	44,000	2.00%	880
Construction	4,800,000	3.75%	180,120
	$5,020,000		$225,000

Estimated total contract revenue is computed as follows:

Engineering	
8000 hours at $20	$160,000
Allowance for indirect costs	16,000
Procurement	
2000 hours at $20	40,000
Allowance for indirect costs	4,000
Construction, including labor, materials, subcontract, and indirect costs	4,800,000
	$5,020,000
Fixed fee	225,000
	$5,245,000

The contractor meets the criteria for segmenting. In addition to the contract specifying the separate phases of the work, such phases are frequently contracted separately, and the contractor has a significant history of providing the engineering services to other customers separately. Such a history shows a relatively stable pricing policy. The similarity of services and prices on the contract segments to services and the prices of such services to other customers contracted separately are documented and verifiable. In the past, the contractor's normal fees have been 15 percent on engineering, 2 percent on procurement, and 5 percent on construction. Those rates are commensurate with the different levels of risk attributable to the separate phases of the work. A comparison of the aggregate of the values of the separate phases of the contract that would have been produced from such a fee structure to the contractual fee arrangement is as follows:

		Contract Revenue	*Fee*
Engineering			
Direct costs	$160,000		
Allowance for indirect costs	16,000		
	$176,000		
Normal fee, at 15%	26,400	$202,400	$26,400
Procurement			
Direct costs	$40,000		
Allowance for indirect costs	4,000		
	$44,000		
Normal fee, at 2%	880	44,880	880
Construction (total costs)	$4,800,000		
Normal fee, at 5%	240,000	5,040,000	240,000
		$5,287,280	$267,280

	Contract Revenue	Fee
Estimated total contract revenue and fee	5,245,000	225,000
Excess of the sum of the prices of the separate elements over estimated total contract revenues	$42,280	$42,280

This excess is attributable to cost savings incident to performance as a single project. The contractor segments revenues into the 3 profit centers in the manner set forth in the following table. Note that the contract-provision stipulating a 25 percent profit margin for engineering is not used because that margin is not supported by historical experience.

	Engineering	Procurement	Construction	Total
Normal historical fee as stated previously	$26,400	$880	$240,000	$267,280
Less reduction to reflect allocation of the excess amount in proportion to the preceding prices	(4,176)	(139)	(37,965)	(42,280)
Adjusted fee	$22,224	$741	$202,035	$225,000
Estimated total cost	176,000	44,000	4,800,000	5,020,000
Estimated total contract revenue, as adjusted	$198,224	$44,741	$5,002,035	$5,245,000

For purposes of this illustration, it is assumed that there are no changes in estimates of contract revenues, costs, and labor hours for the duration of the contract. The contractor uses the labor-hours method in determining measure of progress. Construction hours include the hours of the construction manager, the general contractor, and all subcontractors. At the end of the first year, the following is the contract status:

Profit Center	Labor Hours Incurred to Date	Estimated Total Labor Hours	Measure of Progress
Engineering	40,000	44,000	90.9%
Procurement	5,500	11,000	50.0%
Construction	75,000	600,000	12.5%
	120,500	655,000	18.4%

Recognized revenues, costs, and gross profit for the first fiscal period are as follows:

Profit Center	*Recognized Revenues*	*Cost Incurred*	*Gross Profit*
Engineering			
90.9% of estimated total revenues	$180,186		
Total costs		$159,984	$20,202
Procurement			
50.0% of estimated total revenues	$22,370		
Total costs		$22,000	$370
Construction			
12.5% of estimated total revenues	$625,254		
Total costs	$—	$600,000	$25,254
	$827,810	$781,984	$45,826

Assuming the contract is completed in the second fiscal period, recognized revenues, costs, and gross profit for the two fiscal periods would be as follows:

Profit Center	*Year 1*	*Year 2*	*Total*
Engineering			
Earned revenue	$180,186	$18,038	$198,224
Cost of earned revenue	159,984	16,016	176,000
Gross profit	$20,202	$2,022	$22,224
Procurement			
Earned revenue	$22,370	$22,371	$44,741
Cost of earned revenue	22,000	22,000	44,000
Gross profit	$370	$371	$741
Construction			
Earned revenue	$625,254	$4,376,781	$5,002,035
Cost of earned revenue	600,000	4,200,000	4,800,000
Gross profit	$25,254	$176,781	$202,035
Total Contract			
Earned revenue	$827,810	$4,417,190	$5,245,000
Cost of earned revenue	781,984	4,238,016	5,020,000
Gross profit	$45,826	$179,174	$225,000

If the contract had not been segmented, recognized revenues for year 1 would have been revised as follows:

Earned revenue (18.4% complete × $5,245,000)	$965,080
Costs of revenue	781,984
Gross profit without segmenting	$183,096
Gross profit under segmenting	45,826
Reduction in gross profit under segmenting year 1	$137,270

Appendix G

Example of Change in Accounting Estimate

This appendix is nonauthoritative and is included for informational purposes only.

FASB *Accounting Standards Codification* (ASC) 250-10-45-17 states that a change in accounting estimate should be accounted for in the period of change if the change affects that period only, or in the period of the change and future periods if the change affects both. FASB ASC 250-10-50-4 provides that the effect on income from continuing operations, net income, and any related per-share amounts of the current period should be disclosed for a change in accounting estimate that affects several future periods, such as a change in service lives of depreciable assets. Disclosure of those effects is not necessary for accounting estimates made each period in the ordinary course of accounting for items such as uncollectible accounts or inventory obsolescence; however, disclosure is required if the effect of a change in the estimate is material.

An illustrative example of the calculation and disclosure of the effects of an accounting change is as follows:

Assume, at the end of year 1:	(in thousands)
Contract revenue, at 50% complete	$50,000
Contract costs	45,000
Recognized profit	$5,000
Assume, at the end of year 2:	
Contract revenue (cumulative), at 90% complete	$105,000
Contract costs (cumulative)	90,000
Recognized profit, cumulative	$15,000
Recognized profit, year 2	$10,000

At the end of year 1, contract revenues at completion were estimated to be $100,000,000 (contract price), and contract costs at completion were estimated to be $90,000,000. However, at the end of year 2, contract revenues at completion were estimated to be $116,667,000, and contract costs were estimated to be $100,000,000. A change order agreed to in the second year added $16,667,000 to estimated total revenues and $7,000,000 to estimated total costs. Because of inefficiencies not known at the end of year 1, it was later determined that estimated total contract costs (excluding the change order) should have been $93,000,000 and that the percentage of completion should have been 48.4 percent rather than 50 percent at the end of year 1.[1]

[1] Note that AU-C section 540, *Auditing Accounting Estimates, Including Fair Value Accounting Estimates, and Related Disclosures* (AICPA, *Professional Standards*) notes that management often is able to demonstrate good reason for a change in an accounting estimate. What constitutes a good reason and the adequacy of support for management's contention that there has been a change in circumstances that warrants a change in an accounting estimate are matters of judgment. Consideration of potential deficiencies in related controls or the use of inappropriate assumptions may indicate the revision would more appropriately be deemed a correction of an error.

	Revenues ($ in thousands)	*Costs (in thousands)*
Change order (agreed to in second year)	$16,667	$7,000
Revised estimate (made after change order)		3,000
Estimates of revenues and cost at completion—year 1	100,000	90,000
Estimates of revenues and costs at completion—year 2	$116,667	$100,000

The calculation of the effects of the changes in estimates on year 2 net income follows. The effect of the change order is excluded from the calculation because it is clearly a year 2 event. However, in most circumstances, change orders would not have to be eliminated because their effect would be immaterial.

	(in thousands)
At the end of year 1, using revised estimates:	
Contract revenues (original contract)	$100,000
Contract costs (original contract)	93,000
Estimated total profit	$7,000
Percent complete (revised estimate)	48.4
Recognizable profit	$3,388
Profits recognized originally	5,000
Effect of change in estimate, before income taxes	$1,612
Income taxes at 50%	806
Effect of change in estimate	$806

The following is an example of disclosure of the effect of this change:

> Revisions in estimated contract profits are made in the year in which circumstances requiring the revision become known. The effect of changes in estimates of contract profits was to decrease net income of 20X2 by $806,000 ($.12 per share, net of income tax) from that which would have been reported had the revised estimate been used as the basis of recognition of contract profits in the preceding year.

Appendix H

Sample Financial Statements Percentage Contractors, Inc.

This appendix will be revised upon the effective date of FASB Accounting Standards Update No. 2014-09, *Revenue from Contracts with Customers (Topic 606)*. As industry practice develops, updated guidance, as appropriate, will be included in a future edition of this guide.[1]

This appendix is nonauthoritative and is included for informational purposes only.

The following sample financial statements of a construction contractor are included for illustrative purposes only and are not intended to establish reporting requirements. Furthermore, the dollar amounts shown are illustrative only and are not intended to indicate any customary relationship among accounts. The sample financial statements do not include all of the accounts and transactions that might be found in practice. The notes indicate the subject matter generally required to be disclosed, but they should be expanded, reduced, or modified to suit individual circumstances or materiality considerations. In addition to the illustrative notes that are presented, some of which are more or less peculiar to construction contractors, the notes to a construction contractor's financial statements should include information concerning other matters that are not unique to construction contractors, for example, subsequent events, pension plans, postretirement benefits other than pensions, postemployment benefits, stock options, lease commitments, extraordinary items, accounting changes, and off-balance-sheet risks.

Sample Financial Statements Percentage Contractors, Inc.

<u>Independent Auditor's Report</u>[2]

The Shareholders and Board of Directors Percentage Contractors, Inc. and Subsidiaries

---

[1] FASB Accounting Standards Update (ASU) No. 2014-09, *Revenue from Contracts with Customers (Topic 606)*, was issued in May 2014. Public business entities, certain not-for-profit entities, and certain employee benefit plans should apply the guidance in ASU No. 2014-09 as amended by FASB ASU No. 2015-14, *Revenue from Contracts with Customers (Topic 606): Deferral of the Effective Date*, to annual reporting periods beginning after December 15, 2017, including interim reporting periods within that reporting period. Earlier application is permitted only as of annual reporting periods beginning after December 15, 2016, including interim reporting periods within that reporting period.

All other entities should apply the guidance in ASU No. 2014-09 to annual reporting periods beginning after December 15, 2018, and interim reporting periods within annual reporting periods beginning after December 15, 2019. All other entities may apply the guidance in ASU No. 2014-09 earlier as of an annual reporting period beginning after December 15, 2016, including interim reporting periods within that reporting period. All other entities also may apply the guidance in ASU No. 2014-09 earlier as of an annual reporting period beginning after December 15, 2016, and interim reporting periods within annual reporting periods beginning one year after the annual reporting period in which the entity first applies the guidance in ASU No. 2014-09.

Readers are encouraged to read the full text of the FASB ASU, available at www.fasb.org. Readers should apply the appropriate guidance based on their facts and circumstances.

[2] Appendix K, "The Auditor's Report," provides sample auditors' reports for a variety of circumstances.

Report on the Financial Statements

We have audited the accompanying consolidated financial statements of Percentage Contractors, Inc. and its subsidiaries, which comprise the consolidated balance sheet as of December 31, 20X1, and the related consolidated statements of income, changes in stockholders' equity and cash flows for the year then ended, and the related notes to the consolidated financial statements.

Management's Responsibility for the Financial Statements

Management is responsible for the preparation and fair presentation of these consolidated financial statements in accordance with accounting principles generally accepted in the United States of America; this includes the design, implementation, and maintenance of internal control relevant to the preparation and fair presentation of consolidated financial statements that are free from material misstatement, whether due to fraud or error.

Auditor's Responsibility

Our responsibility is to express an opinion on these consolidated financial statements based on our audit. We conducted our audit in accordance with auditing standards generally accepted in the United States of America. Those standards require that we plan and perform the audit to obtain reasonable assurance about whether the consolidated financial statements are free from material misstatement.

An audit involves performing procedures to obtain audit evidence about the amounts and disclosures in the consolidated financial statements. The procedures selected depend on the auditor's judgment, including the assessment of the risks of material misstatement of the consolidated financial statements, whether due to fraud or error. In making those risk assessments, the auditor considers internal control relevant to the entity's preparation and fair presentation of the consolidated financial statements in order to design audit procedures that are appropriate in the circumstances, but not for the purpose of expressing an opinion on the effectiveness of the entity's internal control.[3] Accordingly, we express no such opinion. An audit also includes evaluating the appropriateness of accounting policies used and the reasonableness of significant accounting estimates made by management, as well as evaluating the overall presentation of the consolidated financial statements.

We believe that the audit evidence we have obtained is sufficient and appropriate to provide a basis for our audit opinion.

Opinion

In our opinion, the consolidated financial statements referred to above present fairly, in all material respects, the financial position of Percentage Contractors, Inc. and its subsidiaries as of December 31, 20X1, and the results of their

---

[3] In circumstances when the auditor also has responsibility to express an opinion on the effectiveness of internal control in conjunction with the audit of the consolidated financial statements, this sentence would be worded as follows: "In making those risk assessments, the auditor considers internal control relevant to the entity's preparation and fair presentation of the consolidated financial statements in order to design audit procedures that are appropriate in the circumstances." In addition, the next sentence, "Accordingly, we express no such opinion." would not be included.

operations, changes in their stockholders' equity, and their cash flows for the year then ended in accordance with accounting principles generally accepted in the United States of America.

[*Auditor's signature*]

[*Auditor's city and state*]

June 19, 20X2

Percentage Contractors Inc. and Subsidiaries
Consolidated Balance Sheet
December 31, 20X1

Assets	
Current Assets	
Cash and cash equivalents (Subsidiary B portion – $225,374)[4]	$ 1,160,791
Contracts receivable, net (Subsidiary B portion – $2,546,223)	6,404,128
Costs and estimated earnings in excess of billings on uncompleted contracts (Subsidiary B portion – $533,410)	1,004,598
Current portion of note receivable	113,546
Prepaid expenses and other current assets (Subsidiary B portion – $698,009)	1,781,128
Total Current Assets	10,464,191
Noncurrent Assets	
Note receivable, less current portion	127,287
Cash surrender value of officers' life insurance	1,030,448
Goodwill, net	1,799,109
Deposits and other assets (Subsidiary B portion – $9,234)	80,151
Property and equipment, net of accumulated depreciation and amortization (Subsidiary B portion – $1,445,209)	2,763,945
Deferred tax asset (Subsidiary B portion – $654)[5]	1,837
Total Noncurrent Assets	5,802,777
Total Assets	$ 16,266,968

[4] Per FASB *Accounting Standards Codification* (ASC) 810-10-45-25, a reporting entity shall present each of the following separately on the face of the statement of financial position:

a. Assets of a consolidated variable interest entity (VIE) that can be used only to settle obligations of the consolidated VIE

b. Liabilities of a consolidated VIE for which creditors (or beneficial interest holders) do not have recourse to the general credit of the primary beneficiary.

Note that FASB ASC 810, *Consolidation*, does not provide guidance on how assets and liabilities that meet this separate presentation criteria should be presented in the primary beneficiary's statement of financial position. A reporting entity that is the primary beneficiary of a variable interest entity could present each asset element that meets the separate presentation criteria as one line item and parenthetically disclose the amount of the asset in a variable interest entity, as presented in this example. Alternatively, the reporting entity could present an asset element in two separate line items, one line item for the asset in a variable interest entity that meet the separate presentation criteria and another line item for the reporting entity's corresponding asset. There may be other acceptable alternatives. FASB ASC 810 does not provide any requirements for separate presentation of a consolidated variable interest entity's revenue, expense or cash flow figures.

[5] FASB ASU No. 2015-17, *Income Taxes (Topic 740): Balance Sheet Classification of Deferred Taxes*, was issued in November of 2015.

(continued)

Liabilities and Stockholders' Equity	
Current Liabilities	
Accounts payable (Subsidiary B portion – $1,776,589)	$ 3,173,919
Billings in excess of costs and estimated earnings on uncompleted contracts (Subsidiary B portion – $36,714)	95,876
Line of credit	1,851,590
Accrued expenses (Subsidiary B portion – $1,343,989)	3,638,207
Accrued loss on uncompleted contracts (Subsidiary B portion – $44,390)	105,950
Current maturities of long-term debt	1,253,602
Total Current Liabilities	10,119,144
Noncurrent Liabilities	
Long-term debt, less current maturities	2,975,142
Deferred tax liability (Subsidiary B portion – $98,965)	208,740
Total Noncurrent Liabilities	3,183,882
Total Liabilities	13,303,026
Stockholders' Equity	
Common stock, no par value, 100,000 shares authorized, 23,549 issued and outstanding	2,752,574
Retained earnings	85,561
Total Controlling Interest Stockholders' Equity	2,838,135
Noncontrolling interest in subsidiary	125,807
Total Stockholders' Equity	2,963,942
Total Liabilities and Stockholders' Equity	$ 16,266,968

The accompanying notes are an integral part of these consolidated financial statements.

(footnote continued)

The amendments in ASU No. 2015-17 are effective for public business entities' financial statements issued for annual periods beginning after December 15, 2016, and interim periods within those annual periods. The amendments are effective for all other entities' financial statements issued for annual periods beginning after December 15, 2017, and interim periods within annual periods beginning after December 15, 2018. Earlier application is permitted.

ASU No. 2015-17 applies to all entities that present a classified statement of financial position. The ASU amends FASB ASC 740, *Income Taxes*, to require that deferred tax liabilities and assets be classified as noncurrent in a classified statement of financial position. Readers are encouraged to consult the full text of this ASU on FASB's website at www.fasb.org.

Percentage Contractors Inc. and Subsidiaries
Consolidated Statement of Income
for the Year Ended December 31, 20X1

Revenues	$ 18,178,085
Cost of Revenues	13,057,260
Gross Profit	5,120,825
Selling, General, and Administrative Expenses	3,315,136
Income From Operations	1,805,689
Other Income (Expenses)	
Rental income	55,988
Interest income	34,340
Interest expense	(382,303)
Miscellaneous income, net	286,951
Total Other Expenses, net	(5,024)
Net Income Before Provision for Income Tax Expense	1,800,665
Provision for Income Tax Expense	461,789
Net Income	1,338,876
Net Loss Attributable to Noncontrolling Interest in Subsidiary B	177,140
Net Income Attributable to Controlling Interest	$ 1,516,016

The accompanying notes are an integral part of these consolidated financial statements.

Percentage Contractors Inc. and Subsidiaries
Consolidated Statement of Changes in Stockholders' Equity
for the Year Ended December 31, 20X1

	Common Stock Shares Outstanding	*Common Stock*	*Retained Earnings (Deficit)*	*Noncontrolling Interest*	*Total Stockholders' Equity*
Balance— January 1, 20X1	22,881	$ 2,529,434	$ (1,430,455)	$ 302,947	1,401,926
Issuance of common stock	668	223,140	—	—	223,140
Net income (loss)	—	—	1,516,016	(177,140)	1,338,876
Balance— December 31, 20X1	23,549	$ 2,752,574	$ 85,561	$ 125,807	$ 2,963,942

The accompanying notes are an integral part of these consolidated financial statements.

Percentage Contractors Inc. and Subsidiaries
Consolidated Statement of Cash Flows
for the Year Ended December 31, 20X1

Cash Flows From Operating Activities	
Net income including noncontrolling interests	$ 1,338,876
Adjustments to reconcile net income to net cash provided by operating activities:	
Depreciation and amortization	969,616
Increase in cash surrender value of officers' life insurance	(243,031)
Gain on sale of property and equipment	(216,377)
Provision for deferred income taxes	186,429
Provision for bad debt expense	521,895
Changes in assets and liabilities:	
Contracts receivable	8,339,602
Costs and estimated earnings in excess of billings on uncompleted contracts	(62,009)
Prepaid expenses and other current assets	369,356
Deposits and other assets	51,654
Accounts payable	484,437
Billings in excess of costs and estimated earnings on uncompleted contracts	(3,600,106)
Accrued loss on uncompleted contracts	(4,883,623)
Accrued expenses	(696,184)
Net Cash Provided by Operating Activities	2,560,535
Cash Flows From Investing Activities	
Repayment of note receivable	90,876
Proceeds from sale of property and equipment	83,145
Purchases of property and equipment	(290,300)
Net Cash Used in Investing Activities	(116,279)
Cash Flows From Financing Activities	
Payments on line of credit, net	(1,722,580)
Principal payments on long-term debt	(1,392,257)
Principal borrowings on long-term debt	250,000
Proceeds from issuance of common stock	223,140
Net Cash Used in Financing Activities	(2,641,697)
Net Change in Cash and Cash Equivalents	(197,441)
Cash and Cash Equivalents—Beginning of Year	1,358,232
Cash and Cash Equivalents—Ending of Year	$ 1,160,791
Supplemental Disclosure of Cash Flow Information	
Cash payments for:	
Interest	$ 374,900
Income Taxes	$ 201,488
Supplemental Disclosure of Noncash Investing and Financing Activities	
Purchase of vehicles by entering into long-term debt	$ 151,723

The accompanying notes are an integral part of these consolidated financial statements.

Note 1—Nature of Operations and Significant Accounting Policies

Nature of Operations

Percentage Contractors, Inc. and Subsidiaries ("the Company") operates under the following industries:

> Subsidiary A—Provides construction, maintenance, repair, and upgrade of water and wastewater facilities in the Southeastern United States.
>
> Subsidiary B—Provides installation, service and operation maintenance of equipment sales of water, waste water, and electrical control systems for commercial and residential clients in the Southeastern United States.

Significant Accounting Policies

Basis of Consolidation and Variable Interest Entities

The consolidated financial statements include the accounts of Percentage Contractors, Inc. and its wholly-owned subsidiary Subsidiary A. The Company has identified Subsidiary B as a variable interest entity of Subsidiary A which is considered the primary beneficiary and has a controlling financial interest in Subsidiary B. See Note 13 for additional discussion of Subsidiary B, a variable interest entity. Amounts pertaining to the noncontrolling ownership interests held by equity owners of Subsidiary B in the operating results and financial position of Subsidiary B are reported as noncontrolling interests in the consolidated subsidiary. The consolidation of Subsidiary B does not change any legal ownership, and does not change the assets or liabilities and equity of Percentage Contractors, Inc. as a separate legal entity. All inter-company accounts and transactions have been eliminated in consolidation.

Use of Estimates

The preparation of the consolidated financial statements in conformity with accounting principles generally accepted in the United States of America requires management to make estimates and assumptions that affect the reported amounts of assets and liabilities and disclosure of contingent assets and liabilities at the date of the consolidated financial statements and reported amounts of revenue and expenses during the reporting period. Actual results could differ from those estimates. Management periodically evaluates estimates used in the preparation of the consolidated financial statements for continued reasonableness. Appropriate adjustments, if any, to the estimates used are made prospectively based upon such periodic evaluation. It is reasonably possible that changes may occur in the near term that would affect management's estimates with respect to the percentage of completion method, allowance for doubtful accounts and accrued expenses.

Revisions in estimated contract profits are made in the year in which circumstances requiring the revision become known.

Balance Sheet Classifications

The Company includes in current assets and liabilities retentions receivable and payable under construction contracts that may extend beyond one year. A one-year time period is used as classifying all other current assets and liabilities.

Cash and Cash Equivalents

For purposes of reporting cash flows, the Company considers all highly liquid investments purchased with a maturity of three months or less at acquisition as cash and cash equivalents in the accompanying consolidated balance sheet. The Company has interest bearing deposits in financial institutions that maintained federal insurance in full for all accounts and limited coverage up to $250,000 per financial institution. The portion of the deposits in excess of this amount is not subject to such insurance and represents a credit risk to the Company. At times, balances held at each financial institution may exceed $250,000, which represents a credit risk to the Company. At December 31, 20X1, there were no uninsured deposits.

Contracts Receivable

Contracts receivable from construction, operation and maintenance are based on amounts billed to customers. The Company provides an allowance for doubtful collections which is based upon a review of outstanding receivables, historical collection information, and existing economic conditions. Normal contracts receivable are due 30 days after issuance of the invoice. Contract retentions are usually due 30 days after completion of the project and acceptance by the owner. Contracts receivable past due more than 60 days are considered delinquent. Delinquent contracts receivable are written off based on individual credit evaluation and specific circumstances of the customer.

Unbilled receivables result from the accrual of revenues on the percentage-of-completion method of accounting for which billings have not yet been rendered.

Property and Equipment

Property and equipment is stated at cost. Depreciation is computed using the straight-line method over the estimated useful lives of the assets, which range from 3 to 15 years. Leasehold improvements are amortized on a straight-line basis over the shorter of the estimated useful life of the improvement or the lease term. Additions, renewals, and betterments that significantly extend the life of the asset are capitalized. Expenditures for repairs and maintenance are charged to expense as incurred.

For assets sold or otherwise disposed of, the cost and related accumulated depreciation are removed from the accounts, and any related gain or loss is reflected in income for the period.

Impairment of Long-Lived Assets

The Company reviews long-lived assets for impairment whenever events or circumstances indicate that the carrying value of such assets may not be fully recoverable. Impairment is present when the sum of undiscounted estimated future cash flows expected to result from use of the assets is less than carrying value. If impairment is present, the carrying value of the impaired asset is reduced to its fair value. Fair value is determined based on discounted cash flows or appraised values, depending on the nature of the assets. During the year ended December 31, 20X1, there was no impairment losses recognized for long-lived assets.

Goodwill[6]

Goodwill, which is the excess of cost over the fair value of net assets (including identifiable intangibles) acquired in a business acquisition, is not amortized but rather assessed at least annually for impairment or whenever events or changes in circumstances indicate that the carrying amount of the asset might not be fully recoverable. The Company qualitatively evaluates relevant events and circumstances to determine whether it is more likely than not that the fair value of a reporting unit is less than its carrying amount. If so, the Company quantitatively compares the fair value of the reporting unit to its carrying amount on an annual basis to determine if there is potential goodwill impairment. If the fair value of the reporting unit is less than its carrying value, an impairment loss is recorded to the extent that the implied fair value of the goodwill is less than its carrying value. Fair values for reporting units are determined based on discounted cash flows, market multiples or appraised values. As of December 31, 20X1, there were no events or circumstances that indicated that goodwill impairment exist and the Company has recorded no goodwill impairment loss during the year ended December 31, 20X1.

Debt Issuance Costs

Debt issuance costs of $16,742 are presented on the balance sheet as a direct deduction from the carrying amount of the related debt liability and are being amortized as interest expense using the effective interest method. The debt issuance costs are being amortized over the term of the underlying debt, which is 5 years. Accumulated amortization amounted to $15,878 at December 31, 20X1. Amortization expense for the year ended December 31, 20X1 was $3,406. The remaining unamortized amount will be expensed in the year ending December 31, 20X2.

Revenues and Cost of Revenues

Revenues from fixed-price and cost-plus contracts are recognized on the percentage of completion method, whereby revenues on long-term contracts are recorded on the basis of the Company's estimates of the percentage of completion of contracts based on the ratio of actual cost incurred to total estimated costs. This cost-to-cost method is used because management considers it to be the best available measure of progress on these contracts. Revenues from cost-plus-fee contracts are recognized on the basis of costs incurred during the period plus the fee earned, measured on the cost-to-cost method.

---

[6] If the entity has elected to adopt the accounting alternative presented in FASB ASU No. 2014-02, *Intangibles—Goodwill and Other (Topic 350): Accounting for Goodwill (a consensus of the Private Company Council)*, the disclosure may read:

> Effective January 1, 20X1, the Company changed its method of accounting for goodwill, electing to adopt ASU No. 2014-02, *Intangibles—Goodwill and Other (Topic 350): Accounting for Goodwill (a consensus of the Private Company Council)*. ASU No. 2014-02 amends FASB *Accounting Standards Codification* (ASC) by establishing an accounting alternative under which private companies are allowed to (1) amortize goodwill on a straight-line basis over the useful life of the primary asset acquired in a business combination, not to exceed ten years, and (2) test goodwill for impairment at either the entity-wide level or at the reporting level only when a triggering event occurs indicating that the fair value of an entity or reporting unit may be below its carrying amount. The ASU is effective for new goodwill recognized in annual periods beginning after December 31, 2014, with early adoption permitted. The Company has elected to apply ASU No. 2014-02 to goodwill existing as of January 1, 20X1, and to new goodwill recognized in future periods. ASU No. 2014-02 requires prospective application and accordingly, the election had no effect of the 20X0 consolidated financial position or consolidated results of operations. As a result of the election, the Company recognized $XXX of amortization expense during the year ended December 31, 20X1. Goodwill is amortized over 10 years. There were no impairment charges noted.

Revenues from time-and-material and rate chart contracts are recognized currently as work is performed.

Revenues from maintenance service contracts are recognized on a straight-line basis over the life of the contract once the Company has an agreement, service has begun, the price is fixed or determinable and collectability is reasonably assured.

Cost of revenues include all direct material, sub-contractor, labor, and certain other direct costs, as well as those indirect costs related to contract performance, such as indirect labor and fringe benefits. Selling, general, and administrative costs are charged to expense as incurred. Provisions for estimated losses on uncompleted contracts are made in the period in which such losses are determined. Changes in job performance, job conditions and estimated profitability may result in revisions to cost and income, which are recognized in the period in which the revisions are determined. Changes in estimated job profitability resulting from job performance, job conditions, contract penalty provisions, claims, change orders, and settlements, are accounted for as changes in estimates in the current period. Claims for additional contract revenue are recognized when realization of the claim is probable and the amount can be reasonably determined.

The asset, "costs and estimated earnings in excess of billings on uncompleted contracts" represents revenues recognized in excess of amounts billed. The liability, "billings in excess of costs and estimated earnings on uncompleted contracts," represents billings in excess of revenues recognized.

Advertising Costs

Advertising costs are expensed as incurred. Total advertising costs for the year ended December 31, 20X1 was $101,655.

Income Taxes

Provisions for income taxes are based on taxes payable or refundable for the current year and deferred taxes on temporary differences between the amount of taxable income and pretax financial income and between the tax basis of assets and liabilities and their reported amounts in the financial statements. Deferred tax assets and liabilities are included in the consolidated financial statements at currently enacted income tax rates applicable to the period in which the deferred tax assets and liabilities are expected to be realized or settled. As changes in tax laws or rate are enacted, deferred tax assets and liabilities are adjusted through the provision for income taxes. The deferred tax assets and liabilities represent the future tax consequences of those differences, which will either be taxable or deductible when the assets and liabilities are recovered or settled. Deferred taxes are also recognized for operating losses that are available to offset future income. Valuation allowance are recorded for deferred tax assets when it is more likely than not that such deferred tax assets will not be realized.

If it is probable that an uncertain tax position will result in a material liability and the amount of the liability can be estimated, then the estimated liability is accrued. If the Company were to incur any income tax liability in the future, interest on any income tax liability would be reported as interest expense, and penalties on any income tax would be reported as income taxes. As of December 31, 20X1, there were no uncertain tax positions.

Concentration Risk

At December 31, 20X1, approximately 85 percent of the Company's workforce is union represented subject to collective bargaining agreements of which approximately 63 percent are represented by unions whose existing labor agreements will expire on various dates in 20X2. The individual unions may limit our flexibility in dealing with our workforce. Any work stoppage or instability within the workforce could delay our ability to satisfy our commitments under existing contracts with our customers in the manner management anticipated when developing contract estimates used in preparing these financial statements. This could cause severe negative impacts to the Company, including possible penalties for delayed contract performance, strained relationships with existing customers, impacts on our ability to obtain future contracts, and cause a loss of revenues, any of which could adversely affect our operations.

Subsequent Events

These consolidated financial statements have been updated for subsequent events occurring through June 19, 20X2, which is the date these consolidated financial statements were available to be issued.

Note 2—Contracts Receivable, Net

Contracts receivable consisted of the following at December 31, 20X1:

Completed contracts	$ 3,509,785
Contracts in progress	1,948,445
Unbilled	650,845
	6,109,075
Retentions:	
Completed contracts	214,675
Contracts in progress	727,411
	942,086
	7,051,161
Allowance for doubtful accounts	(647,033)
	$ 6,404,128

Note 3—Costs and Estimated Earnings on Uncompleted Contracts

The following is a summary of contracts in progress at December 31, 20X1:

Costs incurred on uncompleted contracts	$ 17,755,341
Estimated net loss on uncompleted contracts	(2,808,452)
	14,946,889
Billings to date	(14,038,165)
	$ 908,724

This amount is included in the accompanying consolidated balance sheet under the following captions at December 31, 20X1:

Costs and estimated earnings in excess of billings on uncompleted contracts	$ 1,004,598
Billings in excess of costs and estimated earnings on uncompleted contracts	$ (95,876)
	$ 908,724

Note 4—Note Receivable

The Company has a note receivable relating to the sale of certain assets in 20X0. The note receivable bears interest at 6 percent. The note receivable calls for monthly payments of $9,602, including interest, with the balance of all principal and unpaid interest due in December 20X3. At December 31, 20X1, $240,833 was outstanding on the note receivable. Interest income related to the note receivable was $15,874 for the year ended December 31, 20X1.

Future maturity of the note receivable is as follows:

Years ending December 31,	
20X2	$ 113,546
20X3	127,287
	$ 240,833

Note 5—Property and Equipment

Property and equipment consists of the following at December 31, 20X1:

Assets	
Equipment	$ 2,699,813
Vehicles	2,658,477
Software	1,443,485
Furniture and fixtures	1,381,370
Leasehold improvements	782,497
	8,965,642
Accumulated depreciation and amortization	
Equipment	$ 1,867,509
Vehicles	1,838,919
Software	998,484
Furniture and fixtures	955,518
Leasehold improvements	541,267
	6,201,697
Net property and equipment	$ 2,763,945

Note 6—Financing Arrangements

Line of Credit

The Company has a $7,500,000 line of credit bearing interest at an annual rate equal to the Bank's prime rate plus 1.5 percent (4.75 percent at December 31, 20X1). There was $1,851,590 outstanding at December 31, 20X1. The line of credit is secured by the assets of the Company and is guaranteed by the stockholders.

Covenants

The line of credit with the Bank contains certain financial covenants, including a minimum tangible net worth ratio, minimum debt to tangible net worth ratio and a minimum net profit, as defined in the agreements.

Long-Term Debt

Long-term debt consists of the following notes payable at December 31, 20X1:

	Principal
Various notes payable to Lender A due in monthly installments ranging from $264 to $18,558, including interest, ranging from 1.90 to 6.24 percent, expiring at various dates through May 20X6. The notes are secured by certain vehicles and equipment.	$ 2,187,163
Various unsecured notes payable to Lender B due in monthly installments ranging from $704 to $4,437, including interest at 3.25 percent, expiring at various dates through April 20X6.	1,383,410
Note payable to Lender C due in monthly installments of $4,110, including interest at 1.90 percent, expiring in July 20X4. The note is secured by equipment.	410,745
Various notes payable to various financing institutions, due in monthly installments ranging from $458 to $711, including interest, ranging from 1.99 to 4.69 percent, expiring at various dates through July 20X5. The notes are secured by certain vehicles.	248,290
	4,229,608
Current maturities of long-term debt	(1,253,602)
Less unamortized debt issuance costs	(864)
	$ 2,975,142

Aggregate Maturities

Aggregate maturities of all long-term financing arrangements are as follows:

Years ending December 31,	
20X2	$ 1,253,602
20X3	1,029,838
20X4	952,920
20X5	785,094
20X6	207,290
	$ 4,228,744

Note 7—Stock Redemption Agreements

The Company has stock redemption agreements with all of its shareholders. Under the terms of the agreement, the Company is required to purchase all of the stockholder's shares upon death, disability, retirement, or termination. Additionally, beginning at age 63 through age 67, shareholders are required to sell their stock back to the Company. The Company annually establishes a per share transaction value based upon a formula established in the stockholder agreements and approved by the Board of Directors. At December 31, 20X1, the Company has outstanding stock purchase commitments with its stockholders totaling 10,383 shares at purchase prices ranging up to $384.04 per share.

Note 8—Retentions Payable

Accounts payable includes amounts due to subcontractors of $313,090 at December 31, 20X1, that has been retained pending the completion and customer acceptance of the contracts.

Note 9—Leases

Operating Leases—Lessor

The Company has various noncancelable sublease agreements with lessees to occupy space in various operating facilities. The sublease agreements call for monthly payments ranging from $350 to $3,900. The subleases expire at various times through November 20X3. The agreements do not contain price escalations.

Total rental income amounted to $55,988 for the year ended December 31, 20X1.

Future minimum rental income is as follows:

Years ending December 31,	
20X2	$ 39,067
20X3	5,483
	$ 44,550

Operating Leases—Lessee

The Company rents its main operating facility under a noncancellable lease. Monthly rent payments are $54,789. The lease expires in June 20X4. Rent expense related to this operating facility for the year ended December 31, 20X1 was $657,468.

In addition, the Company has various noncancellable operating leases for operating facilities. Monthly lease payments range from $1,650 to $16,161. The leases expire at various times through April 20X7. Rent expense related to the operating facilities for the year ended December 31, 20X1 was $1,029,073.

The Company has various noncancellable operating leases for office equipment. Monthly lease payments range from $129 to $1,836. The leases expire at various times through November 20X4. Rent expense related to the office equipment for the year ended December 31, 20X1 was $85,437.

Future Minimum Lease Payments

Aggregate future minimum lease payments on all noncancellable operating leases are as follows:

Years ending December 31,	
20X2	$ 1,822,951
20X3	545,756
20X4	269,589
20X5	45,748
20X6	44,271
Thereafter	19,296
	$ 2,747,611

Total rent expense, including equipment rental, for the year ended December 31, 20X1 was $2,200,710.

Note 10—Income Taxes

Significant components of the Company's deferred income tax assets and liabilities are as follows at December 31, 20X1:[7]

	Current	*Long-Term*
Deferred tax asset		
Other	—	3,843
Net operating loss	—	222,401
Valuation allowance	—	(222,401)
Total	—	3,843
Deferred tax liability		
Other	—	(3,150)
Book-tax depreciation	—	(207,596)
Total	—	(210,746)
Net Deferred Tax Liability	—	$ (206,903)

The provision for income tax expense for the year ended December 31, 20X1 consists of the following:

Current	$ 275,360
Deferred	186,429
Total Provision for Income Tax Expense	$ 461,789

The Company has accumulated state taxable loss carryforwards of approximately $6,901,000 at December 31, 20X1. These loss carryforwards expire

[7] See footnote 5.

beginning in 20X2. A valuation allowance has been provided against the state net operating loss carryforward as it is currently uncertain as to when the losses will be utilized by the Company. Subsidiary A also has federal and state operating loss carryforwards of approximately $1,263,000. These loss carryforwards will expire in 20X3.

Note 11—Retirement Plans

Employee Benefit Plan

The Company sponsors a 401(k) plan (the plan) that covers substantially all nonunion employees of the Company. Contributions to the plan totaled $272,445 for the year ended December 31, 20X1. In addition, the Company may elect to make a discretionary contribution to the plan. For the year ended December 31, 20X1, no discretionary contributions were made to the plan.

Union Sponsored Pension Plans

The Company participates in various multiemployer defined benefit pension plans under the terms of collective bargaining agreements covering most of its union-represented employees. The risks of participation in these multiemployer plans are different than single-employer plans in the following aspects:

a. Assets contributed to the plan by a company may be used to provide benefits to participants of other companies,

b. If a participating company discontinues contributions to a plan, other participating employers may have to cover any unfunded liability that may exist, and

c. If the Company stops participating in some of its multiemployer pension plans, the Company may be required to pay those plans an amount based on the underfunded status of the plan, referred to as a withdrawal liability

Information with respect to the multiemployer plans providing pension benefits in which the Company participates is shown in the following table.

	Certified Zone Status			
Name of Plan, Plan Number and Employer ID Number	*20X1*	*Improvement or Rehabilitation Plan Pending / Implemented*	*Surcharge Paid*	*Expiration Date of Collective Bargaining Agreement*
Plan A, 111, 11-1111	Yellow	Yes	No	4/30/20X2
Plan B, 222, 22-2222	Green	No	No	7/31/20X3
Plan C, 333, 33-3333	Green	No	No	6/30/20X5
Plan D, 444, 44-4444	Green	No	No	12/31/20X2
Plan E, 555, 55-5555	Green	No	No	12/31/20X2

The zone status is based on information that the Company received from each of the plans. Among other factors, plans in the red zone are generally less than 65 percent funded, plans in the yellow zone are less than 80 percent funded and plans in the green zone are at least 80 percent funded. The "Improvement or Rehabilitation Plan Pending/Implemented" column indicates plans for which a financial improvement or a rehabilitation plan is either pending or has been implemented.

Contributions made are as follows:

	20X1
Plan A	$—
Plan B	543,121
Plan C	766,119
Plan D	231,223
Plan E	—
Other Plans	93,153
	$ 1,633,616

Note 12—Commitments and Contingencies

The Company, as conditions for entering into certain construction contracts, purchased surety bonds. The bonds are guaranteed by contracts receivable of the Company.

The Company is subject to various claims and legal proceeding covering a wide range of matters that arise in the ordinary course of its business activities. Management believes that any liability that may ultimately result from the resolution of these matters will not have a material effect on the financial condition or results of operations of the Company.

The Company is contingently liable to a surety company under a general indemnity agreement. The Company agrees to indemnify the surety for any payments made on contracts of surety ship, guarantee, or indemnity. The Company believes that all contingent liabilities will be satisfied by their performance on the specific bonded contracts.

Certain contracts are subject to government review of cost and overhead rates as defined in various federal cost regulations. Management of the Company believes that there are no adjustments that would materially impact the Company's financial position and results of operations as a result of a review of government contracts.

The Company has a purchase commitment with a vendor whereby the Company committed to purchase minimum amounts of office supplies used in its normal operations. Future annual minimum purchases remaining under the purchase commitment are $120,000 for the two-year years ending December 31, 20X3. During the year ended December 31, 20X1, total purchases under the purchase commitment were $94,434.

Note 13—Variable Interest Entity

Management analyzes the Company's variable interests including loans, guarantees and equity investments, to determine if the Company has any variable interests in variable interest entities. This analysis includes both qualitative and quantitative reviews. Qualitative analysis is based on the evaluation of the design of the entity, its organizational structure, including decision making ability, and financial agreements. Quantitative analysis is based on forecasted net cash flows. A reporting entity is required to consolidate a variable interest entity when the reporting entity has a variable interest that provides it with a controlling financial interest in the variable interest entity. The entity that consolidates a variable interest entity is referred to as the primary beneficiary of that variable interest entity. The Company also uses qualitative and quantitative analysis to determine if it is the primary beneficiary of variable interest entities in which the Company holds one or more explicit or implicit variable interests.

Subsidiary B is a related party installation company that has common controlling ownership with the Company. The Company uses the services of Subsidiary B for installation of water and waste water equipment. The Company has determined that Subsidiary B is a variable interest entity due to lack of sufficient at risk equity. The Company has also determined that it is the primary beneficiary of Subsidiary B because it has the power to direct the activities of Subsidiary B that most significantly impact Subsidiary B's economic performance, including establishing installation rates, and daily management decisions for operations and the awarding of subcontracts and determination of subcontract terms for work performed by Subsidiary B for Subsidiary A in addition to structuring certain arrangements with customers of Subsidiary A for certain work to be structured as separate contracts directly between the customer and Subsidiary B. Additionally, the Company is exposed to the obligation to absorb losses of Subsidiary B and the right to receive benefits of Subsidiary B that could potentially be significant to Subsidiary B through the subcontracts executed by the Company with Subsidiary B and implicitly due to the common controlling ownership. Subcontracts with Subsidiary B that do not provide positive cash flow or sufficient profitability may expose Subsidiary A to a loss. The operations of Subsidiary B are financed by stockholder contributions of equity. Additionally, Subsidiary A has provided necessary financial support to Subsidiary B for operations when needed. During the year ended December 31, 20X1 there was no financial support provided to Subsidiary B that was not previously contractually required other than the access to bonding capacity which is expected to continue in the future.

As the Company has been determined to be the primary beneficiary of this variable interest entity, Subsidiary B's assets, liabilities and results of operations are included in the Company's consolidated financial statements after elimination of intercompany accounts and transactions. The interests of the noncontrolling equity owners of Subsidiary B is reflected in "Noncontrolling interest in subsidiary" and "Net loss attributable to noncontrolling interest in subsidiary" in the accompanying consolidated balance sheet and consolidated statement of income, respectively. The condensed summary of the carrying amount and classification of Subsidiary B's financial information included in the Company's consolidated balance sheet as of December 31, 20X1 is as follows:

Condensed Balance Sheet	
Current assets	$ 4,003,670
Noncurrent assets	1,454,443
Total assets	5,458,113
Current liabilities	3,201,682
Noncurrent liabilities	98,965
Total liabilities	3,300,647
Condensed Results of Operations	
Revenues	$ 6,574,857
Cost of revenues	3,039,483
Net Income	3,535,374

The assets of Subsidiary B can only be used to settle the liabilities of Subsidiary B. Subsidiary B's creditors, other than it's bonding company, do not have recourse to the general credit of the Company and certain assets such as costs and estimated earnings in excess of billings on uncompleted contracts can only be used to satisfy the obligations of Subsidiary B; therefore, Subsidiary B's assets and liabilities have been presented notationally in the Company's consolidated balance sheet.

Note 14—Backlog

The following schedule shows a reconciliation of backlog representing the amount of revenue the Company expects to realize from work to be performed on uncompleted contracts in progress at December 31, 20X1, and from contractual agreements in effect at December 31, 20X1, on which work has not yet begun.

Contract revenues on uncompleted contracts at December 31, 20X0	15,097,685
Contract adjustments	2,688,136
Contract revenues for new contracts, 20X1	4,446,338
	22,232,159
Contract revenues earned, 20X1	(18,178,085)
Backlog at December 31, 20X1	$ 4,054,074

In addition, between January 1, 20X2, and June 19, 20X2, the Company entered into additional construction contracts with revenues of $5,332,800 (unaudited).

Appendix I

Reporting on Supplementary Information in Relation to the Financial Statements as a Whole[1]

This appendix is nonauthoritative and is included for informational purposes only.

When the entity presents the supplementary information with the financial statements, and the auditor is engaged to report on whether supplementary information is fairly stated, in all material respects, in relation to the financial statements as a whole,[2] the auditor should report on the supplementary information in accordance with AU-C section 725, *Supplementary Information in Relation to the Financial Statements as a Whole.*[3] As required by paragraph .09 of AU-C section 725, the auditor should report on the supplementary information in either an other-matter paragraph in accordance with AU-C section 706, *Emphasis-of-Matter Paragraphs and Other-Matter Paragraphs in the Independent Auditor's Report*, or in a separate report on the supplementary information.

Regardless of how the report on supplementary information is presented, in either an other-matter paragraph or separate report, the auditor should include a statement that the audit was conducted for the purpose of forming an opinion on the financial statements as a whole and that the supplementary information is presented for purposes of additional analysis and is not a required part of the financial statements. Further, the auditor should include a statement that the supplementary information is the responsibility of management and was derived from, and relates directly to, the underlying accounting and other records used to prepare the financial statements.

Also included in the report on supplementary information should be a statement that the supplementary information has been subjected to the auditing procedures applied in the audit of the financial statements and certain

---

[1] Technical Questions and Answers section 9180.01, "Required Supplementary Information in Historical Prior Periods and Auditor Independence of the Entity" (*Technical Questions and Answers*), addresses a situation where required supplementary information extends back to any historical prior period (back periods) in which the auditor did not perform an engagement that required independence, addressing whether the auditor required, for purposes of complying with AU-C section 730, *Required Supplementary Information* (AICPA, *Professional Standards*), to be independent of the entity in those back periods.

Generally accepted auditing standards require the auditor to be independent for any period being audited and covered by the auditor's opinion. In the absence of any separate requirement in the particular circumstances of the engagement, the auditor's opinion on the basic financial statements does not cover required supplementary information. In accordance with AU-C section 730, required supplementary information is not part of the basic financial statements. Furthermore, the specified procedures required to be performed on required supplementary information are limited and do not provide the auditor with sufficient appropriate audit evidence to express an opinion or provide any assurance on the required supplementary information.

[2] If the auditor is not engaged to report on whether supplementary information is fairly stated, in all material respects, in relation to the financial statements as a whole, AU-C section 720, *Other Information in Documents Containing Audited Financial Statements* (AICPA, *Professional Standards*), establishes the requirement for the auditor to read the other information of which the auditor is aware because the credibility of the audited financial statements may be undermined by material inconsistencies between the audited financial statements and other information.

[3] All AU-C sections can be found in AICPA *Professional Standards*.

additional procedures, including comparing and reconciling such information directly to the underlying accounting and other records used to prepare the financial statements or to the financial statements themselves and other additional procedures, in accordance with auditing standards generally accepted in the United States of America.

If the auditor issues an unmodified opinion on the financial statements and the auditor has concluded that the supplementary information is fairly stated, in all material respects, in relation to the financial statements as a whole, a statement should be included that, in the auditor's opinion, the supplementary information is fairly stated, in all material respects, in relation to the financial statements as a whole.

If the auditor issues a qualified opinion on the financial statements and the qualification has an effect on the supplementary information, a statement should be included that, in the auditor's opinion, except for the effects on the supplementary information of (refer to the paragraph in the auditor's report explaining the qualification), such information is fairly stated, in all material respects, in relation to the financial statements as a whole.

If the audited financial statements are not presented with the supplementary information, the auditor should report on the supplementary information in a separate report. When reporting separately on the supplementary information, the report should include, in addition to the elements preceding, a reference to the report on the financial statements, the date of that report, the nature of the opinion expressed on the financial statements, and any report modifications.

If the auditor's report on the audited financial statements contains an adverse opinion or a disclaimer of opinion and the auditor has been engaged to report on whether supplementary information is fairly stated, in all material respects, in relation to such financial statements as a whole, the auditor is precluded from expressing an opinion on the supplementary information.

The date of the auditor's report on the supplementary information in relation to the financial statements as a whole should not be earlier than the date on which the auditor completed the procedures required by paragraph .07 of AU-C section 725.

If the auditor concludes, on the basis of the procedures performed, that the supplementary information is materially misstated in relation to the financial statements as a whole, the auditor should discuss the matter with management and propose appropriate revision of the supplementary information.

If management does not revise the supplementary information, the auditor should either modify the auditor's opinion on the supplementary information and describe the misstatement in the auditor's report or, if a separate report is being issued on the supplementary information, withhold the auditor's report on the supplementary information.

Exhibit—Sample Audit Report Including an Other-Matter Paragraph When the Auditor Is Issuing an Unmodified Opinion on the Financial Statements and an Unmodified Opinion on the Supplementary Information

Independent Auditor's Report[4]

The Shareholders and Board of Directors Percentage Contractors, Inc. and Subsidiaries

Report on Financial Statements

We have audited the accompanying consolidated financial statements of Percentage Contractors, Inc. and Subsidiaries, which comprise the consolidated balance sheet as of December 31, 20X1, and the related consolidated statements of income, changes in stockholders' equity, and cash flows for the year then ended, and the related notes to the consolidated financial statements.

Management's Responsibility for the Financial Statements

Management is responsible for the preparation and fair presentation of these consolidated financial statements in accordance with accounting principles generally accepted in the United States of America; this includes the design, implementation, and maintenance of internal control relevant to the preparation and fair presentation of consolidated financial statements that are free from material misstatement, whether due to fraud or error.

Auditor's Responsibility

Our responsibility is to express an opinion on these consolidated financial statements based on our audits. We conducted our audits in accordance with

---

[4] If the auditor opts to present the report on supplementary information in a separate report on the supplementary information, the following example may be used.

Exhibit — Sample Separate Audit Report When the Auditor Is Issuing an Unmodified Opinion on the Financial Statements and an Unmodified Opinion on the Supplementary Information

Independent Auditor's Report

The Shareholders and Board of Directors Percentage Contractors, Inc. and Subsidiaries

We have audited the consolidated financial statements of Percentage Contractors, Inc. and Subsidiaries as of and for the year ended December 31, 20X1, and have issued our report thereon dated June 19, 20X2, which contained an unmodified opinion on those consolidated financial statements. Our audit was performed for the purpose of forming an opinion on the consolidated financial statements as a whole. The consolidated earnings from contracts, consolidated contracts completed, and consolidated contracts in progress information is presented for the purposes of additional analysis and is not a required part of the financial statements. Such information is the responsibility of management and was derived from and relates directly to the underlying accounting and other records used to prepare the consolidated financial statements. The information has been subjected to the auditing procedures applied in the audit of the consolidated financial statements and certain additional procedures, including comparing and reconciling such information directly to the underlying accounting and other records used to prepare the consolidated financial statements or to the consolidated financial statements themselves, and other additional procedures in accordance with auditing standards generally accepted in the United States of America. In our opinion, the information is fairly stated in all material respects in relation to the consolidated financial statements as a whole.

[*Auditor's signature*]
[*Auditor's city and state*]
June 19, 20X2

auditing standards generally accepted in the United States of America. Those standards require that we plan and perform the audit to obtain reasonable assurance about whether the consolidated financial statements are free from material misstatement.

An audit involves performing procedures to obtain audit evidence about the amounts and disclosures in the consolidated financial statements. The procedures selected depend on the auditor's judgment, including the assessment of the risks of material misstatement of the consolidated financial statements, whether due to fraud or error. In making those risk assessments, the auditor considers internal control relevant to the entity's preparation and fair presentation of the consolidated financial statements in order to design audit procedures that are appropriate in the circumstances, but not for the purpose of expressing an opinion on the effectiveness of the entity's internal control. Accordingly, we express no such opinion. An audit also includes evaluating the appropriateness of accounting policies used and the reasonableness of significant accounting estimates made by management, as well as evaluating the overall presentation of the consolidated financial statements.

We believe that the audit evidence we have obtained is sufficient and appropriate to provide a basis for our audit opinion.

Opinion

In our opinion, the consolidated financial statements referred to above present fairly, in all material respects, the financial position of Percentage Contractors, Inc. and Subsidiaries as of December 31, 20X1, and the results of their operations and their cash flows for the year then ended in accordance with accounting principles generally accepted in the United States of America.

Other Matter

Our audit was conducted for the purpose of forming an opinion on the consolidated financial statements as a whole. The consolidated earnings from contracts, consolidated contracts completed, and consolidated contracts in progress information is presented for purposes of additional analysis and is not a required part of the consolidated financial statements. Such information is the responsibility of management and was derived from and relates directly to the underlying accounting and other records used to prepare the consolidated financial statements. The information has been subjected to the auditing procedures applied in the audit of the consolidated financial statements and certain additional procedures, including comparing and reconciling such information directly to the underlying accounting and other records used to prepare the consolidated financial statements or to the consolidated financial statements themselves, and other additional procedures in accordance with auditing standards generally accepted in the United States of America. In our opinion, the information is fairly stated in all material respects in relation to the consolidated financial statements as a whole.

[*Auditor's signature*]
[*Auditor's city and state*]
June 19, 20X2

The following supplementary information examples will be revised, as appropriate, upon the effective date of FASB Accounting Standards Update No. 2014-09, *Revenue from Contracts with Customers (Topic 606)*. As industry practice develops, updated presentation or guidance, as appropriate, will be included in a future edition of this guide.[5]

Percentage Contractors, Inc. and Subsidiaries
Consolidated Earnings From Contracts
December 31, 20X1

	Revenues	*Cost of Revenues*	*Gross Profit (Loss)*
Contracts completed during the year	$ 10,432,966	$ 3,128,852	$ 7,304,114
Contracts in progress at year-end	7,745,119	9,822,458	(2,077,339)
Accrued loss on uncompleted contracts	—	105,950	(105,950)
	$ 18,178,085	$ 13,057,260	$ 5,120,825

[5] FASB Accounting Standards Update (ASU) No. 2014-09, *Revenue from Contracts with Customers (Topic 606)*, was issued in May 2014. Public business entities, certain not-for-profit entities, and certain employee benefit plans should apply the guidance in ASU No. 2014-09 as amended by FASB ASU No. 2015-14, *Revenue from Contracts with Customers (Topic 606): Deferral of the Effective Date*, to annual reporting periods beginning after December 15, 2017, including interim reporting periods within that reporting period. Earlier application is permitted only as of annual reporting periods beginning after December 15, 2016, including interim reporting periods within that reporting period.

All other entities should apply the guidance in ASU No. 2014-09 to annual reporting periods beginning after December 15, 2018, and interim reporting periods within annual reporting periods beginning after December 15, 2019. All other entities may apply the guidance in ASU No. 2014-09 earlier as of an annual reporting period beginning after December 15, 2016, including interim reporting periods within that reporting period. All other entities also may apply the guidance in ASU No. 2014-09 earlier as of an annual reporting period beginning after December 15, 2016, and interim reporting periods within annual reporting periods beginning one year after the annual reporting period in which the entity first ap-plies the guidance in ASU No. 2014-09.

Readers are encouraged to read the full text of the FASB ASU, available at www.fasb.org. Readers should apply the appropriate guidance based on their facts and circumstances.

Percentage Contractors, Inc. and Subsidiaries Consolidated Contracts Completed During the Year Ended December 31, 20X1

	Contract Type A—Fixed-price B—Cost-plus-fee	*Total Contract*			*Prior to January 1, 20X1*			*For the Year Ending December 31, 20X1*		
		Revenues	*Cost of Revenues*	*Gross Profit*	*Revenues*	*Cost of Revenues*	*Gross Profit (Loss)*	*Revenues*	*Cost of Revenues*	*Gross Profit (Loss)*
Subsidiary A										
Contract A	B	$ 5,159,692	$ 3,309,198	$ 1,850,494	$ 2,723,477	$ 2,852,343	$ (128,866)	$ 2,436,215	$ 456,855	$ 1,979,360
Contract B	B	3,253,691	1,468,319	1,785,372	1,540,879	961,742	579,137	1,712,812	506,577	1,206,235
Contract C	A	453,090	336,232	116,858	—	—	—	453,090	336,232	116,858
Contract D	B	439,450	315,625	123,825	—	—	—	439,450	315,625	123,825
Contract E	A	348,964	279,672	69,292	—	—	—	348,964	279,672	69,292
Small contracts		272,085	228,218	43,867	—	—	—	272,085	228,218	43,867
Subsidiary B										
Contract A	B	4,655,660	2,849,081	1,806,579	2,318,930	2,487,826	(168,896)	2,336,730	361,255	1,975,475
Contract B	B	3,888,514	1,580,613	2,307,901	2,446,155	1,491,964	954,191	1,442,359	88,649	1,353,710
Contract C	A	267,322	127,365	139,957	—	—	—	267,322	127,365	139,957
Contract D	A	261,576	150,345	111,231	—	—	—	261,576	150,345	111,231
Contract E	A	209,206	166,567	42,639	—	—	—	209,206	166,567	42,639
Contract F	A	122,098	67,499	54,599	—	—	—	122,098	67,499	54,599
Contract G	A	111,323	79,890	31,433	—	59,196	(59,196)	111,323	20,694	90,629
Small contracts		1,083,865	923,368	160,497	1,064,129	900,069	164,060	19,736	23,299	(3,563)
		$ 20,526,536	$ 11,881,992	$ 8,644,544	$ 10,093,570	$ 8,753,140	$ 1,340,430	$ 10,432,966	$ 3,128,852	$ 7,304,114

Percentage Contractors, Inc. and Subsidiaries Consolidated Contracts in Progress as of December 31, 20X1

		Total Contract		*From Inception to December 31, 20X1*					*At December 31, 20X1*		*Year Ended December 31, 20X1*		
	Contract Type A—Fixed-price B—Cost-plus-fee	*Contract Price*	*Estimated Gross Profit (Loss)*	*Revenues*	*Cost of Revenues*	*Gross Profit (Loss)*	*Billings to Date*	*Estimated Costs to Complete*	*Costs and Estimated Earnings in Excess of Billings*	*Billings in Excess of Costs and Estimated Earnings*	*Revenues*	*Cost of Revenues*	*Gross Profit (Loss)*
Subsidiary A													
Contract A	A	$ 5,561,983	$ (1,816,526)	$ 5,453,561	$ 7,234,676	$ (1,781,115)	$ 5,320,985	$ 143,833	$ 132,576	$—	$ 1,910,753	$ 2,686,566	$ (775,813)
Contract B	A	2,179,077	(103,357)	1,627,779	1,704,987	(77,208)	1,305,119	577,447	322,660	—	918,722	1,055,878	(137,156)
Contract C	B	1,804,030	596,800	725,379	485,413	239,966	776,500	721,817	—	51,121	656,396	428,743	227,653
Contract D	A	1,442,319	550,261	798,126	493,632	304,494	782,175	398,426	15,951	—	177,396	118,618	58,778
Small contracts		398,890	85,235	216,017	169,859	46,158	224,057	143,796	—	8,040	218,271	169,683	48,588
Subsidiary B													
Contract A	A	3,682,939	(2,472,475)	3,616,816	6,044,901	(2,428,085)	3,324,895	110,513	291,921	—	2,650,540	4,468,281	(1,817,741)
Contract B	B	2,649,845	1,137,742	1,697,750	968,801	728,949	1,554,274	543,302	143,476	—	476,913	284,416	192,497
Contract C	A	334,418	113,389	103,832	68,626	35,206	140,546	152,403	—	36,714	87,891	49,642	38,249
Contract D	A	310,572	102,490	278,621	186,675	91,946	267,730	21,407	10,891	—	232,785	165,691	67,094
Contract E	A	228,025	41,819	134,448	109,791	24,657	92,438	76,415	42,010	—	114,165	108,526	5,639
Small contracts		408,865	9,134	294,560	287,980	6,580	249,448	111,751	45,112	—	301,287	286,414	14,873
		$ 19,000,963	$ (1,755,488)	$ 14,946,889	$ 17,755,341	$ (2,808,452)	$ 14,038,167	$ 3,001,110	$ 1,004,597	$ 95,875	$ 7,745,119	$ 9,822,458	$ (2,077,339)

Appendix J

Sample Financial Statements Completed Contractor, Inc.

> This appendix will be revised upon the effective date of FASB Accounting Standards Update No. 2014-09, *Revenue from Contracts with Customers (Topic 606)*. As industry practice develops, updated guidance, as appropriate, will be included in a future edition of this guide.[1]

This appendix is nonauthoritative and is included for informational purposes only.

The following sample financial statements of a construction contractor are included for illustrative purposes only and are not intended to establish reporting requirements. Furthermore, the dollar amounts shown are illustrative only and are not intended to indicate any customary relationship among accounts. The sample financial statements do not include all of the accounts and transactions that might be found in practice. The notes indicate the subject matter generally required to be disclosed, but they should be expanded, reduced, or modified to suit individual circumstances or materiality considerations. In addition to the illustrative notes that are presented, some of which are more or less peculiar to construction contractors, the notes to a construction contractor's financial statements should include information concerning other matters that are not unique to construction contractors, for example, subsequent events, pension plans, postretirement benefits other than pensions, postemployment benefits, stock options, lease commitments, extraordinary items, accounting changes, off-balance-sheet risks.

Independent Auditor's Report[2]

The Shareholders and Board of Directors Completed Contractor, Inc.

Report on Financial Statements

We have audited the accompanying financial statements of Completed Contractor, Inc. which comprise the balance sheet as of December 31, 20X1, and the

---

[1] FASB Accounting Standards Update (ASU) No. 2014-09, *Revenue from Contracts with Customers (Topic 606)*, was issued in May 2014. Public business entities, certain not-for-profit entities, and certain employee benefit plans should apply the guidance in ASU No. 2014-09 as amended by FASB ASU No. 2015-14, *Revenue from Contracts with Customers (Topic 606): Deferral of the Effective Date*, to annual reporting periods beginning after December 15, 2017, including interim reporting periods within that reporting period. Earlier application is permitted only as of annual reporting periods beginning after December 15, 2016, including interim reporting periods within that reporting period.

All other entities should apply the guidance in ASU No. 2014-09 to annual reporting periods beginning after December 15, 2018, and interim reporting periods within annual reporting periods beginning after December 15, 2019. All other entities may apply the guidance in ASU No. 2014-09 earlier as of an annual reporting period beginning after December 15, 2016, including interim reporting periods within that reporting period. All other entities also may apply the guidance in ASU No. 2014-09 earlier as of an annual reporting period beginning after December 15, 2016, and interim reporting periods within annual reporting periods beginning one year after the annual reporting period in which the entity first applies the guidance in ASU No. 2014-09.

Readers are encouraged to read the full text of the FASB ASU, available at www.fasb.org. Readers should apply the appropriate guidance based on their facts and circumstances.

[2] Appendix K, "The Auditor's Report," provides sample auditors' reports for a variety of circumstances.

related statements of income, changes in stockholders' equity and cash flows for the year then ended, and the related notes to the financial statements.

Management's Responsibility for the Financial Statements

Management is responsible for the preparation and fair presentation of these financial statements in accordance with accounting principles generally accepted in the United States of America; this includes the design, implementation, and maintenance of internal control relevant to the preparation and fair presentation of financial statements that are free from material misstatement, whether due to fraud or error.

Auditor's Responsibility

Our responsibility is to express an opinion on these financial statements based on our audit. We conducted our audit in accordance with auditing standards generally accepted in the United States of America. Those standards require that we plan and perform the audit to obtain reasonable assurance about whether the financial statements are free from material misstatement.

An audit involves performing procedures to obtain audit evidence about the amounts and disclosures in the financial statements. The procedures selected depend on the auditor's judgment, including the assessment of the risks of material misstatement of the financial statements, whether due to fraud or error. In making those risk assessments, the auditor considers internal control relevant to the entity's preparation and fair presentation of the financial statements in order to design audit procedures that are appropriate in the circumstances, but not for the purpose of expressing an opinion on the effectiveness of the entity's internal control.[3] Accordingly, we express no such opinion. An audit also includes evaluating the appropriateness of accounting policies used and the reasonableness of significant accounting estimates made by management, as well as evaluating the overall presentation of the financial statements.

We believe that the audit evidence we have obtained is sufficient and appropriate to provide a basis for our audit opinion.

Opinion

In our opinion, the financial statements referred to above present fairly, in all material respects, the financial position of Completed Contractor, Inc. as of December 31, 20X1, and the results of its operations, changes in their stockholders' equity, and its cash flows for the year then ended in accordance with accounting principles generally accepted in the United States of America.

[*Auditor's signature*]
[*Auditor's city and state*]
June 19, 20X2

---

[3] In circumstances when the auditor also has responsibility to express an opinion on the effectiveness of internal control in conjunction with the audit of the financial statements, this sentence would be worded as follows: "In making those risk assessments, the auditor considers internal control relevant to the entity's preparation and fair presentation of the financial statements in order to design audit procedures that are appropriate in the circumstances." In addition, the next sentence, "Accordingly, we express no such opinion." would not be included.

Completed Contractor, Inc.
Balance Sheet
December 31, 20X1

Assets	
Current Assets	
Cash and cash equivalents	$ 837,931
Contracts receivable, net	919,618
Costs in excess of billings on uncompleted contracts	418,700
Current portion of note receivable	113,546
Prepaid expenses and other current assets	189,900
Total Current Assets	2,479,695
Noncurrent Assets	
Note receivable, less current portion	127,287
Cash surrender value of officers' life insurance	73,044
Goodwill, net	656,963
Deposits and other assets	8,792
Property and equipment, net of accumulated depreciation and amortization	476,660
Total Noncurrent Assets	1,342,746
Total Assets	$ 3,822,441
Liabilities and Stockholders' Equity	
Current Liabilities	
Accounts payable	$ 392,384
Billings in excess of costs on uncompleted contracts	34,500
Line of credit	1,026,535
Accrued expenses	135,050
Accrued loss on uncompleted contracts	112,055
Current maturities of long-term debt	37,000
Total Current Liabilities	1,737,524
Noncurrent Liabilities	
Long-term debt, less current maturities	265,082
Deferred tax liability[4]	206,903
Total Noncurrent Liabilities	471,985
Total Liabilities	2,209,509

[4] FASB ASU No. 2015-17, *Income Taxes (Topic 740): Balance Sheet Classification of Deferred Taxes*, was issued in November 2015.

The amendments in ASU No. 2015-17 are effective for public business entities' financial statements issued for annual periods beginning after December 15, 2016, and interim periods within those annual periods. The amendments are effective for all other entities' financial statements issued for annual periods beginning after December 15, 2017, and interim periods within annual periods beginning after December 15, 2018. Earlier application is permitted.

ASU No. 2015-17 applies to all entities that present a classified statement of financial position. The ASU amends FASB ASC 740, *Income Taxes*, to require that deferred tax liabilities and assets be classified as noncurrent in a classified statement of financial position. Readers are encouraged to consult the full text of this ASU on FASB's website at www.fasb.org.

Stockholders' Equity	
Common stock, no par value, 50,000 shares authorized, 23,500 issued and outstanding	1,229,434
Retained earnings	383,498
Total Stockholders' Equity	1,612,932
Total Liabilities and Stockholders' Equity	$ 3,822,441

The accompanying notes are an integral part of these financial statements.

Completed Contractor, Inc.
Statement of Income
for the Year Ended December 31, 20X1

Revenues	$ 9,577,000
Cost of Revenues	7,457,171
Gross Profit	2,119,829
Selling, General, and Administrative Expenses	265,300
Income From Operations	1,854,529
Other Income (Expenses)	
Rental income	55,988
Interest income	91,340
Interest expense	(182,303)
Miscellaneous income	216,188
Total Other Income, net	181,213
Net Income Before Provision for Income Tax Expense	2,035,742
Provision for Income Tax Expense	621,789
Net Income	$ 1,413,953

The accompanying notes are an integral part of these financial statements.

Completed Contractor, Inc.
Statement of Changes in Stockholders' Equity
for the Year Ended December 31, 20X1

	Common Stock Shares Outstanding	*Common Stock*	*Retained Earnings (Deficit)*	*Total Stockholders' Equity*
Balance—January 1, 20X1	24,371	$ 1,276,877	$ (699,910)	$ 576,967
Repurchase of common stock	(871)	(47,443)	(330,545)	(377,988)
Net income	—	—	1,413,953	1,413,953
Balance—December 31, 20X1	23,500	$ 1,229,434	$ 383,498	$ 1,612,932

The accompanying notes are an integral part of these financial statements.

Completed Contractor, Inc.
Statement of Cash Flows
for the Year Ended December 31, 20X1

Cash Flows From Operating Activities	
Net income	$ 1,413,953
Adjustments to reconcile net income to net cash provided by operating activities:	
Depreciation and amortization	107,104
Increase in cash surrender value of officers' life insurance	(296,620)
Provision for deferred income taxes	66,429
Provision for bad debt expense	22,193
Changes in assets and liabilities:	
Contracts receivable	83,396
Costs in excess of billings on uncompleted contracts	(62,009)
Prepaid expenses and other current assets	39,356
Deposits and other assets	(8,346)
Accounts payable	73,770
Billings in excess of costs on uncompleted projects	(56,001)
Accrued loss on uncompleted projects	(68,836)
Accrued expenses	(226,961)
Net Cash Provided by Operating Activities	1,087,428
Cash Flows From Investing Activities	
Repayment on note receivable	32,633
Purchases of property and equipment	(298,892)
Net Cash Used in Investing Activities	(266,259)
Cash Flows From Financing Activities	
Payments on line of credit	(271,390)
Principal payments on long-term debt	(380,688)
Principal borrowings on long-term debt	66,463
Repurchase of common stock	(377,988)
Net Cash Used in Financing Activities	(963,603)
Net Change in Cash and Cash Equivalents	(142,434)
Cash and Cash Equivalents—Beginning of Year	980,365
Cash and Cash Equivalents —Ending of Year	$ 837,931
Supplemental Disclosure of Cash Flow Information	
Cash payments for:	
Interest	$ 142,603
Income Taxes	$ 311,028

The accompanying notes are an integral part of these financial statements.

Note 1—Nature of Operations and Significant Accounting Policies

Nature of Operations

Completed Contractor ("the Company") provides construction, maintenance, repair, and upgrade of water and wastewater facilities and provides installation, service and operation maintenance of equipment sales of water, waste water, and electrical control systems for commercial and residential clients in the Southeastern United States.

Significant Accounting Policies

Use of Estimates

The preparation of the financial statements in conformity with accounting principles generally accepted in the United States of America requires management to make estimates and assumptions that affect the reported amounts of assets and liabilities and disclosure of contingent assets and liabilities at the date of the financial statements and reported amounts of revenue and expenses during the reporting period. Actual results could differ from those estimates. Management periodically evaluates estimates used in the preparation of the financial statements for continued reasonableness. Appropriate adjustments, if any, to the estimates used are made prospectively based upon such periodic evaluation. It is reasonably possible that changes may occur in the near term that would affect management's estimates with respect to the allowance for doubtful accounts and accrued expenses.

Revisions in estimated contract profits are made in the year in which circumstances requiring the revision become known.

Balance Sheet Classifications

The Company includes in current assets and liabilities retentions receivable and payable under construction contracts that may extend beyond one year. A one-year time period is used as classifying all other current assets and liabilities.

Cash and Cash Equivalents

For purposes of reporting cash flows, the Company considers all highly liquid investments purchased with a maturity of three months or less at acquisition as cash and cash equivalents in the accompanying balance sheet. The Company has interest bearing deposits in financial institutions that maintained federal insurance in full for all non-interest bearing accounts and limited coverage up to $250,000 for all interest bearing deposits through December 31, 20X1. The portion of the interest bearing deposits in excess of this amount is not subject to such insurance and represents a credit risk to the Company. At times, balances held at each financial institution may exceed $250,000, which represents a credit risk to the Company. At December 31, 20X1, there were no uninsured deposits.

Contracts Receivable

Contracts receivable from construction, operation and maintenance are based on contracted prices. The Company provides an allowance for doubtful collections which is based upon a review of outstanding receivables, historical collection information, and existing economic conditions. Normal contracts receivable are due 30 days after issuance of the invoice. Contract retentions are usually due 30 days after completion of the project and acceptance by the owner. Receivables past due more than 60 days are considered delinquent. Delinquent receivables are written off based on individual credit evaluation and specific circumstances of the customer.

Unbilled receivables result from the accrual of revenues on the percentage-of-completion method of accounting for which billings have not yet been rendered.

Property and Equipment

Property and equipment is stated at cost. Depreciation is computed using the straight-line methods over the estimated useful lives of the assets, which range from 3 to 15 years. Additions, renewals, and betterments that significantly extend the life of the asset are capitalized. Expenditures for repairs and maintenance are charged to expense as incurred.

For assets sold or otherwise disposed of, the cost and related accumulated depreciation are removed from the accounts, and any related gain or loss is reflected in income for the period.

Impairment of Long-Lived Assets

The Company reviews long-lived assets for impairment whenever events or circumstances indicate that the carrying value of such assets may not be fully recoverable. Impairment is present when the sum of undiscounted estimated future cash flows expected to result from use of the assets is less than carrying value. If impairment is present, the carrying value of the impaired asset is reduced to its fair value. Fair value is determined based on discounted cash flows or appraised values, depending on the nature of the assets. During the year ended December 31, 20X1, there was no impairment losses recognized for long-lived assets.

Goodwill[5]

Goodwill, which is the excess of cost over the fair value of net assets (including identifiable intangibles) acquired in a business acquisition, is not amortized but rather assessed at least annually for impairment or whenever events or changes in circumstances indicate that the carrying amount of the asset might not be fully recoverable. The Company qualitatively evaluates relevant events and circumstances to determine whether it is more likely than not that the fair value of a reporting unit is less than its carrying amount. If so, the Company quantitatively compares the fair value of the reporting unit to its carrying

---

[5] If the entity has elected to adopt the accounting alternative presented in FASB Accounting Standards Update (ASU) No. 2014-02, *Intangibles—Goodwill and Other (Topic 350): Accounting for Goodwill (a consensus of the Private Company Council)*, the disclosure may read:

> Effective January 1, 20X1, the Company changed its method of accounting for goodwill, electing to adopt ASU No. 2014-02, *Intangibles—Goodwill and Other (Topic 350): Accounting for Goodwill (a consensus of the Private Company Council)*. ASU No. 2014-02 amends FASB *Accounting Standards Codification* (ASC) by establishing an accounting alternative under which private companies are allowed to (1) amortize goodwill on a straight-line basis over the useful life of the primary asset acquired in a business combination, not to exceed ten years, and (2) test goodwill for impairment at either the entity-wide level or at the reporting level only when a triggering event occurs indicating that the fair value of an entity or reporting unit may be below its carrying amount. The ASU is effective for new goodwill recognized in annual periods beginning after December 31, 2014, with early adoption permitted. The Company has elected to apply ASU No. 2014-02 to goodwill existing as of January 1, 20X1, and to new goodwill recognized in future periods. ASU No. 2014-02 requires prospective application and accordingly, the election had no effect of the 20X0 consolidated financial position or consolidated results of operations. As a result of the election, the Company recognized $XXX of amortization expense during the year ended December 31, 20X1. Goodwill is amortized over 10 years. There were no impairment charges noted.

amount on an annual basis to determine if there is potential goodwill impairment. If the fair value of the reporting unit is less than its carrying value, an impairment loss is recorded to the extent that the implied fair value of the goodwill is less than its carrying value. Fair values for reporting units are determined based on discounted cash flows, market multiples or appraised values. As of December 31, 20X1, there were no events or circumstances that indicated that goodwill impairment exist and the Company has recorded no goodwill impairment loss during the year ended December 31, 20X1.

Debt Issuance Costs

Debt issuance costs of $6,742 are presented on the balance sheet as a direct deduction from the carrying amount of the related debt liability and are being amortized as interest expense using the effective interest method. The deferred financing fees are being amortized over the term of the underlying debt, which is 5 years. Accumulated amortization amounted to $5,878 at December 31, 20X1. Amortization expense for the year ended December 31, 20X1 was $406. The remaining unamortized amount will be expensed in the year ending December 31, 20X2.

Revenue and Cost of Revenue

Revenue from fixed-price and cost-plus contracts are recognized on the completed-contract method. The Company's contracts are typically completed in two months or less, and financial position and results of operations do not vary significantly from those which would result from the use of the percentage-of-completion method. A contract is considered complete when all costs, except insignificant items, have been incurred, and the installation is operating according to specifications or has been accepted by the customer.

Cost of revenue include all direct material, sub-contractor, labor, and certain other direct costs, as well as those indirect costs related to contract performance, such as indirect labor and fringe benefits. Selling, general, and administrative costs are charged to expense as incurred. Provisions for estimated losses on uncompleted contracts are made in the period in which such losses are determined. Claims for additional contract revenue are recognized when realization of the claim is probable and the amount can be reasonably determined.

The asset, "costs in excess of billings on uncompleted contracts" represents costs incurred on projects in excess of amounts billed. The liability, "billings in excess of costs on uncompleted contracts," represents billings in excess of costs incurred.

Advertising Costs

Advertising costs are expensed as incurred. Total advertising costs for the year ended December 31, 20X1 was $11,655.

Income Taxes

Provisions for income taxes are based on taxes payable or refundable for the current year and deferred taxes on temporary differences between the amount of taxable income and pretax financial income and between the tax basis of assets and liabilities and their reported amounts in the financial statements. Deferred tax assets and liabilities are included in the financial statements at currently enacted income tax rates applicable to the period in which the deferred tax assets and liabilities are expected to be realized or settled. As changes in tax laws or rate are enacted, deferred tax assets and liabilities are adjusted through the provision for income taxes.

The deferred tax assets and liabilities represent the future tax consequences of those differences, which will either be taxable or deductible when the assets and liabilities are recovered or settled. Deferred taxes are also recognized for operating losses that are available to offset future income. Valuation allowance are recorded for deferred tax assets when it is more likely than not that such deferred tax assets will not be realized.

If it is probable that an uncertain tax position will result in a material liability and the amount of the liability can be estimated, then the estimated liability is accrued. If the Company were to incur any income tax liability in the future, interest on any income tax liability would be reported as interest expense, and penalties on any income tax would be reported as income taxes. As of December 31, 20X1, there were no uncertain tax positions.

Concentration Risk

At December 31, 20X1, approximately 85 percent of the Company's workforce is union represented subject to collective bargaining agreements of which approximately 63 percent are represented by unions whose existing labor agreements will expire on various dates in 20X2. The individual unions may limit our flexibility in dealing with our workforce. Any work stoppage or instability within the workforce could delay our ability to satisfy our commitments under existing contracts with our customers in the manner management anticipated when developing contract estimates used in preparing these financial statements. This could cause severe negative impacts to the Company, including possible penalties for delayed contract performance, strained relationships with existing customers, impacts on our ability to obtain future contracts, and cause a loss of revenues, any of which could adversely affect our operations.

Subsequent Events

These financial statements have been updated for subsequent events occurring through June 19, 20X2, which is the date these financial statements were available to be issued.

Note 2—Contracts Receivable, Net

Contracts receivable consisted of the following at December 31, 20X1:

Completed contracts	$ 466,190
Contracts in progress	386,700
	852,890
Retentions:	
Completed contracts	10,928
Contracts in progress	65,800
	76,728
	929,618
Allowance for doubtful accounts	(10,000)
	$ 919,618

Note 3—Costs and Billings on Uncompleted Contracts

The following is a summary of contracts in progress at December 31, 20X1:

Costs incurred on uncompleted contracts	8,411,710
Billings on uncompleted contracts	8,027,510
	$ 384,200

This amount is included in the accompanying balance sheet under the following captions at December 31, 20X1:

Costs in excess of billings on uncompleted contracts	$ 418,700
Billings in excess of costs on uncompleted contracts	(34,500)
	$ 384,200

Note 4—Note Receivable

The Company has a note receivable relating to the sale of certain assets in 20X0. The note receivable bears interest at 6 percent. The note receivable calls for monthly payments of $6,902, including interest, with the balance of all principal and unpaid interest due in December 20X3. At December 31, 20X1, $240,833 was outstanding on the note receivable. Interest income related to the note receivable was $1,874 for the year ended December 31, 20X1.

Future maturity of the note receivable is as follows:

Years ending December 31,	
20X2	$ 113,546
20X3	127,287
	$ 240,833

Note 5—Property and Equipment

Property and equipment consists of the following at December 31, 20X1:

Assets	
Equipment	210,000
Vehicles	178,000
Software	220,000
Furniture and fixtures	123,000
	731,000
Accumulated depreciation	254,340
Net property and equipment	$ 476,660

Note 6—Financing Arrangements

Lines of Credit

The Company has a $2,000,000 bank line of credit bearing interest at an annual rate equal to the Bank's prime rate plus 1.5 percent (4.75 percent at December 31, 20X1). There was $1,026,535 outstanding at December 31, 20X1. The line of credit is secured by the assets of the Company and is guaranteed by the stockholders.

Covenants

The line of credit with the Bank contain certain financial covenants, including a minimum tangible net worth ratio, minimum debt to tangible net worth ratio and a minimum net profit, as defined in the agreements.

Long-Term Debt

Long-term debt consists of the following notes payable at December 31, 20X1:

Various notes payable to Lender A due in monthly installments ranging from $264 to $1,855, including interest, ranging from 1.90 to 6.24 percent, expiring at various dates through May 20X6. The notes are secured by certain vehicles and equipment.	$ 189,493
Various unsecured notes payable to Lender B due in monthly installments ranging from $704 to $1,437, including interest at 3.25 percent, expiring at various dates through April 20X6.	98,341
Note payable to Lender C due in monthly installments of $411, including interest at 1.90 percent, expiring in July 20X4. The note is secured by a vehicle (equipment).	11,074
Various notes payable to various financing institutions, due in monthly installments ranging from $158 to $211, including interest, ranging from 1.99 to 4.69 percent, expiring at various dates through July 20X5. The notes are secured by certain vehicles.	4,038
	302,946
Current maturities of long-term debt	(37,000)
Less unamortized debt issuance costs	(864)
	$ 265,082

Aggregate Maturities

Aggregate maturities of all long-term financing arrangements are as follows:

Years ending December 31,	
20X2	$ 37,000
20X3	89,838
20X4	67,920
20X5	57,094
20X6	50,230
	$ 302,082

Note 7—Leases

Operating Leases—Lessor

The Company has various noncancelable sublease agreements with leases to occupy space in various operating facilities. The sublease agreements call for monthly payments ranging from $350 to $3,900. The subleases expire at various times through November 20X3. The agreements do not contain price escalations.

Total rental income amounted to $55,988 for the year ended December 31, 20X1.

Future minimum rental income is as follows:

Years ending December 31,	
20X2	$ 39,067
20X3	5,483
	$ 44,550

Operating Leases—Lessee

The Company rents its main operating facility under a noncancellable lease. Monthly rent payments are $4,789. The lease expires in June 20X4. Rent expense related to this operating facility for the year ended December 31, 20X1 was $57,468.

In addition, the Company has various noncancellable operating leases for operating facilities. Monthly lease payments range from $1,650 to $3,161. The leases expire at various times through April 20X9. Rent expense related to the operating facilities for the year ended December 31, 20X1 was $129,073.

The Company has various noncancellable operating leases for office equipment. Monthly lease payments range from $129 to $1,836. The leases expire at various times through November 20X4. Rent expense related to the office equipment for the year ended December 31, 20X1 was $8,437.

Future Minimum Lease Payments

Aggregate future minimum lease payments on all noncancellable operating leases are as follows:

Years ending December 31,	
20X2	$ 196,009
20X3	180,958
20X4	165,774
20X5	133,029
20X6	129,657
Thereafter	402,894
	$ 1,208,321

Total rent expense, including equipment rental, for the year ended December 31, 20X1 was $200,710.

Note 8—Stock Redemption Agreements

The Company has a stock redemption agreement with all of its shareholders. Under the terms of the agreement, the Company is required to purchase all of the stockholder's shares upon death, disability, retirement, or termination. Additionally, beginning at age 63 through age 67, shareholders are required to sell their stock back to the Company. The Company annually establishes a per share transaction value based upon a formula established in the stockholder agreements and approved by the Board of Directors. At December 31, 20X1, the Company has outstanding stock purchase commitments with its stockholders totaling 10,383 shares at purchase prices ranging up to $384.04 per share.

Note 9—Retentions Payable

Accounts payable includes amounts due to subcontractors of $313,090 at December 31, 20X1, that has been retained pending the completion and customer acceptance of the contracts.

Note 10—Income Taxes[6]

Significant components of the Company's deferred income tax assets and liabilities are as follows at December 31, 20X1:

	Current	*Long-Term*
Deferred tax asset		
Other	$—	$ 3,843
Net operating loss	—	222,401
Valuation allowance	—	(222,401)
Deferred tax liability		
Other	—	(3,150)
Accrual to cash adjustment	—	(207,596)
Net Deferred Tax Liability	$—	$ (206,903)

The provision for income tax expense for the year ended December 31, 20X1 consists of the following:

Current	$ 455,360
Deferred	166,429
Total Provision for Income Tax Expense	$ 621,789

The Company has accumulated state taxable loss carryforwards of approximately $901,000 at December 31, 20X1. These loss carryforwards expire beginning in 20X2. A valuation allowance has been provided against the state net

[6] See footnote 4.

operating loss carryforward as it is currently uncertain as to when the losses will be utilized by the Company.

Note 11—Retirement Plans

The Company sponsors a 401(k) plan (the plan) that covers substantially all nonunion employees of the Company. Contributions to the plan totaled $72,445 for the year ended December 31, 20X1. In addition, the Company may elect to make a discretionary contribution to the plan.

Union Sponsored Pension Plan

The Company participates in various multiemployer defined benefit pension plans under the terms of collective bargaining agreements covering most of its union-represented employees. The risks of participation in these multiemployer plans are different than single-employer plans in the following aspects:

a. Assets contributed to the plan by a company may be used to provide benefits to participants of other companies,

b. If a participating company discontinues contributions to a plan, other participating employers may have to cover any unfunded liability that may exist, and

c. If the Company stops participating in some of its multiemployer pension plans, the Company may be required to pay those plans an amount based on the underfunded status of the plan, referred to as a withdrawal liability

Information with respect to the multiemployer plans providing pension benefits in which the Company participates is shown in the following table.

	Certified Zone Status			
Name of Plan, Plan Number and Employer ID Number	*20X1*	*Improvement or Rehabilitation Plan Pending / Implemented*	*Surcharge Paid*	*Expiration Date of Collective Bargaining Agreement*
Plan A, 111, 11-1111	Yellow	Yes	No	4/30/20X2
Plan B, 222, 22-2222	Green	No	No	7/31/20X3
Plan C, 333, 33-3333	Green	No	No	6/30/20X5
Plan D, 444, 44-4444	Green	No	No	12/31/20X2
Plan E, 555, 55-5555	Green	No	No	12/31/20X2

The zone status is based on information that the Company received from each of the plans. Among other factors, plans in the red zone are generally less than 65 percent funded, plans in the yellow zone are less than 80 percent funded and plans in the green zone are at least 80 percent funded. The "Improvement or Rehabilitation Plan Pending/Implemented" column indicates plans for which a financial improvement or a rehabilitation plan is either pending or has been implemented.

Contributions made are as follows:

	20X1
Plan A	$—
Plan B	243,121
Plan C	266,119
Plan D	31,223
Plan E	—
Other Plans	93,153
	$ 633,616

Note 12—Commitments and Contingencies

The Company, as conditions for entering into certain construction contracts, purchased surety bonds. The bonds are guaranteed by contracts receivable of the Company.

The Company is subject to various claims and legal proceeding covering a wide range of matters that arise in the ordinary course of its business activities. Management believes that any liability that may ultimately result from the resolution of these matters will not have a material effect on the financial condition or results of operations of the Company.

The Company is contingently liable to a surety company under a general indemnity agreement. The Company agrees to indemnify the surety for any payments made on contracts of surety ship, guarantee, or indemnity. The Company believes that all contingent liabilities will be satisfied by their performance on the specific bonded contracts.

Certain contracts are subject to government review of cost and overhead rates as defined in various federal cost regulations. Management of the Company believes that there are no adjustments that would materially impact the Company's financial position and results of operations as a result of a review of government contracts.

The Company has a purchase commitment with a vendor whereby the Company committed to purchase minimum amounts of office supplies used in its normal operations. Future annual minimum purchases remaining under the purchase commitment are $120,000 for the two-year years ending December 31, 20X3. During the year ended December 31, 20X1, total purchases under the purchase commitment were $94,434.

Note 13—Backlog

The estimated gross revenue on work to be performed on signed contracts was $10,636,012 at December 31, 20X1. In addition to the backlog of work to be performed, there was gross revenue to be reported in future periods under the completed-contract method used by the Company of $1,980,434 at December 31, 20X1.

Appendix K

The Auditor's Report[1, 2]

This appendix is nonauthoritative and is included for informational purposes only.

The objectives of an auditor, as explained in paragraph .10 of AU-C section 700, *Forming an Opinion and Reporting on Financial Statements*,[3] are (*a*) to form an opinion on the financial statements based on an evaluation of the audit evidence obtained and (*b*) to express clearly that opinion on the financial statements through a written report that also describes the basis for that opinion.

In order to meet the first objective of forming an opinion, the auditor should evaluate whether the financial statements are prepared, in all material respects, in accordance with the applicable reporting framework based on the evidence obtained. Paragraphs .15–.18 of AU-C section 700 describe that as part of this evaluation, the auditor should take into consideration whether sufficient appropriate evidence has been obtained, if uncorrected misstatements are material, individually or in the aggregate, and the following:

- Whether the financial statements are prepared, in all material respects, in accordance with the requirements of the applicable reporting framework, considering the qualitative aspects of the entity's accounting practices, including possible bias in management's judgments
- Whether the financial statements adequately disclose the significant accounting policies, the accounting policies are consistent with the applicable reporting framework and are appropriate, management's accounting estimates are reasonable, the information in the financial statements is relevant, reliable, comparable, and understandable, the financial statements provide adequate disclosure, and the terminology used in the financial statements, including the title of each financial statement, is appropriate
- Whether the financial statements achieve fair presentation by considering the overall presentation, structure, and content of the financial statements and whether the financial statements,

---

[1] For more examples of other types of auditor's reports, as well as situational guidance, please refer to the AICPA online tool *The Auditor's Report: Comprehensive Guidance and Examples*.

[2] The AICPA issued Technical Questions and Answers (Q&A) sections 9160.29, "Modification to the Auditor's Report When a Client Adopts a PCC Accounting Alternative," and 9160.30, "Modification to the Auditor's Report When a Client Adopts a PCC Accounting Alternative That Results in a Change to a Previously Issued Report" (*Technical Questions and Answers*), in March 2014 and April 2014, respectively. The Q&A sections were issued to provide nonauthoritative guidance regarding the application of FASB Accounting Standards Update (ASU) No. 2014-02, *Intangibles—Goodwill and Other (Topic 350): Accounting for Goodwill (a consensus of the Private Company Council)*, and No. 2014-03, *Derivatives and Hedging (Topic 815): Accounting for Certain Receive-Variable, Pay-Fixed Interest Rate Swaps—Simplified Hedge Accounting Approach (a consensus of the Private Company Council)*, which amend the FASB *Accounting Standards Codification* to allow for accounting alternatives for private entities that are not classified as public business entities, as defined in FASB ASU No. 2013-12, *Definition of a Public Business Entity—An Addition to the Master Glossary*, and to discuss how application might affect an audit engagement and related reports.

Auditing interpretations are available in the "Research" section of aicpa.org.

[3] All AU-C sections can be found in AICPA *Professional Standards*.

including related notes, represent the underlying transactions and events in a manner that achieves fair presentation

- Whether the financial statements adequately refer to or describe the applicable financial reporting framework

Once the first objective, forming an opinion, is met, then the second objective, expressing the opinion, can be met. If the auditor concludes that the financial statements are presented fairly, in all material respects, in accordance with the applicable financial reporting framework, the auditor should express an unmodified opinion. The guidance related to the basic form of the auditor's report resides in paragraphs .22–.41 of AU-C section 700 and is explained throughout the remainder of this appendix. The unmodified opinion should be in writing and include the following sections:

Title. The title should include the word *independent* to clearly indicate that it is the report of an independent auditor. The reference to independent affirms that the auditor has met all the relevant ethical requirements regarding independence.

Addressee. The auditor's report should be addressed as required by the circumstances of the engagement. The addressee is normally those for whom the report is prepared. It may be addressed to the entity whose financial statements are being audited or those charged with governance. Occasionally, an auditor may be retained to audit the financial statements of an entity that is not a client; in such a case, the report may be addressed to the client and not to those charged with governance of the entity whose financial statements are being audited.

Introductory paragraph. The introductory paragraph should (*a*) identify the entity whose financial statements have been audited, (*b*) state that the financial statements have been audited, (*c*) identify the title of each statement that comprises the financial statements, and (*d*) specify the date or period covered by each financial statement.

The auditor's report covers the complete set of financial statements, as defined by the applicable financial reporting framework. For example, in the case of many general purpose frameworks, the financial statements include a balance sheet, an income statement, a statement of changes in equity, and a cash flow statement, including related notes.

The identification of the title for each statement that the financial statements comprise may be achieved by listing them individually or by referencing the table of contents.

Management's responsibility for the financial statements. This section should be identified with the heading "Management's Responsibility for the Financial Statements" and should include an explanation that management is responsible for the preparation and fair presentation of the financial statements in accordance with the applicable financial reporting framework, which includes the design, implementation, and maintenance of internal control relevant to the preparation and fair presentation of financial statements that are free of material misstatement, whether due to error or fraud.

In some instances, a document containing the auditor's report may include a separate statement by management regarding its responsibility for the preparation of the financial statements. Generally accepted auditing standards (GAAS) do not permit including a reference to any separate statement by management about such responsibilities because this may lead users to erroneously believe that the auditor is providing assurances about representations made by management discussed elsewhere in the document.

Auditor's responsibility. The section with this heading should describe that it is the auditor's responsibility to express an opinion on the financial statements based on the audit. This section should also include a statement that the audit was conducted in accordance with GAAS, should identify the United States of America as the country of origin of those standards, and that those standards require the auditor to plan and perform the audit to obtain reasonable assurance about whether the financial statements are free of material misstatement. The audit should be described by stating

- an audit involves performing procedures to obtain audit evidence about the amounts and disclosures in the financial statements.
- the procedures selected depend on the auditor's judgment, including the assessment of the risks of material misstatement of the financial statements, whether due to fraud or error. In assessing those risks, the auditor considers internal control relevant to the entity's preparation and fair presentation of the financial statements in order to design audit procedures that are appropriate in the circumstances but not for the purpose of expressing an opinion on the effectiveness of the entity's internal control, and, accordingly, no such opinion is expressed. (If the auditor has a responsibility to express an opinion on the effectiveness of the internal control in conjunction with the audit of the financial statements, the auditor should omit the phrase "the auditor's consideration of internal control is not for the purpose of expressing an opinion on the effectiveness of internal control, and accordingly, no such opinion is expressed.")
- an audit also includes evaluating the appropriateness of the accounting policies used and the reasonableness of significant accounting estimates made by management, as well as the overall presentation of the financial statements.

The auditor's report should include a statement about whether the auditor believes that the audit evidence he or she has obtained is sufficient and appropriate to provide a basis for the auditor's opinion.

Auditor's opinion. The auditor's report should include a section with the heading "Opinion." This, when expressing an unmodified opinion, states the auditor's opinion that the financial statements present fairly, in all material respects, the financial position, results of operations, and cash flows in accordance with the applicable reporting framework and identifies the applicable reporting framework.

The auditor's opinion includes the identification of the financial statements as indicated in the introductory paragraph in order to describe the information that is the subject of the auditor's opinion.

Other reporting responsibilities. If the auditor addresses other reporting responsibilities in the auditor's report on the financial statements that are in addition to the auditor's responsibility under GAAS to report on the financial statements, these reporting responsibilities should be addressed in a separate section subtitled "Report on Other Legal and Regulatory Requirements" or otherwise, as appropriate.

If this section is included, all the sections discussed earlier should be under the subtitle "Report on the Financial Statements" and this section should follow it.

Signature of the auditor. The signature should include the manual or printed signature of the auditor's firm. In certain situations, the auditor's report may be required by law or regulation to include the personal name and signature of the auditor, in addition to the auditor's firm.

Auditor's address. The auditor's report should include the name of the city and state where the auditor practices or the issuing office, if different. Note that this requirement may be met by placing the report on firm letterhead that includes the firm's address.

Date of the auditor's report. The auditor's report should be dated no earlier than the date on which the auditor has obtained sufficient appropriate audit evidence on which to base the auditor's opinion on the financial statements, including evidence that the audit documentation has been reviewed, all the financial statements and notes have been prepared, and management has taken responsibility for the financial statements.

Additional Considerations[4]

Auditor's Report for Audits Conducted in Accordance With Both GAAS and Another Set of Auditing Standards

The preceding reporting requirements include a requirement to indicate that the audit was conducted in accordance with GAAS and identify the United

---

[4] Statement on Auditing Standards (SAS) No. 131, Amendment to Statement on Auditing Standards No. 122 Section 700, *Forming an Opinion and Reporting on Financial Statements* (AU-C sec. 700), addresses the format of the auditor's report that should be issued when the auditor conducts an audit in accordance with the standards of the PCAOB, but the audit is not under the jurisdiction of the PCAOB.

An audit is "under the jurisdiction of the PCAOB" if, to perform that audit, the auditor is required to be registered with, and subject to inspection by, the PCAOB. This is required of auditors of certain entities, including issuers and nonissuer brokers and dealers registered with the SEC.

When the audit is under the jurisdiction of the PCAOB, the AICPA Code of Professional Conduct requires members to conduct the audit in accordance with the standards of the PCAOB, and the audit is not required to also be conducted in accordance with generally accepted auditing standards (GAAS).

However, when the audit is not under the jurisdiction of the PCAOB but the entity desires, or is required by an agency, by a regulator, or by contractual agreement, to obtain an audit conducted under PCAOB standards, the AICPA Code of Professional Conduct requires the auditor to also conduct the audit in accordance with GAAS. Examples of entities whose audits are not within the jurisdiction of the PCAOB include clearing agencies and futures commission merchants registered with the Commodity Futures Trading Commission (CFTC), as well as certain other entities registered with the CFTC that are not also SEC-registered brokers and dealers. SAS No. 131 addresses the different reporting requirements of GAAS and the auditing standards of the PCAOB. When the auditor refers to the standards of the PCAOB in addition to GAAS in the auditor's report, SAS No. 131 requires the auditor to use the form of report required by the standards of the PCAOB, amended to state that the audit was also conducted in accordance with GAAS.

States of America as the country of origin of those standards. However, an auditor may indicate that the audit was also conducted in accordance with another set of auditing standards (for example, International Standards on Auditing, the standards of the PCAOB, or *Government Auditing Standards*). Paragraphs .42–.43 of AU-C section 700 address these situations. If the audit was conducted under GAAS and another set of auditing standards, the auditor's report should identify the other set of auditing standards, as well as their origin. The auditor should not refer to having conducted an audit in accordance with another set of auditing standards in addition to GAAS unless the audit was conducted in accordance with both sets of standards in their entirety.

Information Presented in the Financial Statements

In some circumstances, the entity may be required by law, regulation, or standards, or may voluntarily choose, to include in the basic financial statements information that is not required by the applicable financial reporting framework. If the information cannot be clearly differentiated from the financial statements because of its nature and how it is presented, the auditor's opinion should cover this information as required by paragraph .58 of AU-C section 700.

If the information included in the basic financial statements is not required by the applicable financial reporting framework and is not necessary for fair presentation but is clearly differentiated, then such information may be identified as "unaudited" or as "not covered by the auditor's report."

Modification to the Auditor's Report When a Client Adopts a Private Company Council Accounting Alternative

According to paragraphs .07–.12 of AU-C section 708, *Consistency of Financial Statements*, if an entity has adopted a change in accounting principle and that change has a material effect on the financial statements, the auditor should include, in the auditor's report, an emphasis-of-matter paragraph in the period of the change and in subsequent periods until the new accounting principle is applied in all periods presented. If the change in accounting principle is accounted for by retrospective application to the financial statements of all prior periods presented, the emphasis-of-matter paragraph is needed only in the period of such change.

The auditor's emphasis-of-matter paragraph should describe the change in accounting principle and provide a reference to the entity's note disclosure. Following is an illustration of this paragraph when a private company has elected to adopt a change in accounting for goodwill in its December 31, 2014 financial statements (and that change is material and has been disclosed in the financial statements):

Change in Accounting Principle

> As discussed in Note X to the financial statements, the Company has elected to change its method of accounting for goodwill in 2014. Our opinion is not modified with respect to this matter.

Exhibit—An Auditor's Report on Consolidated Comparative Financial Statements Prepared in Accordance With Accounting Principles Generally Accepted in the United States of America[5]

Circumstances include the following:

- Audit of a complete set of general purpose consolidated financial statements (comparative).
- The financial statements are prepared in accordance with accounting principles generally accepted in the United States of America.

Independent Auditor's Report

The Shareholders and Board of Directors Percentage Contractors, Inc. and Subsidiaries

Report on the Financial Statements[6]

We have audited the accompanying consolidated financial statements of Percentage Contractors, Inc. and its subsidiaries, which comprise the consolidated balance sheets as of December 31, 20X1 and 20X0, and the related consolidated statements of income, changes in stockholders' equity, and cash flows for the years then ended, and the related notes to the financial statements.

Management's Responsibility for the Financial Statements

Management is responsible for the preparation and fair presentation of these consolidated financial statements in accordance with accounting principles generally accepted in the United States of America; this includes the design, implementation, and maintenance of internal control relevant to the preparation and fair presentation of consolidated financial statements that are free from material misstatement, whether due to fraud or error.

Auditor's Responsibility

Our responsibility is to express an opinion on these consolidated financial statements based on our audits. We conducted our audits in accordance with auditing standards generally accepted in the United States of America. Those standards require that we plan and perform the audit to obtain reasonable assurance about whether the consolidated financial statements are free from material misstatement.

An audit involves performing procedures to obtain audit evidence about the amounts and disclosures in the consolidated financial statements. The procedures selected depend on the auditor's judgment, including the assessment of the risks of material misstatement of the consolidated financial statements, whether due to fraud or error. In making those risk assessments, the auditor

---

[5] For an illustrative sample of an auditor's report containing an other-matter paragraph applicable when the auditor is issuing an unmodified opinion on the financial statements and an unmodified opinion on included supplementary information, such as backlog information, see appendix I, "Reporting on Supplementary Information in Relation to the Financial Statements as a Whole." For additional exhibits and illustrative sample auditor's reports which meet the requirements of AU-C section 700, *Forming an Opinion and Reporting on Financial Statements*, refer to *The Auditor's Report: Comprehensive Guidance and Examples*.

[6] The subtitle "Report on the Financial Statements" is unnecessary in circumstances when the second subtitle "Report on Other Legal and Regulatory Requirements" is not applicable.

considers internal control relevant to the entity's preparation and fair presentation of the consolidated financial statements in order to design audit procedures that are appropriate in the circumstances, but not for the purpose of expressing an opinion on the effectiveness of the entity's internal control.[7] Accordingly, we express no such opinion. An audit also includes evaluating the appropriateness of accounting policies used and the reasonableness of significant accounting estimates made by management, as well as evaluating the overall presentation of the consolidated financial statements.

We believe that the audit evidence we have obtained is sufficient and appropriate to provide a basis for our audit opinion.

Opinion

In our opinion, the consolidated financial statements referred to above present fairly, in all material respects, the financial position of Percentage Contractors, Inc. and its subsidiaries as of December 31, 20X1 and 20X0, and the results of their operations and their cash flows for the years then ended in accordance with accounting principles generally accepted in the United States of America.

Report on Other Legal and Regulatory Requirements

[*Form and content of this section of the auditor's report will vary depending on the nature of the auditor's other reporting responsibilities.*]

[*Auditor's signature*]
[*Auditor's city and state*]
[*Date of the auditor's report*]

---

[7] In circumstances when the auditor also has responsibility to express an opinion on the effectiveness of internal control in conjunction with the audit of the consolidated financial statements, this sentence would be worded as follows: "In making those risk assessments, the auditor considers internal control relevant to the entity's preparation and fair presentation of the consolidated financial statements in order to design audit procedures that are appropriate in the circumstances." In addition, the next sentence, "Accordingly, we express no such opinion," would not be included.

Appendix L

Information Sources

This appendix is nonauthoritative and is included for informational purposes only.

Further information on matters addressed in this guide is available through various publications and services listed in the table that follows. Many non-government and some government publications and services involve a charge or membership requirement.

Fax services allow users to follow voice cues and request that selected documents be sent by fax machine. Some fax services require the user to call from the handset of the fax machine, others allow the user to call from any phone. Most fax services offer an index document, which lists titles and other information describing available documents.

Recorded announcements allow users to listen to announcements about a variety of recent or scheduled actions or meetings.

All telephone numbers listed are voice lines, unless otherwise designated as fax (f) lines.

Information Sources

Organization	*General Information*	*Fax/Phone Services*	*Website*	*Recorded Announcements*
AICPA	*Order Department* 220 Leigh Farm Road Durham, NC 27707-8110 *Member Service Center* 888.777.7077 *Technical Hotline* 877.242.7212	*General Information* 919.402.4500	aicpa.org www.aicpastore.com	
Financial Accounting Standards Board	*Order Department* 401 Merritt 7 P.O. Box 5116 Norwalk, CT 06856-5116 203.847.0700 (ext. 10)	*General Information* 203.847.0700	www.fasb.org	*Action Alert Telephone Line* 800.462.0393
Public Company Accounting Oversight Board	1666 K Street NW Washington, DC 20006-2803 Phone: 202.207.9100 Fax: 202.862.8430	*General Information* 202.207.9100	www.pcaobus.org	
U.S. Securities and Exchange Commission	*Publications Unit* 100 F Street NE Washington, DC 20549 202.551.4040 *SEC Public Reference Room* 202.551.8090	*Information Line* 800.732.6585	www.sec.gov	*Information Line* 800.732.6585

(continued)

Information Sources—*continued*

Organization	*General Information*	*Fax/Phone Services*	*Website*	*Recorded Announcements*
U.S. Department of Commerce	1401 Constitution Avenue NW Washington, DC 20230	*General Information* 202.482.2000 Bureau of Economic Analysis 1441 L Street NW Washington, DC 20230 202.606.9900	www.commerce .gov www.bea.gov	
Associated General Contractors of America	2300 Wilson Boulevard Suite 400 Arlington, VA 22201	*General Information* 703.548.3118 703.548.3119 (f)	www.agc.org	
Professional Construction Estimators Association	P.O. Box 680336 Charlotte, NC 28216	*General Information* 704.489.1494 704.489.1495 (f)	www.pcea.org	
Construction Financial Management Association	100 Village Blvd. Suite 200 Princeton, NJ 08540	*General Information* 609.452.8000 609.452.0474 (f)	www.cfma.org	

Appendix M

Schedule of Changes Made to the Text From the Previous Edition

This appendix is nonauthoritative and is included for informational purposes only.

As of July 1, 2018

This schedule of changes identifies areas in the text and footnotes of this guide that have been changed from the previous edition. Entries in the table of this appendix reflect current numbering, lettering (including that in appendix names), and character designations that resulted from the renumbering or reordering that occurred in the updating of this guide.

Reference	Change
Preface	Updated.
Various chapters	Update boxes have been added for various pronouncements issued by standard setters.
Chapter 2	Updated due to FASB Accounting Standards Update (ASU) No. 2014-09, *Revenue from Contracts with Customers (Topic 606)*.
Paragraphs 3.03 and 3.08	Updated due to FASB ASU No. 2016-01, *Financial Instruments—Overall (Subtopic 825-10): Recognition and Measurement of Financial Assets and Financial Liabilities*.
Paragraph 3.11	Updated due to FASB ASU No. 2017-05, *Other Income—Gains and Losses from the Derecognition of Nonfinancial Assets (Subtopic 610-20): Clarifying the Scope of Asset Derecognition Guidance and Accounting for Partial Sales of Nonfinancial Assets*.
Paragraphs 3.21 and 3.23	Updated due to FASB ASU No. 2016-01.
Paragraphs 3.25 and 3.43	Revised for clarification.
Paragraph 4.03	Revised for clarification.
Paragraph 5.25	Updated due to FASB ASU No. 2016-19, *Technical Corrections and Improvements*.
Paragraph 5.39	Updated due to FASB ASU No. 2016-01.
Paragraph 5.44	Revised for clarification.
Paragraphs 5.46–.47 and 5.50	Updated due to FASB ASU No. 2016-01.
Paragraphs 5.105–.109	Revised for clarification.

(continued)

Reference	*Change*
Paragraph 6.18	Updated due to FASB ASU No. 2016-01; revised for clarification.
Paragraphs 6.19–.24, 6.26–.27, and 6.29–.31	Updated due to FASB ASU No. 2014-09.
Paragraphs 6.38 and 6.42	Revised for clarification.
Paragraph 6.47	Updated due to FASB ASU No. 2014-09.
Paragraph 6.48	Revised for clarification.
Paragraphs 10.39–.59 and exhibits 10-3 and 10-4	Updated due to FASB ASU No. 2014-09.
Paragraphs 11.19–.27	Revised.
Appendix A	Revised.
Appendix B	Revised.
Appendix C	Revised.
Appendix D	Revised.
Appendix E	Revised.
Appendix F	Revised.
Appendix H	Revised.
Appendix I	Revised.
Appendix J	Revised.
Glossary	Updated.
Index of Pronouncements and Other Technical Guidance	Updated.
Subject Index	Updated.

Glossary

> **© Update *Accounting and Reporting*: Revenue Recognition**
>
> FASB *Accounting Standards Codification* (ASC) 606, *Revenue from Contracts with Customers*, is effective for annual reporting periods of a public business entity, a not-for-profit entity that has issued, or is a conduit bond obligor for, securities that are traded, listed, or quoted on an exchange or an over-the-counter market, and an employee benefit plan that files or furnishes financial statements with or to the SEC should apply the "Pending Content" that links to FASB ASC 606-10-65-1 for annual reporting periods beginning after December 15, 2017, including interim reporting periods within that reporting period. Earlier application is permitted only as of annual reporting periods beginning after December 15, 2016, including interim reporting periods within that reporting period.
>
> For other entities, FASB ASC 606 is effective for annual reporting periods beginning after December 15, 2018, and interim periods within annual periods beginning after December 15, 2019. Other entities may elect to adopt the standard earlier, however, only as of either
>
> - an annual reporting period beginning after December 15, 2016, including interim periods within that reporting period, or
> - an annual reporting period beginning after December 15, 2016, and interim periods within annual periods beginning one year after the annual reporting period in which an entity first applies the "Pending Content" that links to FASB ASC 606-10-65-1.
>
> FASB ASC 606 provides a framework for revenue recognition and supersedes or amends several of the revenue recognition requirements in FASB ASC 605, *Revenue Recognition*, as well as guidance within the 900 series of industry-specific topics, including FASB ASC 910, *Contractors—Construction*. The standard applies to any entity that either enters into contracts with customers to transfer goods or services or enters into contracts for the transfer of nonfinancial assets unless those contracts are within the scope of other standards (for example, insurance or lease contracts).
>
> Readers are encouraged to consult the full text of FASB ASC 606 on FASB's website at www.fasb.org.

The following terms can be found in the FASB ASC glossary:

contractor. A person or entity that enters into a contract to construct facilities, produce goods, or render services to the specifications of a buyer either as a general or prime contractor, as a subcontractor to a general contractor, or as a construction manager.

cost-type contracts. Contracts that provide for reimbursement of allowable or otherwise defined costs incurred plus a fee that represents profit. Cost-type contracts usually only require that the contractor use his best efforts to accomplish the scope of the work within some specified time and some stated dollar limitation.

expected losses. In the context of consolidations (chapter 3, "Accounting for and Reporting Investments in Construction Joint Ventures," of this guide and FASB ASC 810-10), a legal entity that has no history of net losses and expects to continue to be profitable in the foreseeable future can be a variable interest entity (VIE). A legal entity that expects to be profitable will have expected losses. A VIE's expected losses are the expected negative variability in the fair value of its net assets exclusive of variable interests and not the anticipated amount or variability of the net income or loss.

expected losses and expected residual returns. In the context of consolidations (chapter 3 of this guide and FASB ASC 810-10), expected losses and expected residual returns refer to amounts derived from expected cash flows as described in FASB Concepts Statement No. 7, *Using Cash Flow Information and Present Value in Accounting Measurements*. However, expected losses and expected residual returns refer to amounts discounted and otherwise adjusted for market factors and assumptions rather than to undiscounted cash flow estimates. The definitions of expected losses and expected residual returns specify which amounts are to be considered in determining expected losses and expected residual returns of a variable interest entity.

expected residual returns. In the context of consolidations (chapter 3 of this guide and FASB ASC 810-10), a variable interest entity's expected residual returns are the expected positive variability in the fair value of its net assets exclusive of variable interests.

expected variability. In the context of consolidations (chapter 3 of this guide and FASB ASC 810-10), expected variability is the sum of the absolute values of the expected residual return and the expected loss. Expected variability in the fair value of net assets includes expected variability resulting from the operating results of the legal entity.

fixed-price contract. A contract in which the price is not subject to any adjustment by reason of the cost experience of the contractor or his or her performance under the contract.

joint venture. An entity owned and operated by a small group of businesses (the joint venturers) as a separate and specific business or project for the mutual benefit of the members of the group. A government may also be a member of the group. The purpose of a joint venture frequently is to share risks and rewards in developing a new market, product, or technology; to combine complementary technological knowledge; or to pool resources in developing production or other facilities. A joint venture also usually provides an arrangement under which each joint venturer may participate, directly or indirectly, in the overall management of the joint venture. Joint venturers thus have an interest or relationship other than as passive investors. An entity that is a subsidiary of one of the joint venturers is not a joint venture. The ownership of a joint venture seldom changes, and its equity interests usually are not traded publicly. A minority public ownership, however, does not preclude an entity from being a joint venture. As distinguished from a corporate joint venture, a joint venture is not limited to corporate entities.

percentage-of-completion method. A method of recognizing profit for time-sharing transactions under which the amount of revenue recognized (based on the sales value) at the time a sale is recognized is measured by the relationship of costs already incurred to the total of costs already incurred and future costs expected to be incurred.

The preceding paragraph will be deleted upon the effective date of FASB Accounting Standards Update No. 2014-09, *Revenue from Contracts with Customers (Topic 606)*.[1]

profit center. The unit for the accumulation of revenues and costs and the measurement of income. For business entities engaged in the performance of contracts, the profit center for accounting purposes is usually a single contract. However, under some specified circumstances it may be a combination of two or more contracts, a segment of a contract, or of a group of combined contracts.

subcontractor claims. Those obligations of a contractor to a subcontractor that arise from the subcontractor's costs incurred through transactions that were related to a contract terminated but did not result in the transfer of billable materials or services to the contractor before termination.

time-and-material contract. Contracts that generally provide for payments to the contractor on the basis of direct labor hours at fixed hourly rates (that cover the cost of direct labor and indirect expenses and profit) and cost of materials or other specified costs.

unit-price contract. Contracts under which the contractor is paid a specified amount for every unit of work performed. A unit-price contract is essentially a fixed-price contract with the only variable being units of work performed. Variations in unit-price contracts include the same type of variations as fixed-price contracts. A unit-price contract is normally awarded on the basis of a total price that is the sum of the product of the specified units and unit prices. The method of determining total contract price may give rise to unbalanced unit prices because units to be delivered early in the contract may be assigned higher unit prices than those to be delivered as the work under the contract progresses.

The following is a list of additional terms that have been used in this guide:

back charges. Billings for work performed or costs incurred by one party that, in accordance with the agreement, should have been performed or incurred

---

[1] FASB Accounting Standards Update (ASU) No. 2014-09, *Revenue from Contracts with Customers (Topic 606)*, was issued in May 2014. Public business entities, certain not-for-profit entities, and certain employee benefit plans should apply the guidance in ASU No. 2014-09 as amended by FASB ASU No. 2015-14, *Revenue from Contracts with Customers (Topic 606): Deferral of the Effective Date*, to annual reporting periods beginning after December 15, 2017, including interim reporting periods within that reporting period. Earlier application is permitted only as of annual reporting periods beginning after December 15, 2016, including interim reporting periods within that reporting period.

All other entities should apply the guidance in ASU No. 2014-09 to annual reporting periods beginning after December 15, 2018, and interim reporting periods within annual reporting periods beginning after December 15, 2019. All other entities may apply the guidance in ASU No. 2014-09 earlier as of an annual reporting period beginning after December 15, 2016, including interim reporting periods within that reporting period. All other entities also may apply the guidance in ASU No. 2014-09 earlier as of an annual reporting period beginning after December 15, 2016, and interim reporting periods within annual reporting periods beginning one year after the annual reporting period in which the entity first applies the guidance in ASU No. 2014-09.

Readers are encouraged to read the full text of the FASB ASU, available at www.fasb.org. Readers should apply the appropriate guidance based on their facts and circumstances.

by the party to whom billed. Owners bill back charges to general contractors, and general contractors bill back charges to subcontractors. Examples of back charges include charges for cleanup work and charges for a subcontractor's use of a general contractor's equipment.

backlog. The amount of revenue that a contractor expects to be realized from work to be performed on uncompleted contracts, including new contractual agreements on which work has not begun.

bid. A formal offer by a contractor, in accordance with specifications for a project, to do all or a phase of the work at a certain price in accordance with the terms and conditions stated in the offer.

bid bond. A bond issued by a surety on behalf of a contractor that provides assurance to the recipient of the contractor's bid that, if the bid is accepted, the contractor will execute a contract and provide a *performance bond*. Under the bond, the surety is obligated to pay the recipient of the bid the difference between the contractor's bid and the bid of the next lowest responsible bidder if the bid is accepted and the contractor fails to execute a contract or to provide a performance bond.

bid security. Funds or a *bid bond* submitted with a bid as a guarantee to the recipient of the bid that the contractor, if awarded the contract, will execute the contract in accordance with the bidding requirements and the contract documents.

bid shopping. A practice by which contractors, both before and after their bids are submitted, attempt to obtain prices from potential subcontractors and material suppliers that are lower than the contractors' original estimates on which their bids are based or, after a contract is awarded, seek to induce subcontractors to reduce the subcontract price included in the bid.

bidding requirements. The procedures and conditions for the submission of bids. The requirements are included in documents such as the notice to bidders, advertisement for bids, instructions to bidders, invitations to bid, and sample bid forms.

bonding capacity. The total dollar value of construction bonds that a surety will underwrite for a contractor, based on the surety's predetermination of the overall volume of work that the contractor can handle.

bonding company. A company authorized to issue *bid bonds*, *performance bonds*, *labor and materials bonds*, or other types of surety bonds.

bonus clause. A provision in a construction contract that provides for payments to the contractor in excess of the basic contract price as a reward for meeting or exceeding various contract stipulations, such as the contract completion date or the capacity, quality, or cost of the project.

broker. A party that obtains and accepts responsibility as a *general contractor* for the overall performance of a contract but enters into *subcontracts* with others for the performance of virtually all construction work required under the contract.

builders' risk insurance. Insurance coverage on a construction project during construction, including extended coverage that may be added for the contractor's protection or required by the contract for the customer's protection.

building codes. The regulations of governmental bodies specifying the construction standards that buildings in a jurisdiction must meet.

building permit. An official document issued by a governing body for the construction of a specified project in accordance with drawings and specifications approved by the governing body.

change orders. Modifications of an original contract that effectively change the provisions of the contract without adding new provisions. They include changes in specifications or design, method or manner of performance, facilities, equipment, materials, site, and period for completion of work. (See paragraphs 25–27 of FASB ASC 605-35-25.)

claims. Amounts in excess of the agreed contract price that a contractor seeks to collect from customers or others for customer-caused delays, errors in specifications and designs, unapproved change orders, or other causes of unanticipated costs. (See paragraphs 30–31 of FASB ASC 605-35-25.)

completed and accepted. A procedure relating to the time for closing jobs for tax purposes under the completed-contract method of accounting that allows closing a job when construction is physically completed and the customer has formally accepted the project as defined in the contract.

completion bond. A document providing assurance to the customer and the financial institution that the contractor will complete the work under the contract and that funds will be provided for the completion.

construction loan. Interim financing for the development and construction of real property.

construction management contractor. A party who enters into an agency contract with the owner of a construction project to supervise and coordinate the construction activity on the project, including negotiating contracts with others for all the construction work.

contract bond. An approved form of security executed by a contractor and a surety for the execution of the contract and all supplemental agreements, including the payment of all debts relating to the construction of the project.

contract cost breakdown. An itemized schedule prepared by a contractor after the receipt of a contract showing in detail the elements and phases of the project and the cost of each element and phase.

contract item (pay item). An element of work, specifically described in a contract, for which the contract provides either a unit or lump-sum price.

contract overrun (underrun). The amount by which the original contract price, as adjusted by *change orders*, differs from the total cost of a project at completion.

contract payment bond. The security furnished by the contractor to guarantee payment for labor and materials obtained in the performance of the contract. (See **payment (labor and materials) bond**.)

contract performance bond. The security furnished by the contractor to guarantee the completion of the work on a project in accordance with the terms of the contract. (See **performance bond**.)

critical path method. A network scheduling method that shows the sequences and interdependencies of activities. The critical path is the sequence of activities that shows the shortest time path for completion of the project.

draw. The amount of *progress billings* on a contract that is currently available to a contractor under a contract with a fixed payment schedule.

escalation clause. A contract provision that provides for adjustments of the price of specific items as conditions change (for example, a provision that requires wage rates to be determined on the basis of wage levels established in agreements with labor unions).

estimate (bid function). The amount of labor, materials, and other costs that a contractor anticipates for a project, as summarized in the contractor's bid proposal for the project.

estimated cost to complete. The anticipated additional cost of materials, labor, and other items required to complete a project at a scheduled time.

extras (customer's extras). Additional work, not included in the original plan, requested of a contractor that will be billed separately and will not alter the original contract amount.

final acceptance. The customer's acceptance of the project from the contractor on certification by an architect or engineer that the project is completed in accordance with contract requirements. The customer confirms final acceptance by making final payment under the contract unless the time for making the final payment is otherwise stipulated.

final inspection. The final review of the project by an architect or engineer before issuance of the final certificate for payment.

front-end loading. A procedure under which *progress billings* are accelerated in relation to costs incurred by assigning higher values to contract portions that will be completed in the early stages of a contract than to those portions that will be completed in the later stages so that cash receipts from the project during the early stages will be higher than they otherwise would be.

general contractor. A contractor who enters into a contract with the owner of a project for the construction of the project and who takes full responsibility for its completion, although the contractor may enter into *subcontracts* with others for the performance of specific parts or phases of the project.

incentives. (See **bonus clause** and **penalty clause**.)

letter agreement (letter of agreement). A letter stating the terms of an agreement between addressor and addressee, usually prepared for signature by the addressee as indication of acceptance of those terms as legally binding.

letter of intent. A letter signifying an intention to enter into a formal agreement and usually setting forth the general terms of such an agreement.

lien. An encumbrance that usually makes real or personal property the security for payment of a debt or discharge of an obligation.

liquidated damages. Construction contract clauses obligating the contractor to pay specified daily amounts to the project owner as compensation for damages suffered by the owner because of the contractor's failure to complete the work within a stated time.

loss contract. A contract on which the estimated cost to complete exceeds the contract price.

maintenance bond. A document given by the contractor to the owner guaranteeing to rectify defects in workmanship or materials for a specified time following completion of the project. A one-year bond is normally included in the performance bond.

mechanics lien. A lien on real property, created by statute in many areas, in favor of persons supplying labor or materials for a building or structure, for the value of labor or materials supplied by them. In some jurisdictions, a mechanics lien also exists for the value of professional services. Clear title to the property cannot be obtained until the claim for the labor, materials, or professional services is settled. Timely filing is essential to support the encumbrance, and prescribed filing dates vary by jurisdiction.

negotiated contract. A contract for construction developed through negotiation of plans, specifications, terms, and conditions without competitive bidding.

payment (labor and materials) bond. A bond executed by a contractor to protect suppliers of labor, materials, and supplies to a construction project.

penalty clause. A provision in a construction contract that provides for a reduction in the amount otherwise payable under a contract to a contractor as a penalty for failure to meet targets or schedules specified in the contract or for failure of the project to meet contract specifications.

performance bond. A bond issued by a surety and executed by a contractor to provide protection against the contractor's failure to perform a contract in accordance with its terms.

prequalification. The written approval of an agency seeking bids on a project that authorizes a contractor to submit a bid on the project in circumstances in which bidders are required to meet certain standards.

prime contract. A contract between an owner of a project and a contractor for the completion of all or a portion of a project under which the contractor takes full responsibility for the completion of the work.

prime contractor. A contractor who enters into a contract with the owner of the project for the completion of all or a portion of the project and who takes full responsibility for its completion. (See **general contractor**.)

progress (advance) billings. Amounts billed in accordance with the provisions of a contract on the basis of progress to date under the contract.

punch list. A list made near the completion of work indicating items to be furnished or work to be performed by the contractor or subcontractor in order to complete the work as specified in the contract.

quantity takeoffs. An itemized list of the quantities of materials and labor required for a project, with each item priced and extended, which is used in preparing a bid on the project.

retentions. Amounts withheld from progress billings until final and satisfactory project completion.

specifications (specs). A written description of the materials and workmanship required on a project (as shown by related working drawings), including standard and special provisions related to the quantities and qualities of materials to be furnished under the contract.

stop order. A formal notification to a contractor to discontinue some or all work on a project for reasons such as safety violations, defective materials or workmanship, or cancellation of the contract.

subcontract. A contract between the *prime contractor* and another contractor or supplier to perform specified work or to supply specified materials in accordance with plans and specifications for the project.

subcontractor bond. A bond executed by a subcontractor and given to the *prime contractor* to assure the subcontractor's performance on the *subcontract*, including the payment for all labor and materials required for the *subcontract*.

substantial completion. The point at which the major work on a contract is completed and only insignificant costs and potential risks remain. Revenue from a contract is recognized under the completed-contract method when the contract is substantially completed. (See paragraphs 96–97 of FASB ASC 605-35-25.)

surety. (See **bonding company**.)

turnkey project. A project for which a contractor undertakes under contract to deliver a fully operational and tested facility before being entitled to payment.

unbalanced bid. A bid proposal under which the contract price is allocated to phases or items in the contract on a basis other than that of cost plus overhead and profit for each bid item or phase. A common practice is to *front-end load* a bid proposal to obtain working capital to finance the project. Another form of unbalanced bid on unit-price contracts assigns higher profits to types of work for which the quantities are most likely to be increased during the performance of the contract.

waiver of lien. An instrument by which the holder of a *mechanics or materials* lien against property formally relinquishes that right.

warranty (maintenance) period. A specified period, which is normally specified in the contract, after the completion and acceptance of a project, during which a contractor is required to provide maintenance construction, and for which the contractor is required to post a *maintenance bond*.

Index of Pronouncements and Other Technical Guidance

A

Title	Paragraphs
560, *Subsequent Events and Subsequently Discovered Facts*	9.95, 10.58, 10.59, 11.34
570, *The Auditor's Consideration of an Entity's Ability to Continue as a Going Concern*	11.18–.19, 11.22
580, *Written Representations*	10.65
600, *Special Considerations—Audits of Group Financial Statements (Including the Work of Component Auditors)*	11.08, 11.12, 11.14
620, *Using the Work of an Auditor's Specialist*	10.02, 10.40, 10.59
700, *Forming an Opinion and Reporting on Financial Statements*	9.96, Appendix K
705, *Modifications to the Opinion in the Independent Auditor's Report*	11.09, 11.27, 11.27, 11.46
706, *Emphasis-of-Matter Paragraphs and Other-Matter Paragraphs in the Independent Auditor's Report*	10.61, Appendix I
725, *Supplementary Information in Relation to the Financial Statements as a Whole*	10.61, 11.28, 11.35, Appendix I
800, *Special Considerations—Audits of Financial Statements Prepared in Accordance With Special Purpose Frameworks*	11.49
940, *An Audit of Internal Control Over Financial Reporting That Is Integrated With an Audit of Financial Statements*	9.02

E

Title	Paragraphs
EU Directive 2002/96/EC	5.117

F

Title	Paragraphs
FASB ASC	
205, *Presentation of Financial Statements*	
205-20	5.62–.63, 5.65, 5.68, 5.69–.70

Title	*Paragraphs*
205-40	6.36, 6.42
210, *Balance Sheet*	6.01, 6.06
210-10	6.01, 6.08, 6.09, 6.17, 6.26, 6.34
250, *Accounting Changes and Error Corrections*	2.30, 5.15, 5.74, 5.112, 6.27
250-10	5.75, 6.27, Appendix G
275, *Risks and Uncertainties*	6.47
275-10	6.47
280, *Segment Reporting*	5.69
320, *Equity Method Investments*	3.08
320-10	3.08, 6.08
323, *Investments-Equity Method and Joint Ventures*	5.88, 5.107, 6.26, 11.09
323-10	3.03–.07, 3.09, 3.18, 3.21, 3.23, 3.38, 3.40, 3.43–.44
323-30	3.38
325, *Investments—Other*	
325-20	3.21, 3.44
350, *Intangibles—Goodwill and Other*	5.74
350-20	5.77, 5.78, 5.87, 5.88, 5.90, 5.93, 5.96
350-30	5.80, 5.81, 5.102–.104
360, *Property, Plant, and Equipment*	5.39, 5.65, 8.24
360-10	5.63, 5.71–.76, 5.103, 5.104, 5.118
410, *Asset Retirement and Environmental Obligations*	
410-20	5.116–.121
410-30	5.118
450, *Contingencies*	6.51, 8.26
450-30	6.31
470, *Debt*	
470-10	6.09
480, *Redeemable Financial Instruments*	5.123–.124

Title	*Paragraphs*
480-10	5.123
605, *Revenue Recognition*	6.26
605-35	1.09, 2.01–.10, 2.18, 2.20–.23, 2.25–.32, 6.10, 6.19–.20, 6.27, 6.29, 6.31, 6.47, 10.03, 10.15, 10.39, 10.42–.45, 10.47, 10.53–.54, 12.21–.22, Appendix D
606, *Revenue from Contracts with Customers*	2.37, 10.59
606-10	2.31, 10.59
606-25	10.59
715, *Compensation—Retirement Benefits*	
715-80	6.51–.60
720, *Other Expenses*	
720-15	2.25, 6.26
740, *Income Taxes*	5.125, 5.130, 5.132
740-10	4.09, 5.126, 5.131–.132, 6.18, 6.35
805, *Business Combinations*	3.32, 5.78, 5.113, 5.115
805-20	3.34, 3.35, 5.105, 5.109
805-30	5.88
805-50	3.09, 5.110, 5.112, 5.114
810, *Consolidations*	3.06, 4.03
810-10	3.06, 3.21, 3.25–.31, 3.33–.34, 3.36–.37, 3.40, 3.44, 4.03, 4.04–.05
815, *Derivatives and Hedging*	5.51
815-10	5.52, 5.55
815-15	5.47
815-20	5.53–.54
815-45	6.49
820, *Fair Value Measurements*	5.02–.03, 5.19–.20, 5.31, 5.73
820-10	5.04–.33, 5.36–.46
825, *Financial Instruments*	5.02, 5.30

S

Subject Index

A

J

K

L

N

O

P

S

T